Judgments Over Time

JUDGMENTS OVER TIME
The Interplay of Thoughts, Feelings, and Behaviors

Edited by
Lawrence J. Sanna and Edward C. Chang

OXFORD
UNIVERSITY PRESS
2006

OXFORD
UNIVERSITY PRESS

Oxford University Press, Inc., publishes works that further
Oxford University's objective of excellence
in research, scholarship, and education.

Oxford   New York
Auckland   Cape Town   Dar es Salaam   Hong Kong   Karachi
Kuala Lumpur   Madrid   Melbourne   Mexico City   Nairobi
New Delhi   Shanghai   Taipei   Toronto

With offices in
Argentina   Austria   Brazil   Chile   Czech Republic   France   Greece
Guatemala   Hungary   Italy   Japan   Poland   Portugal   Singapore
South Korea   Switzerland   Thailand   Turkey   Ukraine   Vietnam

Copyright © 2006 by Lawrence J. Sanna and Edward C. Chang

Published by Oxford University Press, Inc.
198 Madison Avenue, New York, New York 10016

www.oup.com

Oxford is a registered trademark of Oxford University Press

Library of Congress Cataloging-in-Publication Data
Judgments over time : the interplay of thoughts, feelings, and behaviors / edited
by Lawrence J. Sanna and Edward C. Chang.
p.   cm
Includes bibliographical references and index.
ISBN-13 978-0-19-517766-4
ISBN 0-19-517766-5
1. Time—Psychological aspects.   2. Thought and thinking.   3. Emotions.   4.
Human behavior.   I. Sanna, Lawrence J.   II. Chang, Edward C. (Edward Chin-Ho)

BF468.J83 2006
153.7'53—dc22   2005016400

9 8 7 6 5 4 3 2 1
Printed in the United States of America
on acid-free paper

To my wife, Lucia, and daughter, Thereza, who make my time pass so enjoyably.

—*Lawrence J. Sanna*

To Tae Myung-Sook and Chang Suk-Choon who gave me the gift of time and who took time from their own lives to allow me to be what I have been, what I am, and what I am becoming. I will always be grateful for their support, guidance, and love. To my wife, the only one who is able to stop time whenever I look into her eyes. And last, but not least, to my little princess Olivia Dae Chang, who I hold very close and dear to me each moment of my life. As the world grows, let's keep laughing about those fun-filled daddy-day-care days spent eating a blueberry bagel in the morning, playing with a sea of Polly Pockets on the carpet floor, running our own restaurant with French Vanilla and the Cook, and daydreaming of building sand castles along the Pacific Ocean in Wailea. As long as I exist in time, you will always have my time at the mere asking.

—*Edward C. Chang*

Foreword

Parallel Worlds

GEORGE LOEWENSTEIN

"How do you feel?"

"How do I feel," he repeated, and scratched his head. "I cannot say I feel ill. But I cannot say I feel well. I cannot say I feel anything at all. . . ."

"You feel alive though?"

" 'Feel alive' . . . Not really. I haven't felt alive for a very long time."

Oliver Sacks

This gem of a book addresses the ways in which *thinking* about the past and the future profoundly shapes our sense of self and, indirectly, our behavior. Having edited two books on "choice over time," I opened *Judgments over Time* expecting to read about decisions that involve time, such as dieting, saving, or getting an education. I was surprised. Judgment, as I should have known, is not the same as choice. It occurs in the mind, though it may move the body. The chapters in this book provide an amazingly comprehensive overview of the internal processes of assessment and evaluation that hum along internally as we live in the external world. As novelists have long understood, human beings inhabit two parallel worlds—a "material world" of decisions and an internal world of evaluation that is infused with the past and alert to the future. An amnesic with no memories of whole decades, as Oliver Sacks discovered, not only lacked a past but also a future and, without past and future, did not feel alive.

In my home discipline—economics—the life of the mind is seen as subservient to, and derivative of, the material world; economics adheres to the instrumentalist assumption that the purpose of thinking is to inform choice. Economists posit that human beings try to foretell the shape of the future (e.g., how wealthy will I be?) to make better decisions, such as about how much to work or play and how much to save or spend. They recall the past mainly to predict the future. If one has suffered long bouts of unemployment, for example, one might want not to bank on sustained employment in the future but instead put more current earnings into the bank.

As the chapters in this book make clear, however, thinking about the future and the past is much more than an input into decisions. Thinking about the past and the future is an important source of pleasure and pain in its own right. In economic parlance, we derive "utility" from memory and from anticipation, and in thinking about the past and future we naturally and automatically construct a narrative of our own life—a life story that, as Jerome Bruner expresses it, "achieve[s] the power to structure perceptual experience, to organize memory, to segment and purpose-build the very 'events' of a life." "In the end," Bruner argues, "we become the autobiographical narratives by which we 'tell about' our lives."[1]

One of the mysteries of the life of the mind is what constraints hold it in check. The constraints of the *material world* are pretty obvious. Besides the much lamented certainties of death and taxes, we can count on there being only 24 hours in a day. There are also many limits on how much money we can spend, which depend in part on how many of the 24 hours we devote to income-earning work. We are also constrained in the real world by health, strength, intelligence, looks, and personality. The nerdy academic, sad to say, is highly unlikely to secure a date with the movie star of his or her dreams.

On the face of it, the life of the mind seems less constrained. What's to stop us from *imagining* a date with our favorite star, even if she *has* been dead for 43 years, 5 days (and counting). Indeed, some fantasy-prone people who enjoy imaginations so vivid that they experience fantasies as "real as real" can, if they choose to, create a world that is as good as they want it to be. And who has not met the occasional Pangloss who imagines not only that everything is already for the best but also that it will continue to get better. As Pangloss's student Candide learned, however, optimism can exact a price—intense disappointment—when reality inevitably falls short of one's fantasies. Hope, in other words, can bear an emotional cost in the future, just as immediate gratification can take a real toll. It seems, then, that constraints on the life of the mind can bear an eerie resemblance to limits on the material world. This may be why, as chapter 2 discusses, people often maintain low expectations, or strategically lower their expectations, as the "moment of truth" draws near.

In some ways, in fact, the life of the mind is far *crueler* than the material world (at least the material world inhabited by the affluent). In the material world, we may experience real setbacks, but we can usually recover from them. In the mind, in contrast, we often wallow in our own miseries. We ruminate about our failures and inadequacies (chapter 9), hold ourselves to unrealistic standards (chapter 4), drive ourselves crazy with regret over what could have been had we only been smart enough to see it (chapters 10 and 12), and drive ourselves *extra* crazy because, as discussed in chapter 13, with the benefit of hindsight the best course of actions seems to have been blindingly obvious at the outset. Fortunately, the world of the mind isn't entirely unforgiving. Over time, as we learn in chapter 14, our memories tend to edit out the worst things we endure and the mind envelops the past in a warm aura of nostalgia. Furthermore, as discussed in chapter 7, there is always psychotherapy to make us feel subjectively better about our objective reality.

These parallel worlds are, needless to say, linked. The life of the mind conditions the material world. You need to think about the future to act on it (chapter 6), though, as discussed in chapter 5, there is good evidence that we mispredict both how we will feel and how we will behave (albeit in opposite directions). It also seems to require some degree of optimism to take action (chapters 8 and 15) and some explanatory processing (chapter 11). If, however, you are *too* happy with your existence—if you do manage to persuade yourself that it is the best of all possible worlds—then you will have a hard time motivating self-improvement. In fact, as discussed in chapter 3, defensive pessimism can not only protect us from disappointment but can also perform a motivational function: the unrealistic prospect of ignominious failure can drive us to greater effort. And rumination may be miserable but, as emphasized in chapter 9, it may help us learn the lessons of the past.

The material world, likewise, conditions the life of the mind. Except for the fantasy-prone or insane (assuming these to be distinct categories), most people have only limited ability to make up a life of the mind that is divorced from reality. If you are an unemployed drug addict, it takes serious effort to convince yourself that it's the best of all possible worlds. Nor do we seem to have much capacity to decide on our own wants and desires. We would all be much better off to lust after the objects that no one else wants and to thumb our noses at those that everyone else desires. Yet few of us are constituted in such a fashion. Indeed, quite the opposite, the moment that we see that everyone else wants something, the value of that thing is likely to automatically increase in our minds.

I've never been one to ask "a penny for your thoughts," and I have never shared the desire that I've heard many people express to be able to read other people's minds. But, reading about the real life of the mind is, happily, less threatening than the prospect of discovering that your mild-mannered office-mate entertains fantasies of murdering you. For a general understanding of the judging mind, I cannot imagine a better source than the volume before you.

Notes

Epigraph source: Sacks, O. (1984, February 16). From an interview with an amnesiac who has no memories of the last 40 years. The lost mariner. *New York Review of Books 31*(2).

1. Bruner, J. (1987). Life as narrative. *Social Research, 54*, 11–32 (quote from page 15). For a fuller discussion of this point, see pp. 67–70 of Karlsson, N., Loewenstein, G. and McCafferty, J. (2004). The economics of meaning. *Nordic Journal of Political Economy, 30*(1), 61–75.

Preface

It was our goal in this book to bring together in one volume some of the exciting and diverse theory and research related to people's judgments over time. Research on temporal variables has been somewhat fragmented, isolated, and even provincial. It seemed to us that there were a lot of interesting ideas related to judgments over time, but it also seemed that there was less attention being paid to potential commonalities across traditional research boundaries. We hoped that bringing together this theory and research into a single volume would correspondingly help bring greater awareness and appreciation of possible conceptual relations between seemingly disparate areas, topics, and traditions.

As with any book, especially one encompassing a broad topic, we could not include everything related to judgments over time. However, we provide readers with a representative sampling of theory and research on many of the most exciting and intriguing issues within these areas. We have generally organized our book around people's thoughts about the future and past. The chapters focus on specific temporal variables and are written by leading experts. Although particular chapters naturally may focus on one temporal orientation over others, all give strong consideration to the future, present, and past. These are related to the interplay between people's thoughts, feelings, and behaviors as chapters warrant. In short, we hoped our book could take a broader perspective on people's judgments over time. Because of this, our book should be of interest not only to theorists and researchers but also to anyone who simply is interested in learning more about relations between thoughts, feelings, and behaviors over time.

We gratefully acknowledge the support, guidance, and insights proffered by the chapter contributors, as they are responsible for any success this book might have. Without their time, efforts, and enthusiasm for thinking outside of what has become routine and conventional, this book simply would not have been possible. We thank Catharine Carlin, Karen Capria, Jennifer Rappaport, and others at Oxford University Press for giving us the opportunity to edit this volume and for their support, encouragement, and assistance throughout the process. Sanna also acknowledges time spent as a visiting scholar at the Fuqua School of Business, Duke University, which was instrumental in aiding the completion of this book. Finally, we thank the many people, including the chapter contributors, who continue to help shape and guide our excitement about the future of research on judgments over time more generally and on the interplay between people's thoughts, feelings, and behaviors over time in particular.

Contents

Contributors

Daniel Balliet
Department of Psychology
Washington State University
Pullman, WA 99164-4820

Fred B. Bryant
Department of Psychology
Loyola University Chicago
Chicago, IL 60626

Patrick J. Carroll
Department of Psychology
Ohio State University
Columbus, OH 43210

Seth E. Carter
Department of Psychology
University of North Carolina
    at Chapel Hill
Chapel Hill, NC 27599-3270

Edward C. Chang
Department of Psychology
University of Michigan
Ann Arbor, MI 48109-1109

Adam DeHoek
Department of Psychology
Loyola University Chicago
Chicago, IL 60626

Christina A. Downey
Department of Psychology
University of Michigan
Ann Arbor, MI 48109 1109

John E. Edlund
Department of Psychology
Northern Illinois University
DeKalb, IL 60115

Jeffrey A. Joireman
Department of Psychology
Washington State University
Pullman, WA 99164-4820

Joanne Kane
Department of Psychology
University of Colorado at Boulder
Boulder, CO 80309-0345

Heather C. Lench
Psychology and Social Behavior
University of California, Irvine
Irvine, CA 92697-7085

Linda J. Levine
Psychology and Social Behavior
University of California, Irvine
Irvine, CA 92697-7085

Elizabeth Y. Lin
Department of Psychology
University of Michigan
Ann Arbor, MI 48109-1109

George Loewenstein
Department of Social & Decision
  Sciences
Carnegie Mellon University
Pittsburgh, PA 15213

Bertram F. Malle
Department of Psychology &
Institute of Cognitive and Decision
  Sciences
University of Oregon
Eugene, OR 97403-1227

Leonard L. Martin
Department of Psychology
University of Georgia
Athens, GA 30605

Julie K. Norem
Department of Psychology
Wellesley College
Wellesley, MA 02481

Gabriele Oettingen
Department of Psychology
New York University
New York, NY 10003

Rik Pieters
Department of Economic and Social
  Psychology
Tilburg University
5000-LE Tilburg
The Netherlands

Kevin L. Rand
Department of Psychology
University of Kansas
Lawrence, KS 66045-2462

Lorie A. Ritschel
Department of Psychology
University of Kansas
Lawrence, KS 66045-2462

Lawrence J. Sanna
Department of Psychology
University of North Carolina
  at Chapel Hill
Chapel Hill, NC 27599-3270

Martin A. Safer
Department of Psychology
The Catholic University of America
Washington, DC 20064

James A. Shepperd
Department of Psychology
University of Florida
Gainesville, FL 32611-2250

John J. Skowronski
Department of Psychology
Northern Illinois University
DeKalb, IL 60115

Eulena M. Small
Department of Psychology
University of North Carolina
  at Chapel Hill
Chapel Hill, NC 27599-3270

Shannon Smith
Clinical and Social Sciences in
  Psychology
University of Rochester
Rochester, NY 14627-0266

C. R. Snyder
Department of Psychology
University of Kansas
Lawrence, KS 66045-2462

Alan Strathman
Department of Psychological
  Sciences
University of Missouri–Columbia
Columbia, MO 65211

Kate Sweeny
Department of Psychology
University of Florida
Gainesville, FL 32611-2250

Chuck Tate
Department of Psychology &
Institute of Cognitive and Decision
   Sciences
University of Oregon
Eugene, OR 97403-1227

Abraham Tesser
Department of Psychology
University of Georgia
Athens, GA 30605

Jennifer Thorpe
Department of Psychology
New York University
New York, NY 10003

Leaf Van Boven
Department of Psychology
University of Colorado at Boulder
Boulder, CO 80309-0345

W. Richard Walker
Department of Social Sciences
Winston-Salem State University
Winston-Salem, NC 27110

Marcel Zeelenberg
Department of Economic and Social
   Psychology
Tilburg University
5000-LE Tilburg
The Netherlands

Judgments Over Time

1

Past as Prologue

An Introduction to Judgments Over Time

LAWRENCE J. SANNA
EDWARD C. CHANG

Time present and time past
Are both perhaps present in time future,
And time future contained in time past.
T. S. Eliot (1941)

Past. Present. Future. Time pervades every aspect of people's lives. We all are affected by remnants of our pasts, assessments of our presents, and forecasts of our futures. Our thoughts, feelings, and behaviors over time inexorably intertwine and intermingle, determining varied reactions such as affect and emotions, judgments and decisions, and plans and future behaviors. As just a few common examples illustrate, temporal variables are critical when people are considering the antecedents and consequences of their interpersonal relationships (e.g., thinking about possibilities resulting from staying in or leaving a marriage), intrapersonal concerns (e.g., contemplating likely outcomes of a new exercise regimen), economic circumstances (e.g., assessing the potential results of selling or investing in property or the stock market), or broader societal issues (e.g., determining the effectiveness of a neighborhood crime prevention program). In each of these situations, and in many other everyday settings, people's thoughts, feelings, and behaviors inescapably influence—and are influenced by—their conceptions of the past, present, and future. This interaction is the subject of this book.

Brief Philosophical and Psychological History

In looking at the past as prologue, we can begin our discussion by mentioning a little about the historical philosophical and psychological importance of time.

3

Without question, ideas about time have both inspired and burdened human beings throughout recorded history. For example, according to Martin Heidegger (1927/1962), the great twentieth-century German philosopher, questions about time are critical to the more basic and fundamental question, What does it mean to be? Heidegger (1927/1962) attempted to answer this central question in his magnum opus, *Being and Time*. His conclusions were simultaneously simple and complex. In his view, "to be" was essentially defined by our temporality. In short, human beings exist as a function of time. Heidegger argued that it is our potentiality, not our actuality, which most directly defines our temporality or being. Beyond this, as temporal beings, we are more than the simple sum of our past and present trajectories. According to philosophers such as Heidegger and others (Merleau-Ponty, 1945/1962; Sartre, 1943/1956), we are beings that are influenced by our past and present as we project ourselves into the constantly unfolding and self-created future.

Psychologists have also embraced the importance of time in their theorizing. But sometimes this recognition has been explicit, and in many cases it has remained merely implicit. Nevertheless, a more focused interest in temporal factors within psychology and other related sciences may be increasing. We attempted to bring together in this edited volume some of the current theory and research on temporal variables from a psychological perspective. It is interesting that issues of time have played a role within several major schools of psychological thought. For example, psychodynamic theorists such as Freud (1923/1962) argued that transformations between primary and secondary processes transpire over time. Jung (1951/1981, 1952/1973) incorporated temporal notions such as the collective unconscious and synchronicity into his theorizing, whereas Adler (1964) spoke much about the importance of people's future orientation with strivings for superiority. Early on, Kurt Lewin (1951) also proposed that persons within situations can be fully understood only within the context of time ("psychological distance"). Behavioral theorists have picked up on these ideas by demonstrating, for example, that the relations between rewards and punishments may change dramatically over time (Ainslie, 1975; Miller, 1944), a theme also espoused more recently by behavioral economists (Chapman, 1996; Thaler, 1981).

Humanistic theorists, such as Carl Rogers (1961), have proposed that one critical component to optimal psychological functioning is getting people to distinguish between real and ideal selves, which can be viewed as determining relations between present and future selves in a developing and evolving world (see also the more recent theorizing of Higgins, 1987, and Markus and Nurius, 1986). The temporal component of positive mental health and potential psychopathology has certainly been echoed by psychologists with a cognitive orientation. People must, for example, sometimes delay immediate gratification to service more long-term objectives in order to function optimally (Mischel, 1974; Mischel, Shoda, & Rodriguez, 1989). People's life courses are determined by their expectations for the future (Bandura, 1997; Nuttin, 1985; Rotter,

1954), as well as by their attributions about the past (Abramson, Seligman, & Teasdale, 1978; Weiner, 1986). These expectations and attributions can have grave consequences, including depression (Abramson, Metalsky, & Alloy, 1989; Peterson & Seligman, 1984; Seligman, 1975) and other psychopathologies (Gottesman, 1991; Zubin, Magaziner, & Steinhauer, 1983). It is thus clear that time not only is an unavoidable element of individual human experience but that it also has been an unavoidable element of psychological theorizing.

Bringing Together Current Ideas

Our point, of course, is not to discuss historical perspectives in an attempt to review everything related to time. That may be impossible. We simply wish to illustrate how time has been considered in previous psychological theorizing. Our book attempts to provide a rich and unique array of current and emerging topics in psychology that are drawn together by a common effort to illustrate how time may be, or should be, integrated into our efforts to better understand and predict people's thoughts, feelings, and behaviors; that is, in our human ways of being.

This volume is divided into two major sections, "Thinking About the Future" and "Thinking About the Past." However, within each section, authors were asked to describe the implications of their theorizing and research for past, present, and future perspectives. That is, variables normally associated mainly with future perspectives (abandoning optimism, defensive pessimism, perfectionism, predicting feelings and choices, considering future consequences, hope, and fantasy realization) are discussed also with a concern for the present and the past. Conversely, variables normally associated mainly with a past perspective (rumination, counterfactuals, attribution, regret, hindsight bias, autobiographical memory, and remembering emotions) are discussed also with a concern for the present and the future. In short, all chapter authors take a truly integrative approach to judgments over time and their relation to people's thoughts, feelings, and behaviors.

Overview of "Thinking About the Future"

This section begins with chapter 2, in which Shepperd, Sweeny, and Carroll focus on the fascinating processes involved in abandoning optimism. Their idea is that people lower earlier positive predictions for future events as the proximity to performance or feedback gets closer. These authors provide a thoughtful discussion of when and why people shift from optimism to pessimism in their predictions. According to these authors, most individuals abandon their optimism in an effort to prepare or brace themselves against the uncertainty that negative outcomes will result. The authors also describe several possible mechanisms that may underlie this phenomenon.

Chapter 3, by Norem and Smith, discusses the strategy of defensive pessimism, a process whereby some high-achieving individuals harness their anxiety to attain positive future outcomes. Ironically, thinking about the possibility of negative outcomes actually motivates these persons to perform at their best. According to these authors, defensive pessimists do not spend much time celebrating past successes. Instead, they focus more on the challenges of obtaining continued success in the future. By anticipating future challenges and considering the possibility of failure, defensive pessimists display a variety of proactive behaviors, allowing them to effectively attain their desired goals.

In chapter 4, Chang, Downey, and Lin take a critical look at past studies on maladaptive perfectionism, the notion that high standards of performance are pathological. They argue instead for a new multifunctional model. According to these authors, perfectionism is informed by both positive and negative past experiences. In turn, perfectionism is believed to develop into a complex variable that involves both positive and negative features linked to important future affective, cognitive, and behavioral elements.

Van Boven and Kane, in chapter 5, examine the fascinating relations between people's predicted feelings and choices. They suggest that people overestimate the influence of affectively arousing situations when predicting future feelings but that they underestimate the influence of affectively arousing situations on their future choices and preferences. Thus people may more readily predict changed feelings than changed choices. The authors additionally outline a number of potentially important variables (e.g., cultural differences, type of affect) that may help to explain these intriguing differences.

In chapter 6, Joireman, Strathman, and Balliet describe consideration of future consequences, the extent to which people think about distant results of their current behaviors. According to these authors, individual variations in considering future consequences can be linked to a variety of important behaviors (e.g., academic achievement, prosocial behaviors). The authors also provide an integrative model describing various potential developmental antecedents and mediating mechanisms, bringing together several ideas from diverse literatures.

Chapter 7, by Snyder, Rand, and Ritschel, provides an overview of research on hope. According to these authors, hope is a multidimensional future-oriented construct that is based on thoughts about agency (e.g., "I will do it") and pathways (e.g., "There are many different ways I can succeed"). In their conceptualization, hope is also strongly guided by past and present experiences. The authors thus argue for the importance of blending past and present experiences into therapy and other settings in order to instill greater hope and foster more psychological and physical adjustment.

Last within this section is chapter 8, in which Oettingen and Thorpe describe their intriguing ideas about fantasy realization. They make a critical distinction between people's beliefs about the future (expectancy judgments) and simple images of the future (fantasies). These authors suggest how the past guides motivation and commitment in the service of helping people pursue or resolve a variety of divergent life problems. Within their model, a variety of mental simulations may be used to describe relations between the future and the present.

Overview of "Thinking About the Past"

The second section begins with chapter 9, in which Martin and Tesser review the literature on rumination, normally thought of as a chronic tendency to focus on negative or unpleasant thoughts. However, these authors show convincingly that ruminations can also have a positive component. Ruminations can be goal-directed, can relate to a person's authentic needs, and can even foster psychological growth. Thus thinking about the past can help some individuals to reevaluate their current and future goals to ensure continued progress or movement toward what is most valued.

In chapter 10, Sanna, Carter, and Small take a comprehensive view of counterfactual thinking. The authors situate counterfactual thinking within a broader framework that considers the many processes of mental simulations over time. They present an integrative model that suggests that although counterfactuals and other mental simulations may serve a variety of functions, they sometimes are just simply reactive. The broader implications of this for judgments and decisions over time are discussed.

Chapter 11, by Malle and Tate, describes a unique perspective on the processes of explanation and prediction. Building on classic attribution theories, these authors propose a theory of explanations that accounts for both past and the future. Explanations are situated within a multilayered model that incorporates modes of explanations, psychological processes, and linguistic expressions. Important parallels between explanations and predictions are drawn, and theoretical and applied issues are discussed.

Zeelenberg and Pieters, in chapter 12, describe theory and research on regret, an emotion felt when people realize that the past could have been better had they acted differently. As these authors illustrate, regret is a multifaceted and multifunctional variable that has become of great interest to researchers. A novel model of regret regulation is presented that seeks to integrate experiences of the past, present, and future, involving strategies that focus on the prevention and management of regret experiences.

In chapter 13, Bryant and DeHoek review research on the hindsight bias, the tendency for people to reappraise events after the fact as if they had been known all along. These authors move to an expanded discussion that focuses on factors that may influence the hindsight bias. The authors clarify the processes associated with when and how foresight turns into hindsight as an event unfolds over time, and they point to the different cognitive and motivational variables that may affect those processes.

In chapter 14, Skowronski, Walker, and Edlund look at autobiographical memory. These authors focus their discussion on two related lines of research: namely, fading affect bias—the tendency for negative emotions associated with autobiographical memory to fade more than for positive emotions—and the processes by which people remember and date when events have occurred. The authors point to a number of possible factors that may account for these phenomena, including self-relevance of emotional events and the dispositions of the individual persons.

Chapter 15, by Levine, Safer, and Lench, takes an intriguing and novel perspective on people's memories for past emotions. These authors address the question of why it is important to sometimes remember, forget, and reconstruct past emotional events. They also describe how misremembering past emotional events can in some cases foster greater future goal-directed behavior when dealing with challenging situations.

Finally, in chapter 16, we conclude the volume by underscoring and expanding on the need to consider people's conceptions of the past, present, and future, along with the intersecting dimensions of feelings, thoughts, and behaviors. They further describe the implications of this approach while suggesting a number of emerging questions and possibilities that may be examined in future research.

Summary

In ending this introductory prologue, we want simply to make explicit our main goal for this book. Our major objective was simple. We wished to put together in a comprehensive volume the ideas of some of the leading psychologists who have been studying how people's thoughts, feelings, and behaviors are influenced by time. It is our hope that by bringing together some of the most contemporary theories and research on these issues, readers will become similarly intrigued with studying the role of time in people's judgments. The authors of the chapters have put forward their most promising work addressing these interesting temporal questions. Many of the chapters propose new and intriguing models and methods that may help to map a journey to even greater understanding. Each in their own way tells us all a little bit more about how time past, present, and future are contained within each other.

References

Abramson, L. Y., Metalsky, G. I., & Alloy, L. B. (1989). Hopelessness depression: A theory-based subtype of depression. *Psychological Review, 96*, 358–372.

Abramson, L. Y., Seligman, M. E. P., & Teasdale, J. D. (1978). Learned helplessness in humans: Critique and reformulation. *Journal of Abnormal Psychology, 87*, 49–74.

Adler, A. (1964). Striving for superiority. In H. L. Ansbacher & R. R. Ansbacher (Eds.), *The individual psychology of Alfred Adler* (pp. 101–125). New York: Harper & Row.

Ainslie, G. (1975). Specious reward: A behavioral theory of impulsiveness and impulse control. *Psychological Bulletin, 82,* 463–496.

Bandura, A. (1997). *Self-efficacy: The exercise of control.* New York: Freeman.

Chapman, G. B. (1996). Temporal discounting and utility of health and money. *Journal of Experimental Psychology: Learning, Memory, and Cognition, 22,* 771–791.

Eliot, T. S. (1941). *Burnt Norton.* London: Faber & Faber.

Freud, S. (1962). The ego and the id. In J. Strachey (Ed. & Trans.), *The standard edition of the complete psychological works of Sigmund Freud* (Vol. 19, pp. 3–66). New York: Norton. (Original work published 1923)

Gottesman, I. I. (1991). *Schizophrenia genesis: The origins of madness.* New York: Freeman.

Heidegger, M. (1962). *Being and time* (J. Macquarrie & E. Robinson, Trans.). New York: Harper & Row. (Original work published 1927)

Higgins, E. T. (1987). Self-discrepancy: A theory relating self and affect. *Psychological Review, 94,* 319–340.

Jung, C. G. (1973). *Synchronicity: An acausal connecting principle* (R. F. C. Hull, Trans.). Princeton, NJ: Princeton University Press. (Original work published 1952)

Jung, C. G. (1981). *The archetypes and the collective unconscious* (R. F. C. Hull, Trans.). Princeton, NJ: Princeton University Press. (Original work published 1951)

Lewin, K. (1951). *Field theory in social science.* New York: Harper.

Markus, H., & Nurius, P. (1986). Possible selves. *American Psychologist, 41,* 954–969.

Merleau-Ponty, M. (1962). *The phenomenology of perception* (C. Smith, Trans), London: Routledge & Kegan Paul. (Original work published 1945)

Miller, N. E. (1944). Experimental studies of conflict. In M. V. Hunt (Ed.), *Personality and the behavior disorders* (pp. 431–465). New York: Ronald Press.

Mischel, W. (1974). Processes in the delay of gratification. *Advances in Experimental Social Psychology, 7,* 249–292.

Mischel, W., Shoda, Y., & Rodriguez, M. L. (1989). Delay of gratification in children. *Science, 244,* 933–938.

Nuttin, J. (1985). *Future time perspective and motivation: Theory and research method.* Hillsdale, NJ: Erlbaum.

Peterson, C., & Seligman, M. E. P. (1984). Causal explanations as a risk factor for depression: Theory and evidence. *Psychological Review, 91,* 347–374.

Rogers, C. (1961). *On becoming a person.* Boston: Houghton Mifflin.

Rotter, J. B. (1954). *Social learning and clinical psychology.* Englewood Cliffs, NJ: Prentice-Hall.

Sartre, J.-P. (1956). *Being and nothingness.* (H. E. Barnes, Trans.). New York: Philosophical Library. (Original work published 1943)

Seligman, M. E. P. (1975). *Helplessness: On depression, development, and death.* San Francisco: Freeman.

Thaler, R. H. (1981). Some empirical evidence on dynamic inconsistency. *Economic Letters, 8,* 201–207.

Weiner, B. (1986). *An attributional theory of motivation and emotion.* New York: Springer-Verlag.

Zubin, J., Magaziner, J., & Steinhauer, S. R. (1983). The metamorphosis of schizophrenia: From chronicity to vulnerability. *Psychological Medicine, 13,* 551–571.

PART I

THINKING ABOUT THE FUTURE

2

Abandoning Optimism in Predictions About the Future

JAMES A. SHEPPERD
KATE SWEENY
PATRICK J. CARROLL

The books and stories that parents read or tell their children often communicate subtly (or not so subtly) the important values and beliefs of the society. These values can range from the consequences of sharing to the benefits of frugality to the importance of self-reliance. Although a perusal of the children's section of a bookstore or library suggests that Western cultures cherish a variety of values and beliefs, one value stands out clearly —optimism. Protagonists who have an optimistic outlook or positive expectations are successful in their endeavors and prevail over adversity, as evident in the story of *The Little Engine That Could* (Piper, 1930), in which a little train's positive expectations allow it to ascend a steep, imposing hill. Protagonists who have a pessimistic outlook or negative expectations are unsuccessful in their endeavors and sometimes are met with grim consequences, as evident in the story of *Chicken Little* (Hadler & Hadler, 1990), whose pessimistic prognostication that the sky is falling ultimately proves disastrous for Chicken Little and her followers.

Given these children's stories, it is perhaps no surprise that people are not evenhanded in their predictions of the future but rather are overwhelming biased toward optimism. The bias toward optimism takes many shapes, including *comparative optimism*, whereby people predict that they will experience more positive outcomes and fewer negative outcomes than will other people (Weinstein, 1980); *dispositional optimism*, whereby people display an enduring tendency to expect that every cloud has a silver lining (Carver & Scheier, 1981); and *unrealistic optimism*, whereby people predict that their future outcomes will be better than the future suggested by objective indicators (Armor & Taylor,

13

1998; Buehler, Griffin, & MacDonald, 1997). Some researchers have proposed that an optimistic outlook characterizes normal human functioning (S. E. Taylor & Brown, 1988). Accordingly, normal people possess social and cognitive filters that screen and distort information in a self-serving manner (Greenwald, 1980; Pyszczynski & Greenberg, 1989; S. E. Taylor & Brown, 1988), providing the most positive visions of the future within the limits of reason.

Moreover, an optimistic outlook has emotional and health benefits. People who are optimistic are happier, better adjusted, and less anxious than people who are not optimistic (Alloy & Ahrens, 1987; Aspinwall & Taylor, 1992; Carver & Scheier, 1981; Segerstrom, Taylor, Kemeny, & Fahey, 1998; Scheier & Carver, 1988). People who are optimistic also show a variety of health benefits compared with people who are not optimistic. For example, compared with people who score low in dispositional optimism, people who score high in dispositional optimism show better recovery from coronary events and are more successful at reducing their risk for future coronary events (Shepperd, Morato, & Pbert, 1996).

Although an optimistic outlook may be pervasive and beneficial and may seem to characterize normal thinking, we propose that people are not always optimistic about the future and at times will favor a less optimistic or even a pessimistic outlook. Specifically, mounting evidence suggests that people will shelve an optimistic outlook in favor of a more conservative outlook when they anticipate that their optimism might be challenged. We further propose that a downward shift from optimism, although incurring some costs, also offers several benefits.

In this chapter we present research showing that people are not always optimistic and will sometimes surrender their optimism for a less favorable outlook. Next we discuss when people shift from optimism and why the shift occurs. This discussion of the shift is followed by an exploration of the costs and benefits of surrendering an optimistic outlook. Finally, we organize the disparate explanations for the shift under a single adaptive purpose and discuss directions for future research.

In discussing the downward shift from optimism we do not focus on whether judgments about the future are objectively optimistic, realistic, or pessimistic relative to some external criterion. When predicting future outcomes, people often have little sense of what objectively represents an optimistic versus a pessimistic prediction, making it meaningless to define one point as objectively optimistic and another as objectively pessimistic. Thus, when examining judgments across time, the transition between points is more important than starting and end points. Our review explores the *process* by which judgments become progressively lower relative to an initial judgment. Because an optimistic outlook appears to represent the ambient state for most people, we employ the term *optimism* to refer to the initial judgment.

Departures From Optimism

Studies that measure predictions over time in anticipation of approaching feedback illustrate the surrender of optimism. For instance, students in one study estimated the score they would receive on an in-class exam at four periods in time. At Time 1, a month prior to the exam, students were quite optimistic in the scores they predicted receiving. At Time 2, just after they had completed the exam, students were more realistic in their estimates, and they remained realistic at Time 3, five days later at the beginning of class on the day the graded exams were returned. However, at Time 4 (50 minutes later), as the professor called students by name to return the graded exams, the students revised their final predictions significantly below the predictions they made at Times 2 and 3 and significantly below the scores they actually received (Shepperd, Ouellette, & Fernandez, 1996, Studies 2 & 3; see also Gilovich, Kerr, & Medvec, 1993; Sackett, 2002; Sanna, 1999).

Other studies find similar results and extend the findings from judgments about performance to judgments about risk. For example, participants in a medical study believed that they either would or would not be tested for a fictitious medical condition (TAA deficiency) with severe consequences. All participants learned that 20% of students test positive for TAA deficiency, then estimated the probability that they would test positive. Only participants who anticipated testing supplied an estimate significantly greater than 20%. Moreover, as time passed, the estimates of the test participants climbed even higher, whereas the estimates of no-test participants remained the same (K. M. Taylor & Shepperd, 1998).

Still other studies show shifts in predictions of starting salaries (Shepperd, Ouellette, & Fernandez, 1996), corporate earnings (Calderon, 1993), performance on laboratory tasks (Gilovich et al, 1993; Savitsky, Medvec, Charlton & Gilovich, 1998), performance on a driving test (McKenna & Myers, 1997), the results of a scavenger hunt (Armor & Sackett, 2005), smoking risks (Grace & Pennington, 2000), and interpersonal feedback from others (Terry & Shepperd, 2004). Taken together, these investigations demonstrate that, although optimism might be the rule, there are plenty of exceptions in which people surrender their optimism.

When Do People Lower Their Predictions?

Several circumstances prompt a downward shift from optimism. These factors include the proximity of performance and feedback, the importance of the outcome, the ease with which people can imagine negative outcomes, the controllability of the outcome, the person's level of self-esteem, and whether people possess competing motives to maintain optimistic predictions. We discuss each of these circumstances in turn.

First, shifts from optimism appear to correspond closely to the temporal proximity of behavior that bears on the outcome, as well as the temporal proximity of the outcome itself. For example, aspiring premed students may be quite confident in their ability to land a spot in a desirable medical school when the admission deadline is several months away. However, after they take the MCAT and begin the arduous application process, they may entertain a more conservative forecast, as they identify shortcomings in their application materials or learn more about the selective nature of medical schools. In addition, once the behavior is complete (the application is sent out in the mail), these aspiring premed students may show further declines resulting from the fact that the process has moved out of their hands into the hands of an admissions committee. Finally, at the moment of truth, people may abandon any remaining ray of optimism. On the day on which they hope to learn their admissions decision, the hopeful premed students may be thinking about the virtues of a career in law in anticipation that the decision will be unfavorable.

Second, evidence suggests that people are more inclined to shift from optimism when the outcome is important or consequential. For example, in the study described earlier in which participants predicted their likelihood of testing positive for a medical condition, participants who anticipated receiving their test results immediately shifted their predictions downward, but only when they believed that the medical condition had severe consequences. When they believed the medical condition had benign consequences, their predictions remained unchanged (K. M. Taylor & Shepperd, 1998).

The importance of an outcome can vary across people, as well as across situations. Consistent with this idea are the results from a study that examined predictions in anticipation of a pending financial event. Students were led to believe (falsely) that a billing error in the registrar's office meant that 25% of the student body would soon receive a bill in the mail for $78. When asked to estimate their chances of being one of the unlucky students who would receive a bill, financially needy students, who had trouble making financial ends meet and for whom the bill would create new hardships, estimated that their chances were 42%. In contrast, non-needy students, for whom the bill would have few consequences, estimated that their chances were 17%. Moreover, these effects were replicated even after controlling for past experiences with billing errors with the university and for past experiences with receiving unexpected bills (Shepperd, Findley-Klein, Kwavnick, Walker, & Perez, 2000).

Third, shifts from optimism are influenced by the ease with which people can imagine or mentally simulate alternative outcomes. Research finds that people display less confidence in their predictions the more they think about things that will lead to undesired outcomes (Sanna, 1999). For example, students in one study reported several weeks prior to an exam, and again on the exam day, their exam performance confidence and their mental simulations of things that could affect their performance. Students reported more thoughts about things that would undermine their performance and were less confident on the day of the exam than during the earlier period (Sanna, 1999).

Although the ability to simulate alternative outcomes may come easily for most people, it is not innate. Rather, mental simulation requires skills that do not fully develop until adulthood. These skills include the ability to conceptualize causal relationships, the ability to mentally reverse a situation and understand which action caused an outcome (Wadsworth, 1996), and the ability to engage in hypothetical thinking (Piaget, 1972). Perhaps most important is the ability to distinguish goals from reality and thereby recognize that what one wants to happen may not happen and that what one wants not to happen may happen (Harter & Pike, 1984).

Fourth, people are likely to maintain an optimistic outlook when they perceive that they have some control over the outcomes they are predicting. This perception may center on control over the outcome, whereby people believe they can increase the occurrence of a desired outcome and avoid the occurrence of an undesired outcome. Indeed, perceptions of outcome control likely contributed to the substantial optimism found in students' predictions of their exam scores at the beginning of the semester (Shepperd, Ouellette, & Fernandez, 1996). As a test or performance draws near, control over the outcome often declines (e.g., people have less time to prepare), as does optimism. And when performance is over, control over the outcome, as well as any remaining sliver of optimism, often ends.

On the other hand, the perception can also center on control over the consequences of the outcome, and evidence suggests that people will maintain an optimistic outlook when they perceive the consequences as controllable. Specifically, participants in one study were led to believe that because they had an enzyme deficiency, they faced a 50% chance of developing a serious medical problem. However, whereas some participants believed that they could control the problem (i.e., the consequences) through medication, others believed that they could not. Participants predicted that they were less likely to develop the medical problem when the consequences were controllable than when they were uncontrollable (Shepperd, Carroll, Tobin, & Findley-Klein, 2003). Importantly, participants also viewed the outcome as less serious when the consequences were controllable, suggesting that control over the consequences may influence the shift in predictions by affecting how seriously people regard the consequences.

Fifth, several studies find that people with low self-esteem surrender their optimism more readily than do people with high self-esteem (Sanna, Turley-Ames, & Meier, 1999; Shepperd, Ouellette, & Fernandez, 1996; Spencer & Steele, 1994). For instance, in the weeks prior to an exam, both people with high and with low self-esteem were optimistic in their exam-score estimates. However, in the moments prior to receiving their exam feedback, people with low self-esteem were more likely than people with high self-esteem to underestimate the exam scores they would receive. Moreover, just prior to receiving their exams, people with low self-esteem reported more thoughts about things that would lead to a poor exam score, whereas people with high self-esteem reported more thoughts about things that would lead to a good exam score (Sanna, 1999).

The greater propensity for people with low self-esteem to shift their future outlook may stem from their well-documented tendency to be uncertain about where they stand (Baumgardner, 1990; Campbell, 1990; Campbell & Lavallee, 1993). Their uncertainty may elicit sensitivity to external self-relevant feedback, which in turn may prompt people with low self-esteem to more readily entertain the possibility that an optimistic outcome might be disconfirmed. On the other hand, some researchers have argued that people with low self-esteem regulate their affect by proactively anticipating and preparing for possible future negative outcomes (Blaine & Crocker, 1993). Thus they more readily shift from optimism to regulate possible negative feelings that can arise when outcomes turn out poorly.

Why Do People Reduce Their Optimism?

So far we have identified a variety of circumstances that influence *when* people reduce their optimism. However, in light of the mental filters that channel people toward optimism and of the numerous benefits linked to having an optimistic outlook, the more intriguing question is *why* people would ever reduce their optimism. Although we can think of a variety of reasons, all fall into two broad categories of explanations (see Table 2.1). The first category comprises reasons that reflect a response to information. The second category comprises reasons that reflect an attempt to brace for possible bad news. Importantly, we do not perceive one category as right and the other as wrong but rather find truth in both categories of explanations.

Table 2.1.　*Explanations for Downward Shifts in Future Outlooks*

Response to Information
　　Acquiring new data bearing on future outcomes
　　Mood as information about future outcomes
　　Greater scrutiny of existing information

Bracing for Undesired Outcomes
　　Avoiding disappointment
　　Magical thinking intended to influence the outcome
　　Mobilizing resources via defensive pessimism to avoid an undesired outcome

Responding to Information

The downward shift in predictions sometimes reflects nothing more than having new information on which to base judgments or better clarity about existing information. The reduction in optimism reflects a recalibration of judgments in light of this information. The information may originate from one of three sources: (1) the acquisition of new data bearing directly on the judgments, (2) mood as information, and (3) more careful consideration of existing information.

Acquiring New Data   When outcomes are distant, people often have some information on which to base their judgments, but the information is often vague and allows flexibility in predictions. This flexibility, coupled with cognitive filters that people possess for screening information (Greenwald, 1980; Pyszczynski & Greenberg, 1989; S. E. Taylor & Brown, 1988), allows people to be optimistic in their predictions. With the passage of time, people may acquire new data bearing directly on their judgments, and the new data often result in less optimistic predictions. For example, sophomores, juniors, and seniors in one study estimated the starting salaries of their first jobs after graduation on two occasions: once 4 months prior to the date the seniors would graduate, and again just 2 weeks prior to graduation. All participants were optimistic in their predictions 4 months prior to graduation. However, 2 weeks prior to graduation, sophomores and juniors remained optimistic, whereas seniors did not. The decline in optimism among seniors likely arose from having greater information 2 weeks prior to graduation than they had 4 months prior to graduation. At the end of the term, many of the seniors had acquired postgraduation jobs, were in the throes of looking for jobs, or had friends looking for jobs. Unlike sophomores and juniors, the seniors thus had a better sense of what jobs were available and what salaries were likely, prompting a recalibration of predictions (see also Grace & Pennington, 2000; Pennington, Thompson, & Thoman, 2002).

Of note, as the moment of truth draws near, people often acquire a second type of information—information about their diminishing ability to control their outcomes. With the passage of time, control over forthcoming outcomes often declines, with some control opportunities disappearing and others becoming restricted. For example, in the weeks prior to an exam, students may predict earning high grades based on their plans to attend class, read the assigned text, and set aside plenty of time to study. However, on the day of the exam, the opportunities to attend class, read the text, and study have passed. With these traditional avenues for influencing exam performance no longer available, students must base their predictions on what they have done (and perhaps still can do) rather than on what they plan to do.

Mood as Information   It is noteworthy that people will sometimes reduce their optimism even in the apparent absence of new information (Shepperd, Ouellette, & Fernandez, 1996, Studies 2 and 3; K. M. Taylor & Shepperd, 1998). For example, in the exam-score-estimate study, participants reduced their estimates from Time 3 (50 minutes prior to receiving their exam scores) to Time 4 (moments prior to receiving their exam scores), even though they had learned nothing new about the exam during the intervening period. Yet, although people learned nothing about the exam, they nevertheless may have gained information pertinent to their estimates. Specifically, some researchers have proposed that current mood states can function as information and that people draw inferences about themselves and their outcomes based on their moods (Schwarz & Clore, 1988). From this perspective, when predicting an approaching outcome, people note their rising anxiety and infer that, if they are feeling this anxious, it must be because they did poorly. Thus people interpret their anxiety as important information about what the outcome will be (Gilovich et al., 1993).

Greater Scrutiny of Existing Data   People may sometimes revise their optimism after more careful consideration of existing data, either in response to accountability pressures or because they construe distant events differently from near events.

Accountability pressures refer to pressures to explain or justify one's judgments, beliefs, or actions. The pressures may originate externally, but they may also originate internally, as people attempt to explain or justify their judgments, beliefs, and actions to themselves (Tetlock, 1992). When accountability pressures are high, people engage in more complex and thorough information processing. They think about issues more carefully, entertain alternative outcomes, and engage in more self-critical thinking. Accountability pressures prompt a reduction in biases in perception and decision processes (Tetlock & Kim, 1987). Indeed, the mere anticipation of a challenge to one's outlook on the future can spark accountability pressures, leading people to evaluate their future less optimistically (Armor, 2002; McKenna & Myers, 1997; Armor & Sackett, 2005). As the moment of truth draws near, accountability pressures increase, eliciting more conservative predictions.

With the passage of time, people often shift in the way they construe events. According to temporal construal theory (Liberman & Trope, 1998), people attend to different information and think about events differently when the events are in the distant future than when the events are in the immediate future. People construe distant events more abstractly and base predictions on factors such as what they desire to happen. Thus predictions about distant events are often optimistic. As events draw near, people construe events more concretely, and feasibility becomes more central in predictions of what will happen. The shift in construal from abstract to concrete and from desirable to feasible can result in less optimistic predictions.

Although people sometimes shift their predictions in response to new information, this is not always the case. In many instances, the shift in outlook represents a recognition and response to the possibility of an undesired outcome. Specifically, people sometimes reduce their optimism in an attempt to position or *brace* themselves for the possibility that things may not turn out as hoped. With bracing, people shift their predictions downwardly either to influence the occurrence of an undesired outcome or to manage how they feel about that outcome. As such, bracing is distinct from self-handicapping, which involves proactively claiming or creating barriers to performance so as to provide a non-ability explanation for failure, should it occur (Leary & Shepperd, 1986). Whereas the focus of self-handicapping is on the explanation made for a poor performance, the focus of bracing is on the reducing the likelihood of an undesired outcome or managing how one feels about that outcome.

Bracing has three manifestations: (1) it reflects an attempt to avoid disappointment; (2) it reflects a form of magical thinking intended to influence the outcome, and (3) it reflects the cognitive strategy of defensive pessimism in which people mobilize resources to avoid the undesired outcome or to minimize its consequences.

Avoiding Disappointment   How people feel about their outcomes is to some degree influenced by their expectations. When outcomes exceed expectations, people are satisfied. When outcomes fall short of expectations, people are dissatisfied. This point was made clear over a century ago by William James (1890), who argued that self-esteem represents the ratio of successes to pretensions. When personal successes exceed pretensions, self-esteem is high. When personal successes fall short of pretensions, self-esteem is low. Other theorists have echoed this sentiment (e.g., Diener, Colvin, Pavot, & Allman, 1991; Feather, 1969; Locke, 1967; Mellers & McGraw, 2001; Pyszczynski, 1982; Thibaut & Kelley, 1959).

Although people often embrace an optimistic outlook, particularly when events and outcomes are some distance away, as events draw near, people have less freedom to believe whatever they want. Instead they face the possibility that their optimistic outlook might be disconfirmed, that things may not turn out as hoped. Bad news is, by definition, unpleasant. However, it is particularly unpleasant when it is unexpected (Shepperd & McNulty, 2002).

When expectations exceed outcomes, people feel disappointment, which is a powerful negative emotion. As is evident from several studies, people will proactively reduce their optimism when performance and feedback draw near to reduce or avoid feelings of disappointment (Shepperd, Ouellette, & Fernandez, 1996; K. M. Taylor & Shepperd, 1998). It is also possible that people brace to avoid regret should their actions or inactions fail to produce desired outcomes

(Gilovich & Medvec, 1995). However, we feel that people more often brace to avoid disappointment than to avoid regret. People feel regret in response to their actions and inactions; they feel disappointment when their expectations exceed their outcomes (van Dijk, Zeelenberg, & van der Pligt, 1999). Yet people brace even when they have no actions or inactions to regret. For example, in the study that examined predictions in anticipation of feedback regarding a medical condition, people reduced their optimism at the moment of truth even though the event was completely out of personal control. That is, the situation offered no opportunity for action or inaction and thus no opportunity to experience regret (K. M. Taylor & Shepperd, 1998).

As events draw near, the durability bias may magnify anticipated disappointment and the subsequent reduction in optimism. The durability bias refers to the tendency for people to overestimate the duration of emotions they are experiencing (Gilbert, Pinel, Wilson, Blumberg, & Wheately, 1998). For example, people overestimate how long they will feel bad should they experience a relationship breakup (Gilbert et al., 1998). Evidence suggests that the durability bias may occur in predictions for hypothetical forthcoming negative events, with people overestimating how long they will feel bad should a negative event occur (Blanton, Axsom, McClive, & Price, 2001). Accordingly, we suspect that as outcomes become proximate, people's estimates of the duration of their disappointment may increase, making them even more motivated to reduce their optimism to avoid disappointment.

Magical Thinking   Sometimes people believe that the predictions they voice can influence the outcomes that occur. Most notably, people sometimes believe that making an optimistic prediction will somehow diminish the chances that the optimistic prediction will be fulfilled. They thus make dire predictions to avoid "jinxing" (i.e., putting an unfavorable curse on) the forthcoming outcome. The belief that one's predictions can influence one's outcomes represents a type of magical thinking—a belief in causal forces operating outside the realm of normal physical laws (Rozin & Nemeroff, 1990). It represents a secondary control strategy (Rothbaum, Weisz, & Snyder, 1982) that people turn to in an attempt to influence outcomes when primary control opportunities are unavailable. With superstitious control, people recognize that things may not turn out well. They brace in the belief that their reduced optimism will serve as an intervention that can affect the outcome that eventually occurs.

People need not actually believe the negative predictions they express publicly. Instead, they may believe that by merely making negative predictions they diminish the possibility that the negative outcome will transpire. In addition, the circumstances that instigate this form of bracing (e.g., declining primary control opportunities) likely increase as the moment of truth draws near. Thus bracing as a form of superstitious control is likely greatest when all other opportunities to control the outcome have passed.

Defensive Pessimism   In some instances bracing represents the cognitive strategy of defensive pessimism (Norem & Cantor, 1986), an individual difference strategy akin to fear of failure (Atkinson & Raynor, 1974). Defensive pessimists are generally highly capable people who nevertheless make grim predictions. The grim predictions, however, serve a function. They create anxiety, and the defensive pessimists apply the anxiety toward behaviors that ensure that the negative predictions do not come to pass. Defensive pessimism serves to mobilize resources to reduce the likelihood of an undesired outcome or to address the consequences.

Although theorizing on defensive pessimism has focused on responses prior to performance, it is likely that defensive pessimism has implications that go beyond managing outcomes to managing the consequences of outcomes. Defensive pessimism may also come into play even when control over outcomes has passed. The gloom-and-doom predictions of defensive pessimists may prompt action to minimize the negative consequences of an undesired outcome.

The Economics of Abandoning Optimism

A downward shift in predictions functions to prepare people for uncertain outcomes, thereby enhancing their readiness to respond to misfortune. The shift, however, has both costs and benefits. Moreover, the extent to which the downward shift serves its intended function depends on whether people shift at the right time and in the right amount.

Benefits and Costs

A downward shift in outlook at the moment of truth offers several benefits. First, irrespective of whether the shift reflects a response to information or an attempt to brace for an undesired outcome, one fact remains: How people feel about their outcomes is influenced by their expectations (Mellers, Schwartz, Ho, & Ritov, 1997; Shepperd & McNulty, 2002). Receiving a $1,000 bonus produces elation if the person expected only $500 but produces disappointment if the person expected $1,500. When expectations exceed outcomes, people feel disappointed. A downward shift in expectations, regardless of why it occurs, serves to reduce the likelihood of disappointment and thus can increase satisfaction should the outcome exceed expectations. Moreover, the more unexpected the event, the greater the potential for producing elation and disappointment (van Dijk & van der Pligt, 1997; van Dijk et al., 1999; Mellers et al., 1997). The benefit of a downward shift in outlook is that it allows people to circumvent their disappointment by "expecting" bad news.

A second benefit of shifting predictions downward involves the potential to inspire action in preparation for a negative outcome. Although we discussed this idea earlier as being independent of new information and reflecting a type of bracing, it nevertheless can occur in response to new information. Expecting a negative outcome can prompt people to take action or arrange their circumstances to mitigate or counter the harm, allowing them to recover more quickly than if they persist in the belief that everything will turn out well (Showers & Ruben, 1990). For example, people who expect that they face a high chance of being laid off during an economic downturn are likely to postpone large purchases, to save money, and to be frugal in their spending in preparation. In short, grim predictions can produce actions directed at reducing the trauma of the negative outcome should it occur.

Although a downward shift in predictions has benefits, it also carries costs. As we noted at the outset, a number of studies have documented the psychological and health benefits of an optimistic outlook (S. E. Taylor & Brown, 1988). One cost of abandoning an optimistic outlook is that it may require forfeiting the numerous benefits of optimism. For example, studies show that an optimistic outlook is related to a short-term rise in positive affect (Robins & Beer, 2001). Temporary positive affect, in turn, is linked to physical and behavioral outcomes that include perceptions of pain and immune functioning (e.g., Austin, MacLeod, & Dunn, 2004; Segerstrom, Castañeda, & Spencer, 2003). People forfeit the positive affect and all its attendant physical and behavioral dividends by shifting their predictions downward at the moment of truth. A second cost of a downward shift in predictions is that entertaining thoughts of negative outcomes promotes anxiety and negative affect. Thus, not only does a downward shift forfeit the benefits of optimism, but it also entails negative emotional costs. This anxiety can be debilitating to the extent that people become obsessed with the possibility of receiving bad news and are unable to function. Obsessing over possibly getting bad news such as failing an exam, being passed over for a promotion, or learning that a medical screening test reveals cancer may distract people from the countless other tasks they must accomplish each day (e.g., preparing dinner, getting the kids to school). Finally, people tend to like other people less if the other people are pessimistic than if the other people are optimistic (Helweg-Larsen, Sadeghian, & Webb, 2002; Carver, Kus, & Scheier, 1994). Thus a downward shift in predictions can also carry the risk of greater social rejection.

Balancing the Benefits and Costs

Although a downward shift in predictions can be psychologically costly even in anticipation of feedback, the benefits can nevertheless outweigh the costs, making the shift adaptive when done at the right time in the right amount. Shifting from optimism *too early* (i.e., long before the outcome is known) is problematic in that it can prolong the accompanying stress and negative affect unnecessarily. A downward shift in predictions perhaps serves the person best when adopted as late as possible. Circumstances, of course, often force people to brace early, such as when a person must wait days, weeks, or even months before learning about an outcome that has life-changing consequences. For example, patients may have to wait days before learning the results of a cancer biopsy and, if they test positive, several more days or weeks before they can meet with an oncologist to discuss treatment options. Likewise, new law school graduates are often forced to wait six weeks or more after the state bar exam before learning whether they passed and are thus certified to practice law. In instances such as these, people must contemplate and prepare for the possibility of a negative outcome that can produce dramatic consequences well before they learn whether that negative possibility will be a reality. Not only do people in such circumstances experience negative affect and dread over the prospect of bad news, but they also often put their lives on hold as they await news of their fate. Although it is understandable that a person awaiting news such as the results of a biopsy would obsess over the possibility of a negative outcome, assuming the worst for weeks on end could compromise other life tasks, such as maintaining social relationships and meeting family and work obligations. Ultimately, prolonged obsession over possible bad news could result in job loss, seclusion from family and friends, and even depression or debilitating anxiety, all of which would be for naught should the outcome ultimately be inconsequential.

Shifting *too much* is also problematic in that it can intensify the accompanying negative affect. Although extremely negative expectations can be rewarding when reality proves that the expectations were unfounded, there likely comes a point when the relief from having one's worst fears disconfirmed is no match for the stress and anxiety of harboring those fears in the first place. Believing that every call in the middle of the night will announce the death of a loved one, or that every time a lover wants to talk about the relationship it is to announce a breakup, is immensely stressful. Negative expectations certainly have their place, but excessive doom-and-gloom predictions can be debilitating.

On the other hand, when the shift reflects bracing, either to avoid disappointment or to mobilize resources toward action, there may be few things worse than shifting *too little*. Many researchers can tell horror stories of receiving an encouraging priority score on a grant proposal and making all the recommended changes to the proposal. When the next round of reviews is available, the researcher wisely braces for the possibility that the priority score might not improve, only to be cut at the knees when the priority score actually goes down. Managing emotional reactions to bad news is difficult enough when people are prepared to receive it. Managing bad news that they are not prepared to receive can be overwhelming. Indeed, we suspect that the symptoms of post-traumatic stress disorder (PTSD) may partly arise from a failure to adequately prepare for bad news. We do not propose that the victims of PTSD are the architects of their own condition but rather suggest that PTSD can be an extreme consequence of being emotionally unprepared for a negative event. The initial emotional shock can snowball as attempts at mood management divert attention resources from other areas of life. Life does not stop when people are caught emotionally unprepared. Most people who lose loved ones still have jobs and families to attend to. As such, people may be well served by negative expectations that, however disconcerting, prepare them to move forward when tragedy occurs.

Finally, although people may occasionally make colossal errors in judgments, it seems doubtful that people display a habit of making absurdly optimistic predictions about their outcomes, even when their predictions face no challenge. When people do display optimism in their predictions, the optimism likely reflects only a modest departure from reality. As Kunda (1990) aptly noted, people are not at liberty to believe whatever they want. Rather, they will believe something only if they can marshal enough evidence to support the belief. In short, reality considerations constrain the extent to which people display optimism. In a similar vein, we suspect that reality considerations constrain the extent to which people shift their predictions at the moment of truth. An A student awaiting the return of an exam will likely brace by predicting a B or perhaps even a C. However, predicting anything lower is likely to exceed credibility. Although theoretically the A student can reap greater affective rewards in the form of relief or surprise from predicting an F than from predicting a B, predicting an F falls outside the boundary of believability.

Broader Issues and Unanswered Questions

Preparedness and Outcome Predictions

Although we have discussed two distinct categories of reasons why people shift their predictions downward, we believe that both categories generally serve a single goal—the goal of preparedness. Preparedness is a goal state of readiness to respond to uncertain outcomes. It can involve not only being equipped for setbacks should they occur but also a readiness to capitalize on opportunity should it knock. The future holds the possibility of an infinite number of outcomes. Although people do not know what outcome will occur, they can orient toward outcomes. Intuitive prediction allows people to anticipate, plan, and prepare for events before they happen.

The goal of preparedness serves to organize within a single framework the various explanations for why people shift from optimism. Consider, for example, the information-based explanations. Being prepared can involve adjusting explanations in response to new information or in response to more careful consideration or scrutiny of existing information. By adjusting predictions toward greater accuracy, people are better prepared for what lies ahead. Being prepared can also involve responding to mood as a source of information about what lies ahead. Although these internal feelings may sometimes be misleading, they nevertheless can function as important cues to recalibrate predictions.

Preparedness also accounts for the various bracing explanations whereby people alter predictions in response to the possibility that things may not turn out as hoped. For example, people prepare for the negative emotional consequences of undesired outcomes when they brace to avoid regret or disappointment. With magical thinking and defensive pessimism, people attempt to prepare for undesired outcomes by proactively influencing the outcome rather than dealing with the aftermath. In the case of magical thinking, people make predictions that enlist the favors of metaphysical agents to supplement conventional control tactics. In the case of defensive pessimism, people direct emotional energy toward avoiding the outcome.

The specific reasons for declining predictions focus on specific motives, cognitive mechanisms, or a combination of motives or mechanisms. Importantly, we do not propose that preparedness replace these individual reasons. Rather we propose that the larger need of preparedness helps organize the various individual reasons under a single framework. The various information-based explanations and bracing-based explanations for the shift in predictions are all viable means to the same end of being prepared.

Although we thus far have described how preparedness accounts for declines in predictions either in response to new information or in response to possible setbacks, the ambient state for most people appears to be optimism. Moreover, sometimes people shift their predictions upward rather than downward. For example, research on mindsets reveals that, once people have decided on a course of action, they typically move from a deliberative mindset to an implemental mindset. An implemental mindset is characterized by a shift to an optimistic outlook, which facilitates goal pursuit and attainment (S. E. Taylor & Gollwitzer, 1995). People also appear to display shifts toward optimism as they approach life transition points such as the start of a new job, a new relationship, or a new year or the birth of a new baby. We propose that the ambient state of optimism, as well as upward adjustments in predictions, can also serve preparedness—preparedness for possible opportunity. Optimistic expectations orient people toward enhancement and allow them to capitalize on positive openings when they present themselves. Moreover, an optimistic outlook provides the emotional energy needed to persevere toward hard-to-reach goals. Finally, at an intuitive level people likely recognize the emotional, health, and behavioral benefits of an optimistic outlook and may move toward or maintain an optimistic outlook to seize these benefits.

In sum, downward shifts in predictions can reflect a response to new information and an attempt to brace for the possibility that outcomes may not turn out as desired. Both serve the larger purpose of preparing people to respond to uncertainty. Preparedness sometimes involves being equipped for setbacks should they occur, but at other times it involves a readiness to capitalize on opportunity should it knock. As such, preparedness can account for optimism and pessimism in predictions, as well as shifts between the two.

Implications for Present and Past

Thus far, we have focused on future-oriented thoughts, feelings, and behaviors. Abandoning optimism is future oriented in that it reflects an expectation about a future outcome. The expectation is often prompted by concerns over avoiding future negative emotions such as disappointment. However, thoughts about the future also influence how people behave and feel in the present and how they feel about their past. Abandoning optimism reflects a change in present expectations, a change that can occur in response to current information or current anxiety. This change may prompt a change in behavior as people undertake behaviors to avoid or reduce the impact of the undesired outcome. For example, the woman who shifts towards pessimism in her expectations about her current job situation may turn her attention to the present as she experiences stress related to her pessimistic beliefs and readjusts her self-beliefs to account for the new information. She may also attempt to intervene in ways that circumvent a job loss, postpone purchases in light of her uncertain economic future, or initiate a search for a new job.

Furthermore, people who brace for bad news by shifting away from optimism are in essence dictating how they will feel about their past. The husband who braces for the possibility that his wife may leave him sets himself up to feel better about the separation if it occurs. Rather than thinking, "If only I had seen this coming," or "If only I had acted differently," he can find some peace in knowing that he was not caught flat-footed. Shifts away from optimism cannot change past behavior, but they can change how people feel about the past when faced with a negative outcome.

Future Directions

A number of topics related to shifts away from optimism await further research. First, when during development do people learn to brace? Children may learn the benefits of preparing for the worst from experience, they may learn from the instruction of others, or bracing may simply rise out of the capacity to consider future outcomes and feelings about future events. Research with children and adolescents is required to answer this question. Second, we can conceptualize shifts in thinking about the future in a number ways. The existing research focuses primarily on shifts in expectations about future outcomes, but research currently in progress examines shifts in people's standards for acceptable and unacceptable outcomes and finds that people similarly shift their standards downward as feedback draws near (Terry & Shepperd, 2004). Further research will attempt to delineate these conceptualizations of bracing.

Third, future research must address the specific consequences of bracing versus maintaining an optimistic outlook. We speculate that people can reduce feelings of disappointment and regret by lowering their expectations, but we lack empirical support for this claim. Finally, we recognize the need to replicate the existing findings across cultures. Although it seems that disappointment is a universal experience and that people would universally attempt to avoid it, cross-cultural research must support this presumption.

Summary

Although an optimistic outlook has a multitude of benefits and appears to be the rule rather than the exception in how people think about the future, people are not always optimistic and will sometimes shift their predictions downward. For the shift to occur, people must be capable of perceiving a link between their expectations and feelings. In addition, the shift occurs when performance and feedback are proximal, when the outcome is consequential, and when people perceive no control over the outcome or its consequences. Other studies reveal that people with low levels of self-esteem change their outlooks more readily than people with high self-esteem. Finally, competing goals may derail the shift in outlooks, leading people to maintain optimism even at the moment of truth.

The shift in outlooks can reflect a response to new information or an attempt to brace for the possibility that things may not turn out as desired. Both of these responses ultimately help people prepare for an uncertain world. Although shelving an optimistic outlook carries costs, regardless of why it occurs, it can prompt action to mitigate or avoid the undesired outcome and can help people avoid negative emotions such as disappointment. However, the costs of shifting from optimism outweigh the benefits when people shift too early (which prolongs the unpleasant affect), too much (which can intensify negative affect), or not enough (which produces negative affect without the return of a decrease in disappointment). Finally, the various reasons we presented for the shift from optimism in personal predictions serve the common goal of preparing people for what may lie ahead, allowing people to anticipate, plan, and prepare for events before they happen.

References

Alloy, L. B., & Ahrens, A. H. (1987). Depression and pessimism for the future: Biased use of statistically relevant information in predictions for self versus others. *Journal of Personality and Social Psychology, 52*, 366–378.

Armor, D. A., & Sackett, A. (2005). *Accuracy, error, and bias in predictions for real versus hypothetical events.* Unpublished manuscript, Yale University.

Armor, D. A., & Taylor, S. E. (1998). Situated optimism: Specific outcome expectancies and self-regulation. In M. P. Zanna (Ed.), *Advances in experimental social psychology* (Vol. 30, pp. 309–379). New York: Academic Press.

Aspinwall, L. G., & Taylor, S. E. (1992). Modeling cognitive adaptation: A longitudinal investigation of the impact of individual differences and coping on college adjustment and performance. *Journal of Personality and Social Psychology, 63*, 989–1003.

Atkinson, J. W., & Raynor, J. O. (1974). *Motivation and achievement.* Washington, DC: Winston.

Austin, J. K., MacLeod, J., & Dunn, D. W. (2004). Daily mood and stress predict pain, health care use, and work activity in African American adults with sickle-cell disease. *Epilepsy and Behavior, 5*, 472–482.

Baumgardner, A. H. (1990). To know oneself is to like oneself: Self-certainty and self-affect. *Journal of Personality and Social Psychology, 58*, 1062–1072.

Blaine, B., & Crocker, J. (1993). Self-esteem and self-serving biases in reactions to positive and negative events: An integrative review. In R. F. Baumeister (Ed.), *Self-esteem: The puzzle of low self-regard* (pp. 55–85). New York: Plenum.

Blanton, H., Axsom, D., McClive, K. P., & Price, S. (2001). Pessimistic bias in comparative evaluations: A case of perceived vulnerability to the effects of negative life events. *Personality and Social Psychology Bulletin, 27*, 1627–1636.

Buehler, R., Griffin, D., & MacDonald, H. (1997). The role of motivated reasoning in optimistic time predictions. *Personality and Social Psychological Bulletin, 23*, 238–247.

Calderon, T. G. (1993). Predictive properties of analysts' forecasts of corporate earnings. *Mid-Atlantic Journal of Business, 29*, 41–58.

Campbell, J. D. (1990). Self-esteem and clarity of the self-concept. *Journal of Personality and Social Psychology, 59*, 538–549.

Campbell, J. D., & Lavallee, L. F. (1993). Who am I? The role of self-concept confusion in understanding the behavior of people with low self-esteem. In R. F. Baumeister (Ed.), *Self-esteem: The puzzle of low self-regard* (pp. 3–20). New York: Plenum.

Carver, C. S., Kus, L. A., & Scheier, M. F. (1994). Effects of good versus bad mood and optimism versus pessimistic outlook on social acceptance versus rejection. *Journal of Social and Clinical Psychology, 13*, 138–151.

Carver, C. S., & Scheier, M. F. (1981). *Attention and self-regulation: A control-theory approach to human behavior.* New York: Springer-Verlag.

Diener, E., Colvin, C. R., Pavot, W. G., & Allman, A. (1991). The psychic costs of intense positive affect. *Journal of Personality and Social Psychology, 61*, 492–503.

Feather, N. T. (1969). Attribution of responsibility and valence of success and failure in relation to initial confidence and task performance. *Journal of Personality and Social Psychology, 13,* 129–144.

Gilbert, D. T., Pinel, E. C., Wilson, T. D., Blumberg, S. J., & Wheately, T. P. (1998). Immune neglect: A source of durability bias in affective forecasting. *Journal of Personality and Social Psychology, 75,* 617–638.

Gilovich, T., Kerr, M., & Medvec, V. H. (1993). Effect of temporal perspective on subjective confidence. *Journal of Personality and Social Psychology, 64,* 552–560.

Gilovich, T., & Medvec, V. H. (1995). The experience of regret: What, when, and why. *Psychological Review, 102,* 379–395.

Grace, J., & Pennington, J. (2000, February). *Exploring the factors that may reduce optimism among smokers.* Paper presented at the annual meeting of the Society for Personality and Social Psychology, Nashville, TN.

Greenwald, A. G. (1980). The totalitarian ego: Fabrication and revision of personal history. *American Psychologist, 35,* 603–618.

Hadler, B., & Hadler, E. (1990). *Chicken little.* New York: Smith.

Harter, S., & Pike, R. (1984). The pictorial scale of perceived competence and social acceptance for young children. *Child Development, 55,* 1969–1982.

Helweg-Larsen, M., Sadeghian, P., & Webb, M. A. (2002). The stigma of being pessimistically biased. *Journal of Social and Clinical Psychology, 21,* 92–107.

James, W. (1890). *The principles of psychology* (Vol. 1). New York: Holt.

Kunda, Z. (1990). The case for motivated reasoning. *Psychological Bulletin, 108,* 480–498.

Leary, M. R., & Shepperd, J. A. (1986). Self-handicapping: A conceptual note. *Journal of Personality and Social Psychology, 51,* 1265–1268.

Liberman, N., & Trope, Y. (1998). The role of feasibility and desirability considerations in near and distant future decisions: A test of temporal construal theory. *Journal of Personality and Social Psychology, 75,* 5–18.

Locke, E. A. (1967). Relationship of success and expectation to affect on goal-seeking task. *Journal of Personality and Social Psychology, 7,* 125–134.

McKenna, F. P., & Myers, L. B. (1997). Illusory self-assessments: Can they be reduced? *British Journal of Psychology, 88,* 39–51.

Mellers, B. A., & McGraw, A. P. (2001). Anticipated emotions as guides to choice. *Current Directions in Psychological Science, 10,* 210–214.

Mellers, B. A., Schwartz, A., Ho, K., & Ritov, I. (1997). Decision affect theory: Emotional reactions to the outcomes of risky options. *Psychological Science, 8,* 423–429.

Norem, J. K., & Cantor, N. (1986). Defensive pessimism: Harnessing anxiety and motivation. *Journal of Personality and Social Psychology, 51,* 1208–1217.

Pennington, J., Thompson, J., & Thoman, D. (2002, February). *The consequences of increasing and reducing health optimism among smokers.* Paper presented at the third annual meeting of the Society for Personality and Social Psychology, Savannah, GA.

Piaget, J. (1972). Intellectual evolution from adolescence to adulthood. *Human Development, 15,* 1–12.

Piper, W. (1930). *The little engine that could.* New York: Platt & Munk.

Pyszczynski, T. (1982). Cognitive strategies for coping with uncertain outcomes. *Journal of Research in Personality, 16,* 386–399.

Pyszczynski, T., & Greenberg, J. (1989). Toward an integration of cognitive and motivational perspectives on social inference: A biased hypothesis testing model. In L. Berkowitz (Ed.) *Advances in experimental social psychology* (Vol. 20, pp. 297–340). New York: Academic Press.

Robins, R. W., & Beer, J. S. (2001). Positive illusions about the self: Short-term benefits and long-term costs. *Journal of Personality and Social Psychology, 80,* 340–352.

Rothbaum, F., Weisz, J. R., & Snyder, S. S. (1982). Changing the world and changing the self: A two-process model of perceived control. *Journal of Personality and Social Psychology, 42,* 5–37.

Rozin, P., & Nemeroff, C. (1990). The laws of sympathetic magic: A psychological analysis of similarity and contagion. In J. W. Stigler, R. A. Shweder, & G. H. Herdt (Eds.), *Cultural psychology: Essays on comparative human development* (pp. 205–232). New York: Cambridge University Press.

Sackett, A. M. (2002). *Optimism and accuracy in performance predictions: An experimental test of the self-protection hypothesis.* Unpublished master's thesis, Yale University.

Sanna, L. J. (1999). Mental simulations, affect, and subjective confidence: Timing is everything. *Psychological Science, 10,* 339–345.

Sanna, L. J., Turley-Ames, K. J., & Meier, S. (1999). Mood, self-esteem, and simulated alternatives: Thought-provoking affective influences on counterfactual direction. *Journal of Personality and Social Psychology, 76,* 543–558.

Savitsky, K., Medvec, V. H., Charlton, A. E., & Gilovich, T. (1998). "What, me worry?": Arousal, misattribution, and the effect of temporal distance on confidence. *Personality and Social Psychology Bulletin, 24,* 529–536.

Scheier, M. F., & Carver, C. S. (1988). A model of behavioral self-regulation: Translating intention into action. In L. Berkowitz (Ed.), *Advances in experimental social psychology* (Vol. 21, pp. 303–346). New York: Academic Press.

Schwarz, N., & Clore, G. L. (1988). How do I feel about it? Informative functions of affective states. In K. Fiedler & J. Forgas (Eds.), *Affect, cognition, and social behavior* (pp. 44–62). Toronto, Ontario, Canada: Hogrefe.

Segerstrom, S. C., Castañeda, J. O., & Spencer, T. E. (2003). Optimism effects on cellular immunity: Testing the affective and persistence models. *Personality and Individual Differences, 35,* 1615–1624.

Segerstrom, S. C., Taylor, S. E., Kemeny, M. E., & Fahey, J. L. (1998). Optimism is associated with mood, coping, and immune change in response to stress. *Journal of Personality and Social Psychology, 74,* 1646–1655.

Shepperd, J. A., Carroll, P., Tobin, S., & Findley-Klein, C. F. (2003). [Bracing and the controllability of outcomes]. Unpublished raw data.

Shepperd, J. A., Findley-Klein, C., Kwavnick, K. D., Walker, D., & Perez, S. (2000). Bracing for loss. *Journal of Personality and Social Psychology, 78,* 620–634.

Shepperd, J. A., & McNulty, J. K. (2002). The affective consequences of expected and unexpected outcomes. *Psychological Science, 13,* 85–88.

Shepperd, J. A., Morato, J. J., & Pbert, L. A. (1996). Dispositional optimism as a predictor of health changes among cardiac patients. *Journal of Research in Personality, 30,* 517–534.

Shepperd, J. A., Ouellette, J. A., & Fernandez, J. K. (1996). Abandoning unrealistic optimism: Performance estimates and the temporal proximity of self-relevant feedback. *Journal of Personality and Social Psychology, 70,* 844–855.

Showers, C., & Ruben, C. (1990). Distinguishing defensive pessimism from depression: Negative expectations and positive coping mechanisms. *Cognitive Therapy and Research, 14,* 385–399.

Spencer, S. J., & Steele, C. M. (1994). *Self-esteem functioning: The role of affirmational resources in self-evaluation.* Unpublished manuscript, State University of New York, Buffalo.

Taylor, K. M., & Shepperd, J. A. (1998). Bracing for the worst: Severity, testing and feedback as moderators of the optimistic bias. *Personality and Social Psychology Bulletin, 24,* 915–926.

Taylor, S. E., & Brown, J. D. (1988). Illusion and well being: A social psychological perspective on mental health. *Psychological Bulletin, 103,* 193–210.

Taylor, S. E., & Gollwitzer, P. M. (1995). The effects of mindset on positive illusions. *Journal of Personality and Social Psychology, 69,* 213–226.

Terry, M., & Shepperd, J. A. (2004, January). *Changing standards: Adjusting the definition of an acceptable outcome.* Paper presented at the annual meeting of the Society for Personality and Social Psychology, Austin, TX.

Tetlock, P. E. (1992). The impact of accountability on judgment and choice: Toward a social contingency model. In M. P. Zanna (Ed.), *Advances in experimental social psychology* (Vol. 25, pp. 331–376). New York: Academic Press.

Tetlock, P. E., & Kim, J. I. (1987). Accountability and judgment processes in a personality prediction task. *Journal of Personality and Social Psychology, 52,* 700–709.

Thibaut, J. W., & Kelley, H. (1959). *The social psychology of groups.* New York: Wiley.

van Dijk, W. W., & van der Pligt, J. (1997). The impact of probability and magnitude of outcome on disappointment and elation. *Organizational Behavior and Human Decision Processes, 69,* 277–284.

van Dijk, W. W., Zeelenberg, M., & van der Pligt, J. (1999). Not having what you want versus having what you do not want: The impact of type of negative outcome on the experience of disappointment and related emotions. *Cognition and Emotion, 13,* 129–148.

Wadsworth, B. (1996). *Piaget's theory of cognitive and affective development* (5th ed.). White Plains, NY: Longman.

Weinstein, N. D. (1980). Unrealistic optimism about future life events. *Journal of Personality and Social Psychology, 39,* 806–820.

3

Defensive Pessimism

Positive Past, Anxious Present, and Pessimistic Future

JULIE K. NOREM
SHANNON SMITH

The ability to think about the past and the future, as well as about one's immediate situation, is a hallmark of human cognition. Understanding how we make judgments over time is vital to understanding what we do and how we feel. Our past becomes a pivotal character in our ongoing life stories, and "its" experiences help to define the ongoing plots we pursue (McAdams, 1987). We evaluate our present experiences relative to our understanding of the past and what we are working toward in the future. The futures we imagine include particular outcomes and possible selves, the avoidance or achievement of which influence the ways in which our stories are comedies or tragedies (Markus & Ruvolo, 1989).

Individuals differ in the kinds of information and experience they emphasize as they interpret their lives over time. This chapter discusses how individual differences in the strategies people use to pursue their goals are related to the judgments they make about their past, present, and future circumstances. The focus is on these judgments and related affect, motivation, and behavior among those using the strategy of defensive pessimism.

Defensive Pessimism as a Strategy

Defensive pessimism is a strategy used by those who feel anxious and out of control in situations related to their personal goals (Cantor, Norem, Niedenthal, Langston, & Brower, 1987; Norem, 2001a, 2001b). These individuals set pessimistic expectations (even though they have typically done well in the past), and they spend considerable time and energy thinking through possible outcomes—particularly negative possible outcomes.

Although dispositional and attributional pessimism are often related to poorer outcomes across a variety of domains (Scheier & Carver, 1993; Seligman, 1998), research on defensive pessimism has repeatedly shown that people who use this strategy typically perform as well as their optimistic counterparts do. They also perform better when they use the strategy than when they try to be more optimistic, more cheerful, or less reflective (Norem & Cantor, 1986a, 1986b; Norem & Illingworth, 1993, 2004; Sanna, 1998; Spencer & Norem, 1996).

Those who use defensive pessimism are anxious, and understanding that is key to understanding the strategy. Anxiety is often debilitating: It may lead us to avoid situations we fear; or, even if we gather our courage to try, it can impede our progress by disrupting concentration, interfering with motor coordination, or making us appear less competent to others. Rather than running away or feeling immobilized because they are apprehensive about what might happen, however, defensive pessimists use their mental simulations of dire possibilities to plan and act effectively. Anxious individuals who use defensive pessimism tend to cope more effectively, perform better, and experience more satisfaction and higher self-esteem over time than equivalently anxious or pessimistic individuals who do not use defensive pessimism (Elliot & Church, 2003; Eronen, Nurmi, & Salmela Aro, 1998; Norem, 2001a, 2001b; Norem & Andreas Burdzovic, in press; Showers & Ruben, 1990).

Understanding that defensive pessimism can be an effective affect regulation strategy, however, is only one step in the process of making sense of defensive pessimism. The strategies that individuals use to pursue their goals do not exist in a vacuum, independent of other aspects of their past experience, personalities, self-knowledge, attributions, beliefs about the world, or hopes and fears for the future. Deeper understanding of defensive pessimism comes from a more complete examination of how defensive pessimists make sense of their world.

Defensive Pessimism and Judgments About the Past

Construal of Past Experience

As noted earlier, defensive pessimists typically perform well. From the perspective of an outside observer, defensive pessimism can seem particularly irrational for this reason. Why would someone who has done well in the past be pessimistic about the future? Why wouldn't consistent, repeated success lead to greater optimism? The persistence of negative expectations among defensive pessimism is multidetermined. We can begin to explore that persistence by raising the question of whether a defensive pessimist is likely to concur with an external observer's judgment that the defensive pessimist has done well.

Defensive pessimists do seem to acknowledge that they have done well in the past (Showers, 1992). Indeed, the questionnaire used to measure defensive pessimism has always included an item that asks respondents to rate how well they have performed in the past, and rating one's own performance relatively highly (e.g., a 5 or above on a 7-point scale, on which higher ratings indicate better performance) has been used as an explicit criterion to distinguish *defensive* pessimists (those whose pessimism is not justified by poor past performance) from *realistic* or *justified* pessimists (those whose past performance was poor, thus justifying pessimistic predictions about future performance; see Norem, 2001a).

Defensive pessimists' evaluations of their performances also correlate well with their actual performances (Norem, 2001a). Their strategy does not seem to interfere with or grossly distort their perceptions of how well they have done; moreover, they interpret their performances more positively (and more accurately) when they use their strategy than when they do not (Norem & Illingworth, 1993).

Left to their own devices, however, defensive pessimists do not typically spend much time thinking about the past. Showers and Ruben (1992) have shown that defensive pessimists' rumination does not persist once a situation is over. Defensive pessimism is actually related to *less* recall of past unsuccessful performances among anxious individuals, further supporting the contention that defensive pessimism is not normally maintained by retrospection about past negative events (Schoneman, 2002).

In a series of studies, Sanna found further evidence that, compared with more optimistic individuals, defensive pessimists are less likely to engage in *counterfactual* thinking, which is mental simulation of alternative outcomes after the real outcome has occurred. When they did engage in counterfactual thinking as a result of experimental manipulations, they were more likely to generate *upward* counterfactuals, which are mental simulations of outcomes that are *better* than the outcome that actually occurred; in contrast, more optimistic individuals were more likely to generate *downward* counterfactuals, in which they mentally simulate outcomes that are worse than the actual outcome (Sanna, 1996, 1998).

The fact that defensive pessimists do not typically ruminate about the past is likely to be an important reason that they do not appear to suffer the depressogenic effects that can accompany rumination. Especially given that, when they do think about what has happened in the past, they engage in mental simulations that are likely to increase negative affect, not thinking about the past would appear to be adaptive for defensive pessimists.

Another implication of these findings is that judgments about the past are likely to have relatively less influence on defensive pessimists' present and future behavior than might be the case for others. For example, one would not necessarily expect positive performance to decrease subsequent pessimism among defensive pessimists if their focus when anticipating upcoming events does not include much review of past events. Successful past performance is also less likely to decrease subsequent pessimism if, when it does come to mind, defensive pessimists emphasize thoughts of what could have gone better rather than the success itself. Finally, even when defensive pessimists are thinking about successful past performances, given that their primary goal tends to be avoiding failure (see later discussion), their typical thoughts are not likely to be "I was successful in the past" but "At least I didn't blow it that time."

As attribution theorists have taught us, the implications of a prior outcome for predicting future outcomes depend on what we perceive to have caused that prior outcome. Defensive pessimists can and do make attributions about their past outcomes, of course. When they do, their attributions are complex. For example, they tend toward internal rather than external attributions (Norem, 2001a). Whether outcomes are positive or negative, defensive pessimists tend to attribute particular performance outcomes to ability (internal and stable) and their effort (internal and variable). Even if they believe they are smart or competent in a particular domain, they also believe that they had to work hard to achieve what they have in the past. Interestingly, defensive pessimists report that their parents tend to believe that intelligence is not a fixed or stable entity. If defensive pessimists internalize their parents' views, they may not conceive of their ability as stable (Norem, 1991).

Further evidence suggests that defensive pessimists view the world as a tricky and unpredictable place and other people as somewhat uncontrollable (Norem, 2001a). In a sample of undergraduates, defensive pessimism was moderately associated with less endorsement of just-world beliefs and less assertion that one can predictably control other people's behavior or influence outcomes in broader social and political domains (Norem, 1992). Their home environment may have reinforced uncertainty about the rest of the world in that defensive pessimism is associated with reports of less cohesive family environments (Norem, 1991).

As they contemplate new situations, then, defensive pessimists continue to face the problem or task of motivating themselves to work hard, because they perceive that hard work was the key to their past success. Even if they believe they have been and will continue to be able to control their own behavior, the unpredictability of the world means that they cannot necessarily generalize from past experience to the present. Indeed, friends and family who try to argue defensive pessimists out of their dire predictions frequently hear in response that "this time is different—really!" (Norem, 2001b).

These attributional tendencies and beliefs about the world should mitigate against strong relationships between particular past performances and predictions about present and future circumstances. According to defensive pessimists, in other words, the past is *not* the best predictor of the future.

Affect and Retrospection

Not surprisingly, the judgments that defensive pessimists make about their past experiences are colored both by their affect during those experiences and by the affective implications of the interpretations they construct. Even though, relative to others' evaluations and to objective standards, defensive pessimists accurately evaluate their (generally good) performances, they do tend to be less satisfied with their performances relative to more optimistic individuals (Norem & Cantor, 1986a,b; Norem & Illingworth, 1993). Making things even more complicated, their performances are actually worse when they are in positive moods (Norem & Illingworth, 2004; Sanna, 1998; see later discussion). Congruent with their goal orientation (to avoid disaster), relief dominates their postperformance affect when they are successful, and the satisfaction they do experience coexists with memories of the anxiety they felt. This affect reinforces the judgment that past experience is characterized by uncertainty, and thus it has tenuous status as a basis for prediction of the future.

Remembering past success means remembering the hard work and worry that went into that success, reinforcing defensive pessimists' need to manage anxiety and prepare themselves for what might go wrong next time. Furthermore, they feel more enjoyment and satisfaction and relatively less anxiety when they use their strategy than when they do not (Norem & Illingworth, 1993). Thus thinking about past situations in which they used their strategy is unlikely to reassure defensive pessimists, but remembering times when they did *not* use their strategy may exacerbate negative affect. Given that retrospection about positive experiences is unlikely to serve either mood-enhancement or mood-repair functions, it is not surprising that defensive pessimists typically refrain from such retrospection.

Judgments About Past Behavior

As may already be clear from the previous discussion, for defensive pessimists, the key to past success is persistence and hard work. Indeed, given their high levels of anxiety and beliefs about the uncertainty of the world, their interpretations of their past behavior can be expressed succinctly: "I worked hard, and thus avoided disaster." Given that they do not tend to indulge in counterfactuals, they are unlikely to think about how they might have done well without so much effort, nor are they likely to consider that disaster may not have been so imminent (and thus their hard work not so crucial) in the first place. When they were more optimistic or more cheerful, their performances were likely to have been worse, probably because this positive perspective signaled less need for effort, which led to poorer performance (Norem & Illingworth, 2004).

As described earlier, Sanna (1996) has shown that when defensive pessimists are induced to generate counterfactuals, they are more likely to generate upward counterfactuals; that is, to mentally simulate how things might have been better. Their typical attributions and beliefs about the world and the relationship between their affect and performance conspire to lead defensive pessimists to decide that good outcomes were a function of not getting too cocky and working very hard and that better outcomes would have occurred with greater persistence and more hard work. In other words, from the defensive pessimists' perspective, they either worked hard, did not work hard enough, or could have worked harder.

Defensive Pessimism, Anxiety, and Performance in the Present

Pessimistic Thoughts and Planning for the Worst

Defensive pessimists' thoughts, emotions, and motivations exert reciprocal influences as their strategy unfolds in performance situations. As the name of the strategy indicates, their initial expectations are pessimistic relative to those of more optimistic individuals with similar performance histories or available information (Norem & Cantor, 1986a,b). These negative expectations then initiate extensive mental rehearsal of possible outcomes.

In initial theorizing about defensive pessimism, the hypothesis was that defensive pessimists reflected only about possible negative outcomes; subsequent research showed, however, that they play through both positive and negative outcomes in concrete and specific detail (Norem, 2001a). Thus a student preparing for a test may first simply predict that she will fail the exam. If she is a defensive pessimist, however, she will then begin to mentally rehearse precisely *how* that could happen (Showers, 1992). She imagines not getting through the entire study guide, misunderstanding key concepts, blanking out during the test, and running out of time on the final essay. As her mental review continues, however, she can also begin to envision specific behaviors that might prevent the negative events she imagines. The specificity of her mental simulation itself points to effective alternative plans.

Figuring out how to avoid failing an exam seems like an amorphous and potentially overwhelming problem. In contrast, figuring out how to ensure that one has sufficient time to work through the entire study guide is considerably more manageable. The process of imagining how to avoid disaster for each specific task (e.g., break the study guide into sections, schedule time each day for one section, check frequently to see whether schedule is working realistically, etc.) also illustrates how more positive outcomes might happen.

Sanna (1998) has shown that defensive pessimists generate more upward prefactuals than optimists; that is, prior to a performance, they mentally simulate outcomes that are better than those they initially expect. His research also shows that this prefactual simulation leads to *better* performance for defensive pessimists (but not for optimists). This research converges with other studies that show that this process of reflecting on possible outcomes is integral to good performance for defensive pessimists (Norem & Illingworth, 1993; Spencer & Norem, 1996).

Organizing goal-relevant or self-relevant knowledge in terms of specifics may be a general tendency among defensive pessimists. Yamawaki, Tschanz, and Feick (2004) found that defensive pessimists had a higher ratio of negative-to-positive academically relevant self-thoughts than optimists. This finding converges with research that shows that when defensive pessimists list characteristics that describe themselves, they list more negative characteristics than optimists do. Although their self-concepts and self-knowledge are more negative than those of optimists, however, both the positive and negative characteristics they list are also more specific than those listed by the optimists (Norem & Whitney, 1992).

Breaking down knowledge about the self—especially negative information that may be distressing—can be a very effective way both to allow that information into awareness without overwhelming distress and to figure out how to change negative characteristics. Although negative self-characteristics may be salient to them, defensive pessimists also seem to emphasize self-improvement and working to change those negative characteristics more than do either optimists or anxious individuals who do not use defensive pessimism. Among those three groups, defensive pessimists rate the aspects of themselves that they are working on changing as more important than their other existing characteristics, but the reverse is true for the other two groups. Defensive pessimists also report more positive change in those characteristics over a period of several months than do other anxious individuals. More generally, defensive pessimists are more likely to identify personal-growth-related goals and to report progress toward those goals than are either optimists or anxious persons (Norem, 2002).

The defensive pessimists' awareness of the negative encompasses more than just their understanding of themselves; it also extends to their construal of the other goals they pursue. Cantor and her colleagues found that defensive pessimists, compared with optimists, are more likely to perceive their life tasks as conflicting with one another (Cantor et al., 1987). At a more general level, Elliot and Church (2003) found that defensive pessimists, motivated by their fear of failure, adopted both approach- and avoidance-focused performance goals. In contrast to self-handicappers, however, their avoidance-focused goals were not associated with poor performance.

Affect and Goal Pursuit

Typical daily affect is more negative for defensive pessimists than for optimists (Cantor et al., 1987; Norem & Illingworth, 1994, 2004), and defensive pessimism is consistently correlated with higher trait anxiety and greater neuroticism (e.g., Norem & Cantor, 1986a; Norem, 2001a). The strategy itself does not appear either to reduce anxiety or to decrease fear of failure, at least in the long term. What it seems to do, however, is to transform those typically detrimental affects into more positive influences on performance.

Several studies have shown that the negative feelings that defensive pessimists experience during goal pursuit are facilitative rather than detrimental. Defensive pessimists certainly experience positive affect, and it is not difficult to induce more positive moods in them experimentally. For defensive pessimists, however, the effect of positive mood is to decrease performance (Norem & Illingworth, 2004; Sanna, 1998). Sanna's work showing reciprocal relations between prefactual thinking and mood states suggests that one of the ways in which defensive pessimists' negative moods facilitate their performance is by reinforcing mental rehearsal as a preparatory process (prefactual simulations). When defensive pessimists are in positive moods, they are less likely to engage in their typical mental simulations. As a consequence, they may be less well prepared for subsequent tasks because they did not think through potential problems. They may interpret their positive affect as a signal that they do not need to persist or work as hard as they typically do, which could further impair their performances.

Defensive pessimism may sometimes maintain or exacerbate negative affect. In particular, thinking about what might go wrong may temporarily increase anxiety, even if continued mental rehearsal ultimately moves anxiety to an optimal level. Those using the strategy may be less able or less motivated to use the kinds of mood-repair and mood-maintenance strategies used by optimists. Nevertheless, defensive pessimism as a strategy seems more aptly viewed as an adaptive response to chronically negative, failure-oriented thoughts and moods, as opposed to a cause of that negativity. The consistently better outcomes that defensive pessimists experience relative to other, equivalently anxious individuals lend support to this interpretation.

Judgments About Past Behavior: If It Worked Once, It Can Work Again

The behavioral imperative for defensive pessimists is to mobilize themselves to overcome the inhibitions caused by anxiety and fear of failure. The argument that defensive pessimism is adaptive for anxious individuals finds its greatest support in research that demonstrates that defensive pessimists engage in effective, *proactive* behavior that helps them ward off the disasters they fear and mentally simulate. Much of that research focuses on actual task performance among defensive pessimists, and it has already been mentioned. Across several domains (social, academic, recreational), defensive pessimists perform better when they set low expectations and reflect extensively about possible outcomes prior to their performance (Norem & Cantor, 1986a,b; Norem & Illingworth, 1993, 2004; Sanna, 1996; Sanna, 1998; Showers, 1992; Spencer & Norem, 1996).

Other recent research provides convergent evidence that the defensive pessimists' pessimism and reflectivity promote effective behavior. Schoneman (2002), for example, found that among socially anxious people, defensive pessimists showed less avoidance of social situations than did those who did not use defensive pessimism. Norem (2002) found increased use of college support services among defensive pessimists, as well as better subsequent social, academic, and health-related outcomes, relative to anxious students who did not use defensive pessimism. W. C. Chang and colleagues showed that defensive pessimism was associated with greater SARS-related fear among Singaporeans but was also related to more preventative health-related behaviors that were directly relevant to SARS (W. C. Chang & Sivam, 2004). E. C. Chang argues that the pessimism reported by Asian American individuals is similar to defensive pessimism and found that it was associated with active problem-solving approaches to stressors (E. C. Chang, 1996).

How Bright Is the Future?

Defensive Pessimists' Possible Selves

It is difficult to draw a sharp distinction between the judgments that defensive pessimists make about their current situations and those that they make about the future, because the strategy itself is directed toward upcoming events. Anxiety is fundamentally an anticipatory emotion: It arises from the perception that danger, physical or psychological, lurks ahead at some point. The pessimism and reflectivity that characterize defensive pessimists are prompted by their anxiety as they face an impending performance situation.

One can get a sense of how defensive pessimism influences views beyond the confines of the near future, though, by considering the possible selves that defensive pessimists construct. Possible selves organize our beliefs about what we might become in the future and may represent long-term goals and expectations that provide comparison points for judgment and evaluation of the present (Wurf & Markus, 1991).

There are numerous potential ways we can think about ourselves in the future. Previous researchers have considered, for example, individuals' *ideal* possible selves (i.e., ourselves as we would ideally like to become), *ought* selves (ourselves as we believe we should be), and *feared* selves (negative selves we are worried we might become; Cross & Markus, 1994).

Among a sample of undergraduate women during their first semester of college, ratings of the controllability, likelihood, and importance of ideal, ought, and feared possible selves reveal intriguing differences between constructions of those selves by defensive pessimists and more optimistic individuals on the one hand and by defensive pessimists and equally anxious women who do not use defensive pessimism on the other. Defensive pessimists and optimists both appraise their ideal and ought selves as more important than their feared selves; nevertheless, defensive pessimists and other anxious individuals report that they consider their feared possible selves to be more important than optimists consider theirs to be. This finding is not surprising, given that avoidance motivation should be stronger for those high in anxiety and that feared possible selves should be cognitive representations of the specific self-relevant outcomes one is motivated to avoid. Defensive pessimists differ from the other anxious respondents, however, in that they report that all of their possible selves are potentially more under their control. Correspondingly, defensive pessimists report that their positive possible selves (ideal and ought) are more likely, and their feared possible selves less likely, to be realized than other anxious students reported for their correlate possible selves (Norem, 1994).

There is some suggestion, then, that even when defensive pessimists look beyond impending situations, they continue to be vigilant about potential negative outcomes, as reflected in the relative importance they assign to their feared possible selves. Attributions that their effort has been integral to past success, however, may lead them—in contrast to other anxious individuals—to believe that with continued vigilance and persistence they can ward off the feared possible selves that might otherwise appear.

Just as with their beliefs about their actual or present selves, the defensive pessimists express a mixture of positive and negative conceptions concerning their future selves. Their judgments about past, present, and future are *not* monolithically negative, despite their persistent pessimism. Moreover, there is considerable hopefulness imbedded in their ongoing sense that, even if they cannot control everything and there is always the potential for negative outcomes, their own actions can help to prevent those outcomes.

Affect and Strategy Stability or Change

As discussed earlier in this chapter, the defensive pessimist's general tendency to avoid extensive counterfactual thinking can be viewed as effective affect regulation in the short term. If their retrospection is negatively tinged because of past anxiety, or if they primarily generate upward counterfactuals, then that retrospection would be likely to exacerbate negative affect.

One might predict that repeated success over time would lower subsequent anxiety: If one reviews a string of past successes, one might very well conclude that there is no reason to be anxious in the future. Yet if defensive pessimists do not dwell on or internalize the fact that they have been successful, their anxiety may reappear in future situations, once again initiating the strategy. Even if they do reflect, if their conclusion is that they have been successful with respect to the goal of narrowly avoiding disaster, the implications for the future are that vigilance and effort continue to be the only bulwarks against doom, the potential for which is ample basis for continued anxiety.

The cycle of motivation, affect, and cognition that characterizes defensive pessimism should be somewhat self-perpetuating. To the extent that defensive pessimists continue to feel anxious, they should continue to use their strategy. This may be an advantage in that it might ward off complacency and motivate continued hard work. Using a strategy that has worked well in the past is often a good choice.

This does not imply, of course, that there is no potential for strategy change. Rather, it implies that change is more likely to be a function of affective response to performance situations than a direct result of performance outcome. There has not yet been extensive research on strategy change. Two studies, however, have found patterns of change that provide some support for the description offered here. Over a 2-year period, Martin, Marsh, and Debus (2001) found that less anxiety and increased feelings of control predicted decreases in defensive pessimism. Eronen et al. (1998) found that satisfaction with achievement predicted similar changes.

Defensive Pessimists' Judgments and Judging Defensive Pessimism

Very little is known about how much success or habituation, under what conditions, might be necessary before defensive pessimists begin to feel less anxious. Habit, and perhaps belief that anxiety is necessary for good performance, may maintain the strategy beyond the time at which the individual using it is so anxious the he or she needs to prevent anxiety from interfering with performance.

It is not clear that changing strategies is necessarily desirable or beneficial for defensive pessimists. The problems they encounter may have more to do with others' lack of understanding of how their strategy works for them and their chronic affective tendencies than they have to do with defensive pessimism (Gagne & Norem, 2005). One could argue that their anxiety is unwarranted, or that they "should" be more optimistic, given their performance histories. This judgment of defensive pessimism, however, ignores the motivation for the strategy and the way that it is embedded in the defensive pessimists' experience and worldview. To the extent that their performance is important to them and that their motivational orientation is toward avoiding failure, defensive pessimism seems to work well in helping individuals to pursue their goals.

References

Cantor, N., Norem, J. K., Niedenthal, P. M., Langston, C. A., & Brower, A. (1987). Life tasks, self-concept ideals, and cognitive strategies in a life transition. *Journal of Personality and Social Psychology, 53*(6), 1178–1191.

Chang, E. C. (1996). Evidence for the cultural specificity of pessimism in Asians vs Caucasians: A test of a general negativity hypothesis. *Personality and Individual Differences, 21*(5), 819–822.

Chang, W. C., & Sivam, R.-W. (2004). Constant vigilance: Heritage values and defensive pessimism in coping with severe acute respiratory syndrome in Singapore. *Asian Journal of Social Psychology, 7*, 35–53.

Cross, S. E., & Markus, H. R. (1994). Self-schemas, possible selves, and competent performance. *Journal of Educational Psychology, 86*, 423–438.

Elliot, A. J., & Church, M. A. (2003). A motivational analysis of defensive pessimism and self-handicapping. *Journal of Personality, 71*(3), 369–396.

Eronen, S., Nurmi, J. E., & Salmela Aro, K. (1998). Optimistic, defensive-pessimistic, impulsive and self-handicapping strategies in university environments. *Learning and Instruction, 8*(2), 159–177.

Gagne, F. M., & Norem, J. K. (2005, January). *"Thanks for your support (not)": When partner strategy and social support don't mix.* Paper presented at the annual meeting of the Society for Personality and Social Psychology, New Orleans, LA.

Markus, H. R,, & Ruvolo, A. (1989). Possible selves. Personalized representation of goals. In L. A. Pervin (Ed.), *Goal concepts in personality and social psychology* (pp. 211–241.). Hillsdale, NJ: Erlbaum.

Martin, A. J., Marsh, H. W., & Debus, R. L. (2001). Self-handicapping and defensive pessimism: Exploring a model of predictors and outcomes from a self-protection perspective. *Journal of Educational Psychology, 93*(1), 87–102.

McAdams, D. P. (1987). A life story model of identity. In R. Hogan & W. H. Jones (Eds.), *Perspectives in personality* (Vol. 2, pp. 15–50). Greenwich, CT: JAI Press.

Norem, J. K. (1991, August). *Parental beliefs and children's endeavors.* Paper presented at the annual meeting of the American Psychological Association, San Francisco, CA.

Norem, J. K. (1992). Correlation matrix. Unpublished data.

Norem, J. K. (1994, August). *Who is in pursuit of what? Relationships among goal constructs, self-knowledge, and life outcomes.* Paper presented at the meeting of the American Psychological Association, Los Angeles, CA.

Norem, J. K. (2001a). Defensive pessimism, optimism, and pessimism. In E. C. Chang (Ed.), *Optimism and pessimism: Implications for theory, research and practice* (pp. 77–100). Washington, DC: American Psychological Association.

Norem, J. K. (2001b). *The positive power of negative thinking.* New York: Basic Books.

Norem, J. K. (2002). *Defensive pessimism and personal growth: From negative thinking to positive outcomes.* Unpublished manuscript, Wellesley College.

Norem, J. K., & Andreas Burdzovic, J. A. (in press). Understanding journeys: Individual growth analysis as a tool for studying individual differences in change over time. In A. D. Ong & M. V. Dulmen (Eds.), *Handbook of methods in positive psychology.* London: Oxford University Press.

Norem, J. K., & Cantor, N. (1986a). Anticipatory and post hoc cushioning strategies: Optimism and defensive pessimism in "risky" situations. *Cognitive Therapy and Research, 10*(3), 347–362.

Norem, J. K., & Cantor, N. (1986b). Defensive pessimism: Harnessing anxiety as motivation. *Journal of Personality and Social Psychology, 51,* 1208–1217.

Norem, J. K., & Illingworth, K. S. S. (2004). Mood and performance among defensive pessimists and strategic optimists. *Journal of Research in Personality, 38,* 351–366.

Norem, J. K., & Illingworth, K. S. S. (1993). Strategy-dependent effects of reflecting on self and tasks: Some implications of optimism and defensive pessimism. *Journal of Personality and Social Psychology, 65,* 822–835.

Norem, J. K., & Whitney, D. M. (1992, April). *Specificity of self: Emotional and behavioral implications.* Paper presented at the Eastern Psychological Association, Boston, MA.

Sanna, L. J. (1996). Defensive pessimism, optimism, and simulating alternatives: Some ups and downs of prefactual and counterfactual thinking. *Journal of Personality and Social Psychology, 71*(5), 1020–1036.

Sanna, L. J. (1998). Defensive pessimism and optimism: The bitter-sweet influence of mood on performance and prefactual and counterfactual thinking. *Cognition and Emotion, 12*(5), 635–665.

Scheier, M. F., & Carver, C. S. (1993). On the power of positive thinking: The benefits of being optimistic. *Current Directions in Psychological Science, 2*(1), 26–30.

Schoneman, S. W. (2002). The role of the cognitive coping strategy of defensive pessimism within the social-evaluative continuum. (Doctoral dissertation, Texas Tech University, 1990). *Dissertation Abstracts International, 63,* 3024.

Seligman, M. E. P. (1998). The prediction and prevention of depression. In D. K. Routh (Ed.), *The science of clinical psychology: Accomplishments and future directions* (pp. 201–214). Washington, DC: American Psychological Association.

Showers, C. (1992). The motivational and emotional consequences of considering positive or negative possibilities for an upcoming event. *Journal of Personality and Social Psychology, 63*(3), 474–484.

Showers, C., & Ruben, C. (1990). Distinguishing defensive pessimism from depression: Negative expectations and positive coping mechanisms. *Cognitive Therapy and Research, 14*(4), 385–399.

Spencer, S. M., & Norem, J. K. (1996). Reflection and distraction: Defensive pessimism, strategic optimism, and performance. *Personality and Social Psychology Bulletin, 22*(4), 354–365.

Wurf, E., & Markus, H. R. (1991). Possible selves and the psychology of personal growth. In D. J. Ozer & J. M. J. Healy (Eds.), *Perspectives in personality* (Vol. 3, pp. 39–62). Philadelphia: Kingsley.

Yamawaki, N., Tschanz, B. T., & Feick, D. L. (2004). Defensive pessimism, self-esteem instability, and goal strivings. *Cognition and Emotion, 18,* 233–249.

4

Pursuing a Path to a More Perfect Future

On Causes, Correlates, and Consequences of Perfectionism

EDWARD C. CHANG
CHRISTINA A. DOWNEY
ELIZABETH Y. LIN

During the Middle Kingdom (1991–1778 B.C.) in Egypt, the perfect individual was defined as one who was *"effective* because his life [was] in harmonious attunement to society and nature, the universal order . . ." (La Rondelle, 1971, p. 8). By actively living in step with the grandest and most valued of ideals, the perfect individual was expected to naturally accumulate greater positive than negative experiences throughout his or her life.

Within the culture of the ancient Greeks, the pursuit of perfection was both implicitly and explicitly tied to notions of seeking the good life (*summum bonum*). Among the Greeks, the idea of perfectionism was often equated with their concept of excellence (*areté*). For example, according to Aristotle, happiness (*eudaemonia*) was, for most rational beings, derived from living a deliberate life guided by virtuous actions, whereas unhappiness resulted for those who lived a life guided by vices. Importantly, among the different moral virtues identified, Aristotle believed that excellence or perfection was the highest virtue possible.

Similar notions of perfectionism and of the process of trying to perfect oneself as a good or a virtue can also be found in the classical writings of Buddha and Confucius (e.g., Aitken, 1994; Ratnayaka, 1978). In contrast to classical views that have marked the pursuit of high standards of performance as a good (Hurka, 1993), modern notions, often clinically focused, have tended to represent perfectionism as undesirable and dysfunctional (e.g., Burns, 1980; Frost, Marten, Lahart, & Rosenblate, 1990; Hewitt & Flett, 1991; Hollender, 1965; Shafran, Cooper, & Fairburn, 2002).

The Present Correlates and Future Consequence of Perfectionism

Perfectionism as Distressful

One of the most popular models of perfectionism is the one presented by Frost et al. (1990). According to these investigators, perfectionism is composed of six distinguishable dimensions: (1) concern over mistakes, (2) personal standards, (3) doubts about actions, (4) organization, (5) parental expectations, and (6) parental criticism. Another popular model of perfectionism is the one presented by Hewitt and Flett (1991). According to these investigators, perfectionism is composed of three distinguishable dimensions: (1) self-oriented perfectionism, (2) socially prescribed perfectionism, and (3) other-oriented perfectionism. Although these two popular models are not identical, they share some common conceptual underpinnings. First, both models recognize that the source of perfectionistic thoughts can be both self-oriented and socially prescribed. In addition, both models are based on a fundamental assumption that perfectionism represents a maladaptive construct. Indeed, studies based on using measures derived from these two conceptual models (viz., Frost Multidimensional Perfectionism Scale [FMPS] and the Multidimensional Perfectionism Scale [MPS], respectively) have provided consistent support for the notion that perfectionism is maladaptive.

Findings from mostly cross-sectional studies have shown that perfectionism is associated with a variety of maladaptive cognitive, affective, and behavioral correlates. Perfectionism has been found to be positively linked to a number of maladaptive behavior patterns, including the use of dysfunctional coping strategies. For example, studies of young adults have shown that perfectionism is associated with the use of greater ineffective or avoidant coping strategies (e.g., Chang, 2002; Dunkley & Blankstein, 2000; Dunkley, Blankstein, Halsall, Williams, & Winkworth, 2000; Dunkley, Zuroff, & Blankstein, 2003). In young adult females, studies have also shown that greater perfectionism is associated with greater bulimic patterns, including greater binging and purging behaviors (e.g., Garner, Olmstead, & Polivy, 1983; Joiner, Heatherton, Rudd, & Schmidt, 1997; Minarik & Ahrens, 1996). Similarly, in a study of married adult couples, Haring, Hewitt, and Flett (2003) found that perfectionism in both husbands and wives is linked to the use of greater maladaptive marital behavior patterns (e.g., self-blaming, being sarcastic to partner). In addition, perfectionism has been linked to a host of broad and specific maladaptive cognitions. For example, studies of adults have shown that greater perfectionism is linked to greater irrational thinking (Flett, Hewitt, Blankstein, & Koledin, 1991), negative automatic thinking (Flett, Hewitt, Blankstein, & Gray, 1998), and greater dysfunctional attitudes (Ashby & Rice, 2002). Furthermore, some studies have shown that greater perfectionism is specifically linked to greater body image dissatisfaction (Vohs et al., 2001), hopelessness and suicide ideation (Chang, 1998, 2002; Hewitt, Flett, & Weber, 1994), negative problem orientation (Chang, 1998), rumination (Flett, Madorsky, Hewitt, & Heisel, 2002), and greater worry (Chang, 2000). In addition, perfectionism has recently been linked to what has been referred to as "not just right experiences." Specifically, perfectionism has been found in studies of young adults to be associated with greater obsessive-like perceptions of things not being just right (e.g., perception that one is not recalling the past accurately; Coles, Frost, Heimberg, & Rhéaume, 2003). Thus, overall, perfectionism in adults appears to be associated with a range of dysfunctional behavior patterns, maladaptive thoughts, and thinking processes. Beyond this set of associations, the most robust and reliable associations to emerge from the empirical literature in the past decade have been between perfectionism and negative affective conditions. Findings from a number of studies have consistently linked perfectionism to greater concurrent experiences of negative affect (e.g., Chang & Rand, 2000; Frost, Heimberg, Holt, Mattia, & Neubauer, 1993). For example, Chang, Watkins, and Banks (2004) found that perfectionism was associated with greater experiences of global negative affect in both White and Black female college students. Moreover, studies examining specific negative affective conditions in adults have provided additional evidence for a maladaptive link. For example, researchers have found that perfectionism in clinical and nonclinical adult samples is associated with greater depressive symptoms (e.g., Chang & Sanna, 2001; Cheng, 2001; Enns & Cox, 1999; Frost et al., 1993; Frost et al., 1990; Hewitt & Flett, 1991, 1993; Joiner & Schmidt, 1995). Similarly, researchers have found a link between perfectionism and greater experiences of anxiety in adults (e.g., Flett, Hewitt, & Dyck, 1989; Frost et al., 1990; Hewitt & Flett, 1991; Saboonchi & Lundh, 1997). In addition, researchers have also identified a link between perfectionism and greater stress (e.g., Chang, 2000; Dunkley et al., 2000; Lynd-Stevenson & Hearne, 1999; Mitchelson & Burns, 1998). Taken together, these convergent findings have tended to represent perfectionism as a distressing personality variable that is associated with chronic negative affective conditions, including experiences of depressive symptoms, anxiety, and stress.

Perfectionism as a Future Distress Maker

Apart from the notion that being perfectionistic is concurrently associated in time with distressing experiences, some researchers have argued that being perfectionistic may even lead to greater distressing experiences over time. Specifically, Hewitt, Flett, and Ediger (1996) have contended that "perfectionistic behavior can generate stress that stems, in part, from the tendency for perfectionists to evaluate stringently, focus on negative aspects of performance, and

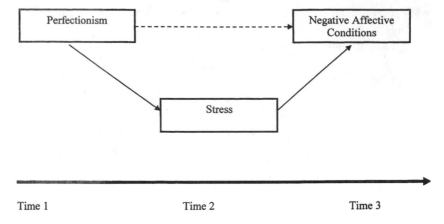

Figure 4.1. A model of how stress may mediate the association between perfectionism and negative affective conditions across time.

experience little satisfaction" (p. 276). This stress-generation model of perfectionism, or the notion that perfectionism may generate stress that in turn leads to greater negative affective conditions over time, is illustrated in Figure 4.1. To date, a number of studies have attempted to test this model in adults. In one study, Chang (2000) examined the extent to which stress experiences mediated the associations between perfectionism and general negative affect in young and middle-aged adult samples and found evidence for partial mediation. Specifically, stress experiences were found to account for much of the variance in the associations between perfectionism and negative affect across these two adult groups, but they did not eliminate the direct links between perfectionism and negative affect. In a more recent study focusing on young adult females, Chang et al. (2004) again found that stress partially mediated the link between perfectionism and negative affect in a sample of White female college students. However, for Black female college students, stress was found to fully mediate the link between perfectionism and negative affect. Thus the finding obtained for Black females was strongly in line with the stress-generation model of perfectionism proposed by Hewitt et al. (1996). Similarly, Dunkley and his associates (Dunkley et al., 2000; Dunkley et al., 2003; cf. Dunkley & Blankstein, 2000) have also found support for the notion that the link between perfectionism and negative affective conditions is mediated by greater stressful experiences or hassles in young adults. Unfortunately, most of these findings are based on studies using a cross-sectional design (e.g., Chang, 2000; Dunkley et al., 2000), or are based on studies using aggregated responses of stress and negative affective conditions across a very short period of time (e.g., 8 days; Dunkley, Zuroff, & Blankstein, 2003). Thus, despite these promising findings, no large scale multi-wave study has yet been conducted that seeks to investigate perfectionism in generating stress experiences that are believed to result later in the experience of greater negative affective conditions in adults.

Beyond a stress-generation model of perfectionism, it has also been argued that perfectionism may combine or interact as a vulnerability factor or diathesis with concurrent stress experiences to predict greater negative affective conditions in the future (Hewitt et al., 1996). Findings from several cross-sectional studies of adults have provided support consistent with this view (e.g., Chang & Rand, 2000; Dunkley et al., 2000; Hewitt & Flett, 1993) even across different cultural groups. For example, Cheng (2001) also found perfectionism to interact with stress experiences to predict depressive symptoms in a sample of Chinese adults. Moreover, in a longitudinal study of adult patients, Hewitt et al. (1996) found that perfectionism interacted with stress to predict depressive experiences 4 months later in this group. Thus recent findings based on studies of both stress-generation models and diathesis-stress models of perfectionism provide some support for the general notion that perfectionism may lead to or interact with stress experiences, which in turn may lead to the development of greater negative affective experiences in adults. In all, in contrast to classical views of perfectionism as a virtue (Hurka, 1993), findings from recent studies have tended to highlight perfectionism as if it were a modern vice (Blatt, 1995; Shafran & Mansell, 2001).

Considering Perfectionism as a Positive Construct: Learning From the Past

Thus far, our review of perfectionism has tended to underscore the conventional view of adult perfectionism as maladaptive (i.e., it is associated with concurrent distress and may lead to greater distress over time). However, there have been growing concerns that a more inclusive model is needed, one that takes into consideration the possibility of perfectionism as both maladaptive and adaptive (Chang, 2003). Indeed, decades before researchers conducted numerous studies that examined the relationship between perfectionism and psychological functioning, Hamachek (1978) made an important theoretical distinction between normal, or adaptive, and neurotic, or maladaptive, perfectionism:

> Persons who might fit under the label "normal perfectionists" (whom we could just as easily refer to as skilled artists or careful workers or masters of their craft) are those who derive a very real sense of pleasure from the labors of a painstaking effort and *who feel free to be less precise as the situation permits*. . . .

. . . This is not, however, apt to be true for neurotic perfectionists. Here we have the sort of people whose efforts—even their best ones—never seem quite good enough, at least in their own eyes. . . . They are unable to feel satisfaction because in their own eyes they *never seem to do things good enough to warrant that feeling.* (p. 27)

In keeping with this earlier and more inclusive psychological notion of perfectionism, some researchers who focus less on psychopathology and maladjustment have increasingly begun to explore the possibility that perfectionism can be both positive or adaptive *and* negative or maladaptive (Slade & Owens, 1998). In one study involving a college student population, Frost et al. (1993) found that scores on the FMPS subscales and the MPS subscales loaded onto two distinguishable factors, which they subsequently identified as reflecting positive strivings and maladaptive evaluation concerns. Specifically, these investigators found that FMPS scores on Personal Standards and Organization and MPS scores on Self-Oriented Perfectionism and Other-Oriented Perfectionism all loaded highest onto the adaptive perfectionism dimension, whereas FMPS scores on Concern over Mistakes, Parental Expectations, Parental Criticism, and Doubts about Actions and MPS scores on Socially Prescribed Perfectionism all loaded highest onto the maladaptive perfectionism dimension. Indeed, other researchers have found growing value in distinguishing between these two broad aspects of perfectionism using the FMPS subscales in both normal populations (e.g., Chang et al., 2004; Rice, Ashby, & Slaney, 1998; Rice & Dellwo, 2002) and clinical populations (e.g., Norman, Davies, Nicholson, Cortese, & Malla, 1998; Purdon, Antony, & Swinson, 1999).

In addition to these findings for the FMPS and MPS, other researchers have found value in making distinctions between adaptive and maladaptive perfectionism using alternative measures (e.g., Lynd-Stevenson & Hearne, 1999; Rice & Preusser, 2002; Slaney, Rice, Mobley, Trippi, & Ashby, 2001; Terry-Short, Owens, Slade, & Dewey, 1995). Accordingly, some researchers have begun increasingly to point to a need to distinguish between adaptive and maladaptive aspects of perfectionism when studying perfectionism (e.g., Enns, Cox, & Clara, 2002; Rice et al., 1998; see Chang, 2003, for a recent review). It is interesting to note that this growing trend in studies of perfectionism appears to parallel recent efforts to attain an inclusive understanding of psychological health and well-being (e.g., Chang & Sanna, 2003; Keyes & Haidt, 2003; McCullough & Snyder, 2000; Seligman & Csikszentmihalyi, 2000; Sheldon & King, 2001). Below, we present some exciting new theoretical and empirical work on performance perfectionism.

Identifying a Multidimensional and Multifunctional Model of Perfectionism: Performance Perfectionism Theory

In the absence of a comprehensive model and measure to study adaptive and maladaptive perfectionism, Chang (2005a) proposed a new model of perfectionism based on linking high standards of performance to outcome cognitions. In the following we present some of the key theoretical underpinnings behind this new model and then review some emerging findings.

High Standards of Performance: What Source Matters Most?

Currently, more than two dozen different conceptualizations of perfectionism have emerged in the literature (Flett & Hewitt, 2002). Of these, as mentioned earlier, two of the most popular conceptualizations (and measures) of a model of perfectionism have been those proffered by Frost et al. (1990) and Hewitt and Flett (1991). Although these two models and measures (viz., FMPS and MPS) advanced by Frost et al. (1990) and Hewitt and Flett (1991) do not fully map onto each other (Frost et al., 1993), two important conceptual similarities seem readily apparent. First, socially prescribed high standards of performance seem to define parental expectations, parental criticism, and socially prescribed perfectionism. Second, self-oriented high standards of performance seem to define concern over mistakes, personal standards, doubts about action, organization, and self-oriented perfectionism. Thus both of these popular models and measures of perfectionism place emphasis on self-oriented and socially prescribed sources of perfectionism. References to self-oriented or socially prescribed aspects of perfectionism can also be found in other models and measures of perfectionism (e.g., Joiner & Schmidt, 1995; Rice & Preusser, 2002; Slaney et al., 2001; Terry-Short et al., 1995). The emphasis on self-oriented perfectionism is not only in keeping with classical notions of perfectionism as a striving to attain an excellence of one's soul, but it is also in keeping with modern views which have consistently associated perfectionistic attributes with the setting of high personal standards of performance (e.g., Burns, 1980; Hollender, 1965; Hamachek, 1978; Pacht, 1984). Alternatively, the emphasis on socially prescribed perfectionism is in keeping with classical notions of perfectionism as involving harmony and attunement with the high ideals of others. This emphasis is also in keeping with modern views that have linked perfectionistic strivings with the challenges of meeting and achieving high social ideals and standards (e.g., Adler, 1931; Maslow, 1954; Rogers, 1961). In sum, although many different aspects or dimensions of perfectionism have been examined in the literature in recent decades, there appears to be some convergence across different models and measures of perfectionism in distinguishing between high standards of performance that are perceived to be self-oriented and standards that are perceived to be socially prescribed in origin.

Integrating Outcome Cognitions to High Standards of Performance: Does Holding Positive Versus Negative Cognitions Make a Difference?

Because much of human behavior is determined by our expectations for reaching future goals (e.g., hope, optimism, pessimism), Chang (2005a) proposed a need to link high standards of performance to positive and negative outcome cognitions for identifying potential adaptive and maladaptive aspects of perfectionism. The notion that activation of high standards of performance may operate in conjunction with the activation of outcome cognitions to determine behavior is not new. For some time, researchers have proposed various models of self-regulation that implicate the importance of goal-related standards that may sometimes lead to discrepancy experiences and of outcome cognitions that may direct or motivate behavior in such situations (e.g., Bandura, 1977; Higgins, 1987; Rotter, 1954; Scheier & Carver, 1985). When an individual perceives a discrepancy between some standard and a goal, positive and negative outcome cognitions are believed to play a powerful role in determining approach and avoidance behaviors, respectively (Carver & Scheier, 1982; Scheier & Carver, 1985). Alternatively, outcome cognitions are not thought to play an important role in determining behavior when an individual does not perceive a discrepancy between some standard and a goal. Therefore, it seems quite reasonable to expect that positive and negative outcome cognitions would naturally come into play when perceptions of high standards of performance are involved. Indeed, because negative outcome cognitions are often readily (even explicitly) implicated in items taken from existing measures used to assess for maladaptive perfectionism (e.g., "If I *fail* at work/school, I am a *failure* as a person"; "I *never felt* like I could meet my parents' standards"; "I find it *difficult* to meet others' expectations of me" [italics added]), it may not be surprising that the findings linking maladaptive perfectionism with negative outcomes or conditions have been fairly consistent. In contrast, because positive outcome cognitions are often not readily implicated in items taken from existing measures used to assess for adaptive perfectionism (e.g., "I have extremely high goals"; "One of my goals is to be perfect in everything I do"), it is quite possible that some individuals may appraise these items in light of positive outcome cognitions, negative outcome cognitions, or a mix of the two. In turn, this may help account for the lack of findings supporting a strong or consistent link between adaptive perfectionism and positive outcomes or conditions.

To avoid possible confusion with conventional approaches and definitions of perfectionism (especially those derived largely from pathological foundations), Chang (2005a) used the term *performance perfectionism* to refer to high standards of performance involving positive and negative outcome cognitions. However, performance perfectionism is not thought to represent a singular phenomenon. Rather, it is believed to represent a multifaceted construct that is determined not only by the presence of positive versus negative outcome cognitions but also by the source of high standards of performance, namely, self versus others. Indeed, beyond high standards of performance, a number of different models of perfectionism have all pointed to the importance of distinguishing between self-oriented and socially prescribed sources linked to adjustment and outcome (cf. Shafran et al., 2002; Shafran & Mansell, 2001). Therefore, because performance perfectionism may be determined by the source of high standards of performance (self-oriented vs. socially prescribed) and by the valence (positive vs. negative) of the outcome cognitions involved, four distinguishable aspects of performance perfectionism can be considered. As shown in Figure 4.2, two aspects of performance perfectionism are believed to be adaptive (positive self-oriented performance perfectionism and positive socially prescribed performance perfectionism), and two aspects of performance perfectionism are believed to be maladaptive (negative self-oriented performance perfectionism and negative socially prescribed performance perfectionism). *Positive self-oriented performance perfectionism* is defined by high personal standards of performance that involve positive outcome cognitions for the indi-

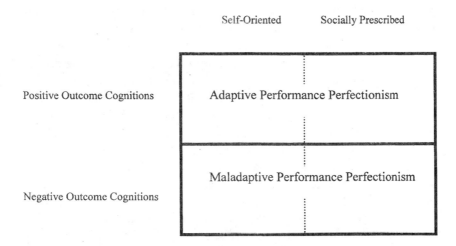

Figure 4.2. A multidimensional and multifunctional model of performance perfectionism based on source of high standards (self-oriented vs. socially prescribed) and valence of outcome cognitions (positive vs. negative).

vidual. *Negative self-oriented performance perfectionism* is defined by high personal standards of performance that involve negative outcome cognitions for the individual. *Positive socially prescribed performance perfectionism* is defined by high standards of performance that involve positive outcome cognitions placed on an individual by others. *Negative socially prescribed performance perfectionism* is defined by high standards of performance that involve negative outcome cognitions placed on an individual by others.

Linking the Past to the Present in Seeking Future Goals: An Outline of a Model of Performance Perfectionism Across Time

Drawing again from various works in social learning theory (e.g., Bandura, 1977; Rotter, 1954), different aspects of performance perfectionism are believed to develop and be associated with outcomes in different but predictable ways. During childhood, one might expect cognitive representations of positive and negative socially prescribed standards of performance perfectionism to become strongly influenced by direct success and failure experiences associated with early efforts to meet the high standards of significant others (e.g., parents, teachers, siblings, friends). As the child moves into adulthood, some of these representations may become assimilated into the individual's core representation of his or her own personal standards of performance perfectionism (Rogers, 1961). A model of this process of internalization is depicted in Figure 4.3. As the figure shows, some of the external high standards experienced during childhood are believed to become internalized by the time an individual reaches adulthood. Although perceptions of external high standards of performance are likely to remain present throughout adulthood, it is believed that self-oriented high standards matter more at this point of development.

There are at least two compelling reasons for believing in the greater involvement of self-oriented aspects of performance perfectionism over socially prescribed aspects of performance perfectionism in determining behaviors and outcomes in adults. First, consistent with cognitive models that link self-focused attention with emotional disorders and distress in adults, results from numerous studies that have attempted to identify vulnerability factors associated with maladjustment have consistently implicated negative self-referent thoughts as a major etiological factor (see Mor & Winquist, 2002, for a recent review). Likewise, a review of findings from other studies has pointed to a robust association between a variety of positive self-referent thoughts and positive psychological functioning (Taylor & Brown, 1988). Second, recent findings based on testing for a proximal-distal model have offered some support for the idea that socially prescribed aspects of perfectionism may lead to self-oriented aspects of perfectionism (Rice, Lopez, & Vergara, in press). For example, in one recent study of college students, Enns et al. (2002) found that a form of socially prescribed per-

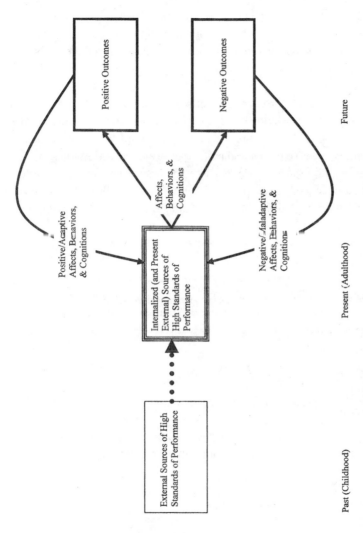

Figure 4.3. A model showing how past external sources affect current high standards in adults, which in turn determine future goal pursuits. The experience of successful or unsuccessful goal pursuits are believed to then inform subsequent appraisals of high standards of performance for the individual.

fectionism (viz., perfectionistic parenting) was related to depression proneness only through self-oriented forms of perfectionism. That is, socially prescribed perfectionism was not found to have a direct link with depression proneness, whereas self-oriented perfectionism was. Accordingly, one should find self-oriented aspects, and not socially prescribed aspects, of performance perfectionism to matter most in determining important outcomes and conditions in adult populations. Moreover, between positive and negative self-oriented aspects of performance perfectionism, it would seem reasonable to expect that the former, involving approach motives, would be more strongly associated with positive outcomes and conditions, whereas the latter, involving avoidance motives, would be more strongly associated with negative outcomes and conditions (Slade & Owens, 1998).

Additionally, within performance perfectionism theory (Chang, 2005a), it is hypothesized that the impact of incurring positive versus negative outcomes should have a meaningful and reciprocal impact on the subsequent accessibility of positive versus negative high standards of performance (see Figure 4.3). For example, dominance of positive over negative self-oriented performance perfectionism is what most likely helps most individuals successfully seek and obtain greater positive than negative outcomes over time. However, if an individual experiences greater negative than positive outcomes across time, then the aggregate consequence of such experiences is likely to make negative self-oriented performance perfectionism more dominant than positive self-oriented performance perfectionism. In turn, the outcome of such a process may then lead to fostering greater negative experiences and outcomes for the individual and result in a vicious downward cycle involving avoidant behaviors, negative thinking, and negative affect.

The Empirical Status of Performance Perfectionism Theory: Some Emerging Findings

Although studies on performance perfectionism have only recently been conducted, some basic and preliminary findings are worth mentioning.

Is Performance Perfectionism Multidimensional?
Development of the Performance Perfectionism
Scale (PPS)

Based on performance perfectionism theory, a pool of items reflecting distinct aspects of performance perfectionism was developed to create the 32-item Performance Perfectionism Scale (PPS; see Chang, 2005a, Studies 1a, 1b). Results from a factor-analytic study of responses provided by 638 college students indicated that the PPS tapped four distinguishable dimensions that mapped onto the expected four-factor model that underlies performance perfectionism theory (Chang, 2005a, Study 1b). Accordingly, the PPS is composed of four subscales, namely, Positive Self-Oriented Performance Perfectionism (e.g., "My desire to do things perfectly ensures my highest level of effectiveness"), Negative Self-Oriented Performance Perfectionism (e.g., "My high standards prevent me from doing my best"), Positive Socially Prescribed Performance Perfectionism (e.g., "I do my best when others push me to meet their high standards"), and Negative Socially Prescribed Performance Perfectionism (e.g., "I can't do anything right when others hold me to their high standards"). In addition to their factor structure, scores on these PPS scales have been found to be internally reliable and temporally stable across a 6-week period (Chang, 2005a, Study 1b).

In a subsequent study, Chang (2005a, Study 2) was able to show that scores on the PPS were not redundant with scores on a variety of measures assessing for alternative personality variables (e.g., optimism, pessimism, five-factor model of personality). In addition, scores on the PPS were found to be unrelated to scores that assess social desirability. In sum, these initial findings indicate that different aspects of performance perfectionism can be distinguished and measured by the PPS and that the PPS is a valid and reliable measure of performance perfectionism that is not redundant with other key personality measures.

Is Performance Perfectionism Multifunctional? A Look at Positive and Negative Psychological Functioning

Unlike most pathological models of perfectionism, a key assumption behind performance perfectionism theory is that some facets of performance perfectionism are adaptive, whereas other facets are maladaptive. Specifically, positive self-oriented and socially prescribed aspects of performance perfectionism are believed to represent important adaptive dimensions. In contrast, negative self-oriented and socially prescribed performance perfectionism are believed to represent important maladaptive dimensions. To determine whether this is true, Chang (2005a, Studies 3a and 3b) examined the associations between PPS scores and scores from measures assessing for both positive and negative psychological functioning in samples of college students. In one study, Chang (2005a, Study 3a) examined the associations between scores on the PPS and scores on several measures of negative psychological functioning, including those that assess negative automatic thinking, negative affect, psychological symptoms, depressive symptoms, and worry. Overall, findings from this study indicated that the two measures that assess aspects of negative performance perfectionism (viz., negative self-oriented and negative socially prescribed performance perfectionism) held positive associations with these and other measures of negative psychological functioning, whereas the two measures that assess positive aspects of performance perfectionism held no associations or negative associations with measures of negative psychological functioning.

In the other study, Chang (2005a, Study 3b) examined the associations between scores on the PPS and on several measures of positive psychological functioning, including those that assess life satisfaction, positive affect, and different representations of psychological well-being. Overall, findings from this study indicated that the two measures that assess aspects of positive performance perfectionism held positive associations with these measures of positive psychological functioning, whereas the two measures that assess negative aspects of performance perfectionism held no associations or negative associations with measures of positive psychological functioning. Thus, taken together, these findings indicate that some aspects of performance perfectionism may be more adaptive than other aspects, whereas some aspects of performance perfectionism may be more maladaptive than other aspects. Indeed, after partial correlations were computed that controlled for covariation between the PPS subscales, one fairly consistent pattern emerged across both studies; namely, that the most robust associations with psychological functioning that remained with measures of performance perfectionism were those involving self-oriented, and not socially prescribed, aspects of performance perfectionism. Accordingly, these findings can be taken to be consistent with the idea that self-oriented aspects, and not socially prescribed aspects, of performance perfectionism have greater involvement in adult behaviors broadly defined. Finally, it is worth mentioning that even after the inclusion of FMPS scores in predicting positive psychological functioning, PPS scores continued to predict significant additional variance in measures of positive psychological functioning beyond FMPS scores (Chang, 2005a, Study 3b). Therefore, the PPS does not seem to be wholly redundant with popular measures of perfectionism such as the FMPS.

Does Performance Perfectionism Predict Future Outcomes? A Look at Academic Achievement and Depressive Symptoms

Another important tenet of performance perfectionism theory is that performance perfectionism is believed to affect future outcomes. To investigate this possibility, two studies were conducted. First, Chang (2005a, Study 4) examined the prospective associations between PPS scores (taken during the first day of class) and academic achievement (across an academic term) in a sample of college students. As expected, this investigator found that positive self-oriented performance perfectionism was the only dimension to be consistently associated with greater academic achievement across time. Specifically, positive self-oriented performance perfectionism was found to be positively associated with outcome scores on four out of five exams and with final course grade. Moreover, these associations remained significant and in most cases unchanged even after controlling for scores on a measure of general intellectual ability. Thus these findings point to the importance of performance perfectionism as a potential determinant of positive outcomes.

In another study, Chang (2005b) examined the prospective associations between performance perfectionism and subsequent depressive symptoms in a sample of European American and Japanese college students. For both groups, negative self-oriented performance perfectionism was found to be strongly associated with concurrent depressive symptoms. Moreover, this dimension of performance perfectionism was found to also be associated with depressive symptoms in both groups 2months later, even after controlling for initial levels of depressive symptoms. Thus these findings are consistent with the notion that performance perfectionism is a potential determinant of negative outcomes. In sum, findings from these two studies support the notion of performance perfectionism as multifunctional and as a future determinant of important outcomes.

Some Concluding Thoughts

Although studies over the past decade have been based on a clinically derived view of perfectionism as pathological, there has been a growing acceptance by researchers of a multifunctional model of perfectionism, one that defines perfectionism as involving both adaptive and maladaptive features. As presented in this chapter, there is emerging evidence in favor of a model of perfectionism as both adaptive and maladaptive, as is the case in recent studies of performance perfectionism.

However, there remain many unanswered questions that have yet to be addressed in studies of perfectionism. For example, little is known about potential factors that may determine when and how socially prescribed standards experienced in childhood transform themselves to become self-oriented standards later on in adulthood. Thus there is an important need to understand the natural progression of perfectionism across the life span. Relatedly, some emerging works suggest that it may also be important to examine group variations in perfectionism. For example, most studies on perfectionism have been limited to the study of Whites or European Americans. In the few studies in which cultural or racial variations have been considered, researchers have increasingly found significant differences in levels or functions of perfectionism between different cultural and racial groups (e.g., Castro & Rice, 2003; Chang, 2005b; Chang et al., 2004). Therefore, in the effort to establish an inclusive theory of perfectionism, it may be particularly useful to test for potential group variations in the manner in which perfectionism unfolds over time. In this way, researchers and practitioners alike may be able to play effective roles in identifying and assisting diverse individuals in their efforts to pursue meaningful paths to a future that is more nearly perfect than the past or present.

References

Adler, A. (1931). *What life should mean to you.* Boston: Little, Brown.

Aitken, R. (1994). *The practice of perfection: The Pāramitās from a Zen Buddhist perspective.* New York: Pantheon Books.

Ashby, J. S., & Rice, K. G. (2002). Perfectionism, dysfunctional attitudes, and self-esteem: A structural equations analysis. *Journal of Counseling and Development, 80,* 197–203.

Bandura, A. (1977). Self-efficacy: Toward a unifying theory of behavioral change. *Psychological Review, 84,* 191–215.

Blatt, S. J. (1995). The destructiveness of perfectionism. *American Psychologist, 50,* 1003–1020.

Burns, D. D. (1980, November). The perfectionist's script for self-defeat. *Psychology Today, 14,* 34–52.

Carver, C. S., & Scheier, M. F. (1982). Control theory: A useful conceptual framework for personality-social, clinical, and health psychology. *Psychological Bulletin, 92,* 111–135.

Castro, J. R., & Rice, K. G. (2003). Perfectionism and ethnicity: Implications for depressive symptoms and self-reported academic achievement. *Cultural Diversity and Ethnic Minority Psychology, 9,* 64–78.

Chang, E. C. (1998). Cultural differences, perfectionism, and suicidal risk in a college population: Does social problem solving still matter? *Cognitive Therapy and Research, 22,* 237–254.

Chang, E. C. (2000). Perfectionism as a predictor of positive and negative psychological outcomes: Examining a mediation model in younger and older adults. *Journal of Counseling Psychology, 47,* 18–26.

Chang, E. C. (2002). Examining the link between perfectionism and psychological maladjustment: Social problem solving as a buffer. *Cognitive Therapy and Research, 26,* 581–595.

Chang, E. C. (2003). On the perfectibility of the individual: Going beyond the dialectic of good versus evil. In E. C. Chang & L. J. Sanna (Eds.), *Virtue, vice, and personality: The complexity of behavior* (pp. 125–143). Washington, DC: American Psychological Association.

Chang, E. C. (2005a). *Conceptualization and measurement of adaptive and maladaptive aspects of performance perfectionism: Relations to personality, psychological functioning, and academic achievement.* Manuscript submitted for publication.

Chang, E. C. (2005b). *Does performance perfectionism predict depressive symptoms across cultures? A prospective test of a model in Westerners and Easterners.* Manuscript submitted for publication.

Chang, E. C., & Rand, K. L. (2000). Perfectionism as a predictor of subsequent adjustment: Evidence for a specific diathesis-stress mechanism among college students. *Journal of Counseling Psychology, 47,* 129–137.

Chang, E. C., & Sanna, L. J. (2001). Negative attributional style as a moderator of the link between perfectionism and depressive symptoms: Preliminary evidence for an integrative model. *Journal of Counseling Psychology, 48,* 490–495.

Chang, E. C., & Sanna, L. J. (Eds.). (2003). *Virtue, vice, and personality: The complexity of behavior.* Washington, DC: American Psychological Association.

Chang, E. C., Watkins, A. F., & Banks, K. H. (2004). How adaptive and maladaptive perfectionism relate to positive and negative psychological functioning: Testing a stress-mediation model in Black and White female college students. *Journal of Counseling Psychology, 51,* 93–102.

Cheng, S. K. (2001). Life stress, problem solving, perfectionism, and depressive symptoms in Chinese. *Cognitive Therapy and Research, 25,* 303–310.

Coles, M. E., Frost, R. O., Heimberg, R. G., & Rhéaume, J. (2003). "Not just right experiences": Perfectionism, obsessive-compulsive features and general psychopathology. *Behaviour Research and Therapy, 41,* 681–700.

Dunkley, D. M., & Blankstein, K. R. (2000). Self-critical perfectionism, coping, hassles, and current distress: A structural equation modeling approach. *Cognitive Therapy and Research, 24,* 713–730.

Dunkley, D. M., Blankstein, K. R., Halsall, J., Williams, M., & Winkworth, G. (2000). The relation between perfectionism and distress: Hassles, coping, and perceived social support as mediators and moderators. *Journal of Counseling Psychology, 47,* 437–453.

Dunkley, D. M., Zuroff, D. C., & Blankstein, K. R. (2003). Self-critical perfectionism and daily affect: Dispositional and situational influences on stress and coping. *Journal of Personality and Social Psychology, 84,* 234–252.

Enns, M. W., & Cox, B. J. (1999). Perfectionism and depression symptom severity in major depressive disorder. *Behaviour Research and Therapy, 37,* 783–794.

Enns, M. W., Cox, B. J., & Clara, I. (2002). Adaptive and maladaptive perfectionism: Developmental origins and association with depression proneness. *Personality and Individual Differences, 33,* 921–935.

Flett, G. L., & Hewitt, P. L. (Eds.). (2002). *Perfectionism: Theory, research, and treatment.* Washington, DC: American Psychological Association.

Flett, G. L., Hewitt, P. L., Blankstein, K. R., & Gray, L. (1998). Psychological distress and the frequency of perfectionistic thinking. *Journal of Personality and Social Psychology, 75,* 1363–1381.

Flett, G. L., Hewitt, P. L., Blankstein, K. R., & Koledin, S. (1991). Dimensions of perfectionism and irrational thinking. *Journal of Rational-Emotive and Cognitive Behavior Therapy, 9,* 185–201.

Flett, G. L., Hewitt, P. L., & Dyck, D. G. (1989). Self-oriented perfectionism, neuroticism, and anxiety. *Personality and Individual Differences, 10,* 731–735.

Flett, G. L., Madorsky, D., Hewitt, P. L., & Heisel, M. (2002). Perfectionism cognitions, rumination, and psychological distress. *Journal of Rational-Emotive and Cognitive-Behavior Therapy, 20,* 33–47.

Frost, R. O., Heimberg, R. G., Holt, C. S., Mattia, J. I., & Neubauer, A. L. (1993). A comparison of two measures of perfectionism. *Personality and Individual Differences, 14,* 119–126.

Frost, R. O., Marten, P., Lahart, C., & Rosenblate, R. (1990). The dimensions of perfectionism. *Cognitive Therapy and Research, 14,* 449–468.

Garner, D. M., Olmsted, M. P., & Polivy, J. (1983). Development and validation of a multidimensional eating disorder inventory for anorexia nervosa and bulimia. *International Journal of Eating Disorders, 2,* 15–34.

Hamachek, D. E. (1978). Psychodynamics of normal and neurotic perfectionism. *Psychology: A Journal of Human Behavior, 15,* 27–33.

Haring, M., Hewitt, P. L., & Flett, G. L. (2003). Perfectionism, coping and quality of intimate relationships. *Journal of Marriage and Family, 65,* 143–158.

Hewitt, P. L., & Flett, G. L. (1991). Perfectionism in the self and social contexts: Conceptualization, assessment, and association with psychopathology. *Journal of Personality and Social Psychology, 60,* 456–470.

Hewitt, P. L., & Flett, G. L. (1993). Dimensions of perfectionism, daily stress, and depression: A test of the specific vulnerability hypothesis. *Journal of Abnormal Psychology, 102,* 58–65.

Hewitt, P. L., Flett, G. L., & Ediger, E. (1996). Perfectionism and depression: Longitudinal assessment of a specific vulnerability hypothesis. *Journal of Abnormal Psychology, 105,* 276–280.

Hewitt, P. L., Flett, G. L., & Weber, C. (1994). Dimensions of perfectionism and suicide ideation. *Cognitive Therapy and Research, 18,* 439–460.

Higgins, E. T. (1987). Self-discrepancy: A theory relating self and affect. *Psychological Review, 94,* 319–340.

Hollender, M. H. (1965). Perfectionism. *Comprehensive Psychiatry, 6,* 94–103.

Hurka, T. (1993). *Perfectionism.* New York: Oxford University Press.

Joiner, T. E., Heatherton, T. F., Rudd, M. D., & Schmidt, N. B. (1997). Perfectionism, perceived weight status, and bulimic symptoms: Two studies testing a diathesis-stress model. *Journal of Abnormal Psychology, 106,* 145–153.

Joiner, T. E., Jr., & Schmidt, N. B. (1995). Dimensions of perfectionism, life stress, and depressed and anxious symptoms: Prospective support for diathesis-stress but not specific vulnerability among male undergraduates. *Journal of Social and Clinical Psychology, 14,* 165–183.

Keyes, C. L. M., & Haidt, J. (Eds.). (2003). *Flourishing: Positive psychology and the life well-lived.* Washington, DC: American Psychological Association.

La Rondelle, H. K. (1971). *Perfection and perfectionism: A dogmatic-ethical study of biblical perfection and phenomenal perfectionism.* Berrien Spring, MI: Andrews University Press.

Lynd-Stevenson, R. M., & Hearne, C. M. (1999). Perfectionism and depressive affect: The pros and cons of being a perfectionist. *Personality and Individual Differences, 26,* 549–562.

Maslow, A. (1954). *Motivation and personality.* New York: Harper & Row.

McCullough, M. E., & Snyder, C. R. (2000). Classical sources of human strength: Revisiting an old home and building a new one. *Journal of Social and Clinical Psychology, 19,* 1–10.

Minarik, M. L., & Ahrens, A. H. (1996). Relations of eating and symptoms of depression and anxiety to the dimensions of perfectionism among undergraduate women. *Cognitive Therapy and Research, 20,* 155–169.

Mitchelson, J. K., & Burns, L. R. (1998). Career mothers and perfectionism: Stress at work and at home. *Personality and Individual Differences, 25,* 477–485.

Mor, N., & Winquist, J. (2002). Self-focused attention and negative affect: A meta-analysis. *Psychological Bulletin, 128,* 638–662.

Norman, R. M. G., Davies, R., Nicholson, I. R., Cortese, L., & Malla, A. K. (1998). The relationship of two aspects of perfectionism with symptoms in a psychiatric outpatient population. *Journal of Social and Clinical Psychology, 17,* 50–68.

Pacht, A. R. (1984). Reflections on perfectionism. *American Psychologist, 39,* 386–390.

Purdon, C., Antony, M. M., & Swinson, R. P. (1999). Psychometric properties of the Frost Multidimensional Perfectionism Scale in a clinical anxiety disorder sample. *Journal of Clinical Psychology, 55,* 1271–1286.

Ratnayaka, S. (1978). *Two ways of perfection: Buddhist and Christian.* Sri Lanka, India: Lake House.

Rice, K. G., Ashby, J. S., & Slaney, R. B. (1998). Self-esteem as a mediator between perfectionism and depression: A structural equations analysis. *Journal of Counseling Psychology, 45,* 304–314.

Rice, K. G., & Dellwo, J. P. (2002). Perfectionism and self-development: Implications for college adjustment. *Journal of Counseling and Development, 80,* 188–196.

Rice, K. G., Lopez, F. G., & Vergara, D. (in press). Parental/social influences on perfectionism and adult attachment orientations. *Journal of Social and Clinical Psychology.*

Rice, K. G., & Preusser, K. J. (2002). The Adaptive/Maladaptive Perfectionism Scale. *Measurement and Evaluation in Counseling and Development, 34,* 210–222.

Rogers, C. (1951). *Client-centered therapy: Its current practice, implications, and theory.* Boston: Houghton Mifflin.

Rotter, J. B. (1954). *Social learning and clinical psychology.* Englewood Cliffs, NJ: Prentice Hall.

Saboonchi, F., & Lundh, L. G. (1997). Perfectionism, self-consciousness and anxiety. *Personality and Individual Differences, 22,* 921–928.

Scheier, M. F., & Carver, C. S. (1985). Optimism, coping, and health: Assessment and implications of generalized outcome expectancies. *Health Psychology, 4,* 219–247.

Seligman, M., & Csikszentmihalyi, M. (2000). Positive psychology: An introduction. *American Psychologist, 55,* 5–14.

Shafran, R., Cooper, Z., & Fairburn, C. G. (2002). Clinical perfectionism: A cognitive-behavioural analysis. *Behaviour Research and Therapy, 40,* 773–791.

Shafran, R., & Mansell, W. (2001). Perfectionism and psychopathology: A review of research and treatment. *Clinical Psychology Review, 21,* 879–906.

Sheldon, K. M., & King, L. A. (2001). Why positive psychology is necessary. *American Psychologist, 56,* 216–217.

Slade, P. D., & Owens, R. G. (1998). A dual process model of perfectionism based on reinforcement theory. *Behavior Modification, 22,* 372–390.

Slaney, R. B., Rice, K. G., Mobley, M., Trippi, J., & Ashby, J. S. (2001). The Revised Almost Perfect Scale. *Measurement and Evaluation in Counseling and Development, 34*, 130–145.

Taylor, S. E., & Brown, J. D. (1988). Illusion and well-being: A social psychological perspective on mental health. *Psychological Bulletin, 103*, 193–210.

Terry-Short, L. A., Owens, R. G., Slade, P. D., & Dewey, M. E. (1995). Positive and negative perfectionism. *Personality and Individual Differences, 18*, 663–668.

Vohs, K. D., Voelz, Z. R., Pettit, J. W., Bardone, A. M., Katz, J., Abramson, L. Y., et al. (2001). Perfectionism, body dissatisfaction, and self-esteem: An interactive model of bulimic symptom development. *Journal of Social and Clinical Psychology, 20*, 476–497.

5

Predicting Feelings Versus Choices

LEAF VAN BOVEN
JOANNE KANE

In his essay on "self-command," Thomas Schelling wrote, "An important part of the consumer's task is . . . treating himself as though he were occasionally a servant who might misbehave" (1984, p. 5). The need to subjugate oneself as an errant servant arises, in Schelling's view, because the self sometimes behaves in ways it would rather not. We eat chocolate cake when we should content ourselves with salad. We smoke cigarettes when we should chew gum. We fail to exercise when we fully intend to do so. We plan to be the life of the party, but then stand in the corner instead of gyrating on the dance floor. In short, we routinely behave against our better judgment, and these misbehaviors often feel as though they were committed by someone other than our true salad-eating, nonsmoking, exercising, dancing selves. It seems that the current, well-behaved, masterly self often has difficulty anticipating and controlling the behavior of the future, errant-servant self.

Figuring out why people fail to anticipate the misbehavior of future selves is a persistent pastime of researchers of judgment and decision making over time. One reasonable explanation is that the current self doesn't always have a good idea of how the future self will feel and make decisions. The current sated self doesn't want cake and fails to realize that the future hungry self will long for buttery chocolate. The current noncraving self doesn't want a smoke and fails to predict the future self's unpleasant craving. The current outgoing self wishes to be an extroverted social butterfly and fails to anticipate the future self being paralyzed by fear of embarrassment.

This chapter reviews the recent flurry of research on people's predictions of their feelings and choices. Specifically, we review research on people's predictions when they are in an affectively unaroused "cold" state about what they would feel and choose in affectively arousing "hot" situations. Understanding how, and how well, people make predictions across the cold/hot divide would go a long way toward understanding why current (cold) selves fail to anticipate the feelings and behavior of future (hot) selves.

Our review indicates that, whereas people in a cold state tend to *overestimate* the influence of affective situations on the intensity and duration of their feelings, people *underestimate* the influence of affective situations on their choices and preferences. People overestimate how anxious they would feel if asked to sing karaoke in front of coworkers. But they also underestimate how willing they would be to fake a sudden onset of laryngitis to avoid singing. We discuss the different ways in which affective arousal influences feelings versus choice and suggest that predicted feelings and choices are subject to different constraints and moderators. Specifically, we posit that because choices are intuitively more stable and correspond more to dispositions than to feelings, people are more reluctant to predict changing choices than to predict changing feelings. We then raise three important questions for future research before concluding with some practical suggestions for research on the interplay among thoughts, feelings, and behavior over time.

Impact Bias in Predicted Feelings

People easily predict the quality of their feelings in different situations. Professors know they will be sad if they don't get tenure and happy if they do. Dieters know they will be tempted if they enter Ben and Jerry's. And people know they will be embarrassed if they sing popular music from the 1980s in front of coworkers. But people are less adept at predicting the intensity and duration of their feelings. A spate of recent research, much of it by Gilbert, Wilson, and their colleagues, indicates that people who are not affectively aroused overestimate the influence of affective events on the intensity and duration of their feelings.

This *impact bias* has been demonstrated among various populations (college students, laypeople, and professors, to name a few) and in response to various types of events (Wilson & Gilbert, 2003). The impact bias occurs both when people predict their reactions to extreme events such as severe injury or winning the lottery (Brickman, Coates, & Janoff-Bulman, 1978) and when they predict the influence of more mundane events such as taking an exam (Buehler & McFarland, 2001). People exhibit the impact bias in predicting their reactions to once-in-a-lifetime events (e.g., the death of a child; Suh, Diener, & Fujita, 1996) and to day-to-day events (e.g., watching a football game; Wilson, Wheatley, Meyers, Gilbert, & Axsom, 2000). They also exhibit the bias when predicting their reactions to events that are personally relevant (e.g., testing positive for HIV; Sieff, Dawes, & Loewenstein, 1999) and socially diffuse (e.g., gubernatorial election outcomes; Gilbert, Pinel, Wilson, Blumberg, & Wheatley, 1998).

The impact bias' ubiquity stems partly from people's difficulty in learning from previous mispredictions of feelings (Wilson, Meyers, & Gilbert, 2001). One might expect individuals to learn that regularly occurring events such as watching football or taking tests influence the intensity and duration of their feelings less than they expected. But they don't. Instead, people continually expect football losses and stressful exams to produce intense, long-term disaffection. Why?

Like other psychological phenomena, the impact bias is multiply determined. Two causes can explain many instances of the impact bias. One is that people generally don't realize the extent to which their "psychological immune systems" work quickly to minimize reactions to negative events (Gilbert et al., 1998). People predict that their feelings will hurt for a long time after a coworker insults their intellectual abilities in part because they don't anticipate that their psychological defenses will "kick in" (they will quickly realize the colleague is a buffoon), thereby dissipating negative feelings. Because the psychological mechanisms that diminish negative feelings are often necessarily opaque, people usually are not fully cognizant of those defenses. People consequently overestimate how long their feelings will be influenced by affective events.

This "immune neglect" is exacerbated when individuals overlook contextual features that moderate the operation of psychological defenses (Gilbert, Liberman, Morewedge, & Wilson, 2004). For example, hearing from the department chair that one's intellect is sophomoric is a major insult, so defense mechanisms are quickly mustered, the chair's talents are called into question ("She opted for an administrative post!"), and severely hurt feelings are dissipated. In contrast, hearing from an undergraduate student that one's intellect is sophomoric is clearly a relatively minor insult. Defense mechanisms are therefore less likely to kick in, and the slightly hurt feelings can linger longer than severely hurt feelings—in contrast to the intuition that big events and severely hurt feelings linger longer than small events and slightly hurt feelings (Gilbert et al., 2004).

Another moderator of the psychological immune system that is often overlooked is the extent to which the feelings are associated with an event that can be undone (Gilbert & Ebert, 2002). People are extraordinarily good at reconstruing events and decisions in a way that paints the chosen alternative in the most positive light (Aronson, 1969; Festinger, 1957). Dissonance reduction is more successful when decisions cannot be undone than when they can (Frey, 1981; Frey, Kumpf, Irle, & Gniech, 1984). People overlook this critical fact, however, preferring to retain the option to reverse their decisions. As a result, people overestimate how satisfied they will be with reversible decisions.

A second reason people exhibit the impact bias is that when predicting feelings they focus on salient features of affective events and neglect minor but potent features. This focalism (Wilson et al., 2000) or focusing illusion (Schkade &

Kahneman, 1998) is part of a more general judgmental tendency to overweight more salient features and to underweight less salient features. When it comes to affective events, people overweight the salient hedonic attributes (a close-knit family dinner at Thanksgiving) and underweight the less salient attributes (2-year-olds' tantrums, arrogant brothers-in-law, and so on; Mitchell, Thompson, Peterson, & Cronk, 1997). In one study, participants overestimated the degree to which California living would make them happier than Midwest living because they focused on the superior California weather and neglected other factors that influence well-being, such as job prospects, educational opportunities, and traffic (Schkade & Kahneman, 1998).

Focalism can be especially difficult to avoid because predicting feelings makes salient the distinctions between different situations—that is, the situation one currently is in and future situations—whereas people actually experience only one situation (Hsee & Zhang, 2004). For instance, the shorter commute makes a new apartment 5 minutes from work seem much better than one's current apartment 25 minutes from work because the 20-minute difference in commute is salient even though the two apartments, and hence one's feelings while living in them, are overwhelmingly similar (Dunn, Wilson, & Gilbert, 2003).

Taken together, studies of the impact bias indicate that people expect affective events to have a greater impact on their feelings than they actually do. In other words, people overestimate the influence of affective events on their feelings. To the extent that predicted feelings influence predicted choices, it follows that people would also overestimate the influence of affective situations on their choices.

Empathy Gaps in Predicted Choice

Follow it may seem, but follow it does not. Whereas research on the impact bias indicates that people overestimate the influence of affective situations on the intensity and duration of feelings, other research indicates that people *underestimate* the influence of affective situations on their choices. Specifically, when people are in a nonaffective cold state they underestimate the influence of being in an affectively arousing hot situation on their own choices and preferences.

These hot/cold *empathy gaps* have been documented across a variety of affective situations. For instance, when predicting how they would react if they were lost in the woods without extra food or extra water, people who are just about to exercise and are in a relatively neutral state predict that they would regret choosing not to bring extra food more than extra water; people who have just exercised, in contrast, predict that they would regret choosing not to bring extra water more than food (Van Boven & Loewenstein, 2003). People who are sated because they have just eaten are less likely than hungry people who have not eaten to choose a high-calorie snack to consume at a well-defined time in the future (Gilbert, Gill, & Wilson, 2002; Read & van Leeuwen, 1998). And men who are not sexually aroused predict they would be less likely to engage in sexually aggressive behavior compared with the predictions made by men who are sexually aroused (Loewenstein, Nagin, & Paternoster, 1997).

People also exhibit empathy gaps when they predict their choices and preferences in situations that involve emotions unrelated to bodily drives. For instance, people who are not affectively aroused predict that they would be more willing to engage in embarrassing public performances—miming dancing, and telling jokes—than they actually are in the "moment of truth" (Van Boven, Loewenstein, & Dunning, 2005; Van Boven, Loewenstein, Dunning, & Welch, 2004). And people who do not own an object underestimate how much money they would demand to part with it if they owned the object (Loewenstein & Adler, 1995; Van Boven, Dunning, & Loewenstein, 2000).

Empathy gaps, like the impact bias in predicted feelings, are multiply determined. For one thing, affective arousal may directly influence behavior, independent of and outside of conscious awareness (Bechera, Damasio, Kimball, & Damasio, 1997; Frijda, Kuipers, & ter Schure, 1989; Ledoux, 1996), so people may have limited opportunities to learn about affective influences. Second, when people in a cold state mentally simulate being in a hot, affective situation, they may infer that the stability of their current preferences is informative about what choices they would make if they were actually in an affective situation (Finucane, Alhakami, Slovic, & Johnson, 2000; Schwarz, 2001, 2002; Schwarz & Clore, 1988; Slovic, Finucane, Peters, & MacGregor, 2002).

Finally, affective arousal can increase the accessibility of affective information by, for instance, inhibiting attention to nonaffective information (Fox, Russo, & Bowles, 2001; Fox, Russo, & Dutton, 2002) and narrowing visual attention (Basso, Schefft, Ris, & Dember, 1996; Derryberry, 1993; Derryberry & Reed, 1998; Derryberry & Tucker, 1994; Tucker & Derryberry, 1992). The increased accessibility of affectively relevant information can directly increase the weight of that information in choice (Schwarz et al., 1991; Tversky & Kahneman, 1973). People can easily think of many reasons why dancing in front of friends and colleagues is a bad idea when the music is pumping and the dancing is imminent compared with the prospect of dancing in front of an audience next week. People consequently give more weight to the reasons not to dance in the here and now than in the distant future.

Taken together, studies of empathy gaps indicate that people in a cold, unaroused state systematically underestimate the influence of hot, affective situations on their choices and preferences. This underestimation is somewhat at odds with the results of the impact bias studies in which people in cold states overestimate the influence of affective situations on the intensity and duration of feelings. When predicting their reactions to being in an affective situation, why might people *overestimate* the influence on their feelings (impact bias) but *underestimate* the influence on their choices (empathy gaps)?

Why Do Predicted Feelings and Choices Differ?

In ascertaining why people exhibit divergent biases when they predict feelings versus choices, one should appreciate that feelings and choices are different psychological constructs. Feelings refer to the phenomenological manifestation of affective arousal. The affect aroused just before taking a turn at the karaoke machine can produce feelings of fear and anxiety—an experiential awareness that one's affect is aroused. Sneaking out of the room just before one's turn at the karaoke machine, in contrast, is a choice influenced by one's affective state of fear and arousal.

Choice refers to the selection of one alternative over other alternatives, each of which may differ on various attributes. A particular feeling is but one attribute in the selection of alternatives. As an extreme example, affective states can be nonconscious, influencing choices and preferences outside of conscious awareness (Berridge & Winkielman, 2003; Kihlstrom, 1999). To be sure, feelings of fear and anxiety are relevant to the decision to sing or not. But so are the feelings associated with the costs of renting the karaoke machine, the anticipated regret associated with "chickening out," and so on. Choices, in other words, are based on the relative costs and benefits of various alternatives; feelings are but one attribute that comprises costs and benefits.

The conceptual distinction between feelings and choice is important because it clarifies that there is no logical inconsistency in overestimating the influence of affect on feelings and underestimating the influence of affect on choice. Feelings and choices may be subject to different moderators and mediators. We suggest that the predicted feelings and predicted choices are differentially caused and constrained in at least two ways.

Choices Are Intuitively More Stable

First, people may intuitively expect their choices to be more stable than their feelings over time and context. Feelings are, almost by definition, fleeting. Emotional experience is generally considered to be intense, discrete, and integrally associated with a hedonic event (Lerner & Keltner, 2000, 2001). We suspect that individuals intuitively recognize the instability of feelings. Indeed, in some contexts people expect their feelings to fluctuate regularly over time, such as women's beliefs about the discomfort of menstruation (Igou, 2004; McFarland, Ross, & DeCourville, 1989; Ross, 1989). It would not seem odd to a person if his or her best friend woke up cheerful or got bored during morning classes, grumpy after a lunchtime argument, embarrassed while giving a presentation, and then proud after receiving an A on an exam. Fluctuating feelings are normal.

Choices, in contrast, are intuitively more stable over time and context. Social scientists now know that choices are based on constructed preferences and are not stable over time and context (Slovic, 1995; Tversky & Kahneman, 1986; Tversky, Sattath, & Slovic, 1988). But for much of our intellectual history, psychologists, economists, and other social scientists believed that people's choices revealed preferences that were stable over time, context, descriptions of the alternatives, and so on. Without knowing the research literature (and sometimes despite knowing the research literature!), the stability of choice and preference may have enduring intuitive appeal for social scientists and lay people alike. Indeed, the normative principle of invariance is central to theories of rational choice, which still hold sway in many of the social sciences. It would seem odd to a person if his or her best friend chose to dance in front of an audience in the morning, refused to dance at lunchtime, and was again ready to show his or her moves after dinner. Fluctuating choices are not normal.

Because individuals' intuitions about stability can influence their predictions of their feelings and choices (Nisbett & Wilson, 1977; Wilson, Laser, & Stone, 1982), these intuitions can help explain the discrepancy between the impact bias and empathy gaps. When predicting feelings, people's intuitive theory of instability provides a reason why, in a different affective situation, they would feel very different from the way they currently feel. When predicting choices, people's intuitive theory of stability provides a reason why, in a different affective situation, they would make the same choice as they would in their current nonaffective state.

Choices Are More Dispositional

The intuitive belief that choices are more stable than feelings may be part and parcel of another difference between feelings and choice, namely, that choices and behaviors correspond more to individuals' enduring dispositions than feelings do. Heider (1958) wrote that "Dispositional properties are the invariances that make possible a more or less stable, predictable, and controllable world. They refer to the relatively unchanging structures and processes that characterize and underlie phenomena" (p. 80). If our assertion is correct that choices are intuitively more stable than feelings, it follows that choices are intuitively more dispositional than feelings.

To be sure, there are dispositional differences in feelings. Some people are more prone to experience negative feelings than others (Wason & Clark, 1984), and some people generally experience stronger feelings than others (Larsen, Diener, & Emmons, 1986). The point is that, phenomenologically, feelings are transient consequences of evocative situations, whereas choices are manifestations of enduring preferences, attitudes, and beliefs. For example, one's anticipated feelings when imagining a reaction to a positive HIV test are likely to be attributed to the properties of the external stimulus ("having HIV is very bad, so I would be extremely upset") more than to one's dispositions. In contrast, one's anticipated choices and behaviors in the same situation are likely to be attributed to one's dispositions and personalities ("because I'm the type of person who likes to keep busy, I'd probably go about my daily routine") more than to the external stimulus.

That choices more than feelings may be associated with dispositions is important because it is well established that people are motivated to maintain the consistency of their dispositions and self-concept (Aronson, 1969; Festinger, 1957; Greenwald & Ronis, 1978; Steele, 1988; Thibaut & Aronson, 1992). If people regard choices as more dispositional than feelings, they may be more motivated to maintain consistent choices and behaviors over time and context than to maintain consistent feelings. It may arouse more dissonance to have inconsistent choices than to have inconsistent feelings. The motivated maintenance of choice and behavior may contribute to the inconsistency between predicted feelings and choices. People may more readily admit that they would feel differently in another situation than that they would behave differently in another situation.

Future Research

Our postulations, of course, are preliminary and should be held to empirical scrutiny. One task for future research is to document, with regard to the same affective situation, both overestimation of the influence on feelings and underestimation of the influence on choice. For instance, do people considering the prospect of singing karaoke in front of an audience simultaneously overestimate how fearful and anxious they would feel and underestimate the actions they would take to avoid singing?

Future research should also take care to equate the time frames in which people predict future feelings and choice. Whereas research on the impact bias shows that people overestimate the influence of affective situations on both the intensity and duration of feelings, research on empathy gaps shows that people underestimate the influence of affective situations on choices in the "heat of the moment." If commuters overestimate the duration of their displeasure at missing the express bus, do they also underestimate the duration for which they'd be willing to pay for a cab instead? We suspect that three additional categories of questions will garner researchers' attention in the near future.

Developmental Differences

First, as individuals develop, do they learn to predict more accurately their feelings and choices? As individuals mature, they more readily recognize that others' feelings and choices might differ from their own (e.g., Bernstein, Atance, Loftus, & Meltzoff, 2004; Birch & Bloom, 2003; Gopnik & Wellman, 1994; Royzman, Cassidy, & Baron, 2003). Because making predictions about the self in different times and contexts is analogous to making predictions about other people (Gopnik, 1993; Loewenstein, 1996; O'Connor et al., 2002; Schelling, 1984), the recognition that others may have feelings and choices that differ from one's own may correspond to the recognition that one's own feelings and choices may differ across time and context. If mature people more readily recognize their own shifting preferences and choices, they may be less likely to underestimate the impact of affective situations on their choices. The discrepancy between predicted feelings and predicted choices might therefore diminish over the course of maturation.

Cultural Differences

Another looming question is whether individuals from different cultures differ in the ways and means of predicting feelings and choices. Of particular relevance, East Asians in collectivist cultures, compared with individualistic Westerners, are less prone to construe individuals in terms of enduring dispositions (Chiu, Hong, & Dweck, 1997). East Asians are also less likely to exhibit cognitive dissonance (Heine & Lehman, 1997), partly because collectivists are less motivated to maintain favorable self-views (Heine et al., 2001; Heine, Lehman, Markus, & Kitayama, 1999). If, as we suggest, predictions of preferences are constrained by the motivation to maintain personal consistency, these cultural differences imply that East Asians may be less likely than Westerners to underestimate the influence of affective situations on their choices. East Asians may therefore exhibit closer correspondence between their predicted feelings and choices in response to affective situations.

Different Types of Affect

A final question concerns potential differences between predictions of feelings and choices associated with different types of affective states. We have discussed affective states in a broad, inclusive way in this chapter. However, the distinction between biological drives and "higher order" emotions (Buck, 1999) might be a particularly important consideration in future research. Obviously, both drives and emotions influence feelings and choices: We feel thirsty and choose water over crackers just as we feel embarrassed and choose not to sing karaoke in exchange for applause and admiration. But the influence of drives on choice may be less complex than the impact of emotion on choice.

The influence of drives on choice is straightforward: Thirst increases our preference for liquids over food; cold increases our preference for wool caps over shorts; exhaustion increases our preference for sleep over work; and so on. In contrast, the influence of emotions on choice depends importantly on the particular appraisal associated with the emotion (Keltner, Ellsworth, & Edwards, 1993; Lerner & Keltner, 2001; Tiedens & Linton, 2001). For example, because fear is generally associated with higher risk and uncertainty than anger (Tiedens & Linton, 2001), the decisions made by frightened individuals are more risk-averse, whereas the choices made by both angry and happy individuals are more risk-tolerant (Lerner & Keltner, 2001). That similarly valenced emotions (fear and anger) can have divergent influences on risk preferences is just one reason why the relation between emotion and choice may be more complex than the relation between drives and choice. These differences in complexity raise the possibility that predictions of the influence of emotion on choice may be more biased than the influence of drives on choice.

Another consideration is that mentally stimulating situations that arouse drives may be less likely to make people feel "as if" they were actually in the situation than do mentally simulating situations that arouse "higher order" emotions. Thinking about the last time one was thirsty does not arouse thirst in the same way that thinking about the last time one was embarrassed arouses embarrassment. To the extent that people predict their feelings and choices by mentally simulating what they would feel and want in an affective situation (Schwarz, 2001, 2002; Schwarz & Clore, 1988; Slovic et al., 2002), the difficulty of experiencing "as if" drives may impede predictions of feelings and choices in drive-arousing situations more than emotion-arousing situations.

Summary

Psychologists know a lot about how people predict their feelings and choices. Among other things, we know that people do not fully appreciate their ability to cope with and "get over" negative events (Gilbert et al., 1998). We know that people do not anticipate how much daily distractions and nonsalient but affecting attributes will neutralize future feelings (Schkade & Kahneman, 1998; Wilson et al., 2000). And we know that people project their current preferences onto their predictions of how they would behave in a different affective situation (Loewenstein, 1996; Loewenstein, O'Donoghue, & Rabin, 2003).

But there is a lot we don't know. This chapter has focused on one area of ignorance, namely, why people in affectively unaroused (cold) states mispredict their feelings and choices in opposite ways, overestimating the influence of affective situations on feelings but underestimating the influence of affective situations on their choices. We suggested that inconsistent predictions of feelings versus choices are borne of the different moderators and mediators that cause and constrain predicted feelings versus predicted choices.

There are many other open questions regarding the prediction of feelings and choices. Obviously there is much work to be done and many lessons to be learned.

In closing, it is worth noting one important practical lesson already learned from the study of predicted feelings and choices. Researchers often use hypothetical vignettes to study judgment and decision making in affectively relevant situations. Research on the impact bias and empathy gaps suggests that this practice is untenable. Because people systematically mispredict how they will feel and what they will choose, affective judgment and choice cannot be compellingly studied, to our minds, in the absence of affect. It's time for those of us who study judgment and decision making to "get real."

References

Aronson, E. (1969). The theory of cognitive dissonance: A current perspective. In L. Berkowitz (Ed.), *Advances in experimental social psychology* (Vol. 4, pp. 1–34). New York: Academic Press.

Basso, M. R., Schefft, B. K., Ris, M. D., & Dember, W. N. (1996). Mood and global-local visual processing. *Journal of the International Neuropsychological Society, 2,* 249–255.

Bechera, A., Damasio, H., Kimball, M. S., & Damasio, A. R. (1997). Deciding advantageously before knowing the advantageous strategy. *Science, 275,* 1293–1295.

Bernstein, D. M., Atance, C., Loftus, G. R., & Meltzoff, A. N. (2004). We saw it all along: Visual hindsight bias in children and adults. *Psychological Science, 15,* 264–267.

Berridge, K. C., & Winkielman, P. (2003). What is an unconscious emotion? The case for unconscious "liking." *Cognition and Emotion, 17,* 1181–1211.

Birch, S. A. J., & Bloom, P. (2003). Children are cursed: An asymmetric bias in mental-state attribution. *Psychological Science, 14,* 283–286.

Brickman, P., Coates, D., & Janoff-Bulman, R. (1978). Lottery winners and accident victims: Is happiness relative? *Journal of Personality and Social Psychology, 36,* 917–927.

Buck, R. (1999). The biological affects: A typology. *Psychological Review, 106,* 301–336.

Buehler, R., & McFarland, C. (2001). Intensity bias in affective forecasting: The role of temporal focus. *Personality and Social Psychology Bulletin, 27,* 1480–1493.

Chiu, C., Hong, Y., & Dweck, C. S. (1997). Lay dispositionalism and implicit theories of personality. *Journal of Personality and Social Psychology, 73*(1), 19–30.

Derryberry, D. (1993). Attentional consequences of outcome-related motivational states: Congruent, incongruent, and focusing effects. *Motivation and Emotion, 17*, 65–89.

Derryberry, D., & Reed, M. A. (1998). Anxiety and attentional focusing: Trait, state, and hemispheric influences. *Personality and Individual Differences, 25*, 745–761.

Derryberry, D., & Tucker, D. M. (1994). Motivating the focus of attention. In P. M. Niedenthal & S. Kitayama (Eds.), *The heart's eye: Emotional influences on perception and attention* (pp. 167–196). San Diego, CA: Academic Press.

Dunn, E. W., Wilson, T. D., & Gilbert, D. (2003). Location, location, location: The misprediction of satisfaction in housing lotteries. *Personality and Social Psychology Bulletin, 29*(11), 1421–1432.

Festinger, L. (1957). *A theory of cognitive dissonance.* Stanford, CA: Stanford University Press.

Finucane, M. L., Alhakami, A., Slovic, P., & Johnson, S. M. (2000). The affect heuristic in judgments of risks and benefits. *Journal of Behavioral Decision Making, 13*, 1–17.

Fox, E., Russo, R., & Bowles, R. (2001). Do threatening stimuli draw or hold visual attention in subclinical anxiety? *Journal of Experimental Psychology: General, 130*, 681–700.

Fox, E., Russo, R., & Dutton, K. (2002). Attentional bias for threat: Evidence for delayed disengagement from emotional faces. *Cognition and Emotion, 16*, 355–379.

Frey, D. (1981). Reversible and irreversible decisions: Preference for consonant information as a function of attractiveness of decision alternatives. *Personality and Social Psychology Bulletin, 7*, 621–626.

Frey, D., Kumpf, M., Irle, M., & Gniech, G. (1984). Re-evaluation of decision alternatives dependent upon the reversibility of a decision and the passage of time. *European Journal of Social Psychology, 15*, 447–450.

Frijda, N. H., Kuipers, P., & ter Schure, E. (1989). Relations among emotion, appraisal, and emotional action readiness. *Journal of Personality and Social Psychology, 57*, 212–228.

Gilbert, D. T., & Ebert, J. E. J. (2002). Decisions and revisions: The affective forecasting of changeable outcomes. *Journal of Personality and Social Psychology, 82*(4), 503–514.

Gilbert, D. T., Gill, M. J., & Wilson, T. D. (2002). The future is now: Temporal correction in affective forecasting. *Organizational Behavior and Human Decision Processes, 88*, 430–444.

Gilbert, D. T., Liberman, M. D., Morewedge, C., & Wilson, T. D. (2004). The peculiar longevity of things not so bad. *Psychological Science, 15*(1), 14–19.

Gilbert, D. T., Pinel, E. C., Wilson, T. D., Blumberg, S. J., & Wheatley, T. P. (1998). Immune neglect: A source of durability bias in affective forecasting. *Journal of Personality and Social Psychology, 75*, 617–638.

Gopnik, A. (1993). How we know our minds: The illusion of first-person knowledge of intentionality. *Behavioral and Brain Sciences, 16*, 1–14.

Gopnik, A., & Wellman, H. M. (1994). The theory theory. In L. A. Hirschfeld & S. A. Gelman (Eds.), *Mapping the mind: Domain specificity in cognition and culture* (pp. 257–293). New York: Cambridge University Press.

Greenwald, A. G., & Ronis, D. L. (1978). Twenty years of cognitive dissonance: Case study of the evolution of a theory. *Psychological Review, 85,* 53–57.

Heider, F. (1958). *The psychology of interpersonal relations.* New York: Wiley.

Heine, S., Kitayama, S., Lehman, D., Takarta, T., Ide, E., Leung, C., et al. (2001). Divergent consequences of success and failure in Japan and North America: An investigation of self-improving motivations and malleable selves. *Journal of Personality and Social Psychology, 81,* 599–615.

Heine, S., & Lehman, D. (1997). Culture, dissonance, and self-affirmation. *Personality and Social Psychology Bulletin, 23,* 389–400.

Heine, S., Lehman, D., Markus, H., & Kitayama, S. (1999). Is there a universal need for positive self-regard? *Psychological Review, 106,* 766–794.

Hsee, C. K., & Zhang, J. (2004). Distinction bias: Misprediction and mischoice due to joint evaluation. *Journal of Personality and Social Psychology, 86*(5), 680–697.

Igou, E. R. (2004). Lay theories in affective forecasting: The progression of affect. *Journal of Experimental Social Psychology, 40*(4), 528–534.

Keltner, D., Ellsworth, P., & Edwards, K. (1993). Beyond simple pessimism: Effects of sadness and anger on social perception. *Journal of Personality and Social Psychology, 64,* 740–752.

Kihlstrom, J. F. (1999). The psychological unconscious. In L. A. Pervin & O. P. John (Eds.), *Handbook of personality: Theory and research* (2nd ed., pp. 424–442). New York: Guilford Press.

Larsen, R. J., Diener, E., & Emmons, R. A. (1986). Affect intensity and reactions to daily life events. *Journal of Personality and Social Psychology, 51,* 803–814.

Ledoux, J. (1996). *The emotional brain.* New York: Simon & Schuster.

Lerner, J., & Keltner, D. (2000). Beyond valence: Toward a model of emotion-specific influences on judgment and choice. *Cognition and Emotion, 14,* 473–493.

Lerner, J., & Keltner, D. (2001). Fear, anger, and risk. *Journal of Personality and Social Psychology, 81,* 146–159.

Loewenstein, G. (1996). Out of control: Visceral influences on behavior. *Organizational Behavior and Human Decision Processes, 65,* 272–292.

Loewenstein, G., & Adler, D. (1995). A bias in the prediction of tastes. *Economic Journal, 105,* 929–937.

Loewenstein, G., Nagin, D., & Paternoster, R. (1997). The effect of sexual arousal on predictions of sexual forcefulness. *Journal of Crime and Delinquency, 32,* 443–473.

Loewenstein, G., O'Donoghue, T., & Rabin, M. (2003). Projection bias in predicting future utility. *Quarterly Journal of Economics, 118,* 1209–1248.

McFarland, C., Ross, M., & DeCourville, N. (1989). Women's theories of menstruation and biases in recall of menstrual symptoms. *Journal of Personality and Social Psychology, 57,* 522–531.

Mitchell, T. R., Thompson, L., Peterson, E., & Cronk, R. (1997). Temporal adjustments in the evaluation of events: The "rosy view." *Journal of Experimental Social Psychology, 33,* 421–448.

Nisbett, R. E., & Wilson, T. D. (1977). Telling more than we can know: Verbal reports on mental processes. *Psychological Review, 84,* 231–259.

O'Connor, K. M., De Dreu, C. K. W., Schroth, H., Barry, B., Lituchy, T. R., & Bazerman, M. H. (2002). What we want to do versus what we think we should do: An empirical investigation of intrapersonal conflict. *Journal of Behavioral Decision Making, 15,* 403–418.

Read, D., & van Leeuwen, B. (1998). Time and desire: The effects of anticipated and experienced hunger and delay to consumption on the choice between healthy and unhealthy snack food. *Organizational Behavior and Human Decision Processes, 76,* 189–205.

Ross, M. (1989). Relation of implicit theories to the construction of personal histories. *Psychological Review, 96,* 341–357.

Royzman, E. B., Cassidy, K. W., & Baron, J. (2003). "I know, you know": Epistemic egocentrism in children and adults. *Review of General Psychology, 7,* 38–65.

Schelling, T. C. (1984). Self-command in practice, in policy, and in a theory of rational choice. *American Economic Review, 74,* 1–11.

Schkade, D. A., & Kahneman, D. (1998). Does living in California make people happy? A focusing illusion in judgments of life satisfaction. *Psychological Science, 9,* 340–346.

Schwarz, N. (2001). Feelings as information: Implications for affective influences on information processing. In L. L. Martin & G. L. Clore (Eds.), *Theories of mood and cognition: A user's handbook* (pp. 159–176). Mahwah, NJ: Erlbaum.

Schwarz, N. (2002). Feelings as information: Moods influence judgments and processing strategies. In T. Gilovich, D. Griffin, & D. Kahneman (Eds.), *Heuristics and biases: The psychology of intuitive judgment* (pp. 534–547). New York: Cambridge University Press.

Schwarz, N., Bless, H., Strack, F., Klumpp, G., Rittenauer-Schatka, H., & Simmons, A. (1991). Ease of retrieval as information: Another look at the availability heuristic. *Journal of Personality and Social Psychology, 61,* 195–202.

Schwarz, N., & Clore, G. L. (1988). How do I feel about it? Informative function of affective states. In K. Fiedler & J. Forgas (Eds.), *Affect, cognition, and social behavior* (pp. 44–62). Toronto, Ontario, Canada: Hogrefe International.

Sieff, E. M., Dawes, R. M., & Loewenstein, G. (1999). Anticipated versus actual reactions to HIV test results. *American Journal of Psychology, 112*(2), 297–311.

Slovic, P. (1995). The construction of preference. *American Psychologist, 50,* 364–371.

Slovic, P., Finucane, M., Peters, E., & MacGregor, D. (2002). The affect heuristic. In T. Gilovich, D. Griffin, & D. Kahneman (Eds.), *Heuristics and biases: The psychology of intuitive judgment* (pp. 397–420). New York: Cambridge University Press.

Steele, C. M. (1988). The psychology of self-affirmation: Sustaining the integrity of the self. In L. Berkowitz (Ed.), *Advances in experimental social psychology* (Vol. 21, pp. 261–302). San Diego, CA: Academic Press.

Suh, E., Diener, E., & Fujita, F. (1996). Events and subjective well-being: Only recent events matter. *Journal of Personality and Social Psychology, 70*(5), 1091–1102.

Thibaut, J. W., & Aronson, E. (1992). Taking a closer look: Reasserting the role of the self-concept in dissonance theory. *Personality and Social Psychology Bulletin, 18,* 591–602.

Tiedens, L. Z., & Linton, S. (2001). Judgment under emotional certainty and uncertainty: The effects of specific emotions on information processing. *Journal of Personality and Social Psychology, 81*, 973–988.

Tucker, D. M., & Derryberry, D. (1992). Motivated attention: Anxiety and the frontal executive functions. *Neuropsychiatry, Neuropsychology, and Behavioral Neurology, 5*, 233–252.

Tversky, A., & Kahneman, D. (1973). Availability: A heuristic for judging frequency and probability. *Cognitive Psychology, 5*, 207–232.

Tversky, A., & Kahneman, D. (1986). Rational choice and the framing of decisions: Part 2. *Journal of Business, 59*, 251–278.

Tversky, A., Sattath, S., & Slovic, P. (1988). Contingent weighting in judgment and choice. *Psychological Review, 80*, 204–217.

Van Boven, L., Dunning, D., & Loewenstein, G. (2000). Egocentric empathy gaps between owners and buyers: Misperceptions of the endowment effect. *Journal of Personality and Social Psychology, 79*, 66–76.

Van Boven, L., & Loewenstein, G. (2003). Social projection of transient drive states. *Personality and Social Psychology Bulletin, 29*, 1159–1168.

Van Boven, L., Loewenstein, G., & Dunning, D. (2005). The illusion of courage in social predictions: Underestimating the impact of fear of embarrassment on other people. *Organizational Behavior and Human Decision Processes, 96*, 130–141.

Van Boven, L., Loewenstein, G., Dunning, D., & Welch, N. (2004). *The illusion of courage. Underestimating the impact of fear of embarrassment on the self.* Unpublished manuscript, University of Colorado, Boulder.

Wason, D., & Clark, A. E. (1984). Negative affectivity: The disposition to experience aversive emotions. *Journal of Personality and Social Psychology, 96*, 441–476.

Wilson, T. D., & Gilbert, D. T. (2003). Affective forecasting. In L. Berkowitz (Ed.), *Advances in experimental social psychology* (Vol. 35, pp. 345–411). San Diego, CA: Academic Press.

Wilson, T. D., Laser, P. S., & Stone, J. L. (1982). Judging the predictions of one's own mood: Accuracy and the use of shared theories. *Journal of Experimental Social Psychology, 18*, 537–556.

Wilson, T. D., Meyers, J., & Gilbert, D. T. (2001). Lessons from the past: Do people learn from experience that emotional reactions are short-lived? *Personality and Social Psychology Bulletin, 27*(12), 1648–1661.

Wilson, T. D., Wheatley, T., Meyers, J. M., Gilbert, D. T., & Axsom, D. (2000). Focalism: A source of the durability bias in affective forecasting. *Journal of Personality and Social Psychology, 78*, 821–836.

6

Considering Future Consequences

An Integrative Model

JEFF JOIREMAN
ALAN STRATHMAN
DANIEL BALLIET

M any decisions pose a conflict between the immediate and delayed consequences of one's actions (e.g., smoking). Given their far-reaching implications, understanding decision-making in such "temporal dilemmas" constitutes an important task. To advance this work, we review research on a theoretically relevant personality variable known as the *consideration of future consequences* (CFC; Strathman, Gleicher, Boninger, & Edwards, 1994) and offer a model of the antecedents and consequences of CFC. The model integrates work on CFC with past theory and research in the areas of broader personality dimensions, temporal construal, intertemporal choice, delay of gratification, and self-control in an effort to outline several cognitive and affective mechanisms that may account for and explain the operation of individual differences in CFC.

Defining and Measuring the Consideration of Future Consequences

Individual differences in CFC reflect "the extent to which people consider the potential distant outcomes of their current behaviors and the extent to which they are influenced by these potential outcomes" (Strathman et al., 1994, p. 743). The 12-item CFC scale is shown in table 6.1.

As we detail here, research suggests that CFC is a reliable, stable, and valid

Table 6.1. *The Consideration of Future Consequences Scale*

1. I consider how things might be in the future and try to influence those things with my day-to-day behavior.
2. Often I engage in a particular behavior in order to achieve outcomes that may not result for many years.
3. I only act to satisfy immediate concerns, figuring the future will take care of itself.
4. My behavior is only influenced by the immediate (i.e., a matter of days or weeks) outcomes of my actions.
5. My convenience is a big factor in the decisions I make or the actions I take.
6. I am willing to sacrifice my immediate happiness or well-being in order to achieve future outcomes.
7. I think it is important to take warnings about negative outcomes seriously even if the negative outcome will not occur for many years.
8. I think it is more important to perform a behavior with important distant consequences than a behavior with less important immediate consequences.
9. I generally ignore warnings about possible future problems because I think the problems will be resolved before they reach crisis level.
10. I think that sacrificing now is usually unnecessary since future outcomes can be dealt with at a later time.
11. I only act to satisfy immediate concerns, figuring that I will take care of future problems that may occur at a later date.
12. Since my day-to-day work has specific outcomes, it is more important to me than behavior that has distant outcomes.

Scale Instructions: "For each of the statements shown, please indicate whether or not the statement is characteristic of you. If the statement is extremely uncharacteristic of you (not at all like you) please write a "1" in the space provided to the right of the statement; if the statement is extremely characteristic of you (very much like you) please write a "7" in the space provided. And, of course, use the numbers in the middle if you fall between the extremes."

Scoring: After reverse scoring items 3, 4, 5, 9, 10, 11, 12, researchers should average the items, as this will aid in the interpretation of the level of CFC.

---

construct with implications for a range of significant behaviors. Individuals low in CFC attach a high degree of importance to the immediate consequences of behavior and little importance to the delayed consequences of their behavior. Individuals high in CFC attach great importance to the future consequences of behavior and very little importance to the immediate consequences of behavior.

Strathman et al. (1994) reported exploratory and confirmatory factor analyses that support the presence of a single underlying factor (cf. Petrocelli, in press). In addition, Strathman et al. reported internal reliabilities for the 12-item scale ranging from .80 to .86 and test-retest correlations of .76 (2 weeks) and .72 (5 weeks). Subsequent studies have found similar internal and 5-week test-retest reliabilities (e.g., Joireman, Sprott, Spangenberg, & Balliet, 2004).

Studies that have examined links between CFC and related constructs also provide evidence for its convergent and discriminant validity. For example, individuals who score high on CFC also score higher on delay of gratification (Strathman et al., 1994) and a general future time orientation (e.g., Strathman et al., 1994; Zimbardo & Boyd, 1999) and lower on the present-hedonistic and present-fatalistic subscales of the Zimbardo Time Perspective Inventory (ZTPI) (Zimbardo & Boyd, 1999). Individuals who score high on CFC also report lower levels of impulsiveness (Joireman, Anderson, & Strathman, 2003) and temporal discounting of future monetary gains (Joireman, Sprott, & Spangenberg, in press) and higher levels of conscientiousness (Strathman et al., 1994). Strathman et al. (1994) provided evidence for the discriminant validity of the CFC Scale by demonstrating its ability to predict environmental behavior, health concern, and cigarette or alcohol use, over and above conscientiousness, optimism, hope, and a general future orientation. Although few subsequent studies have examined the predictive ability of CFC over and above theoretically related scales, many studies have supported the validity of the CFC scale by demonstrating its association with meaningful outcomes involving a conflict between immediate and delayed outcomes.

Awareness and Concern Models of CFC

Subsequent research has tended to evaluate the validity of the CFC Scale by testing two theoretically relevant models (see figure 6.1). According to the *awareness* (or *mediation*) *model,* individual differences in CFC influence the perceived consequences of an action, which in turn influence the outcome of interest. For example, an individual high in CFC may be less likely to smoke because he or she is aware that smoking has detrimental long-term consequences for one's health. According to the *concern* (or *moderation*) *model,* CFC influences the sensitivity to immediate versus delayed consequences of an action. In this case, two individuals, one low, the other high in CFC may be equally convinced that smoking is bad for their health, but those high in CFC are less likely

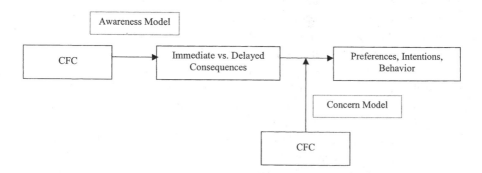

Figure 6.1. Awareness and concern models of CFC

to smoke because they are more concerned with those delayed consequences. It is also possible that both the models apply simultaneously.

Validity of CFC Across Four Domains

In this section, we review studies the support the validity of the CFC construct. We organize our review around four behavioral domains. In addition to highlighting the validity of CFC across a variety of contexts, these studies underscore the validity of the CFC construct for problems at the individual, dyadic, group, and societal levels of analysis.

Health Behavior, Risk Taking, and Academic Achievement

As noted earlier, Strathman et al. (1994) provided evidence for the validity of the CFC Scale in part by demonstrating that individuals high on the CFC Scale reported greater general concern with health and lower use of alcohol and cigarettes. Consistent with these earlier findings, subsequent research has demonstrated that individuals who score high in CFC report exercising more frequently (Ouellette, 2005), getting better sleep (Peters, Joireman, & Ridgway, 2005), being less susceptible to peer pressure to engage in drinking behavior (Reifman, 2001), and less likely to engage in risky sexual practices (Dorr, Krueckeberg, Strathman, & Wood, 1999). Individuals who score high in CFC are also more likely to get HIV tests (Dorr et al., 1999). High levels of CFC have also been linked with lower scores on various forms of sensation seeking, most notably boredom susceptibility and disinhibition (Joireman, Anderson, & Strathman, 2003), and with higher GPAs (Joireman, 1999; Peters et al., in press). Although promising, past studies have not tested the awareness or concern models of CFC in this domain. Thus one important future direction in this domain will be to determine whether individual differences in CFC predict different beliefs about various health-related practices (awareness) and/or differential responsiveness to such concerns (concern).

Aggression

Individual differences in CFC also have important implications for well-being in relationships. As an example, in a series of recent studies, we have found that high levels of CFC are associated with lower levels of hostility, anger, and aggression (Joireman, Anderson, & Strathman, 2003; Joireman, Werner, & Kwon, 2004). In the former study, CFC interacted in systematically meaningful ways with the perceived consequences of aggression to predict participants' responses to a hypothetical conflict situation in which participants imagined they had been insulted by an experimenter. Participants were told that they could evaluate the experimenter under one of four conditions that differed in terms of a possible meeting with the experimenter who would go over their evaluation forms. When participants were led to believe that they would never meet the experimenter again, CFC was unrelated to aggression (i.e., negative evaluations of the experimenter who insulted them). By contrast, when led to believe that they would meet the experimenter in the distant future, individuals high in CFC became significantly less aggressive relative to their own levels of aggression in the no-interaction condition and relative to individuals scoring low in CFC. Interestingly, when led to believe that they would meet the experimenter immediately after completing the evaluation, the pattern was reversed, with individuals low in CFC becoming significantly less aggressive relative to their own levels of aggression in the no-consequences condition and relative to individuals high in CFC. A similar pattern of results was obtained in a recent lab study involving reactions to a confederate who criticized the participant's essay on abortion (Joireman, Becker, Barbosa-Leiker, & Duell, 2005).

Although not directly related to aggression, one other study suggests that individuals low in CFC are likely to experience more blame and regret when they consider counterfactuals that could have changed an outcome (Boninger, Gleicher, & Strathman, 1994). Thus it is possible that individuals low in CFC may be more likely to engage in aggression and then later regret their decisions, creating a cyclical process in which shortsighted actions produce negative consequences, including regret, which subsequently predict greater levels of aggression in the future (e.g., via negative affect).

Prosocial Organizational Behavior

Moving to the group level of analysis, several recent studies indicate that CFC predicts willingness to engage in prosocial organizational behavior (Joireman, Daniels, George-Falvy, & Kamdar, 2004; Joireman, Kamdar, Daniels, & Duell, 2004) and knowledge sharing in organizations (Joireman, Kamdar, Barbosa-Leiker, & Daniels, 2004). In these studies, CFC was positively related to *organizational citizenship behaviors* (OCBs) and *knowledge sharing* (KS) when participants anticipated staying with the company for the foreseeable future, whereas CFC was negatively related to OCBs and KS when individuals adopted a short-term horizon (e.g., anticipated leaving the organization in 3 months), a pattern of results consistent with the concern model of CFC.

Proenvironmental Attitudes and Behavior

At the final level of analysis, individual differences in CFC have been linked with a variety of behaviors with important societal consequences, namely actions that affect the natural environment. For example, in their original article, Strathman et al. (1994) linked high levels of CFC with higher levels of a composite measure of proenvironmental behaviors (e.g., recycling). More important, Strathman and colleagues demonstrated an interaction between CFC and the perceived consequences of an environmentally relevant decision, offshore drilling. In this study, Strathman and colleagues (1994) manipulated the expected time course of costs and benefits associated with offshore drilling. Results revealed that individuals low in CFC had more favorable attitudes toward offshore drilling when the advantages were immediate (and the disadvantages were delayed). By contrast, individuals high in CFC had more favorable attitudes toward drilling when the advantages were delayed (and the disadvantages were immediate). Additional analyses revealed that individuals low (vs. high) in CFC did not differ significantly in the number of positive thoughts they generated about drilling, but individuals high in CFC generated significantly more negative thoughts about drilling than did individuals low in CFC. Subsequent research has provided additional support for the link between CFC and proenvironmental beliefs and intentions. For example, individuals high in CFC report greater willingness to recycle (Ebreo & Vining, 2001; Lindsay & Strathman, 1997), greater proenvironmental political intentions and behavior (Joireman, Lasane, Bennett, Richards, & Solaimani, 2001), and stronger preferences for public transportation (Joireman, Van Lange, & Van Vugt, 2004). An additional study has shown complex, but meaningful, links between CFC and support for structural solutions to transportation dilemmas (Joireman, Van Lange, et al., 2001). Several of these studies support both the awareness model (Joireman, Lasane, et al., 2001; Joireman, Van Lange, & Van Ungt, 2004), as well as the concern model of CFC (Strathman et al., 1994; Joireman, Lasane, et al., 2001; Joireman, Van Lange, et al., 2001). For example, studies supporting the awareness model have shown that the relationship between CFC and proenvironmental behavior is reduced after controlling for the perceived (long-term) consequences of the proenvironmental actions, whereas research testing the concern model has demonstrated that individuals scoring high on the CFC Scale are more likely to engage in proenvironmental behaviors only when they believe that such behaviors can help them avoid negative consequences in the future (e.g., Joireman, Lasane, et al., 2001; Joireman, Van Lange, & Van Vugt, 2004; Strathman et al., 1994). Furthermore, individuals high in CFC actually evidence lower levels of proenvironmental behavior than those low in CFC when the negative consequences of their actions are merely immediate (e.g., Joireman, Lasane, et al., 2001;

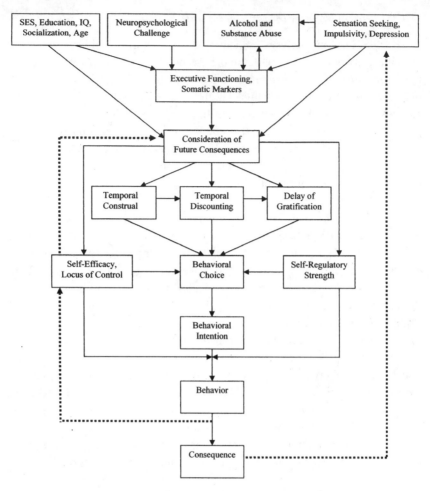

Figure 6.2. Integrative model illustrating precursors and mediating mechanisms of CFC.

Strathman et al., 1994). Although encouraging, future research relating CFC to proenvironmental behavior would likely benefit by examining how and why high CFCs become more aware of the delayed consequences of actions that affect the environment and whether individuals who are low in CFC are differentially affected by tailored interventions that emphasize immediate versus delayed consequences of their actions.

Theoretical Integrations
and Refinements

The preceding discussion has highlighted the importance of CFC across a variety of behavioral domains with important implications. What is less well understood is how CFC develops, how it operates, and where it fits within the broader literature on intertemporal choice. Next, we integrate the CFC construct within a larger model of how people make decisions over time. The model builds on past theory and research in the areas of broad dimensions of personality, temporal construal, temporal discounting, delay of gratification, and self-control (see figure 6.2).

Precursors of CFC

Although our main concern in the model is to determine how CFC manifests itself in people's thoughts, feelings, and actions, we see value in first considering how CFC may develop. To date, little research has directly examined this question. However, past research has demonstrated that individuals who score high in CFC also score lower on sensation seeking, impulsivity, depression, temporal discounting, and drug abuse and higher on delay of gratification, future orientation, and academic achievement, and at least one study has reported a positive correlation between CFC and age during adolescence. Although there is not a one-to-one relationship between CFC, delay of gratification, future orientation, and temporal discounting, the connection between these constructs allows us to speculate on the development of CFC, as numerous studies have examined developmental precursors of delay of gratification, future orientation, and temporal discounting. For example, previous studies have linked ability to delay gratification with IQ, interest in intellectual endeavors, and better academic achievement (e.g., Funder & Block, 1989; Rodriguez, Mischel, & Shoda, 1989; Wulfert, Block, Santa Ana, Rodriguez, & Colsman, 2002). Past research has also shown positive relationships between future orientation and recollections of positive experiences with parents (e.g., Agarwal, Tripathi, & Srivastava, 1983; Trommsdorff, 1983; cf. Tangney, Baumeister, & Boone, 2004) and age (Zimbardo & Boyd, 1999) and negative relationships between future orientation and psychopathology (Braley & Freed, 1971; cf. Greaves, 1971) and depression (Zimbardo & Boyd, 1999). On a related note, recent research reveals that people become more inclined to emphasize short-term outcomes when in a negative emotional state (Gray, 1999; Tice & Bratslavsky, 2000; Tice, Bratslavsky, & Baumeister, 2001). Also relevant are the findings from previous research that the tendency to discount the value of future outcomes is inversely associated with age (Green, Myerson, & Ostaszewski, 1999; Read & Read, 2004) and income (Green, Myerson, Lichtman, Rosen, & Fry, 1996). Finally, from a neuropsychological perspective, it is relevant to note that damage to the prefrontal cortex (Bechara, Damasio,

Damasio, & Anderson, 1994) and substance abuse (Bechara & Damasio, 2002) are both associated with a reduced concern with the future consequences, and drug abuse is also associated with an increase in temporal discounting (Kirby, Petry, & Bickel, 1999). This pattern of findings suggests that CFC is likely to be influenced by a combination of developmental factors (e.g., socialization, education, IQ, aging), neuropsychological challenge, substance abuse, and biologically based personality predispositions (e.g., sensation seeking, impulsivity, depression), as illustrated in figure 6.2.

Assuming that the factors just discussed do predict an individual's predisposition to consider future consequences, the next question is, Why? Part of the explanation may be that these factors affect an individual's level of executive functioning, as indexed by working memory capacity and the ability to form somatic markers that help guide decision making (e.g., learning to avoid costly negative consequences). In line with this reasoning, recent research has demonstrated a negative relationship between impulsivity and working memory capacity (Whitney, Jameson, & Hinson, 2004). Moreover, research has shown that executive control problems are associated with experiencing more negative consequences from alcohol use (Whitney, Hinson, & Jameson, 2002). Other studies indicate that taxing working memory increases temporal discounting (Hinson, Jameson, & Whitney, 2003) and interferes with the ability to form somatic markers that help people avoid costly negative consequences in gambling tasks involving delayed punishments (Hinson, Jameson, & Whitney, 2002).

Although these findings are suggestive, future research will be necessary to clearly establish how these factors may affect the development of CFC. What we do know, however, is that young adults in college show reliable and stable individual differences in the tendency to consider immediate versus delayed consequences, differences that predict a host of important outcomes. We now turn to the downstream cognitive and motivational processes that may mediate CFC and behavioral outcomes.

Temporal Construal, Temporal Discounting, and Delay of Gratification

The model in figure 6.1 suggests several routes through which CFC may operate. To begin, it seems reasonable to assume that by directing attention to either the immediate or delayed consequences of one's actions, CFC influences the way individuals construe their behavioral options. In fact, recent research reveals that an individual's construal of an action depends, in part, on the action's temporal distance (Trope & Liberman, 2003). In this research, a distinction is drawn between two levels of construal: *Low-level construals* are concrete, complex, secondary, subordinate, and goal-irrelevant, whereas *high-level construals* are more abstract, simple, primary, superordinate, and goal-relevant. According to Trope and Liberman's construal level theory (CLT), actions anticipated to occur close in temporal proximity (e.g., going to a movie today) are more likely to result in low-level construals, whereas actions anticipated to occur in the distant future (e.g., going to a movie next month) are more likely to result in high-level construals (Liberman, Sagristano, & Trope, 2002). These construals, in turn, have been demonstrated to have important implications for the value that people assign to various courses of action. Specifically, research indicates that the value attached to an action anticipated to occur in the near future is more likely to be based on low-level features (e.g., feasibility), whereas the value of actions anticipated to occur in the distant future are more likely to be based on high-level features (e.g., desirability; see, e.g., Liberman & Trope, 1998; Trope & Liberman, 2000). Extending this analysis to the CFC construct, individuals low in CFC should be more likely to evaluate behavioral options in terms of features associated with low-level construals, whereas those high in CFC should more often evaluate options in terms of features associated with high-level construals. These differences, in turn, may make individuals low in CFC more likely to prefer easy but less rewarding courses of action and those high in CFC more likely to choose difficult but rewarding courses of action. This may explain, for example, why individuals high in CFC perform better in college (Joireman, 1999; Peters et al., in press).

Temporal construal also influences people's preferences when faced with a choice between a smaller but certain outcome (e.g., $100) and a larger but less certain outcome with a higher expected utility (e.g., a 90% chance of $200): People who are focused on the near future place more emphasis on the certainty of the outcome and are more likely to choose the certain $100, whereas people who are focused on the distant future are more likely to evaluate the outcomes in terms of amounts and so are more likely to choose the 90% probability of $200 (Sagristano, Trope, & Liberman, 2002). Based on these findings, we recently predicted and found that when given a series of choices between smaller but certain and larger but less certain outcomes, individuals high in CFC were more likely than those low in CFC to prefer the larger but less certain outcome (Joireman & Balliet, 2004).

One final implication of CLT is that high-level construals are likely to reduce people's tendency to discount the value of future outcomes and, correspondingly, increase people's ability to delay gratification (Trope & Liberman, 2003). In sum, CFC may influence an individual's preferences via temporal construal, temporal discounting, and delay of gratification. Consistent with this reasoning, as noted earlier, high levels of CFC have already been shown to predict lower discount rates (Joireman, Sprott, & Spangenberg, in press) and higher scores on a delay-of-gratification scale (Strathman et al., 1994). Additional research examining the relationship between CFC and temporal construal and the interrelationships between construal, discounting, and delay of gratification could greatly expand our understanding of the influence of temporal factors on decision making.

Self-Regulatory Strength, Self-Efficacy, and Locus of Control

Previously we focused primarily on the temporal cognitive processes that might mediate between CFC and people's preferences for various courses of action. It is also possible that CFC influences people's choices to engage in various courses of actions via its influence on self-regulatory strength, self-efficacy, and locus of control. These factors may help to explain why people with high CFC would be more likely to put their intentions into action and persevere in the face of obstacles to goal attainment.

According to the depletion model, self-regulation operates like a muscle, such that engaging in self-regulation in one context may reduce an individual's ability to self-regulate in a subsequent context (Baumeister & Heatherton, 1996). Indeed, many studies using various manipulations of self-regulation depletion (e.g., emotion suppression, attention regulation) have shown that when people are required to regulate their behavior in one domain, their ability to regulate in another domain diminishes (e.g., Muraven & Baumeister, 2000; Muraven, Tice, & Baumeister, 1998; Schmeichel, Vohs, & Baumeister, 2003), in part because people believe that time passes slowly when one is engaging in self-regulation (Vohs & Schmeichel, 2003). These findings are important, as CFC might be one indicator of self-regulatory strength. In support of this hypothesis, those scoring high in CFC also score higher on Tangney et al.'s (2004) self-control scale (Schultz, 2001). It is also relevant to note that there is some evidence that people can, over time, build up self-regulatory strength by practicing self-regulation (Baumeister, Muraven, & Tice, 2000; Muraven, Baumeister, & Tice, 1999). This suggests that if people high in CFC are more likely than people low in CFC to engage in various forms of self-regulation, they may build up a stronger ability to self-regulate. We found support for this hypothesis in a recent study evaluating the ability of CFC to moderate the impact of self-regulation depletion on temporal discounting. People who were low and those who were high in CFC watched an amusing video clip and were instructed to either react naturally or to suppress their emotional reactions to the clip. Following the clip, participants completed a measure of temporal discounting in which they made a series of choices between a smaller amount of money they could receive in the near future and a larger amount of money they could receive at a later date. Results revealed that self-regulation depletion increased temporal discounting among those low in CFC but had no effect on discounting among those high in CFC, suggesting that people high in CFC were less depleted after engaging in self-regulation (Joireman, Balliet, Sprott, Spangenberg, & Schultz, 2004).

Another reason that CFC may predict higher motivation and more persistence toward long-term goals is that individuals high in CFC may hold higher levels of self-efficacy (Bandura, 1997) and an internal locus of control (Rotter, 1966). This follows from the reasoning that individuals high in CFC have learned over time the connection between their actions and outcomes, even outcomes that may not occur for some time. As such, individuals high in CFC should be more likely to perceive a connection between an immediate behavior and a long-term outcome. This understanding of the contingencies between one's own effort and long-term outcomes could make people high in CFC more motivated to pursue long-term goals and more persistent in the face of obstacles. Indeed, individuals scoring high in CFC also score higher on internal locus of control than do those scoring low in CFC (Strathman et al., 1994). Future research examining how self-regulatory strength, self-efficacy, and locus of control may mediate the relationship between CFC and goal selection and persistence could help to explain why individuals high in CFC set higher goals and seem better able to resist temptations in pursuit of longer term goals.

Feedback Loops and the Relevance of the Past

The final portion of the model shown in figure 6.2 assumes several feedback loops emanating from the consequences of one's actions. To the extent that the consequences of one's actions are negative and that one sees very little connection between one's behavior and the outcomes one is experiencing, an individual should be more likely to experience negative affect, a reduced sense of self-efficacy, and a shift toward a more external locus of control, each of which may result in a subsequent shift toward emphasizing more immediate consequences on future occasions. Thus individuals who initially fail to consider the future consequences of their actions may experience a downward spiral in which the delayed consequences of their actions are negative and in which they are less likely to appreciate the connection between their actions and delayed consequences, both of which lead them to an increased emphasis on immediate consequences (cf. Joireman, Anderson, & Strathman, 2003; Joireman, Werner, & Kwon, 2004). Future longitudinal work exploring the possibility of a downward spiral among individuals low in CFC may help to identify interventions aimed at breaking a cycle that may serve to perpetuate an individual's "myopia for the future." In connection with this line of reasoning, it is relevant to recall that individuals high in CFC appear to be better able to deal with counterfactuals (Boninger et al., 1994), as they use such counterfactuals as a means through which they can better prepare for the future.

The Role of Feelings

To this point, our emphasis on the underlying mechanisms of CFC has primarily been on cognitive processes. However, feelings are also potentially relevant to the way CFC affects decision making and behavior. We have already noted, for example, that negative affect can lead people to emphasize immediate gains over larger delayed outcomes (Gray, 1999). Indeed, it has long been assumed that (hot) emotions can interfere with an individual's capacity to think and act in a (cool) rational fashion and subsequently engage in self-control (e.g., Metcalfe & Mischel, 1999). Given this, it seems reasonable to predict that individuals high in CFC may be better able than those low in CFC to override emotions in favor of a more rational strategy. However, recent research suggests that the role of emotion in decisions with delayed consequences may be more complex. In attempting to understand how affect relates to people's consideration of future consequences, it seems relevant to address two related questions: First, how does affect enter into the decision-making process in general and, second, which types of emotions can encourage people to maximize their long-term interests? Clearly, the answers to these questions are complex and are well beyond the scope of this chapter. Nevertheless, briefly considering these questions promises to advance our understanding of the CFC construct.

To address the first question, we draw on a recent model outlined by Loewenstein and Lerner (2003). Loewenstein and Lerner's model suggests that decision making is influenced by both *expected emotions* (i.e., how a certain course of action will make an individual feel in the future) and *immediate emotions* (i.e., how an individual feels at the time of the decision). Immediate emotions, in turn, are influenced by both anticipatory considerations (how thinking about the future consequences makes an individual feel at the time of decision making) and incidental influences such as temporary fluctuations in mood. Loewenstein and Lerner (2003) also note how immediate emotions can influence the expected consequences and emotions of a given action. Rather than assuming that emotion will always have a positive or negative impact on decision making, Loewenstein and Lerner (2003) argue that expected emotions can serve as useful guides to decision making to the extent that the expected emotions take all relevant feelings into account, whereas immediate emotions can serve to facilitate decision making by helping an individual take into account considerations that are difficult to articulate (e.g., aesthetic value). Expected and immediate emotions can also be problematic, because people do not always accurately predict how a certain event will make them feel, and people are often not aware of how current mood can influence judgments. In short, Loewenstein and Lerner (2003) argue that, under optimal circumstances, both immediate and expected emotions can facilitate decision making.

How do positive and negative affect influence an individual's ability to consider future consequences? To address this question, we draw on a recent series of studies by Giner-Sorolla (2001). Giner-Sorolla asked participants to describe two delayed-cost dilemmas (e.g., eating fatty foods) and two delayed-benefit dilemmas (e.g., exercising), to write down the thoughts they had in connection with these dilemmas, and to indicate how much self-control they exerted when faced with such dilemmas. Within the delayed-cost dilemmas, Giner-Sorolla

(2001) found that positive hedonic (fun, exciting) and positive self-conscious (respect) affect predicted lower self-control, whereas negative self-conscious affect (guilt, regret) predicted greater self-control. Within the delayed-benefit dilemmas, Giner-Sorolla (2001) found that hedonic negative (boring) affect predicted less self-control. These results illustrate that positive and negative affect can both encourage and discourage people from maximizing their long-term interests. Integrating individual differences in CFC with this work would be likely to help us to better understand the role of emotion in the link between CFC and decision making.

Summary and Comments

Our goal has been to review the literature on individual differences in the consideration of future consequences and to integrate this construct within a broader model specifying both its possible antecedents and consequences. A great deal of research has already been conducted to address each element of the integrative model (for additional detail, see Baumeister & Vohs, 2004; Loewenstein, Read, & Baumeister, 2003; Metcalfe & Mischel, 1999; Rachlin, 2000; Strack & Deutsch, 2004; Strathman & Joireman, 2005; Trope & Liberman, 2003; Zuckerman, 1994). At the same time, it seems that there have been few attempts to integrate these related lines of inquiry within a broader model. It is hoped that the integrative model proposed herein can serve as a springboard for future theory and research that attempts to understand the cognitive, affective, and motivational factors that influence how individuals make judgments and decisions that involve a temporal dimension. In our view, this is an especially important topic of study, as a quick look around will reveal that many, if not most, of our decisions involve a temporal element and, furthermore, that our personal and societal well-being often hinge on our ability to see past the immediate and into the future. Future research will be the judge of whether this effort has moved us in that direction.

Acknowledgments

Preparation of this chapter was supported, in part, by an Initiation and Completion Grant to Joireman from Washington State University.

References

Agarwal, A., Tripathi, K. K., & Srivastava, M. (1983). Social roots and psychological implications of time perspective. *International Journal of Psychology, 18,* 367–380.

Bandura, A. (1997). *Self-efficacy: The exercise of control.* New York: Freeman.

Baumeister, R. F., & Heatherton, T. F. (1996). Self-regulation failure: An overview. *Psychological Inquiry, 7,* 1–15.

Baumeister, R. F., Muraven, M., & Tice, D. M. (2000). Ego depletion: A resource model of volition, self-regulation, and controlled processing. *Social Cognition, 18,* 130–150.

Baumeister, R. F., & Vohs, K. D. (2004). *Handbook of self-regulation: Research, theory, and applications.* New York: Guilford Press.

Bechara, A., Damasio, A. R., Damasio, H., & Anderson, S. W. (1994). Insensitivity to future consequences following damage to human prefrontal cortex. *Cognition, 50,* 7–15.

Bechara, A., & Damasio, H. (2002). Decision-making and addiction: Part 1. Impaired activation of somatic states in substance dependent individuals when pondering decisions with negative future consequences. *Neuropsychologia, 40,* 1675–1689.

Boninger, D. S., Gleicher, F., & Strathman, A. (1994). Counterfactual thinking: From what might have been to what may be. *Journal of Personality and Social Psychology, 67,* 297–307.

Braley, L. S., & Freed, N. H. (1971). Modes of temporal orientation and psychopathology. *Journal of Consulting and Clinical Psychology, 36,* 33–39.

Dorr, N., Krueckeberg, S., Strathman, A., & Wood, M. D. (1999). Psychosocial correlates of voluntary HIV antibody testing in college students. *AIDS Education and Prevention, 11,* 14–27.

Ebreo, A., & Vining, J. (2001). How similar are recycling and waste reduction? Future orientation and reasons for reducing waste as predictors of self-reported behavior. *Environment and Behavior, 33,* 424–448.

Funder, D. C., & Block, J. (1989). The role of ego-control, ego-resiliency, and IQ in delay of gratification in adolescence. *Journal of Personality and Social Psychology, 57,* 1041–1050.

Giner-Sorolla, R. (2001). Guilty pleasures and grim necessities: Affective attitudes in dilemmas of self-control. *Journal of Personality and Social Psychology, 80,* 206–221.

Gray, J. R. (1999). A bias toward short-term thinking in threat-related negative emotional states. *Personality and Social Psychology Bulletin, 25,* 65–75.

Greaves, G. (1971). Temporal orientation in suicidal patients. *Perceptual and Motor Skills, 33,* 1020.

Green, L., Myerson, J., Lichtman, D., Rosen, S., & Fry, A. (1996). Temporal discounting in choice between delayed rewards: The role of age and income. *Psychology and Aging, 11,* 79–84.

Green, L., Myerson, J., & Ostaszewski, P. (1999). Discounting of delayed rewards across the life span: Age differences in individual discounting functions. *Behavioural Processes, 46,* 89–96.

Hinson, J. M., Jameson, T. L., & Whitney, P. (2002). Somatic markers, working memory, and decision making. *Cognitive, Affective, and Behavioral Neuroscience, 2,* 341–353.

Hinson, J. M., Jameson, T. L., & Whitney, P. (2003). Impulsive decision making and working memory. *Journal of Experimental Psychology: Learning, Memory, and Cognition, 29,* 298–306.

Joireman, J., & Balliet, D. (2004). *Preference for certain but smaller vs. less certain but larger outcomes as a function of individual differences in the consideration of future consequences.* Manuscript in preparation.

Joireman, J., Balliet, D., Sprott, D., Spangenberg, E., & Schultz, J. (2004). *Ego depletion, consideration of future consequences, and decision-making preferences: Implications for the self-regulation of behavior.* Manuscript in preparation.

Joireman, J., Becker, C., Barbosa-Leiker, C., & Duell, B. (2005, January). *Aggression as a function of concern with future consequences and anticipated interaction with an aggressive peer.* Poster presented at the annual convention of the Society of Personality and Social Psychology, New Orleans, LA.

Joireman, J., Kamdar, D., Barbosa-Leiker, C., & Daniels, D. (2004). *Willingness to share knowledge in organizations as a function of empathy, future orientation, time horizon, and social identity: A social dilemma analysis.* Unpublished manuscript, Washington State University.

Joireman, J., Kamdar, D., Daniels, D., & Duell, B. (2004). *Good citizens to the end? It depends: Empathy minimizes and concern with future consequences magnifies the negative impact of a short-term time horizon on OCBs.* Manuscript under review.

Joireman, J., Sprott, D., & Spangenberg, E. (2003). *Fiscal responsibility and the consideration of future consequences.* Manuscript under review.

Joireman, J., Werner, N. E., & Kwon, P. (2004). *A longitudinal study on the cycle of aggression: When the world fights back against bored and disinhibited sensation seekers.* Unpublished manuscript, Washington State University.

Joireman, J. A. (1999). Additional evidence for validity of the Consideration of Future Consequences Scale in an academic setting. *Psychological Reports, 84,* 1171–1172.

Joireman, J. A., Anderson, J., & Strathman, A. (2003). The aggression paradox: Understanding links among aggression, sensation seeking, and the consideration of future consequences. *Journal of Personality and Social Psychology, 84,* 1287–1302.

Joireman, J. A., Daniels, D., George-Falvy, J., & Kamdar, D. (in press). Organizational citizenship behaviors as a function of empathy, consideration of future consequences, and employee time horizon: An initial exploration using an in-basket simulation of OCBs. *Journal of Applied Social Psychology.*

Joireman, J. A., Lasane, T. P., Bennett, J., Richards, D., & Solaimani, S. (2001). Integrating social value orientation and the consideration of future consequences within the extended norm activation model of proenvironmental behavior. *British Journal of Social Psychology, 40,* 133–155.

Joireman, J. A., Van Lange, P.A.M., & Van Vugt, M. (2004). Who cares about the environmental impact of cars? Those with an eye toward the future. *Environment and Behavior, 36,* 187–206.

Joireman, J. A., Van Lange, P.A.M., Van Vugt, M., Wood, A., Vander Leest, T., & Lambert, C. (2001). Structural solutions to social dilemmas: A field study on commuters' willingness to fund improvements in public transit. *Journal of Applied Social Psychology, 31,* 504–526.

Kirby, K. N., Petry, N. M., & Bickel, W. K. (1999). Heroin addicts have higher discount rates for delayed rewards than non-drug-use controls. *Journal of Experimental Psychology: General, 128*, 78–87.

Liberman, N., Sagristano, M. D., & Trope, Y. (2002). The effect of temporal distance on level of mental construal. *Journal of Experimental Social Psychology, 38*, 523–534.

Liberman, N., & Trope, Y. (1998). The role of feasibility and desirability considerations in near and distant future decisions: A test of the temporal construal theory. *Journal of Personality and Social Psychology, 75*, 5–18.

Lindsay, J. J., & Strathman, A. (1997). Predictors of recycling behavior: An application of a modified health belief model. *Journal of Applied Social Psychology, 27*, 1799–1823.

Loewenstein, G., & Lerner, S. (2003). The role of affect in decision making. In D. J. Davidson, K. R. Scherer, & H. H. Goldsmith (Eds.), *Handbook of affective sciences.* New York: Oxford University Press.

Loewenstein, G., Read, D., & Baumeister, R. (Eds.) (2003). *Time and decision: Economic and psychological perspectives on intertemporal choice.* New York: Russell Sage Foundation.

Metcalfe, J., & Mischel, W. (1999). A hot/cool-system analysis of delay of gratification: Dynamics of willpower. *Psychological Review, 106*, 3–19.

Muraven, M., & Baumeister, R. F. (2000). Self-regulation and depletion of limited resources: Does self-control resemble a muscle? *Psychological Bulletin, 126*, 247–259.

Muraven, M., Baumeister, R. F., & Tice, D. M. (1999). Longitudinal improvement of self-regulation through practice: Building self-control strength through repeated exercise. *Journal of Personality and Social Psychology, 139*, 446–456.

Muraven, M., Tice, D. M., & Baumeister, R. F. (1998). Self-control as limited resource: Regulatory depletion patterns. *Journal of Personality and Social Psychology, 74*, 774–789.

Ouellette, J. A. (2005). Using images to increase exercise behavior: Prototypes vs. possible selves. *Personality and Social Psychology Bulletin, 31*, 610–620.

Peters, B. R., Joireman, J., & Ridgway, R. L. (2005). Individual differences in the consideration of future consequences scale correlate with sleep habits, sleep quality, and GPA in university students. *Psychological Reports, 96*, 817–824.

Petrocelli, J. V. (in press). Factor validation of the Consideration of Future Consequences Scale. *Journal of Social Psychology.*

Rachlin, H. (2000). *The science of self-control.* Cambridge, MA: Harvard University Press.

Read, D., & Read, N. L. (2004). Time discounting over the lifespan. *Organizational Behavior and Human Decision Processes, 94*, 22–32.

Reifman, A. (2001, August). *Future orientation buffers the relationship between network drinking and own drinking.* Poster presented at the annual convention of the American Psychological Association, San Francisco.

Rodriguez, M. L., Mischel, W., & Shoda, Y. (1989). Cognitive person variables in the delay of gratification of older children at risk. *Journal of Personality and Social Psychology, 57*, 358–367.

Rotter, J. B. (1966). Generalized expectancies for internal versus external control of reinforcement. *Psychological Monographs, 80*, 1–28 (Whole No. 609).

Sagristano, M. D., Trope, Y., & Liberman, N. (2002). Time-dependent gambling: Odds now, money later. *Journal of Experimental Psychology: General, 131*, 364–376.

Schmeichel, B. J., Vohs, K. D., & Baumeister, R. F. (2003). Intellectual performance and ego depletion: Role of self in logical reasoning and other information processing. *Journal of Personality and Social Psychology, 85*, 33–46.

Schultz, J. (2001). *The relationship between conscientiousness, self-awareness, the consideration of future consequences and the self-regulation of behavior.* Unpublished doctoral dissertation, Seattle Pacific University, Seattle, WA.

Strack, F., & Deutsch, R. (2004). Reflective and impulsive determinants of social behavior. *Personality and Social Psychology Review, 8*, 220–247.

Strathman, A., Gleicher, F., Boninger, D. S., & Edwards, C. S. (1994). The consideration of future consequences: Weighing immediate and distant outcomes of behavior. *Journal of Personality and Social Psychology, 66*, 742–752.

Strathman, A., & Joireman, J. (Eds.). (2005). *Understanding behavior in the context of time: Theory, research, and application.* Mahwah, NJ: Erlbaum.

Tangney, J. P., Baumeister, R. F., & Boone, A. L. (2004). High self-control predicts good adjustment, less pathology, better grades, and interpersonal success. *Journal of Personality, 72*, 271–322.

Tice, D. M., & Bratslavsky, E. (2000). Giving in to feel good: The place of emotion regulation in the context of general self-control. *Psychological Inquiry, 11*, 149–159.

Tice, D. M., Bratslavsky, E., & Baumeister, R. F. (2001). Emotional distress regulation takes precedence over impulse control: If you feel bad, do it! *Journal of Personality and Social Psychology, 80*, 53–67.

Trommsdorff, G. (1983). Future orientation and socialization. *International Journal of Psychology, 18*, 381–406.

Trope, Y., & Liberman, N. (2000). Temporal construal and time-dependent changes in preference. *Journal of Personality and Social Psychology, 79*, 876–889.

Trope, Y., & Liberman, N. (2003). Temporal construal. *Psychological Review, 110*, 403–421.

Vohs, K. D., & Schmeichel, B. J. (2003). Self-regulation and the extended now: Controlling the self alters the subjective experience of time. *Journal of Personality and Social Psychology, 83*, 217–230.

Whitney, P., Jameson, T., & Hinson, J. M. (2004). Impulsiveness and executive control of working memory. *Personality and Individual Differences, 37*, 417–428.

Whitney, P., Hinson, J. M., & Jameson, T. (2002, November). *From executive control to self-control: Predicting problem drinking by college students.* Paper presented at the annual meeting of the Psychonomic Society, Kansas City, MO.

Wulfert, E., Block, J. A., Ana, E. S., Rodriguez, M. L., & Colsman, M. (2002). Delay of gratification: Impulsive choices and problem behaviors in early and late adolescence. *Journal of Personality, 70*, 533–552.

Zimbardo, P. G., & Boyd, J. N. (1999). Putting time in perspective: A valid, reliable individual differences metric. *Journal of Personality and Social Psychology, 77*, 1271–1288.

Zuckerman, M. (1994). *Behavioral expressions and biosocial bases of sensation seeking.* New York: Cambridge University Press.

7

Hope Over Time

C. R. SNYDER
KEVIN L. RAND
LORIE A. RITSCHEL

Human activities are characterized by the purposeful organization of behaviors in order to achieve future outcomes. As far as we can tell, this future orientation distinguishes humans from other animals. In fact, the majority of the animal kingdom appears to operate in a Zen-like state of ever-present focus. Accordingly, these animal behaviors are aimed at satisfying current need states. Of course, many animals engage in behaviors that are aimed at achieving results in the future. Birds build nests, foxes fashion dens, and spiders spin webs. But one wonders, are animals contemplating the future when doing these things or merely following an impulse of the present moment? In this regard, humans are not unfamiliar with such actions. We understand that behaviors with future benefits need not be the product of forethought. For example, we may pursue sexual encounters to satiate current desires, although the ultimate purpose of sex is to propagate future copies of our genetic code, at least from a gene's point of view (Dawkins, 1989).

Still, much of what we humans do is antithetical to living in the moment. We resist sleep in order to finish manuscripts, we refrain from eating sweets so as not to ruin our appetites for dinner, and we deprive ourselves of immediate material comforts so that our children can go to college. Such behaviors are the result of purposive living for the future. Humans are able to live this way because of our well-developed abilities to abstractly envision future states of affairs. The future is the mental target of most of intentional human behavior. As we show in this chapter, however, our futures are potentiated by our pasts.

Hope Theory: Relations to the Future, Past, and Present

Because we spend our lives pursuing visions of the future, much of our cognitive energy is invested in as-yet unrealized goals. In our minds, we constantly are listing our goals, revising them, developing ways to reach them, or mustering the strength to go after them. Snyder (1994) has operationalized these goal-related thoughts as *hope* and has developed a theory to explain these processes and their sequelae. As we explain in this section, hope is a cognitive motivational state consisting of three interrelated components: *goals, pathways,* and *agency.* Although Snyder's hope theory focuses primarily on how individuals think about goals, these thoughts have important influences on emotions and behaviors, which in turn influence thoughts. Hence, the hope process is iterative, such that thoughts, emotions, and behaviors interact through both feedforward and feedback mechanisms. We explain these interactions within the structure of hope theory and how they should influence well-being. In addition, we explain how this theory can be applied in clinical settings to improve individuals' adjustment.

Hopeful Thinking: Living for the Future

Hopeful thought begins with an abstract mental representation of the future. The individual imagines a state of affairs that has an intermediate likelihood of occurring. This representation may be visual, but it also may consist of a verbal description (Pylyshyn, 1973; Snyder, 2002). In other words, hopeful reveries consist of things that *may* come to pass. Snyder (1994, 2000, 2002) has labeled these imaginings *goals.*

Goals are the mental targets of the cognitive processes that anchor hope theory (Snyder, 1994). Accordingly, these thoughts drive proximal actions to ultimately guide all purposive behavior. Goals vary in terms of their temporal distance from the present, with some goals designed for the short term (e.g., taking a shower) and others for the long term (e.g., graduating from college; Snyder, 2002). In addition, goals vary in the complexity of their construction. Vague goals are difficult to achieve, because they do not lend themselves to the production of either specific pathways or motivations, whereas explicit goals present clearer targets for our actions. Although goals vary in terms of their subjective importance and degrees of difficulty, they always are conceived as attainable, even if they are inherently uncertain.

There are two basic types of goals within hope theory: positive or "approach" goals and negative or "avoidance" goals (Snyder, 2002). Approach goals involve three different conceptualizations of the future. First, an approach goal can involve thoughts pertaining to reaching a state for the first time. For example, a person may want to purchase her first new car. Second, an approach goal can involve projecting a current state into the future. In other words, approach goals sometimes involve sustaining current states. For example, a man may want to maintain his present weight over the next 6 months. Finally, approach goals can involve increasing the progress made on an already achieved goal. For example, a young person wants to make a living as a writer after having sold her first novel (Snyder, 2002).

Avoidance goals, in contrast, involve foreseen futures that are not desired. As a result, the individual wants to forestall such imagined antigoals. One type of avoidance goal reflects the desire to stop something before it happens. For example, an individual may wear her seat belt because the goal is to not be injured in a car accident (Snyder, 2002). The other type of avoidance goal attempts to delay the onset of the undesired event. As a case in point, consider the patient with a progressive physical disease (e.g., multiple sclerosis) who wants to avoid becoming reliant on a wheelchair for as long as possible.

Once an individual has a goal in mind, thoughts interact with behavior. Hopeful thinking involves organizing behavior so as to increase the likelihood of the imagined future state becoming a reality. In other words, present behaviors are organized around their potential influence on future states (Boniwell & Zimbardo, 2004). The enjoyment of the present may be delayed or sacrificed outright in order to facilitate the achievement of the imagined goal. Thus individuals with high as compared with low hope should resist the intense and immediate emotional or biological gratification of certain behaviors (e.g., drug use, procrastination)—especially if these latter behaviors put the future goal at risk of not being realized. The "dark side" of this hopeful process is that it implies that people with high hope are less likely to "waste" time on more present-focused activities such as socializing with family and friends. Hence their preoccupation with the achievement of their future goals may produce social isolation (Boniwell & Zimbardo, 2004; Zimbardo, 2002). In addition, individuals who think hopefully (i.e., are future-oriented) may be more likely to feel subjective stress or "time press" than their less hopeful counterparts (Levine, 1997). Caution should be taken in considering these latter speculations about the "dark side" of hope, however, as all findings to date show that people with higher hope reap benefits in both their performances in various life arenas (e.g., academics, sports, health, etc.) and in their phenomenological enjoyment of their goal pursuits and interpersonal relationships (for review, see Snyder, 2002).

This conceptualization of hope theory fits well with the idea that the potential for abstract cognitions evolved at a later stage than more primal motivational processes. Both emotions and thoughts can interact with behaviors. The emotional processes of humans motivate us to behave in order to gratify our present need states. In contrast, thoughts directly influence behaviors through our ability to use abstract cognitions to project ourselves into the future and override shortsighted desires (Bar-Tal, 2001). The rarity of the relatively large human frontal cortex compared to the ubiquity of the emotional limbic system in most animals suggests that hopeful thought may be unique to human beings (see Zimbardo & Boyd, 1999).

The second component in hope theory is pathways, or the perceived ability to generate one or more viable strategies for attaining a desired goal. If goals are reveries of possible futures, then pathways thoughts involve connecting the present to these potential futures. Hopeful people think about generating usable routes to their goals. This thought process typically involves generating one prominent route to a goal and having confidence that this route can lead to the desired goal effectively (Snyder, 2002). Consequently, people high in hope should be more certain and decisive about the strategies that they use to achieve their goals than their counterparts who are low in hope. The routes to goals of people low in hope are typically poorly articulated.

Research has shown that individuals high in hope believe that they can find a way to get to their goals. If one route is impeded, these people believe that they can generate several alternate routes (Irving, Snyder, & Crowson, 1998; Snyder et al., 1991). This routing capability is crucial in maintaining goal-directed efforts when a particular strategy is impeded. In other words, pathways thought is paramount for guiding behaviors that ultimately will result in success, and related research shows that high hopers are facile at coming up with alternative routes to goals when blocked (Irving et al., 1998; Snyder, 1994; Snyder et al., 1991). Furthermore, as the goal seeker draws nearer to the goal, pathways should become increasingly refined and precise (Snyder, 2002).

The final component of hopeful thought is *agency* thought, which is the perceived ability to initiate and sustain progress toward a goal. As such, agency is the motivational horsepower that drives the hope engine. It typically is manifested in self-statements such as "I know I can do this" and "I will succeed" (see Snyder, Ilardi, Michael, & Cheavens, 2000). Research has shown that people who are high versus low in hope endorse such positive self-talk (Snyder, La-Pointe, Crowson, & Early, 1998). Although high agency is needed during all stages of the goal-pursuit process, it becomes increasingly important when an impediment is encountered because motivational energy must be summoned to begin using the best alternative pathway (Snyder, 1994). Agency thought is the fuel for goal-directed behaviors.

The Importance of the Past

Although hopeful thought is primarily a future-oriented endeavor, the events of the past are paramount to its development and maintenance. An individual's lived past plays an influential role in the formation of his or her dispositional hope. Snyder (2000) reasoned that trait hope is first established in the infant-to-toddler stage. The pathways component of hope is the first to develop, forming over the course of the first year of life. From birth on, a child is inundated with sensory information. This information must be given meaning by the child's mind in order to facilitate survival. Thus sensations are organized by the brain into a perception, which is a cognitive event (see Mussen, Conger, Kagan, & Huston, 1990). As the infant becomes adept at organizing and interpreting incoming information, he or she begins to notice the temporal connections between events. It becomes apparent in the infant's mind that the world can be characterized by many "this follows that" sequences (Snyder, 2000). Soon, infants are able to anticipate the sequelae of different phenomena in their world. For example, an infant will attend to the signs that will lead to her being fed. Such anticipatory thinking appears to be present from the moment of birth, and it is the foundation of pathways thought (Kopp, 1989).

This early pathways thinking begins directing observable behaviors. For example, the infant soon is able to point out particular objects in his or her environment. This pointing behavior purportedly begins as early as 3 months (Stevenson & Newman, 1986), and it certainly exists by the time the child is 12 months of age (Schulman, 1991). Snyder (2000) has interpreted this pointing behavior as the identification of a goal by the infant. Hence, over the course of the first year of life, a child has developed the ability to perceive his or her environment, to learn temporal sequences, and to discern a wanted goal from many other objects in the environment.

Snyder (2000) posited that infants lack personal awareness during the development of pathways thought during the first year of life. Around the age of 12 months, however, a child starts to become self-aware (Kaplan, 1978; Lewis & Brooks, 1978). As self-recognition unfolds, children begin to realize that they can initiate cause-effect sequences. The language used by toddlers at this stage of development suggests that they are aware of their roles as causal agents in the world (Corrigan, 1978). These assertions of personal agency include statements such as "I can" and "Me do it" (van der Meulen, 1987, p. 30). Snyder (2000) proposed that such statements reveal that toddlers possess short-term goals, along with understanding that they will initiate actions to achieve those goals. Through an iterative process, pathways and agency thinking are hypothesized to develop fully by the time a child has reached 30 months of age.

Other Lessons of the Past

In addition to aiding the development of pathways and agency, the past is an important educator in terms of how to deal with goal blockages. Hope does not develop best in people whose lives were idyllic. Instead, hopeful thought is optimized when children are allowed to encounter and attempt to overcome obstacles to their goals. With this in mind, Snyder (2000) recommended that parents and caregivers not act too quickly to help children out of a jam. Learning to navigate the roadblocks that life throws at us, along with the negative emotions that arise from such blockages, are fundamental to the development of hopeful thinking in adult life. When a goal pursuit is impeded during adulthood, memories of how past impediments were or were not overcome will determine how much pathways and agency thinking the person will have at his or her disposal. In other words, the failures of the past are the potential hope lessons of the future.

Another hopeful lesson of the past should be the bond that is formed between a child and an adult caregiver. A secure early attachment between a child and a caregiver relates to a sense of empowerment and goal-oriented thought (Snyder, McDermott, Cook, & Rapoff, 1997). The caregiver serves as a source of instruction for the lessons related to forming goals and pathways (Snyder, Tran, Schroeder, Pulvers, & Adams, 2000). In addition, a caregiver who consistently is responsive to a child's needs gives the child a sense of control in an otherwise large and confusing world. Research findings support Snyder's hypotheses regarding the importance of such early caregiver-child bonds (Shorey, Snyder, Yang, & Lewin, 2003). People high in hope have been found to form strong attachments to others, and their goals are the types of goals that include other people (Snyder, Cheavens, & Sympson, 1997).

Hope in the Present

It may be helpful at this point to summarize the goal-directed thought sequence as it occurs in the present moment and how these thoughts interact with emotions and behaviors. As we have stated previously, pathways and agency thinking develop over the course of a person's childhood and past goal pursuits. With the memories of these past goal pursuits come associated emotions. Hence people bring enduring emotional sets to the goal-pursuit sequence based on prior experience. Individuals who are high in hope bring a set of positive self-referential emotions based on past experiences of successful goal pursuits. These positive emotions energize people and foster an attitude of excitement in meeting future goals (Snyder, Cheavens, & Michael, 1999; Snyder et al., 1991). In other words, these positive emotions interact with people's cognitive processes to give rise to more hopeful thoughts. In contrast, people low in hope have a set of negative emotions connected to their memories of impeded or failed goal-pursuit endeavors. This results in feelings of passivity and dread with regard to future goal pursuits. Hence these negative emotions reduce the behavioral repertoire of the individual with low hope, making goal attainment less likely.

With these dispositional qualities in place, the individual first decides whether the outcome of the goal in question is worth his or her attention (Snyder, 2002). If the person decides that the goal pursuit is worth the cognitive effort, he or she then enters the event sequence analysis phase. In this phase, iterations of pathways and agency thinking are used to formulate strategies, motivate behaviors, and, if necessary, reformulate strategies. Thoughts about the ongoing goal pursuit create emotions within the individual. If the beginning of the goal pursuit is subjectively deemed to be going well, the individual may experience a surge of positive emotions, which then reinforce the goal-directed behaviors and cognitions. If the beginning of the goal pursuit is difficult, however, the resulting negative emotions may beset the individual with apprehension about the goal pursuit. As a result, attention may be diverted quickly from the goal endeavor because the perceived likelihood of achieving the goal is very low. Hence the emotional feedback generated in the goal-pursuit process is crucial for an individual to be able to maintain his or her motivation to achieve his or her goal.

We highlight the importance of the interplay between thoughts and emotions within Snyder's (1994) hope theory. Although they are not part of the cognitive components of hope theory, emotions are conceptualized as feedback mechanisms for the goal pursuits. As such, positive emotions are indicators that progress is being made or that a particular goal has been accomplished. Conversely, negative emotions inform the individual that a goal pursuit is being impeded or that a desired goal is unattainable. The evidence in our laboratory and elsewhere shows that the blockage or lack of progress toward a goal diminishes well-being (Brunstein, 1993; Diener, 1984; Emmons, 1986; Little, 1983, 1989; Palys & Little, 1983; Snyder et al., 1996). Hence, according to hope theory, positive or negative emotional experiences are the result of perceptions about the success of goal pursuits. In this case, thoughts determine emotional experiences.

If a stressor arises during the goal pursuit, negative emotions should ensue. For people with low hope, these negative emotions may derail their goal-pursuit efforts. People with high hope, in contrast, should perceive the stressor as a challenge (Snyder et al., 1991); in turn, these high hopers may generate alternative pathways and channel their motivations so as to implement these new strategies (Snyder, 2002). If the stressor is overcome (or if no stressor emerges), pathways and agency thinking should alternate and summate throughout the goal-pursuit process. As this continues, the individual should have perceptions about the relative success or failure of the goal pursuit. The resulting emotions should cycle back throughout the goal-pursuit process to affect subsequent agency and pathways thinking. Thoughts give rise to emotions, which give rise to further thoughts. The entire process should continue in this cyclical feed-forward and feedback process until the desired goal is either attained or abandoned. The resulting emotions from goal achievement or failure should then feed back to influence the resulting pathways and agency thoughts about future-related goals in identical or similar domains (Snyder, 2002).

In summary, the hope model involves a series of iterative interactions among thoughts, feelings, and behaviors. First, each individual brings a trait-like set of agency and pathways cognitions and emotional sets to the goal-pursuit process.

As the goal pursuit unfolds, feed-forward and feedback emotional mechanisms contribute to sustained or aborted goal-pursuit behaviors based on the perceived success or failure of the ongoing goal pursuit. Hope theory, then, consists of goal-pursuit thoughts and behaviors that, in turn, are responsive to emotional feedback at various points in the temporal sequence (Snyder, 2002).

Stitches in Time: Instilling Hope via Clinical Interventions

Although Snyder's (1994) theory states that hopeful thought results from one's developmental history, it also offers a model for altering one's goal-related thought processes. Because hope theory posits interplay among thoughts, feelings, and behaviors, we argue that the road to emotional well-being and adaptive behaviors is through adjustments in hopeful thought. By using interventions aimed at changing the way that people think about the goals in their lives, therapists should be able to bring about improvements in their clients' psychological and physical adjustment.

Blending the Present and the Future in Psychotherapy

When people decide to seek psychotherapy, they are acknowledging that something is not working in their lives presently and that they need help in solving their problems. Within the framework of hope theory, they have encountered a goal blockage and currently are experiencing a negative emotional state that reflects their lack of progress toward desired goals. Clients frequently attribute the origins of their goal blockages to their worthlessness as people, believing that they are stupid, pathetic, or incompetent instead of considering that a goal may have been poorly defined, unattainable, or incongruous with their personal beliefs. These attributional errors leave them feeling demoralized and lacking the energy necessary to achieve their goals, to seek alternative methods of attaining particular goals, or to reevaluate their goals. Furthermore, therapists find that clients' assimilations of negative self-statements often reflect their previous difficulties in resolving goal blockages. That is to say, clients who "own" responsibility for negative self-talk also have histories of being stymied in goal pursuits.

Because most goal pursuits involve efforts to learn the difference between a present undesired state and a future desired state (see Carver & Scheier, 1999), people who set goals without clear criteria for success take longer to achieve these goals, and they experience fewer positive emotions along the way (Emmons, 1992; Pennebaker, 1989). Some researchers even have speculated that vague standards for success, in and of themselves, may trigger depressive episodes (Semmer & Fresse, 1985). People high in hope have specific and concrete goals, and they are facile at assessing their progress toward those goals (Snyder, 1994; Snyder et al., 1991).

Although levels of both dispositional and situational hope vary from person to person, much of the work to be accomplished in therapy revolves around establishing and evaluating goals, generating pathways toward those goals, and finding and sustaining the energy to reach those goals. We suggest that, at least in part, therapy works because it teaches hopeful thinking. Effective therapies work because they teach clients to reorient temporally by encouraging them to examine themselves and their lives in terms of their future goals. Furthermore, the therapist's role is to convince clients that they can make changes in their present lives and that they can carry forward such goal-directed, hopeful thinking into their futures. In terms of temporal orientation, then, therapists are helping their clients to examine the lessons that they carry from their pasts, to reframe their views of their present lives, and to instill hope into their futures.

Goals: Anchors to the Future

Using hope clinically begins with the establishment of therapeutic goals. After listening to the client describe his or her presenting concerns, the therapist restates the client's problems in terms of what his or her goals are, what goals are being thwarted, and what can be done to overcome current goal blockages. Once the problems are conceptualized as goal-pursuit issues, the therapist can begin working with the client on the optimal strategies for attaining his or her goals. Using the goal concept in therapy models the benefits of using a similar approach in clients' lives more generally.

Part of the value of looking at life from a goal-seeking perspective is that it allows clients to take stock of their goals. The therapist can use this as an opportunity to point out the importance of having several goals in different life domains (e.g., work, spirituality, physical health, relationships, etc.; Snyder, Rand, King, Feldman, & Taylor, 2002). Therapists can explain to their clients that having a variety of goals for the future should engender more positive emotions in their present, ongoing lives. In addition, by having goals in different life domains, people are less likely to become emotionally distraught when a blockage is encountered in a particular goal pursuit. A stock market analogy works well here. Namely, by diversifying their investment of energy in goals across different life arenas, clients then are more likely to feel positive emotions from successes and are less likely to be debilitated by setbacks.

Therapists also can assist their clients in developing strategies for conceptualizing their goals. Many issues that trouble clients are the result of poorly designed goals. The first step is to help the client to clarify his or her life goals, as well as to set goals in terms of concrete language and with well-specified end points. The client must be able to answer two questions: (1) How will I know when this goal is met? and (2) What will it look like when I reach this goal? By answering these questions, the client is forced to develop specific criteria for success. Therapists can explain how abstract goals often yield disappointing results (Rule, 1982). For example, the pursuit of happiness is such a vague and ephemeral goal that its pursuit generally is stressful and unrewarding (Woolfolk & Richardson, 1978). A more adaptive strategy is to pursue specific and concrete goals, the achievement of which will result in the experience of happiness. Hence, if a client's primary goal is to be happier, the therapist should determine the specific elements that the client believes are necessary for having a happy life (e.g., being in good physical shape, having a romantic relationship, or earning more money). Changing the way a client *thinks* ultimately will change the way a client *feels*.

Therapists also can help clients to develop approach- rather than avoidance-oriented goals. Approaching a goal is a far more specific enterprise than avoiding an undesired outcome. A goal of avoiding a stimulus offers very little information in terms of optimal strategies for staying away from it. If a person is pursuing an avoidance goal, such as not smoking, then there is no end point for reinforcement. At what point does a person who is trying not to smoke reach his or her desired goal? Is it after a week of not smoking? A month? A year? In part because the end point of an avoidance goal is unclear, such goal pursuits do not result in positive emotions nor in the general sense of well-being that are the sequelae of approach goals. Instead, a more effective approach is to encourage the client to conceive of his or her goal as a tangible objective toward which he or she can move rather than a stimulus to be avoided. This approach to goal setting gives clients a sense of purpose and direction, which is likely to increase their agency thoughts.

Another advantage to using the approach framework in thinking about goals is that it increases one's ability to reset goals when the original goal is unattainable. Many people may set goals that are beyond their ability levels or that turn out to require more energy than they originally had estimated. For example, a client who sets the goal of earning an A in her French class may conclude that this goal is unattainable after receiving a C on the first test. In this case, the therapist may help the client to reset her goal and to aim instead for a B in the class. Other goals may be within one's grasp but remain unattainable until a preliminary goal is met. At times we are not aware of these preliminary needs until we already have embarked on our goal-pursuit journey. For example, a person may want to travel to Brazil. She may set out to achieve her goal and be making good progress until she learns that she has to get a provisional visa, which will require more time than she is willing to spend. Therefore, she may decide that she would be just as satisfied by resetting her goal to visit Venezuela, which does not require a provisional visa.

Teaching clients to create approach-oriented goals also facilitates thinking of alternative pathways to goal attainment. If a client is striving for a particular objective, chances are that there are reasonable alternatives to reaching that goal. People may generate only one pathway to their goal, however, and they may adhere rigidly to the one pathway that they have deemed the "best" for attaining that goal. Therapists can help clients to generate multiple pathways and teach them that they are less likely to feel bad when falling short of a goal if they have several other pathways, all of which can be tried before a goal is considered truly unreachable.

In addition to enumerating goals and orienting the client to an approach framework, the therapist may teach the client to break his or her goals down into smaller, more manageable subgoals (Snyder, 1994). By doing this, the client is more likely to see the ultimate goal as being readily attainable, rather than becoming preoccupied with the length of time that the long-range goal remains unattained (Vallacher & Wegner, 1987; Vallacher, Wegner, & Somoza, 1989). For example, although the goal of writing a novel may seem intimidating, the goal of writing a chapter seems more manageable. In therapy, the process of subgoaling is particularly important for clients who are struggling with depression or who generally feel incapable of meeting most or all of their life goals. This follows because subgoaling allows such depressed clients to focus on the more tractable portions of the work that needs to be done to achieve both their short- and long-term goals. Moreover, by giving the client subgoals, a therapist offers more opportunities for the client to experience positive emotions as these subgoals are met. Given that the lack of positive events in one's life often is cited as one of the underlying causes of depression, giving clients multiple opportunities to feel a sense of accomplishment may be an effective intervention technique in and of itself. The ancient koan of a journey of a thousand miles beginning with a single step rests on this subgoaling strategy.

After providing an orientation to the goal-seeking perspective and teaching strategies for optimally conceptualizing desired goals, the therapist can help the client evaluate each goal. It is important to help clients to judge their goals across many life domains in addition to helping them set approach-oriented goals with concrete end points.

In regard to establishing a goal that is congruent with the client's value system (Snyder, 2002; Snyder et al., 2002), research has shown that people are more likely to achieve their goals and to be more satisfied with the goal-pursuit process when their goals are consistent with their personal values (Emmons, 1992; Sheldon & Elliot, 1999). Although much research has demonstrated that achieving goals leads to improved well-being (Brunstein, 1993; Carver & Scheier, 1999; Emmons, 1996; Sheldon & Kasser, 1998), this is not the case if the goal lacks integration into the self (Sheldon & Kasser, 1998). Whereas feelings of cheerfulness and improvement in general well-being are derived from the pursuit and attainment of self-concordant goals (Sheldon & Elliot, 1999; Sheldon & Kasser, 1998), the attainment of externally generated goals yields only a fleeting sense of quiescence (Higgins, Shah, & Friedman, 1997). Simply put, people do not feel good when they are pursuing "should" or "ought to" goals that are dictated to them by others (see Sheldon & Elliot, 1999). By pursuing self-congruent goals, however, the client is likely to have more mental energy (i.e., agency; Csikszentmihalyi, 1993; Sheldon & Elliot, 1998). The pursuit of nonconcordant goals, on the other hand, yields a sense of ambivalence that is accompanied by detrimental physical and psychological effects (Emmons & King, 1988). Hence the goals that are based on the client's values not only will be seen as more attractive by the client but are also more likely to be achieved (Snyder, 2002).

In helping clients to select goals that are congruent with their own abilities, then, we increase the likelihood that the client's goal will be attained (Snyder et al., 2002). Ideally, the therapist helps the client to set goals that are maximally congruent with his or her skills, which, in turn, should increase hope and performance (Snyder, 2002; Snyder & Feldman, 2000; Snyder, Feldman, Taylor, Schroeder, & Adams, 2000). This is not to say that the therapist should not help the client to set lofty goals but simply that the client needs to understand the amount of time and effort required for success in a particular goal pursuit. In fact, research suggests that if an individual is sufficiently motivated (i.e., hopeful), then lofty goals are as likely to be reached as are the more mundane ones (Emmons, 1992)—even when controlling for natural ability (see Curry, Snyder, Cook, Ruby, & Rehm, 1997; Snyder et al., 2001; Snyder et al., 1991; Snyder, Hoza, et al., 1997).

Clients also may need help in assessing the importance of their established goals and in prioritizing them accordingly. As we stated previously, clients should be encouraged to have multiple goals in a wide array of life arenas. It is the case, however, that many clients will have difficulties in organizing such a wide variety of goals into hierarchies of importance. Clearly, goals that are central to a person's self-concept should be given the highest priority because their pursuit and achievements (or failures) will have the greatest impact on the individual's well-being. Also, it is important to explore possible incompatibilities in the client's set of goals (Rule, 1982; Snyder, 1994). When two or more goals are in conflict with each other, the result can be debilitating and is likely to increase ruminative thoughts (Emmons & King, 1988). In fact, having conflicting goals is predictive of such psychological problems as depression, neuroticism, and psychosomatic complaints (Emmons & King, 1988; King & Emmons, 1990). Indeed, research has shown that people who are low in life satisfaction often are working on several conflicting projects (Palys & Little, 1983). If goals are prioritized, the client should be better prepared to make informed choices on discovering incompatibles in some of her goals.

To illustrate these points, let us return to our example of a client whose goal is to quit smoking. From the perspective of hope theory, the therapist would first help the client to ascertain the importance of achieving this goal and then would help her to balance this with the other goals in her life (e.g., physical health, work goals, etc.). Next, the therapist would help the client to define the goal as concretely as possible. A client who wants to quit smoking may set an overarching goal of not smoking for a specified time period (e.g., "I will not smoke any cigarettes for one year"). Once this client has defined an end point for her goal, the therapist can work with her to turn an avoidance-oriented goal into an approach-oriented goal. In this case, instead of aiming simply to quit smoking (an avoidance goal), a client may set a goal of saving a certain amount of money (made possible by not having to purchase cigarettes) to be spent on the approach goal of buying a new wardrobe. Another possibility would be for her to establish a goal in a different life domain that would have been difficult, unreasonable, or wasteful if she were still smoking. For example, she may set a physical fitness goal, such as running a half-marathon, which would have been extremely difficult if she were still smoking. Finally, the therapist should help the client to break the large goal into smaller, more manageable subgoals. By reaching these subgoals, the client is more likely to experience positive emotions throughout the goal-pursuit process. For example, the client may set a subgoal of not smoking for 1 week; she then may reset that goal at the end of each week so that she is constantly achieving subgoals on the way to meeting her goal of not smoking for 1 year. After 1 year of not smoking, the client may decide that she would like to establish a maintenance goal of remaining smoke-free for another year.

Pathways: The Roads to Tomorrow

As we mentioned previously, one skill that therapists can teach their clients is to generate multiple strategies for goal attainment. Setting out more than one pathway, even before a goal pursuit is initiated, increases the likelihood that the established goal will be reached. This is due in part to the fact that generating multiple pathways gives the goal seeker options from which to choose. This skill is particularly useful in the event that a particular strategy is thwarted, because the client will have viable substitute pathways at the ready. In addition, generating more than one route to a goal implies that setbacks or blockages are to be expected. Such an expectation reduces frustration when an actual impediment is encountered, and this often is a novel cognitive approach for clients. When blocked, the goal seeker with high hope merely thinks, "Well, I anticipated that this would happen, and now I need to use one of my other options."

There are a number of evaluations about pathways that can be made to help the client become more successful in fulfilling goal pursuits. First, it is important to help clients to determine whether their chosen pathways are congruent with their values. The achievement of goals is likely to be unfulfilling if the means for this achievement are not congruent with the goal seeker's values. Second, the therapist and the client can examine the impact of a pathway on the client's quality of life. In this regard, the client should ask herself, "What is the effect that chasing a goal in this manner has on my lifestyle?" (see Snyder et al., 2002). Likewise, a client may discover that although her goal is appropriate, her planned route will cause her distress. For example, in the case of the student who wanted to get an A in her French class, she may initially decide that the best pathway to use to attain her goal is to cheat on the rest of the tests. This strategy, however, may be wholly incongruent with the student's values and may cause her more distress than she would have experienced if she had gotten a C in the class.

As with goals, it also is important to match the client's pathways with his or her strengths. Frustration will result if the client sets out to achieve a goal via a route for which he or she is ill prepared. As such, clients should be taught to do what they do best in pursuing goals, whether that involves maximizing and refining extant abilities or learning new skills.

Time commitment is another dimension along which pathways efficacy should be evaluated, as is the length of time that a goal pursuit will consume. If a client is taking longer than expected to reach a goal, then a review of the pathway being used is warranted. People with high hope implement alternative pathways when their progress is stalled or delayed (Snyder, 2002). In contrast, people with low hope seem to get stuck in a particular pathway and ruminate about why they are not having success. Of course, the length of time spent on a particular pathway will vary from client to client, so evaluations of pathways must take into account the client's innate abilities. In addition, the pathway of choice may be less efficient than other options, but it may more closely match the client's value system.

When evaluating pathways, the therapist also can assist the client in understanding whether a pathway is, in fact, a goal. Occasionally, what seems to be a strategy for achieving a goal is actually the goal itself. For example, consider a client who works each weekend on rebuilding a classic car. The clinician may feel that the process is taking an inordinate amount of time until she discovers that what the client truly enjoys about working on the car is that his son comes over to help him. When viewed in this light, the client's main goal is spending time with his teenage son rather than getting the car up and running, and the time commitment to getting the car running becomes irrelevant to the goal pursuit.

It is important to help clients to examine the potential of their own pathways. As we have suggested previously, hopeful thought reframes the concept of failure so that it is conceptualized as feedback about a goal pursuit. Sometimes, failure is the only way for a client to accurately appraise the status of his or her goal-pursuit strategy. In this way, hope can be a self-correcting thought process. Thus encountering setbacks is crucial in establishing hope, because many people with high hope learn through trial and error. One of the primary reasons for teaching clients to evaluate their progress and their pathways efficacy appropriately is that failure to attain goals decreases agency thinking.

Agency

Finally, we offer a few suggestions for increasing a client's sense of agency. The easiest starting point is to assess the client's self-talk. This process is similar to strategies used in cognitive therapy (Beck, 1995), in which the client maintains a record of self-talk in order to better understand what she says to herself in certain situations. By examining patterns of self-talk, clients can work at replacing negative self-statements with affirming ones. Thus "I can't" soon turns into "I can try." Also, thinking of potential difficulties ahead of time helps to maintain agency in the face of potential goal blockages. Then, when encountering setbacks, clients are not demoralized but instead are invigorated because they are prepared to handle these impediments.

The agency of the client also will be increased through the therapeutic process itself. It appears that almost all modes of therapy have the effect of increasing agency (Snyder, Ilardi, et al., 2000; Snyder, Michael, & Cheavens, 1999; Snyder & Taylor, 2000). The simple act of listening fosters motivation in people (Snyder, Ingram, & Newburg, 1982). As a result, parents have been encouraged to make strong efforts to listen to their children as a means of building their hopes (McDermott & Snyder, 2000; Snyder, Hoza, et al., 1997). The same suggestion applies to clients and friends: The act of listening helps people to see the goal-related nature of their own behaviors (Rule, 1982). This is one of the reasons that interpersonal relationships are so important in elevating and maintaining agency. In addition to the therapeutic relationship, the clinician and the client should work together to ensure that the client has social connections outside of the session. Higher levels of hope are associated with better social adjustment with friends and family (Kwon, 2002), less loneliness (Sympson, 1999), more social competence (Snyder, Hoza, et al., 1997), and more perceived social support (Barnum, Snyder, Rapoff, Mani, & Thompson, 1998; McNeal, 1997; Snyder, 2002). Thus a functioning social-support network is crucial for a client's sense of agency.

Clients can engage in specific behaviors to help increase their energy levels and thus their agency. Physical exercise provides an emotional boost while simultaneously helping people to see how they can act as causal agents within their environments (Snyder et al., 2002). Clients also should be encouraged to minimize their intake of caffeine and alcohol and to seek antidepressant medication when appropriate. The net effect of these changes is to boost the client's available energy resources, which helps to increase his or her sense of agency.

Summary

To think hopefully is to live for the future. This does not imply, however, that the past and the present are of little or no importance. On the contrary, Snyder's (1994) hope theory offers a paradigm for connecting the past, present, and future in a fluid interplay of well-learned lessons, authentically experienced moments, and adaptive anticipations. Moreover, hope theory offers a model for optimizing the interaction among thoughts, feelings, and behaviors. The principles of hope theory have practical applications, particularly for individuals whose lives have become stuck. The tools provided by hope theory, however, are not reserved for those who are experiencing clinical crises. The lessons of hope can benefit all of us, regardless of our current level of functioning. In this spirit, we would like to echo the sagacious advice of Philip Zimbardo (2002). The extent to which we are able to live the "good life" is equally dependent on reaping the wisdom of the past, savoring the experiences of the present, and sowing the promises of the future.

References

Barnum, D. D., Snyder, C. R., Rapoff, M. A., Mani, M. M., & Thompson, R. (1998). Hope and social support in the psychological adjustment of pediatric burn survivors and matched controls. *Children's Health Care, 27,* 15–30.

Bar-Tal, D. (2001). Why does fear override hope in societies engulfed by intractable conflict, as it does in Israeli society? *Political Psychology, 22,* 601–627.

Beck, J. S. (1995). *Cognitive therapy: Basics and beyond.* New York: Guilford Press.

Boniwell, I., & Zimbardo, P. G. (2004). Balancing one's time perspective in pursuit of optimal functioning. In P. A. Linley & S. Joseph (Eds.), *Positive psychology in practice* (pp. 165–180). Hoboken, NJ: Wiley.

Brunstein, J. C. (1993). Personal goals and subjective well-being: A longitudinal study. *Journal of Personality and Social Psychology, 65,* 1061–1070.

Carver, C. S., & Scheier, M. F. (1999). Optimism. In C. R. Snyder (Ed.), *Coping: The psychology of what works* (pp. 182–204). New York: Oxford University Press.

Corrigan, R. L. (1978). Language development as related to stage 6 object permanence development. *Journal of Child Language, 5,* 173–189.

Csikszentmihalyi, M. (1993). *The evolving self: A psychology for the third millennium.* New York: HarperCollins.

Curry, L. A., Snyder, C. R., Cook, D. L., Ruby, B. C., & Rehm, M. (1997). The role of hope in student-athlete academic and sport achievement. *Journal of Personality and Social Psychology, 73,* 1257–1267.

Dawkins, R. (1989). *The selfish gene.* Oxford: Oxford University Press.

Diener, E. (1984). Subjective well-being. *Psychological Bulletin, 95,* 542–575.

Emmons, R. A. (1986). Personal strivings: An approach to personality and subjective well-being. *Journal of Personality and Social Psychology, 51,* 1058–1068.

Emmons, R. A. (1992). Abstract versus concrete goals: Personal striving level, physical illness, and psychological well-being. *Journal of Personality and Social Psychology, 62,* 292–300.

Emmons, R. A. (1996). Striving and feeling: Personal goals and subjective well-being. In J. Bargh & P. Gollwitzer (Eds.), *The psychology of action: Linking motivation and cognition to behavior* (pp. 314–337). New York: Guilford Press.

Emmons, R. A., & King, L. A. (1988). Conflict among personal strivings: Immediate and long-term implications for psychological and physical well-being. *Journal of Personality and Social Psychology, 54,* 1040–1048.

Higgins, E. T., Shah, J. Y., & Friedman, R. (1997). Emotional responses to goal attainment: Strength of regulatory focus as moderator. *Journal of Personality and Social Psychology, 72,* 515–525.

Irving, L. M., Snyder, C. R., & Crowson, J. J., Jr. (1998). Hope and the negotiation of cancer facts by college women. *Journal of Personality, 66,* 195–214.

Kaplan, L. (1978). *Oneness and separateness.* New York: Simon & Schuster.

King, L. A., & Emmons, R. A. (1990). Ambivalence over expressing emotion: Physical and psychological correlates. *Journal of Personality and Social Psychology, 58,* 864–877.

Kopp, C. B. (1989). Regulation of distress and negative emotions: A developmental view. *Developmental Psychology, 25,* 343–354.

Kwon, P. (2002). Hope, defense mechanisms, and adjustment: Implications for false hope and defensive hopelessness. *Journal of Personality, 70,* 207–231.

Levine, R. (1997). *A geography of time: The temporal misadventures of a social psychologist, or how every culture keeps time just a little bit differently.* New York: Basic Books.

Lewis, M., & Brooks, J. (1978). Self-knowledge and emotional development. In M. Lewis & L. A. Rosenblum (Eds.), *The development of affect* (pp. 205–226). New York: Plenum Press.

Little, B. R. (1983). Personal projects: A rationale and method for investigation. *Environment and Behavior, 15,* 273–309.

Little, B. R. (1989). Personal projects analysis: Trivial pursuits, magnificent obsessions, and the search for coherence. In D. M. Buss & N. Cantor (Eds.), *Personality psychology: Recent trends and emerging directions* (pp. 15–31). New York: Springer-Verlag.

McDermott, D., & Snyder, C. R. (2000). *The great big book of hope: Help your children achieve their dreams.* Oakland, CA: New Harbinger.

McNeal, L. J. (1997). The effects of perceived non-work social support and hope upon oncology nurses' occupational stress. *Dissertation Abstracts International, 58*(4-A), 1209.

Mussen, P. H., Conger, J. J., Kagan, J., & Huston, A. C. (1990). *Child development and personality.* New York: HarperCollins.

Palys, T. S., & Little, B. R. (1983). Perceived life satisfaction and organization of personal projects systems. *Journal of Personality and Social Psychology, 44,* 1221–1230.

Pennebaker, J. W. (1989). Stream of consciousness and stress: Levels of thinking. In J. A. Bargh & J. S. Uleman (Eds.), *Unintended thought* (pp. 327–350). New York: Guilford Press.

Pylyshyn, Z. W. (1973). What the mind's eye tells the mind's brain: A critique of mental imagery. *Psychological Bulletin, 80,* 1–24.

Rule, W. R. (1982). Pursuing the horizon: Striving for elusive goals. *Personnel and Guidance Journal, 61,* 195–197.

Schulman, M. (1991). *The passionate mind.* New York: Free Press.

Semmer, N., & Fresse, M. (1985). Action theory in clinical psychology. In M. Fresse & J. Sabini (Eds.), *Goal directed behavior: The concept of action in psychology* (pp. 503–549). Hillsdale, NJ: Erlbaum.

Sheldon, K. M., & Elliot, A. J. (1998). Not all personal goals are personal: Comparing autonomous and controlled reasons as predictors of effort and attainment. *Personality and Social Psychology Bulletin, 24,* 546–557.

Sheldon, K. M., & Elliot, A. J. (1999). Goal striving, need satisfaction, and longitudinal well-being: The self-concordance model. *Journal of Personality and Social Psychology, 76,* 482–497.

Sheldon, K. M. & Kasser, T. (1998). Pursuing personal goals: Skills enable progress, but not all progress is beneficial. *Personality and Social Psychology Bulletin, 24,* 1319–1331.

Shorey, H. S., Snyder, C. R., Yang, X., & Lewin, M. R. (2003). The role of hope as a mediator in recollected parenting, adult attachment, and mental health. *Journal of Social and Clinical Psychology, 22,* 685–715.

Snyder, C. R. (1994). *The psychology of hope: You can get there from here.* New York: Free Press.

Snyder, C. R. (2000). Hypothesis: There is hope. In C. R. Snyder (Ed.), *Handbook of hope: Theory, measures, and applications* (pp. 3–21). San Diego, CA: Academic Press.

Snyder, C. R. (2002). Hope theory: Rainbows in the mind. *Psychological Inquiry, 13,* 249–275.

Snyder, C. R., Cheavens, J., & Michael, S. T. (1999). Hoping. In C. R. Snyder (Ed.), *Coping: The psychology of what works* (pp. 205–231). New York: Oxford University Press.

Snyder, C. R., Cheavens, J., & Sympson, S. C. (1997). Hope: An individual motive for social commerce. *Group Dynamics: Theory, Research, and Practice, 1,* 107–118.

Snyder, C. R., & Feldman, D. B. (2000). Hope for the many: An empowering social agenda. In C. R. Snyder (Ed.), *Handbook of hope: Theory, measures, and applications* (pp. 402–415). San Diego, CA: Academic Press.

Snyder, C. R., Feldman, D. B., Taylor, J. D., Schroeder, L. L., & Adams, V., III. (2000). The roles of hopeful thinking in preventing problems and enhancing strengths. *Applied and Preventive Psychology, 15,* 262–295.

Snyder, C. R., Harris, C., Anderson, J. R., Holleran, S. A., Irving, L. M., Sigmon, S. T., et al. (1991). The will and the ways: Development and validation of an individual-differences measure of hope. *Journal of Personality and Social Psychology, 60,* 570–585.

Snyder, C. R., Hoza, B., Pelham, W. E., Rapoff, M., Ware, L., Danovsky, M., et al. (1997). The development and validation of the Children's Hope Scale. *Journal of Pediatric Psychology, 22,* 399–421.

Snyder, C. R., Ilardi, S., Michael, S., & Cheavens, J. (2000). Hope theory: Updating a common process for psychological change. In C. R. Snyder & R. E. Ingram (Eds.), *Handbook of psychological change: Psychotherapy processes and practices for the 21st century* (pp. 128–153). New York: Wiley.

Snyder, C. R., Ingram, R. E., & Newburg, C. (1982). The role of feedback in help seeking and the therapeutic relationship. In T. A. Wills (Ed.), *Basic processes in helping relationships* (pp. 287–305). New York: Academic Press.

Snyder, C. R., LaPointe, A. B., Crowson, J. J., Jr., & Early, S. (1998). Preferences of high- and low-hope people for self-referential feedback. *Cognition and Emotion, 12,* 807–823.

Snyder, C. R., McDermott, D., Cook, W., & Rapoff, M. (1997). *Hope for the journey: Helping children through the good times and the bad.* Boulder, CO: Westview.

Snyder, C. R., Michael, S. T., & Cheavens, J. (1999). Hope as a psychotherapeutic foundation for nonspecific factors, placebos, and expectancies. In M. A. Huble, B. Duncan, & S. Miller (Eds.), *Heart and soul of change* (pp. 179–200). Washington, DC: American Psychological Association.

Snyder, C. R., Rand, K. L., King, E., Feldman, D., & Taylor, J. (2002). "False" hope. *Journal of Clinical Psychology, 58,* 1003–1022.

Snyder, C. R., Shorey, H., Cheavens, J., Pulvers, K. M., Adams, V., III, & Wiklund, C. (2001). Hope and academic success in college. *Journal of Educational Psychology, 94,* 820–826.

Snyder, C. R., Sympson, S. C., Ybasco, F. C., Borders, T. F., Babyak, M. A., & Higgins, R. L. (1996). Development and validation of the State Hope Scale. *Journal of Personality and Social Psychology, 70,* 321–335.

Snyder, C. R., & Taylor, J. D. (2000). Hope as a common factor across psychotherapy approaches: A lesson from the Dodo's Verdict. In C. R. Snyder (Ed.), *Handbook of hope: Theory, measures, and applications* (pp. 89–108). San Diego, CA: Academic Press.

Snyder, C. R., Tran, T., Schroeder, L. L., Pulvers, K. M., & Adams, V., III. (2000). Teaching children the hope recipe: Setting goals, finding routes to those goals, and getting motivated. *Today's Youth, 4,* 46–50.

Stevenson, H. W., & Newman, R. S. (1986). Long-term prediction of achievement and attitudes in mathematics and reading. *Child Development, 57,* 646–659.

Sympson, S. (1999). *Validation of the Domain Specific Hope Scale.* Unpublished doctoral dissertation, University of Kansas, Lawrence.

Vallacher, R. R., & Wegner, D. M. (1987). What do people think they're doing? Action identification and human behavior. *Psychological Review, 94,* 3–15.

Vallacher, R. R., Wegner, D. M., & Somoza, M. (1989). That's easy for you to say: Action identification and speech fluency. *Journal of Personality and Social Psychology, 56,* 199–208.

van der Meulen, M. (1987). *Self-references in young children: Content, metadimensions, and puzzlement.* Groningen, Netherlands: Stichting Kinderstudies.

Woolfolk, R., & Richardson, F. (1978). *Stress, sanity, and survival*. New York: Monarch Books.

Zimbardo, P. G. (2002). Just think about it: Time to take our time. *Psychology Today, 35*, 62.

Zimbardo, P. G., & Boyd, J. N. (1999). Putting time in perspective: A valid, reliable individual-differences metric. *Journal of Personality and Social Psychology, 77*, 1271–1288.

8

Fantasy Realization and the Bridging of Time

GABRIELE OETTINGEN
JENNIFER THORPE

"The person who is aware of the past knows about the future!" This statement expresses how psychological research in the past decades has conceived of thinking about the future. Thinking about the future was conceptualized and operationalized as judgments on how likely it is that certain events or behaviors will or will not occur. Such expectancy judgments are held to reflect a person's past experience and performance history (Bandura, 1977; Mischel, 1973). As past behavior has always been a powerful predictor of future behavior, it comes as no surprise that to this date expectancy judgments have been one of the most important cognitive variables for predicting motivation and behavior. Moreover, expectancy judgments, over and above past behavior, have been potent determinants of future behavior. Finally, because expectancy judgments can be precisely and easily assessed via paper-and-pencil measures, they gained enormous popularity in predicting behavior in many areas of psychology.

This chapter has three parts. First, based on William James's distinction between beliefs and images, we differentiate two forms of thinking about the future: expectancy judgments and fantasies. We show that the distinction between expectancy judgments and fantasies is important, because the two forms of thinking about the future differentially predict motivation and performance. Whereas positive expectancy judgments are a precursor of heightened effort and successful performance, positive fantasies pose a clear hindrance. In the second part of the chapter, we argue and show that fantasies about the future can be used as a self-regulatory strategy of goal setting when contrasted with thoughts about impeding reality. After such mental contrasting of future and present reality, expectancy judgments and thus people's performance history become relevant for thought, feeling, and action. The self-regulatory strategies of indulging in the future or dwelling on the present, in contrast, are found to be moderators of the expectancy-behavior link. The third part of the chapter discusses these findings in the context of cultural determinants of the three self-regulatory strategies of goal setting.

Expectations Versus Fantasies

William James characterizes a belief in terms of experienced consent in the truth of a given thought. James (1890/1950) explicates: "Everyone knows the difference between imagining a thing and believing in its existence, between supposing a proposition and acquiescing in its truth. In the case of acquiescence or belief, the object is not apprehended by the mind, but is held to have reality" (James, 1890/1950, vol. 2, p. 283).

Beliefs Versus Images

According to William James, beliefs are the outcome of a reality check of the content of a given thought. James describes believing as an emotional experience of consent. That what has been only thought of so far is now taken as truth. To believe in an idea means "the cessation of theoretic agitation, through the advent of an idea which is inwardly stable, and fills the mind solidly to the exclusion of contradictory ideas" (James, 1890/1950, vol. 2, p. 283). If one believes in something, action may ensue on the basis of the respective idea: "When this is the case, motor effects are apt to follow." (James, 1890/1950, vol. 2, p. 283).

The experienced inner stability that results from believing applies, according to James, as much to believing as to disbelieving. A person is only then disbelieving if he or she believes in something else. Thus the opposite of believing is not disbelieving but doubting and searching: *The true opposites of belief*, psychologically considered, *are doubt and inquiry, not disbelief.*" (James, 1890/1950, vol. 2, p. 284).

A belief is, therefore, different from a sheer image of an event. This implies that consciousness may nourish two distinct relations to an event. The event may simply be focused on in terms of its appearance in thought, or the event may be judged in terms of being true or false (i.e., it is judged in terms of its match to reality). Both relations may be present in consciousness, the sheer thought and the judgment. William James cites I. Brentano:

> But we must insist that, so soon as the object of a thought becomes the object of an assenting or rejecting judgment, our consciousness steps into an entirely new relation towards it. It is then twice present in consciousness, as

thought of, and as held for real or denied. (Brentano, cited in James, 1890/1950, vol. 2, p. 286).

Thus in consciousness the same content may appear in different ways: as a consenting or disagreeing judgment regarding its degree of truth on the one hand, and as the sheer thought or image per se on the other.

Thinking About the Past Versus Thinking About the Future

William James focused on images and beliefs about events and behaviors that happened in the past. Here the distinction between images and beliefs is easy to comprehend. One may more or less embellish past events in one's thoughts, or one arrives at a judgment about whether the events actually took place in the way one has thought about them. Whereas the first way of thinking about the past keeps events in fluctuation, the second way implies a cognitive laying down of the degree of truth of the event, which is a relief to the prior "theoretic agitation" (James, 1890/1950). It is the cognitive determination regarding the degree of truth that distinguishes the belief or judgment from the sheer image or thought.

For thinking about the future, these considerations imply that beliefs are judgments about the likelihood of occurrence of anticipated events. In such likelihood judgments, a person lays down the truth of future events. Like beliefs about the past, these beliefs or judgments about the future should relieve a prior "theoretic agitation" and thus qualify as the foundation for action.

But how can we conceive of the second way of thinking about the future, the sheer thoughts and images? Contrary to expectancy judgments, events depicted in one's thoughts and images about the future are not tested for their degree of truth. Even though the building stones of such fantasies may be based on experiences of the past, fantasies are not constrained by the cognitive mechanisms that make people appraise factual information (Klinger, 1971, 1990; Singer, 1966). Events do not need to be depicted in their wholeness, in their logical consistency, and in their real consequences. A person may thus embellish future events in the mind's eye without worrying about their potentially low feasibility. Similarly, he or she may project wonderful moments of the past into the future without bothering about how likely it is that these moments will actually become true again. Finally, one may enjoy future successes in one's fantasies without thinking about the cumbersome steps that lead to the realization of these successes. In short, one is forced neither to think about what it takes to actually realize one's fantasies about the future nor to consider one's expectations of successfully realizing them.

Some fantasies may come in the form of *Zauberdenken* (i.e., thoughts depicting actions and events that violate natural laws or social norms; Lewin, 1926,

Mahler, 1933). However, people most frequently fantasize about not yet realized but principally possible futures. For example, adolescents may fantasize about becoming brilliant college students, middle-aged adults may see themselves exercising regularly, or subordinates may imagine shaking off the pressure from their superiors. In this sense, fantasies are similar to daydreams (i.e., thoughts pertaining to immediate or delayed desires, including instrumental activities to attain the desired outcomes; Klinger, 1971, 1990). However, even if fantasies depict events that obey natural and social laws, they still may be disconnected from the perceived probabilities of successful realization. In short, people can experience future blessings in their fantasies without considering the probabilities that these blessings will actually occur.

According to William James (1890/1950), the thoughts and images about the past refer to what has happened and what could have happened. Thus they relate to the recent concepts of rumination (Martin & Tesser, 1989; McIntosh, Harlow, & Martin, 1995; Nolen-Hoeksema, 2000; see also Sanna, Stocker, & Clarke, 2003, for a summary) and counterfactual thinking (Kahneman & Miller, 1986; Markman, Gavanski, Sherman, & McMullen, 1993; Markman & McMullen, 2003; Sanna, Chang, & Meier, 2001; Sanna, Meier, & Wegner, 2001; see also Roese, 1997, for a summary). However, there is a decisive difference between images about the past versus those of the future. Images about the past depict events that already have happened (or could have happened) in a certain way, and thus the issue at hand is behaviorally closed (i.e., nothing can be done to change things). Images about the future, to the contrary, may still become true. Therefore, thoughts and images about the future always have potential relevance for action. We therefore postulate that not only do beliefs about the future (expectancy judgments) have relevance for action, but that this is also true for images about the future (fantasies).

The importance of the distinction between these two forms of thinking about the future (i.e., expectancy judgments versus fantasies) would be convincingly demonstrated if we observed that they differentially predict motivation and action. Indeed, a series of studies demonstrated that expectancy judgments versus fantasies differentially relate to one and the same measure of effort and successful performance (Oettingen & Wadden, 1991; Oettingen & Mayer, 2002). Before we describe three of these studies, we delineate why we think that the two ways of thinking about the future have differential motivational consequences.

Motivational Consequences of Expectations Versus Fantasies

A host of findings testify that expectations of successful performance foster effort and successful performance. These results pertain to success in interpersonal relations, to successful academic and professional achievement, and to attaining mental and physical health (see Bandura, 1997; Peterson & Bossio, 1991; Taylor & Brown, 1988; Taylor, Kemeny, Reed, Bower, & Gruenewald, 2000, for summaries). Because high expectations of success are not fabricated but are based on the appraisal of one's own experiences and performances (Bandura, 1977; Mischel, 1973), they signal that future efforts will not be in vain. Low expectations of success, in contrast, hint to the fact that one should hold off one's engagement. Based on these considerations and based on the numerous findings showing performance-enhancing effects of high expectations of success, we hypothesized a positive correlation between high expectations and successful performance.

To the contrary, fantasies should fail to be a valid signpost for engagement. Rather, they tempt the person to mentally enjoy desired futures in the present moment, concealing the necessity to still realize them in actuality. Therefore, fantasizing about one's desired future should trigger little motivation to actually attain the mentally enjoyed future events. Moreover, fantasies about a trouble-free path to success should hinder efforts to prevent potential obstacles and the forming of plans specifying how to overcome hindrances that may ensue. Lacking preparatory action and careful planning should further compromise motivation and successful performance.

Positive fantasies may focus on having achieved success, on moving smoothly toward it, or on both. Regardless of whether such fantasies are outcome-based or process-based, they should produce little motivation and weak performance. If, however, individuals, in more negatively felt fantasies, question a future of successful performance and its smooth attainment, the desired future is no longer experienced as merely enjoyable but as something to be achieved in actuality. People can now lay out the road to success, prepare for setbacks and hindrances, exert effort, and show persistence. In sum, whereas positive expectations of success should predict effortful action and successful performance, positive fantasies should predict low effort and little success.

In the following three studies, we tested this idea of a differential relation of thinking about the future in terms of expectations versus fantasies to actually achieved successes. In each study, thinking about the future in terms of expectations and fantasies was assessed at least a week before we measured effort and successful performance. We operationalized expectations by the perceived probability of attaining success, and we measured fantasies by using idiographic techniques that tap participants' thoughts and images about achieving successful performance in the future.

Academic Achievement

Right before their midterm exams, college students enrolled in an introductory psychology class were asked to indicate the grade they would like to obtain in the course. To measure expectations, we asked participants to indicate the likelihood that they would actually receive this course grade (Oettingen & Mayer, 2002, Study 3). We then assessed course grade-related fantasies. Participants completed a scenario in writing that depicted them as already having taken all the exams and being on their way to the building in which the course grades are posted. Immediately thereafter, participants rated the experienced positivity/negativity of the reported thoughts and images. Performance was measured by change of course grades from midterm (when expectations and fantasies were assessed) to the final exam.

Previous research has amply documented that high expectations of success build academic achievement. This is true for students of different ages and different educational backgrounds, and with respect to a variety of indicators (e.g., standardized tests, course grades, solving intellectual tasks, application of learning strategies; Schunk, 1989; Zimmerman & Martinez-Pons, 1992; see also Bandura, 1997; Multon, Brown, & Lent, 1991, for summaries). The predictive power of positive fantasies for academic achievement, however, has not been analyzed. Following the ideas presented here, we hypothesized and observed that students entertaining high expectations of success invested much study effort and achieved comparatively high course grades, whereas students entertaining positive fantasies failed to study hard and achieved low course grades (from midterm to the final exam).

The predictive relation between positive fantasy and low performance was mediated by a lack of effort, as measured by the number of hours students had spent studying, by their reported study effort, and by the amount of extra-credit work they had been handing in between their midterm and their final exams. Thus positive fantasies led to less studying than more negatively toned fantasies, and this in turn produced lower levels of achievement as measured by course grades.

This study investigated the role of expectations versus fantasies in building intellectual achievement. The next study attempted to conceptually replicate the pattern of results in the domain of professional achievement.

Professional Achievement

German graduating students who did not have jobs yet participated in our study on transition into work life (Oettingen & Mayer, 2002, Study 1). We first asked participants for their expectations of finding a job in their field of interest. To measure the positivity of their work-related fantasies, we then asked participants to generate positive and negative fantasies about their "transition into work life, looking for a job, finding a job" and to write these fantasies down. Thereafter, participants had to indicate how often they recently had such positive and negative thoughts and images. We subtracted the indicated frequency of negative fantasies from the frequency of positive fantasies to arrive at an overall positivity score for work-related fantasies.

Two years later we assessed participants' professional success by asking them how many job offers they had gotten and how high their present salaries were. Partial correlations show that graduates with positive expectations got more job offers and earned higher salaries than participants with negative expectations; graduates with positive fantasies, to the contrary, got fewer job offers and earned less money than participants with negative fantasies. Finally, participants with positive fantasies put less effort into looking for jobs than did participants with negative fantasies: They reported that they sent out fewer job applications.

Can the predicted pattern of results also be observed in domains other than academic and professional achievement? The following study pertains to the health domain. Here, expectations have also been a pivotal predictor of high effort and success (Scheier et al., 2003; Taylor et al., 2000; see also Bandura, 1997; Peterson & Bossio, 1991, for summaries). Participants were older adults, because at this period of the life span achieving health becomes a particularly pressing concern.

Recovery From Surgery

Participants were patients admitted to a hospital to undergo total hip-replacement surgery (Oettingen & Mayer, 2002, Study 4). Total hip-replacement surgery is a commonly performed surgery in patients with osteoarthritis of the hip, which is the most frequent joint disorder and a particular problem in the elderly (Gogia, Christensen, & Schmidt, 1994). The day before surgery, we assessed participants' expectations and fantasies regarding their recovery. First, participants had to answer questions such as how likely they thought it would be that 2 weeks after surgery they would be able to go for a brief walk using an assistive cane. To assess their fantasies, we asked them to imagine, in writing, five scenarios to completion and then to rate the affective tone of their own thoughts and images. The scenarios pertained, for example, to participants' abilities to walk to the hospital newspaper stand or, after being home again, to go on a trip with a friend. After imagining a story to completion and writing down the respective thoughts and images, participants indicated how positively and how negatively they had experienced their thoughts and images.

Two weeks after surgery, while participants were still in the hospital, each physical therapist who was mainly responsible for a particular patient indicated the functional status of her patient's hip (Gogia et al., 1994). Physical therapists used classic indicators such as degree of hip joint motion (e.g., extension and flexion) and competence to walk on stairs (Dekker, Boot, van der Woude, & Bijlsma, 1992). In addition, they evaluated patients' general recovery (e.g., in terms of muscular strength and degree of pain).

Whereas positive expectations were precursors of successful recovery, positive fantasies were a hindrance, and this was true whether patients' recovery was measured via specific criteria (i.e., hip joint motion or walking stairs) or via more general measures (i.e., general recovery). The findings stayed unchanged after controlling for presurgery hip condition (as assessed by the doctors), weight (70% of the sample were overweight), and gender.

Subsequent content analyses of the patients' fantasies revealed that participants had idealized their future recovery with respect to both outcome (they imagined having achieved recovery) and process (they imagined an easy and effortless way to recovery). Though idealization of outcome was more frequent than idealization of process, both were positively related to the subjective positivity of their fantasies. Thus positively felt fantasies contain both outcome and process in its idealized form, that is, recovery as well as effortless and unencumbered progress toward recovery. Most important, however, it was the subjectively experienced fantasies rather than the expressed idealization as picked up by the raters that predicted little success in recovery.

Supportive Evidence

We replicated the differential relation of expectancy judgments and fantasies in further areas of the health domain (e.g., chronic illness, Oettingen & Mayer, 2003; weight loss, Oettingen & Wadden, 1991), as well as in other life domains such as the interpersonal domain (e.g., starting a romantic relationship, Oettingen & Mayer, 2002, Study 2). In all of these studies, expectations and fantasies were measured long before we assessed the final measure of successful performance (up to 4 years).

Research on counterfactual thinking further supports the idea of a harmful relationship between positive fantasies and thought, feeling, and action. McMullen and Markman (2000; Roese, 1994; see Markman & McMullen, 2003, for a summary) observed that positive affect resulting from counterfactual thinking led to complacency, whereas respective negative affect increased motivation. Further, experimentally induced positive images in defensive pessimists (Norem & Cantor, 1986) led to less effort and worse performance in getting to know somebody than induced negative images (Showers, 1992). Those who had positive images used fewer confidence-building strategies than those who elaborated negative images. Though the findings on defensive pessimism apply only to high-achieving students, they still support our contention that positive thoughts and images lead to comparatively little motivation and success. Finally, mental simulations that focus on the glorious attainment of a goal (outcome simulations) are less motivating and led to worse performances than process simulations in which people rehearsed the cumbersome steps to reach successful performance (Taylor, Pham, Rivkin, & Armor, 1998).

Summary

Assessed by expectancy judgments, thinking positively about the future predicted high performance, whereas measured by fantasies, thinking positively
about the future predicted low performance. Effort and persistence mediated the
negative relation between positive fantasies and high performance. These findings underline the importance of William James's (1890/1950) distinction between beliefs and images, which is the foundation of our differentiation
between two forms of thinking about the future: expectancy judgments versus
fantasies.

Mental Contrasting: Linking Future and Present to Activate the Past

Given the results of the previously described studies, positive fantasies about the
future appear to be problematic for realizing a successful future. However, positive fantasies may lead to fantasy realization if they are freed from their purely
enjoyable contents. In the following, we describe a self-regulation strategy, mental contrasting, that turns them into binding goals with subsequent goal striving and goal attainment.

Realizing Fantasies About Positive Futures

Mental contrasting entails the conjoint elaboration of the wished-for future, on
the one hand, and the present reality that stands in the way of realizing the
wished-for future, on the other hand. Through this conjoint elaboration, the
wished-for future and the present reality become simultaneously accessible
(Kawada, 2004). In addition, mental contrasting activates the relational construct (Higgins & Chaires, 1980) of present reality "standing in the way" of realizing the desired future. Thus a necessity to realize the wished-for future
emerges that activates relevant expectations which now will determine
whether people will set themselves the goal of realizing their fantasies. Therefore, after mental contrasting, individuals should display flexible and strategic
behavior, in that they should refrain from setting the goal of realizing their fantasies when expectancy judgments are low but fully commit themselves to fantasy realization when expectancy judgments signal promise.

A necessity to attain the desired future should emerge only after mental contrasting, not after only fantasizing about the future. After such indulging in the
future, expectations will not determine one's goal commitment to realizing
one's fantasies. Rather, the implicit pull should lead to moderate goal commitment that is independent of perceived chances of success. Similarly, a necessity

to act should not emerge and expectations should not be activated after reflecting on impeding reality only. After such dwelling, goal commitment to realizing one's fantasies should solely reflect the implicit push triggered by the negativity of the reality events that are thought about.

Mental contrasting may be conceived as a problem-solving strategy. Newell and Simon (1972) argued that the internal subjective representation of a problem (i.e., the person's problem space) needs to be differentiated from the objective problem (in this case, realizing one's fantasies by overcoming one's obstacles in the present reality). After mental contrasting, the person's problem space entails both the positive future and the negative reality, and the negative reality is perceived as standing in the way of the positive future. The positive future now appears as something to be achieved and the present reality as something to be overcome. Therefore, relevant expectations of overcoming the present reality (with its obstacles and temptations) to reach the desired future are activated. If expectancy judgments are promising, goal commitment to realizing one's fantasies will be strong; if expectancy judgments are unpromising, goal commitment to realizing one's fantasies will fail to appear. Fantasizing about the positive future only (indulging) and reflecting on the negative reality only (dwelling) means construing the problem space as entailing only half of the constituents of the objective problem. Because the future does not appear as to be realized and the present does not appear as to be changed, relevant expectancy judgments will not be activated and used in fantasy realization.

Altogether, mental contrasting involves three variables: fantasies about the desired future, reflections on reality, and expectancy judgments (perceived probabilities of successful fantasy realization). Just as we asked before whether it is meaningful to differentiate between expectations versus fantasies about the future, we may now ask whether it is meaningful to distinguish between expectations and reflections on reality. First, expectations are judgments, whereas reflections on reality are free thoughts. That is, expectations are beliefs in the form of probability judgments, whereas reflections on reality are images about reality events as they appear in the stream of thought. Second, expectations pertain to the future, whereas reflections on reality focus on the present. Thus mental contrasting links the future and the present to make expectancy judgments relevant for people's change behavior. Interestingly, however, expectancy judgments are based on past experiences and performances. This implies that by activating expectations of success, mental contrasting makes the past relevant for future behavior.

A series of experiments on goal setting support these hypotheses. We now present two such studies. They pertain to goal setting in the achievement domain and in the interpersonal domain. Specifically, the two studies investigate the role of mental contrasting, indulging, and dwelling in setting goals to excel in mathematics and in solving an interpersonal problem.

Realizing Fantasies of Excelling in Mathematics

The fantasy theme of the study was excelling in mathematics (Oettingen, Pak, & Schnetter, 2001, Study 4). Participants were male adolescents, freshmen enrolled in two vocational schools for computer programming. Mathematics was the critical subject in the first year of studies. We first measured participants' expectations to improve in mathematics and then asked them to name four positive aspects of improving in mathematics and four negative aspects that impeded their improvement. Thereafter, we established the three experimental groups, a fantasy-reality contrast (mental contrast) group, a fantasy-only (indulging) group, and a reality-only (dwelling) group. In the fantasy-reality contrast group, participants had to mentally elaborate in writing two positive aspects of improving in math and two negative aspects that stand in the way in alternating order, beginning with a positive aspect of the future. In the fantasy-only group, participants had only to mentally elaborate four aspects of improving in math, and in the reality-only group, participants had only to mentally elaborate four aspects of impeding reality.

We measured fantasy realization by affective and behavioral indicators of goal commitment. Directly following the mental exercises, all participants reported whether they felt energized with respect to excelling in mathematics. Two weeks after the experiment, we asked teachers to evaluate each student's effort during the past fortnight (e.g., how much persistent effort the student showed in studying math and how intrinsically interested the student was). In addition, we measured goal attainment by asking teachers for each student's present course grade.

In participants in the mental-contrast group, feelings of energization, exerted effort, and achieved grades were more in line with their expectations than in participants in the indulging and dwelling groups. High-expectancy participants in the mental-contrast group felt most energized and exerted the most effort, and their teachers gave them the highest course grades. Low-expectancy participants felt least energized, exerted least effort, and achieved the lowest course grades. In contrast, participants in the indulging and dwelling groups felt moderately energized independent of their expectations. Similarly, teachers rated them as showing moderate effort and gave them mediocre course grades, no matter whether students had high or low expectations.

For the participating adolescents who were at the beginning of their vocational training and thus still had career options available, mental contrasting seems beneficial. Those who have high chances to excel invest their time and effort in a promising career, whereas those with minor chances to excel do not invest in vain and thus may move on and use their energies otherwise (Carver & Scheier, 1998). The pattern of goal commitment that results from indulging and dwelling seems less beneficial. Being implicitly pulled by the future or pushed by present reality, those with high expectations do not invest enough effort and thus suffer from failing to realize their potential. Those with low expectations, on the other hand, invest too much effort and thus waste their energies in a lost cause. That is, both indulging and dwelling puts people at risk in terms of being out of touch with their potential.

Realizing Fantasies of Solving an Interpersonal Problem

College students had to name their most important interpersonal problem and to indicate their expectations about whether their problem would have a happy ending (Oettingen et al., 2001, Study 3). Participants named, for example, "to get to know someone I like," "to solve a conflict with my partner," or "to improve the relationship with my mother." Thereafter, participants were asked to list four aspects of fantasy realization and four aspects of the negative reality that appeared to stand against fantasy realization. As in the previous experiment, participants in the mental-contrast group had to alternate in their mental elaborations between positive aspects of the desired future and negative aspects of present reality, beginning with a positive aspect. In the indulging group, participants were asked to imagine only positive aspects of a happy ending, and in the negative reality group, participants were asked to reflect only on negative aspects of present reality. In a control group, participants mentally elaborated the negative reality before they fantasized about the positive future. That way the future did not serve as an anchor to which the reality stands in contrast. Thus a relational construct of reality "standing in the way" of the desired future should not be activated, and a necessity to act with subsequent activation of expectations should not emerge. We hypothesized, therefore, that participants in the control group should show the same expectancy-independent pattern of goal commitment as in the indulging and dwelling groups.

Directly following these mental exercises, all participants reported their feelings of energization with respect to solving their interpersonal problems. Two weeks later, to assess the behavioral indicators of commitment, we asked participants to indicate the two most difficult steps they had undertaken to solve their interpersonal problems and to report the exact date they had performed these steps. Immediacy of fantasy realization was defined as the difference in days between the date participants reported to have taken the steps and the date of participation in the experiment.

As in the previous experiment, contrasting participants felt energized and behaved in line with their expectations of success more than did indulging and dwelling participants. High-expectancy participants in the mental-contrast group felt most energized and started right after the experiment to solve their interpersonal problems, whereas low-expectancy participants felt least energized and delayed their steps toward fantasy realization. To the contrary, indulging and dwelling participants felt moderately energized and started fantasy realization after about a week, independently of whether they expected to solve the problem or not. Participants in the control group (who first mentally elaborated the negative reality and only then the positive future) showed the same pattern of results as the indulging and dwelling groups. This finding implies that the relational construct of reality "standing in the way" of the desired future needs to be activated for mental-contrast effects to occur.

Importantly, the pattern of results was not attributable to differential effects of the manipulation on level of expectations. We found an almost perfect correlation between participants' expectations of success measured before and after the experiment. In addition, the manipulation did not differentially change the level of expectations. This implies that mental contrasting fosters fantasy realization by making high expectations of success relevant for goal commitment rather than by changing the level of expectations of success.

Another experiment using the same design replicated the results with respect to cognitive indicators of goal commitment (Oettingen et al., 2001, Study 1). Specifically, we measured the extent to which participants formed plans to realize their fantasies. Immediately following the experiment, all participants were confronted with eight sentence stems presented in random order: Four sentence stems suggested the formulation of plans, and four did not require the formulation of plans. Participants were supposed to complete those four sentence stems that best matched how they were thinking about their interpersonal problems. When counting the number of sentence stems chosen that led to the formulation of plans, we observed expectancy-dependency in the mental-contrast group, but not in the indulging and dwelling groups.

Supportive Evidence

We replicated these results in further experiments. In the academic domain, for example, experiments pertained to studying abroad (Oettingen et al., 2001, Study 2), to combining work and family life (Oettingen, 2000, Study 2), and to acquiring a second language (Oettingen, Hönig, & Gollwitzer, 2000, Study 1). In the interpersonal domain, experiments focused on getting to know an attractive stranger (Oettingen, 2000, Study 1) and to successfully seeking help (Oettingen, Hagenah, et al., 2005, Study 3). In the health domain, experiments concerned the improvement of patient-provider relations (Oettingen, Hagenah, et al., 2005, Study 1) and the reduction of cigarette consumption (Oettingen, Mayer, & Thorpe, 2005).

The results hold for goal commitment assessed by cognitive, affective, and behavioral indicators (e.g., planning, anticipated disappointment in case of failure, financial investment), via self-report or observations, and measured either directly after the experiment or weeks later. Mental contrasting turned out to be an easy-to-apply self-regulatory tool of goal setting, as the described effects were obtained even when participants elaborated the future and the reality only very briefly (i.e., were asked to imagine only one positive aspect of the desired future and one obstacle standing in the way of realizing the desired future; Oettingen et al., 2000, Study 1).

Recent experimental studies (Oettingen & Pak, 2003) show that mental contrasting affects not only the emergence of goal commitments but also the processes of subsequent goal striving. Effective goal striving implies constructive responses to negative feedback (Dweck, 1999; Dweck & Leggett, 1988; Gollwitzer, 1996). We therefore argued that mental contrasting in light of high expectations should foster effective responses to negative feedback. Because negative feedback provides relevant clues on how to achieve the desired future (Gollwitzer, 1996), an effective response would be to appraise such feedback as useful information for goal striving rather than as a sign of low ability (Dweck & Leggett, 1988). Taking feedback as valuable information should, in addition, guarantee that negative news leaves one's self-view of competence intact. Indeed, we observed that mental contrasting in light of high expectations of success led to the effective processing of negative feedback, as well as to successful maintenance of a positive self-view of competence (Oettingen & Pak, 2003).

So far we have shown that fantasies about a positive future contrasted with reflections on negative reality translate into goal commitment to realize the positive future. In the study reported next, we explored whether fantasies about a negative future contrasted with a positive reality are translated into goal commitment to master the negative future.

Mastering Fantasies About Negative Futures

There are many instances in which people entertain fantasies about a future they are unjustly afraid of. One example is perceived threat of out-groups. Gaines and Reed (1995) and Corenblum and Stephan (2001) showed that prejudice led to unfounded fears of future interactions with members of different religions or ethnicities. Another domain of unjustified fear is HIV infection (Glantz, Mariner, & Annas, 1992), wherein HIV-infected medical practitioners may be barred from practicing due to policy decisions based on fear rather than actual risk.

Unjustified fears have predominantly been investigated in the context of anxiety disorders such as panic disorder, posttraumatic stress disorder, phobias, and generalized anxiety disorders, for all of which the development of effective treatments has been attempted. Though these treatments may stem from different schools of psychotherapy, they are largely based on the principle of exposure (see Foa & Kozak, 1986, for a review).

The research described here uses the principle of exposure in combination with mental contrasting. We hypothesized that exposure to the feared stimulus in one's fantasies may trigger goal commitment to approach the feared stimulus. Specifically, people should approach the feared stimulus if the negative fantasies are contrasted with reflections on positive reality that may impede the occurrence of the feared future and if expectations of mastering the negative future are high. Mere fantasies about being exposed to the negative future (indulging) and mere reflections on impeding positive reality (dwelling), on the other hand, should lead to expectancy-independent goal commitment to approach the negative future. In other words, mental contrasting should strengthen goal commitment to approach the negatively perceived future in light of high expectations of success but should lead to giving in to fears in light of low expectations. Indulging in fantasies about a negative future or dwelling on positive impeding reality, in contrast, should make people act toward the negative future independently of expectations.

Mastering Xenophobic Fantasies

We told adolescents in an ethnically homogeneous district of East Berlin, called Weissensee, that foreigners seeking asylum might move into their neighborhood (Oettingen, Mayer, Thorpe, Janetzke, & Lorenz, in press). We then assessed participants' expectations of helping to integrate the foreigners in their district. To induce negative fantasies, all participants were told to imagine the negative personal consequences that the arrival of immigrants in Weissensee might have. They were asked to generate respective fantasies and to write them down. To induce images about the impeding positive reality, participants were confronted with 12 statements, fabricated by us, supposedly stemming from interviews with adolescents who previously had experienced foreigners moving into their neighborhood. These statements depicted positive interactions between the interviewees and the foreigners. One of the statements was: "Playing soccer with these guys was just great. Finally, we had strong and fair opponents (Lars G., 16 years)."

We then established the three experimental groups (mental contrast of negative fantasy with positive reality, indulging in negative fantasy, dwelling on positive reality). In the mental-contrast group, participants were simply asked to write down what thoughts and images came to their mind when they read these statements. This way, the positive reality was forced on participants' thoughts.

To establish the indulging and dwelling groups, we used a reinterpretation paradigm (Oettingen, 2000). Specifically, we varied the point of view from which participants had to work through the statements. In the indulging group, we ensured that participants would trivialize the adolescents' statements. We suggested to participants that the interviewed adolescents were not to be taken seriously. In the dwelling group, we asked participants to generate thoughts that supported the notion that they would get along well with the foreigners in Weissensee. Thus participants' thoughts were tightly linked to the positive reality.

Two weeks after the experiment, we measured various indicators of goal commitment to help integrate the immigrants. To measure affective goal commitment, we asked participants for their felt tolerance. Specifically, we asked how harmful it would be for them if the immigrants moved into their neighborhood. To measure behavioral goal commitment, we asked participants how much effort and time they would be willing to invest in helping to edit a journal about and in collaboration with foreign youths. Finally, to measure cognitive goal commitment, we assessed the number of plans that participants formed in writing about what it would be like to live with the foreign adolescents in their district.

As in the previous experiments on realizing fantasies about a positive future, this experiment on mastering fantasies about a negative future showed strong expectancy dependence in the mental-contrast group but not in the indulging and dwelling groups. When expectations of success were high, students in the mental-contrast group were more tolerant, were more willing to exert effort toward helping to integrate the foreigners, and formed more plans to achieve this goal than mental-contrast-group participants with low expectations, and more so than participants with high and low expectancies in the indulging and dwelling groups.

There has been much research aimed at ameliorating unjustified fears in clinical settings (see Brown, Antony, & Barlow, 1995, for a summary). The present study reaches out into daily life, specifying self-regulatory strategies people can use to rid themselves of their unjustified fears. Specifically, when participants mentally contrasted negative consequences of a given future event with present reality that stands in the way of these negative consequences occurring, they held out against their fearful fantasies and boldly approached the negatively valenced consequences of the future event. However, this was true only if contrasting participants expected to master their fears. If they were plagued by low expectations of mastery, they gave in to their fears.

In contrast to participants in the mental-contrast group, participants in the indulging and dwelling groups did not utilize their expectations in confronting the negative future. Even when their expectations were high, they showed little tolerance and little willingness to help, and they formed only a few plans to integrate the foreigners. These considerations imply that mental contrasting, but not indulging and dwelling, makes people master their fears by taking an active stance that allows them to act in a tolerant and altruistic way toward members of a feared out-group.

The key feature of fear and anxiety disorders is avoidance of situations that evoke the arousal of fear and anxiety. LeDoux and Gorman (2001) suggest that "the trick is to turn avoidance into a successful coping strategy" (p. 1955). In addition, they argue that strategies that enable people to become active whenever threatening thoughts emerge will attenuate the involuntary passive responses to these fear-arousing thoughts. Contrasting negative fantasies with reflections on positive impeding reality might be such a strategy because it helps people to actively cope with the fear-arousing images.

Summary

Conjoint elaboration of the future and impeding reality puts expectancy judgments to work. As expectancy judgments are a summary statement of one's past experiences and performances, the described experimental studies imply that it is the link between future and present that allows the past to come to the fore. When the link between future and present has been formed, the past guides goal commitment in terms of its cognitive, affective, and behavioral indicators. A host of experimental studies from various life domains and using different paradigms support this contention. They show that participants with high expectancies who mentally contrast a positive future with its impeding reality feel energized, initiate action immediately, plan how to go about the realization of the positive future, and exert strong effort. Importantly, they are also successful in attaining the positive future. Mental contrasting in light of low expectancy judgments led participants to refrain from the goal to realize their fantasies. Finally, participants who consider only part of the problem—that is, only the future or only the present—commit themselves to a moderate degree independently of their expectancy judgments.

Mental contrasting may also be used to dispel fantasies about a feared future. In a study with adolescents nourishing xenophobic fantasies, high-expectancy participants in the mental-contrast group showed more tolerance and generosity than low-expectancy participants and indulging and dwelling participants. Apparently, it does not matter whether fantasies pertain to positive or negative futures; the same effects on goal commitment of mental contrasting versus indulging and dwelling are observed. Seen from the problem-solving perspective described previously (Newell & Simon, 1972), indulging and dwelling imply that the internal subjective representation (i.e., the person's problem space) differs from the objective problem. Only if the problem space considers both future and reality and thus corresponds to the objective problem do relevant expectations influence goal commitments.

So far we have demonstrated that mental contrasting is a beneficial strategy when it comes to helping people orient themselves along their performance history. A question we have not raised yet is, What factors determine the emergence of mental contrasting and what is the role of time herein? To speculate on this question, we want to consider how mental contrasting versus indulging may prevail in cultures adhering to different time perspectives.

Mental Contrasting Across Cultures

Cultures differ in the time perspective their members adhere to. Such differences in time perspective may be observed in cultural products such as myths, stories, or songs. In Japanese haiku poems, for example, the time perspective is short, as goals are set in the here and now (Boesch, 1997). This observation is nicely corroborated in a study by H. Azuma and M. Mashima (personal communication, 1996), who asked students in Japan and the United States what they had been thinking about in the past week. Whereas students in Japan reported to have contemplated the next steps in their daily pursuits (e.g., how I will cook tonight for my girlfriend), American students described thoughts about long-term projects (e.g., my future as a medical doctor). We speculate that cultures with a long-term time perspective should foster mental contrasting and indulging, because a long-term time perspective provides plenty of contents for fantasies about the future.

Which factors in cultures with a long-term time perspective, however, will determine whether people tend to mentally contrast or to indulge? Norm orientation should play the decisive role (tight, simple, and collectivist cultures versus loose, complex, and individualist cultures; Triandis, 1994), because norms provide the necessary assurance for action and lay down the boundaries for action. In addition, they convey commitments which determine the direction for acting.

If norms are the basis for action in more traditional cultures, what factors provide the basis for action in more modern, less norm-oriented societies? Here no norms or rituals provide assurance and boundaries, as well as the direction for acting (by laying down who relates to whom, when, where, and how). We suggest that in modern societies in which norms increasingly vanish, expectations are taking over their function. First, by reflecting an individual's personal history, expectations provide the necessary assurance to act and show the boundaries of acting. Second, in their function of turning free fantasies into binding goals, expectations determine the direction to act.

Assuming that expectations take over the action-guiding function of norms in modern societies, we should there find mental contrasting to be the prevalent form of self-regulatory thought. To the contrary, in traditional societies in which norms guide action, there is no need for mental contrasting. Thus indulging in the positive future and dwelling on negative reality should flourish. They turn people away from bleak prospects and thus will make them "stay in the field." Indulging in positive fantasies will, in addition, stabilize the normative cultural environment, because it provides hope for a better future even in light of low economic prospects and restricted living conditions.

Finally, in cultures with a short-term time perspective, none of the three self-regulatory modes of thought should be prevalent. Rather, mental simulation of how to implement short-term goals assigned by normative regulations (strong norm orientation) or by the immediate demands of the situation (weak norm orientation) should be the prevalent way of self-regulatory thought.

Summary

Cultures with a long-term time perspective should foster the emergence of mental contrasting and of indulging, because a long-term time perspective provides the content for plentiful fantasies about the future. Whether a culture is characterized by mental contrasting or indulging should depend on the degree of its norm orientation. In a culture with weak norm orientation, mental contrasting should be prevalent, because expectations guide action, thus making mental contrasting useful. In a culture of strong norm orientation, indulging should be prevalent, because expectations are not needed for action and indulging may provide hope for a less restricted future.

The latter considerations imply that the benefits of mental contrasting versus indulging are context dependent. In modern societies, in which norms increasingly fail to determine action and expectations take over the action-guiding function of norms (i.e., the person is the agent of his or her own development), mental contrasting should be a beneficial strategy. Under normative constraints, to the contrary, indulging in positive fantasies may well prove to be the more beneficial and comforting self-regulatory mode of thought.

Conclusions

Mental contrasting strengthens the link between past performance and future behavior, whereas indulging and dwelling disconnects a person's thoughts, feelings, and actions from his or her own experiences and performances. Just as mental contrasting and indulging differ in their benefits across sociocultural contexts, they might differ in their benefits across tasks. When solving the task at hand affords the consideration of past experiences, mental contrasting may be chosen, whereas indulging and dwelling would qualify for tasks that are better solved without looking back. Finally, indulging and dwelling rather than mental contrasting may be the right strategy if expectations cannot be determined or when they are grossly distorted. Wise individuals, then, may be those who flexibly adjust the use of their self-regulatory strategies to the context they find themselves to be in, to the task at hand, and to the information that is available.

References

Bandura, A. (1977). Self-efficacy: Toward a unifying theory of behavioral change. *Psychological Review, 84*, 191–215.

Bandura, A. (1997). *Self-efficacy: The exercise of control.* New York: Freeman.

Boesch, E. E. (1997). *Von der Sehnsucht* [About longing]. Saarbrücken, Germany: Private Printing.

Brown, T. A., Antony, M. M., & Barlow, D. H. (1995). Diagnostic comorbidity in panic disorder: Effect on treatment outcome and course of comorbid diagnoses following treatment. *Journal of Consulting and Clinical Psychology, 63*, 408–418.

Carver, C. S., & Scheier, M. F. (1998). *On the self-regulation of behavior.* New York: Cambridge University Press.

Corenblum, B., & Stephan, W. G. (2001). White fears and native apprehensions: An integrated threat theory approach to intergroup attitudes. *Canadian Journal of Behavioural Science, 33*, 251–268.

Dekker, J., Boot, B., van der Woude, L. H. V., & Bijlsma, J. W. J. (1992). Pain and disability in osteoarthritis: A review of biobehavioral mechanisms. *Journal of Behavioral Medicine, 15*, 189–214.

Dweck, C. S. (1999). *Self-theories: Their role in motivation, personality, and development.* Philadelphia: Psychology Press.

Dweck, C. S., & Leggett, E. L. (1988). A social-cognitive approach to motivation and personality. *Psychological Review, 95*, 256–273.

Foa, E. B., & Kozak, M. J. (1986). Emotional processing of fear: Exposure to corrective information. *Psychological Bulletin, 99*, 20–35.

Gaines, S. O., & Reed, E. S. (1995). Prejudice: From Allport to DuBois. *American Psychologist, 50*, 96–103.

Glantz, L. H., Mariner, W. K., & Annas, G. J. (1992). Risky business: Setting public health policy for HIV-infected health care professionals. *Milbank Quarterly, 70*, (1), 43–79.

Gogia, P. P., Christensen, C. M., & Schmidt, C. (1994). Total hip replacement in patients with osteoarthritis of the hip: Improvement in pain and functional status. *Orthopedics, 17*, 145–150.

Gollwitzer, P. M. (1996). The volitional benefits of planning. In P. M. Gollwitzer & J. A. Bargh (Eds.), *The psychology of action* (pp. 287–312). New York: Guilford Press.

Higgins, E. T., & Chaires, W. M. (1980). Accessibility of interrelational constructs: Implications for stimulus encoding and creativity. *Journal of Experimental Social Psychology, 16*, 348–361.

James, W. (1890/1950). *The principles of psychology* (2 vols.). New York: Dover.

Kahneman, D., & Miller, D. T. (1986). Norm theory: Comparing reality to its alternatives. *Psychological Review, 93*, 136–153.

Kawada, C. L. K. (2004). *Self-regulatory thought in goal setting: Perceptual and cognitive processes.* Unpublished doctoral dissertation, New York University.

Klinger, E. (1971). *Structure and functions of fantasy.* New York: Wiley.

Klinger, E. (1990). *Daydreaming: Using waking fantasy and imagery for self-knowledge and creativity.* Los Angeles: Tarcher.

LeDoux, J. E., & Gorman, J. M. (2001). A call to action: Overcoming anxiety through active coping. *American Journal of Psychiatry, 158,* 1953–1955.

Lewin, K. (1926). Vorsatz, Wille und Bedürfnis [Intention, will, and need]. *Psychologische Forschung, 7,* 330–385.

Mahler, W. (1933). Ersatzhandlungen verschiedenen Realitätsgrades [Compensatory action based on different degrees of reality]. *Psychologische Forschung, 18,* 27–89.

Markman, K. D., Gavanski, I., Sherman, S. J., & McMullen, M. N. (1993). The mental simulation of better and worse possible worlds. *Journal of Experimental Social Psychology, 29,* 87–109.

Markman, K. D., & McMullen, M. (2003). A reflection and evaluation model of comparative thinking. *Personality and Social Psychology Review, 7,* 244–267.

Martin, L. L., & Tesser, A. (1989). Toward a motivational and structural theory of ruminative thought. In S. Uleman & J. A. Bargh (Eds.), *Unintended thought* (pp. 306–326). New York: Guilford Press.

McIntosh, W. D., Harlow, T. F., & Martin, L. L. (1995). Linkers and nonlinkers: Goal beliefs as a moderator of the effects of everyday hassles on rumination, depression, and physical complaints. *Journal of Applied Social Psychology, 25,* 1231–1244.

McMullen, M. N., & Markman, K. D. (2000). Downward counterfactuals and motivation: The wake-up call and the Pangloss effect. *Personality and Social Psychological Bulletin, 26,* 575–584.

Mischel, W. (1973). Toward a cognitive social learning reconceptualization of personality. *Psychological Review, 80,* 252–253.

Multon, K. D., Brown, S. D., & Lent, R. W. (1991). Relation of self-efficacy beliefs to academic outcomes: A meta-analytic investigation. *Journal of Counseling Psychology, 38,* 30–38.

Newell, A., & Simon, H. A. (1972). *Human problem solving.* Englewood Cliffs, NJ: Prentice-Hall.

Nolen-Hoeksema, S. (2000). The role of rumination in depressive disorders and mixed anxiety/depressive symptoms. *Journal of Abnormal Psychology, 109,* 504–511.

Norem, J. K., & Cantor, N. (1986). Defensive pessimism: Harnessing anxiety as motivation. *Journal of Personality and Social Psychology, 51,* 1208–1217.

Oettingen, G. (2000). Expectancy effects on behavior depend on self-regulator thought. *Social Cognition, 18,* 101–129.

Oettingen, G., Hagenah, M., Mayer, D., Brinkmann, J., Schmidt, L., & Pak, H. (2005). *Fantasies and goal setting in everyday life.* Manuscript in preparation.

Oettingen, G., Hönig, G., & Gollwitzer, P. M. (2000). Effective self-regulation of goal attainment. *International Journal of Educational Research, 33,* 705–732.

Oettingen, G., & Mayer, D. (2002). The motivating function of thinking about the future: Expectations versus fantasies. *Journal of Personality and Social Psychology,* *83,* 1198–1212.

Oettingen, G., & Mayer, D. (2003). *Mastering the consequences of chronic illness: Expectations versus fantasies.* Unpublished manuscript, University of Hamburg, Germany.

Oettingen, G., Mayer, D., & Thorpe, J. S. (2005). *Mental contrasting and the self-regulation of promotion versus prevention goals.* Manuscript in preparation.

Oettingen, G., Mayer, D., Thorpe, J. S., Janetzke, H., & Lorenz, S. (in press). Turning fantasies about positive and negative futures into self-improvement goals, *Motivation and Emotion.*

Oettingen, G., & Pak, H. (2003, September). *Strategies of goal setting affect goal attainment.* Paper presented at the annual meeting of the Society of Experimental Social Psychology, Boston, MA.

Oettingen, G., Pak. H., & Schnetter, K. (2001). Self-regulation of goal setting: Turning free fantasies about the future into binding goals. *Journal of Personality and Social Psychology, 80,* 736–753.

Oettingen, G., & Wadden, T. A. (1991). Expectation, fantasy, and weight loss: Is the impact of positive thinking always positive? *Cognitive Therapy and Research, 15,* 167–175.

Peterson, C., & Bossio, L. M. (1991). *Health and optimism: New research on the relationship between positive thinking and physical well-being.* New York: Free Press.

Roese, N. J. (1994). The functional basis of counterfactual thinking. *Journal of Personality and Social Psychology, 66,* 805–818.

Roese, N. J. (1997). Counterfactual thinking. *Psychological Bulletin, 121,* 133–148.

Sanna, L. J., Chang, E. C., & Meier, S. (2001). Counterfactual thinking and self-motives. *Personality and Social Psychology Bulletin, 27,* 1023–1034.

Sanna, L. J., Meier, S., & Wegner, E. A. (2001). Counterfactuals and motivation: Mood as input to affective enjoyment and preparation. *British Journal of Social Psychology, 40,* 235–256.

Sanna, L. J., Stocker, S. L., & Clarke, J. A. (2003). Rumination, imagination, and personality: Specters of the past and future in the present. In E. C. Chang & L. J. Sanna (Eds.), *Virtue, vice, and personality: The complexity of behavior* (pp. 105–124) Washington, DC: American Psychological Association.

Scheier, M. F., Matthews, K. A., Owens, J. F., Magovern, G. J., Sr., Lefebvre, R. C., Abbott, R. A., et al. (2003). Dispositional optimism and recovery from coronary artery bypass surgery: The beneficial effects on physical and psychological well-being. In P. Salovey & A. J. Rothman (Eds.), *Social psychology of health: Key readings in social psychology* (pp. 342–361). New York: Psychology Press.

Schunk, D. H. (1989). Self-efficacy and cognitive skill learning. In C. Ames & R. Ames (Eds.), *Research on motivation in education: Goals and cognitions* (Vol. 3, pp. 13–44). San Diego, CA: Academic Press.

Showers, C. (1992). The motivational and emotional consequences of considering positive or negative possibilities for an upcoming event. *Journal of Personality and Social Psychology, 63,* 474–484.

Singer, J. L. (1966). *Daydreaming.* New York: Random House.

Taylor, S. E., & Brown, J. D. (1988). Illusion and well-being: A social psychological perspective on mental health. *Psychological Bulletin, 103,* 193–210.

Taylor, S. E., Kemeny, M. E., Reed, G. M., Bower, J. E., & Gruenewald, T. L. (2000). Psychological resources, positive illusions, and health. *American Psychologist, 55,* 99–109.

Taylor, S. E., Pham, L. B., Rivkin, I. D., & Armor, D. A. (1998). Harnessing the imagination: Mental simulation, self-regulation, and coping. *American Psychologist, 53,* 429–439.

Triandis, H. C. (1994). *Culture and social behavior.* New York: McGraw-Hill.

Zimmerman, B. J., & Martinez-Pons, M. (1992) Perceptions of efficacy and strategy use in the self-regulation of academic learning. In D. H. Schunk & J. L. Meece (Eds.), *Student perceptions in the classroom: Causes and consequences* (pp. 185–207). Hillsdale, NJ: Erlbaum.

PART II

THINKING ABOUT THE PAST

9

Extending the Goal Progress Theory of Rumination

Goal Reevaluation and Growth

LEONARD L. MARTIN
ABRAHAM TESSER

Suppose there is some outcome you really want. Perhaps it is a new car, a date with that attractive coworker, or a publication. Now suppose you can't get it. What would you think? How would you feel? Presumably, you would experience negative thoughts and feelings generally related to the unattained outcome. What would happen if you continued to want the outcome but continued to be unable to get it? In that case, it is very likely that you would experience a continuation of your negative thoughts and feelings over time. In other words, the result would be rumination.

Rumination is a provocative topic of investigation for a number of reasons. For example, it seems to violate the basic law of effect. Rumination is often experienced as unpleasant and nonproductive, yet individuals continue to ruminate and may even believe there is some advantage to doing so. Rumination may also be most likely to occur when the best chances of addressing the triggering event (e.g., divorce, loss of job) have passed. A person may get insulted in a shopping center, for example, yet do nothing about the insult—until he or she leaves the shopping center. Then, the person may ruminate about the event for days afterward. Rumination is also interesting because of its association, and even causal connection, with negative affect, unhappiness, and depression (e.g., McIntosh & Martin, 1992). In short, rumination is often (though not always) unpleasant and unproductive, and individuals may not be able to keep themselves from experiencing ruminative thoughts. Such thoughts may continue to occur for years after the initial triggering event.

In previous publications (e.g., Martin, Shrira, & Startup, 2003; Martin & Tesser, 1989, 1996; Martin, Tesser, & McIntosh, 1993), we proposed that individuals ruminate when they fail to make progress toward an important higher order goal and stop ruminating when they attain the goal, resume sufficient progress toward it, or give it up. Although we still endorse this general view of rumination, we now believe that our earlier discussions of it were limited in a number of ways. For example, those discussions centered primarily on an individual's pursuit of a single goal. It is reasonable to assume that most individuals pursue multiple goals simultaneously (e.g., write a paper, get in shape, maintain a relationship). Why does this matter for rumination? It matters because, if progress toward one goal frustrates progress toward other goals, then individuals are more likely to ruminate. Conversely, if progress toward one goal facilitates progress toward other goals, then individuals are less likely to ruminate. Thus any complete understanding of rumination will have to take into consideration the way in which individuals balance simultaneously the pursuit of multiple goals.

In our earlier discussions, we also alluded to the effects of pursuing goals that were not the ones actually driving the rumination. A related issue concerns the effect of pursuing goals that are not congruent with the individual's authentic needs (e.g., Sheldon & Kasser, 2001). A complete theory of rumination should address this issue.

We also noted, in our earlier writings, that individuals can turn off rumination by disengaging from a goal. We did not say, though, how individuals accomplish this. A complete theory of rumination should do so.

Finally, there is a growing literature on the possibility of psychological growth arising out of traumatic experiences. Specifically, a number of studies suggest that, under some conditions, traumatic experiences can lead individuals to reevaluate their goals and to thrive at levels above their pretraumatic state. The implications of this goal reevaluation for rumination should be addressed.

In this chapter, we attempt to integrate these additional considerations into our basic theoretical framework. We begin with a review of our goal progress theory of rumination. Then we use a parallel distributed processing model (Rumelhart & McClelland, 1986) to address the ways in which individuals attempt to balance the simultaneous pursuit of multiple goals. After that, we discuss research showing that a major change (e.g., divorce, marriage) in an individual's life can lead the individual to reevaluate his or her goals. Finally, we integrate these ideas into a theoretical elaboration of our earlier theory of rumination.

The Goal Progress Theory of Rumination

In the context of the goal progress theory, rumination is defined as "conscious thinking directed toward a given object for an extended period of time" (Martin

& Tesser, 1989, p. 306). It is instigated when individuals fail to progress toward important higher order goals and ceases when individuals either attain the goal, resume progress toward it, or disengage from the goal. According to the theory, the proximate underlying cause of rumination is the heightened accessibility of goal-related information. Specifically, failure to attain an important goal keeps information related to that goal highly accessible (Zeigarnik, 1927/1938). In this state the information can easily be cued (Bruner, 1957; Higgins, Rholes, & Jones, 1977; Martin, Strack, & Stapel, 2001). This, in turn, makes it more likely that individuals will attend to and process information related to the unattained goal. Although rumination may not always facilitate the individual's progress back toward the unattained goal, that is its function (Carver, 1996; Schooler, Fallshore, & Fiore, 1995). It does this largely by keeping the goal-related information highly accessible. Once individuals are back on track, the rumination has, in essence, done its job. Therefore, it ceases. More generally, rumination terminates when individuals either attain the higher order goal, make sufficient progress toward it, or give it up.

Evidence Relating Goal Progress to Rumination

Before we discuss our extension of the goal progress theory, we review evidence for the major assumptions of the basic theory.

Rumination Is the Result of Thwarted Goal Progress

The most fundamental assumption of the goal progress theory is that rumination is the result of failure to progress sufficiently toward important higher order goals. We base this assumption directly on Lewin's (1938) seminal proposition that information related to an important unattained goal stays active in memory longer than information related to an attained goal. The heightened activation of information associated with unattained goals has been called the Zeigarnik effect (e.g., Zeigarnik, 1927/1938), and evidence related to this effect has been obtained in a wide variety of studies (for reviews, see Butterfield, 1954; Weiner, 1972).

A particularly clean demonstration of the relation between goal nonattainment and increased accessibility of goal-related information was provided by Rothermund (2003). He hypothesized that the nonattainment of an important goal not only increases the accessibility of goal-related information but also that it does so automatically. In fact, it may do so despite intentional processing to the contrary (Klinger, 1996; Moskowitz, 2002; Riemann & McNally, 1995).

To test this hypothesis, Rothermund (2003) had participants choose, from a set of alternatives, the closest synonym to a series of target words. On some trials, participants were led to believe they had chosen the correct synonym, whereas on other trials they were led to believe they had chosen the incorrect one. To put this performance feedback in goal progress terms, we would say that participants attained their performance goal when they received the success feedback but not when they received the failure feedback. So, if goal nonattainment maintains the accessibility of information related to the unattained goal, then information related to the failure trials should remain more accessible than information related to the success trials.

Rothermund (2003) assessed the accessibility of this information in the second part of the experiment. He instructed participants to name a target word presented on a computer screen and to respond as quickly as they could when they heard a tone. On all trials, the target words were surrounded by two distractor words. These distractor words came from the earlier synonym task. Specifically, some came from trials on which participants had received success feedback, whereas others came from trials on which participants had received failure feedback. If information related to unattained goals automatically attracts attention, then the distractor words from the failure trials should hamper participants' performance on the focal tasks (i.e., name the target word and respond to the tone).

The results were consistent with this hypothesis. Participants named the target words and responded to the tone more slowly when the distractor words had come from the failure trials than when they had come from the success trials. In other words, information associated with goal nonattainment can capture participants' attention even when participants are consciously attempting to focus elsewhere.

The More Important the Unattained Goal, the Greater the Rumination

Presumably, individuals pursue a wide variety of goals over the course of a lifetime and even in the course of a single day (e.g., taking a sick child to the doctor, finding a good parking spot at the supermarket). Not all of these goals will be attained, however. Despite this, individuals do not seem to ruminate about each and every unattained goal. According to the goal progress theory, they ruminate about important higher goals toward which they are not making sufficient progress.

Evidence consistent with this hypothesis was obtained by Lavallee and Campbell (1995) in a real-world diary study. They had participants list the set of higher order goals they were currently pursuing. Then they had participants fill out diaries for 2 weeks in which they described salient events that had happened to them since their previous diary entry. Participants also completed ratings of their moods, of the most bothersome events they had experienced during the rating period, of the extent of their self-concept confusion (e.g., Did the event make you question your beliefs about yourself?), and of the extent of their rumination (e.g., After the situation, did you continue to think about it later on?). At the end of the study, each participant's diary was content analyzed by outside observers for self-focus, the objective seriousness of the reported events, and the relevance of each reported event for each participant's goals.

As expected, events related to the participants' important higher order goals elicited stronger affective and self-regulatory reactions than events unrelated to those goals. More precisely, when participants reported experiencing negative events, and when these events had implications for their higher order goals, the participants reported greater levels of negative affect, self-focused attention, self-concept confusion, and rumination than when they reported negative events unrelated to their goals. Because there were no differences in the objective seriousness of the goal-related and unrelated events (as reflected in the observers' ratings), the results suggest that the heightened affective and self-regulatory effects were due to the subjective implications of the events. In other words, rumination was associated with failure to make progress toward important higher order goals.

Finding a Substitute Means of Attaining a Goal Can Turn off Rumination

According to the goal progress theory, rumination ceases when individuals either attain the goal, resume progress toward it, or give the goal up. A distinction can be made, however, between the means of attaining a goal and the actual desired end state. An individual may study, for example, to get a good grade in class. If the individual's goal is literally getting a good grade, however, then studying is not the only means of attaining that goal. The individual could cheat, for example. More generally, individuals may be able to turn off rumination by attaining the goal in any number of ways, depending on how they construe the goal.

A real-world test of the role of substitution in terminating rumination was provided by Millar, Tesser, and Millar (1988). They reasoned that the transition from high school to college could inhibit progress toward some goals (spending time with old friends) but facilitate progress toward others (making new friends). If so, then students should ruminate about their frustrated goals, but only to the extent that they had not found substitutes for them.

To test this hypothesis, Millar et al. (1988) asked recently arrived college students to identify the person with whom they were closest before coming to the university and then to list activities in which they had regularly engaged with this person. The students were also asked to indicate the activities for which they had been able to find substitutes after coming to the university. Finally, the students rated the extent to which they were ruminating about the person they had left behind (e.g., "Memories of things we did together popped into my mind when I was trying to study"; "I spent time thinking about when we could see each other").

Consistent with the thwarted-progress hypothesis, the more activities the students were no longer able to pursue, the more rumination they reported. Consistent with the substitution hypothesis, the more activities for which the students had found substitutes, the less rumination they reported. In other words, the students ruminated to the extent that their goals were blocked and that they had not found substitute means for attaining those goals.

This substitution logic was used by Koole, Smeets, van Knippenberg, and Dijksterhuis (1999) to show that rumination about a specific task (i.e., an intelligence test) may actually be instigated by thwarted progress toward a broader, higher order goal (i.e., self-worth). They had participants take what ostensibly was an intelligence test and then informed the participants that they had done poorly on this test. Presumably, participants would want to do well as a sign that they were maintaining progress toward their higher order goal of being intelligent. So, receiving negative feedback would frustrate their progress toward this higher order goal and induce rumination. On the other hand, failing to demonstrate one's intelligence can threaten one's self-worth. Perhaps nonattainment of this higher order goal is fueling the rumination as well.

To assess this possibility, Koole et al. (1999) gave all participants a chance to express their values after taking the intelligence test. For some participants, these values were ones they had earlier indicated were central to their self-concept. For others, the values were ones they had earlier indicated were peripheral to their self-concept. Expressing the central values could remind participants that they have still attained their goal of general competence and self-worth despite their poor performance on the intelligence test (Steele, 1988). If so, then participants who expressed their central values should ruminate less about their intelligence than participants who did not express such values.

Koole et al. (1999) measured the accessibility of goal-related information by asking participants to decide as quickly as possible whether a series of letter strings were real words. In cases in which the letter strings were real words, some of the words were related to intelligence. It was assumed that participants who were ruminating about their failure on the intelligence test would recognize these words faster than those who were not ruminating. Consistent with the hypothesis that substitute means of attaining the higher order goal can turn off rumination, participants who had not expressed values central to the self were faster to recognize intelligence-related words than participants who had expressed such values. In short, all participants ostensibly failed the intelligence test, but only those who had not attained the higher order goal (e.g., self-worth) still had this information highly accessible in mind.

Restricting the Means of Attaining a Goal Makes It Difficult to Terminate Rumination

As we have seen, rumination can be turned off when the goal driving that rumination is attained—and when this attainment can be realized through the initial means or through a substitute means. Suppose, though, that there is only one way to attain the goal and that the individual is having difficulty attaining the goal by that means. According to the goal progress theory, the individual is likely to ruminate until he or she somehow succeeds in attaining the goal or disengages from it. A woman who believes she can be happy only if she gives birth to a biologically related baby, for example, will ruminate until she in fact gives birth to a biologically related baby (or gives up the goal). It might seem as if adopting a child could provide a substitute for the woman, but this would not be the case if the woman defined her goal specifically as producing a biologically related child.

Evidence consistent with this example was obtained by Brothers and Maddux (2003). They had infertile women rate the extent to which they believed having a biologically related child was necessary for their happiness and life satisfaction. They also measured the extent to which the women reported ruminating about having a child and the extent to which they experienced emotional distress. As expected, the more the women linked the attainment of a biologically related child to their happiness (i.e., "I can't be happy unless I have a child"), the more rumination and distress they reported. Interestingly, Brother and Maddux (2003) also found that the relationship between linking and distress was reduced when the effects of rumination were statistically removed. In other words, the more the women linked having a biological baby to their happiness, the more they ruminated, and the more they ruminated, the more distress they experienced.

The effects of linking specific lower order goals to the attainment of higher order goals is not necessarily restricted to the effects of specific means and goals (having a baby and happiness). McIntosh and his colleagues (e.g., McIntosh, 1996; McIntosh & Martin, 1992; McIntosh, Martin, & Jones, 2001) found that individuals who generally link specific means to the attainment of the higher order goal of happiness generally experience more rumination and depression than individuals who do not make such links.

McIntosh, Harlow, and Martin (1995), for example, asked participants to complete a general measure of linking. This measure was composed of 19 scenarios, each followed by two possible reactions. For each scenario, participants were asked to select which of the reactions they thought they would be likely to experience. In one scenario, for example, participants read, "One day you realize that you have all the things you want—the job you want, the spouse you want, the free time you want." The possible reactions were: "This will not directly influence how happy I am, because happiness is something I determine, regardless of what happens to me" and "If I have all the things I want, then I will be very happy." The latter is the linking alternative; the former is the nonlinking alternative. Presumably, the more times individuals select the linking reaction, the greater their tendency is to link the attainment of specific means to the attainment of their higher order goals. Thus linkers may generally be more susceptible than nonlinkers to rumination.

McIntosh et al. (1995) had participants complete the linking scale, as well as measures of rumination, daily hassles, and depression. As expected, the more participants linked their happiness to the attainment of specific outcomes, the more they ruminated and the more depression they experienced. Moreover, the relation between hassles and depression was eliminated when the effects of rumination were removed. In other words, the more individuals linked the attainment of lower order goals to the higher order goal of happiness, the more hassles associated with those goals led to rumination, which in turn, led to depression.

Another way in which individuals can constrain their options to progress toward their higher order goals is by reducing the range of acceptable outcomes that count as progress.

Perfectionists, for example, are satisfied by a smaller range of outcomes than nonperfectionists. Thus we might expect perfectionists to ruminate more and experience more depression than nonperfectionists.

Flett, Madorsky, and Hewitt (2002) tested this hypothesis by having participants complete a perfectionism scale, along with indices of rumination, depression, and anxiety. They found that the higher participants scored on the perfectionism inventory, the more they ruminated, and the more depression and anxiety they reported. Flett et al. (2002) also found that the relations between perfectionism and depression and perfectionism and anxiety were reduced when the effects of rumination were statistically removed. In other words, the more perfectionistic the participant was (i.e., the more he or she restricted the range of acceptable outcomes), the more likely he or she was to ruminate, and this, in turn, facilitated depression and anxiety.

Letting Go of a Frustrated Goal
Reduces Rumination

According to the goal progress theory, individuals cease ruminating if they attain their higher order goal (through the initial means or through substitute means), resume progress toward the goal, or let go of the goal. We have seen evidence of the first two assumptions. Evidence that letting go of a goal is associated with reduced rumination was obtained by Wrosch, Scheier, Miller, Schulz, and Carver (2003). Participants began by listing some goals they had stopped pursuing. Then they rated their ability to disengage from the goal (e.g., It's easy for me to reduce my effort toward the goal) and reengage in other goals (e.g., I think about other new goals to pursue). Participants also rated their well-being (e.g., how often they felt nervous and distressed) and the extent to which they ruminated (e.g., I wake up at night thinking about my problems). The greater participants' self-reported disengagement, the lower their rumination and the greater their well-being. Similarly, the greater their self-reported reengagement, the lower their rumination and the greater their well-being. Whereas the linking and perfectionism studies found that locking into specific means maintained rumination, this study found that opening up to new goals reduced rumination.

In sum, a variety of studies from different investigators using various techniques support the major assumptions of the goal progress theory of rumination. We have seen that failure to progress toward one's goals produces rumination or increases the accessibility of information related to the unattained goals. We have also seen that the more important or higher order the goal is, the greater the rumination resulting from nonattainment will be. Conversely, rumination tends to be reduced if individuals discover substitute means to attain the goal or see a large range of outcomes as evidence of goal attainment. Finally, disengagement from unattained goals and the reinvestment in more fruitful goal progress is associated with reduced rumination. Each of these findings is consistent with the basic goal progress theory.

Extending the Goal Progress Theory

Although considerable supporting evidence exists, we still believe that the initial goal progress theory is limited in a number of ways. For example, it focuses primarily on an individual's pursuit of one goal at a time. In the following we use a parallel distributed processing framework (Rumelhart & McClelland, 1986) to address the way in which an individual's pursuit of one goal can facilitate or thwart his or her pursuit of other goals.

Multiple, Mutually Constraining Goals

Generally speaking, parallel distributed processing (PDP) models are generic models that can be instantiated in any number of ways (e.g., perception, understanding). We use the framework to model an individual's simultaneous pursuit of multiple goals. Before discussing this application, however, we briefly discuss PDP models in their generic sense.

PDP models can be represented as a system of elements that are connected to one another by weights. The activation of one element puts pressure on each and every other element in the system to turn on or turn off (depending on the strength of the weight and whether the weight is positive or negative). The pressure from any given element, however, does not always realize its effect on any other given element. The reason is that each element receives pressure from each and every other active element. The weight that connects Element A to Element B, for example, may be high and positive, yet Element B may not become activated when Element A becomes activated. The reason is that Element B is also receiving negative pressure from Elements C, D, and E. The ultimate status of Element B, therefore, depends on the net pressure it receives from all the active elements in the system (positive minus negative weights). This means that at any given time the activation of Element B may or may not be consistent with the pressure emanating from Element A.

The elements of a system tend to activate and deactivate in ways that maximize the consistency or coherence in the entire system. A system would be totally coherent if the activation of each of its elements reflected the sign of the weights connecting it to every other element. The attainment of a fully coherent system is rare, though. Rather, individuals attempt to negotiate states of activation and deactivation that reflect the most coherent configuration they can attain under the circumstances.

In our application, the elements in the PDP model are primarily goals (along with internal and external factors that facilitate or inhibit attainment of those goals). In essence, the application models the way in which pursuit of one goal can facilitate or inhibit pursuit of other goals. In seeking the most coherent solution, individuals are in essence seeking a system in which they can optimize their progress toward all of their important higher order goals given their current internal and external constraints. Of course, it is unlikely that individuals will ever find all of their goals completely satisfied. So they settle on the best compromise they can negotiate. In PDP terms, this compromise is called a local minimum.

The process by which individuals negotiate a local minimum can also be modeled in terms of an energy landscape with hills and valleys. The hills represent states of the system that are more incoherent, whereas the valleys represent states that are more coherent. Changes in the system (i.e., activation and deactivation of elements) move the individual across the landscape. Because the system is always seeking coherence, it tends to move toward the closest valley, a local minimum. A given local minimum, however, is not necessarily the most coherent state available. It may simply reflect the most coherent state in the vicinity (i.e., available to the individual in the absence of dramatic changes in his or her life).

In figure 9.1, for example, if an individual starts at point C, then a relatively minor change will move him or her to a less coherent state (point B or D). So the individual may tend to stay in point C even though it is not the most coherent location on this landscape. There are at least three reasons, though, that the individual does not immediately go to point A, the most coherent spot on the land-

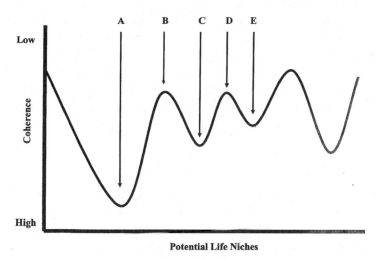

Figure 9.1. If an individual starts at C, a move to B or D decreases coherence. A move past B to A results in increased coherence. A move past D to E places the individual in a less coherent local minimum.

scape. First, the individual may not be aware that there are more coherent niches in the landscape. Second, as mentioned earlier, small changes, even in the direction of point A, lead to less desirable outcomes. Third, even if the individual believes there are more desirable niches, his or her attempts to find these niches are often uninformative. This is because it is difficult for individuals to know whether their tolerance of greater incoherence (i.e., point B or D) is moving them toward a better niche (point A) or toward a niche (point E) that is even less satisfying.

This application of the PDP perspective provides at least one explanation for individuals' often failing to change their situations even though a number of their important goals remain unattained and even though they experience repeated rumination. Their best negotiation process brings them to a local minimum that is not especially coherent. This is the best they can do under the circumstances, yet a number of their goals remain unattained (because of the constraints of pursuing other goals and because of personal and environmental constraints). Moreover, individuals may find that relatively small life changes just make things worse. So they resort to the safety of their local minimum, even when a more dramatic change might have put them into a more coherent local minimum.

To summarize, we are suggesting that rumination is the by-product of what, in PDP terms, would be called a nonoptimal local minimum. Individuals do their best to satisfy simultaneously all of their goals, but they are rarely successful. The reason is that progress toward one goal can hamper progress toward other goals, and contextual factors (e.g., social pressure) can facilitate progress toward one goal (being with friends) while blocking progress toward others (studying). As a result, individuals make a number of trade-offs to arrive at a compromise (i.e., a local minimum) in which at least some (perhaps many) of their important goals are not satisfied. This is why they ruminate and why the rumination persists over time. It may take a large change to move individuals into a more coherent local minimum, yet individuals may have difficulty making such changes on their own. Extra inducement may be needed. One source of such inducement may be traumatic events.

Trauma, Letting Go, and Growth

To the extent that rumination is unpleasant and unproductive, one would think that individuals would quickly abandon their frustrated goals. After all, if individuals cannot attain these goals, then abandoning them would be an effective way to reduce their rumination. As we have seen, though, individuals can have difficulty giving up on their important higher order goals. This, ironically, is where traumatic events may be beneficial. After a serious knee injury, for example, an individual may be forced to give up his goal of playing professional sports. Similarly, a woman who learns she is infertile may have no choice but to give up her goal of having a biologically related child.

As unpleasant as traumatic events may be, they can lead individuals to reevaluate their goals, and this, in turn, may facilitate disengagement from thwarted goals and reengagement in goals that more closely reflect the individual's core values. These changes, in turn, could reduce or eliminate rumination. The lessening of rumination and the other positive outcomes that can follow traumatic experiences have been termed *posttraumatic growth*. Research on posttraumatic growth may have important implications for our understanding of goal pursuit and rumination.

One promising model of posttraumatic growth was proposed by Tedeschi and Calhoun (2004). They begin with the assumption that, as individuals go through life, they build up sets of beliefs about who they are and how the world works. These sets of beliefs can be termed *assumptive worlds* (see also Janoff-Bulman, 1992; Parkes, 1971). One's assumptive world might include beliefs such as that the world is just, that the U.S. mainland is safe from terrorist attacks, and that heart trouble only affects people older than oneself. The problem, of course, is that events in the real world can challenge such beliefs.

When the challenge is great enough, individuals may be forced to drop their beliefs and develop new ones. It is in this context that growth can occur. Subsequent to the trauma, individuals may rebuild their assumptions in ways that map more closely onto the world as it is for them now, and this, in turn, may facilitate future coping. Individuals may also be provided with opportunities they did not see before (e.g., new careers, new relationships). In these ways, and others, it is possible for individuals to experience some growth alongside of, and because of, the loss and pain associated with the trauma. The growth (e.g., improvements in self-efficacy, social support) may in fact result from the individuals' attempts to deal with the trauma.

The Wake-Up Call

There is another form of trauma that can produce psychological growth. In this case, there is no change in the objective status of the individual's life. Individuals may have as much chance of attaining their goals after the trauma as before it. Their abilities and opportunities may not have changed. What have changed are their evaluations of their goals. Individuals may disengage from some goals and increase their effort toward others.

The prototype of such events is a close brush with death. Consider the individual who fell while attempting to climb a mountain (Grof & Halifax, 1977). He was sure he was going to die. During his fall, he was convinced he was experiencing his last few seconds on earth. He landed in a deep snowdrift, though, and walked away unscathed—at least physically. Psychologically, there were important changes. In fact, there are a number of consistencies in the reactions that individuals display following close brushes with death (Martin, Campbell, & Henry, 2004).

At death's door, individuals seem to reevaluate their goals. In the words of Yalom (quoted in Branfman, 1996), individuals facing death "get another perspective on their lives. The important things are really important, and the trivia of life is trivialized." Survivors of a close brush with death often abandon goals that do not seem to be working for them and invest themselves more intensely in goals that seem more authentic. It also seems that the prescription of how to live given by family, culture, profession, religion, or friends loses its grasp (Kuhl, 2002, p. 227).

To the extent that individuals engage in such reevaluations when facing death, the reevaluations may not be easily undone when (if) the individuals get a reprieve, that is, survive the encounter with death. So, even though individuals who have experienced close brushes with death may be able to pursue any of the goals that they had previously pursued, they may find that their desires have changed. The goals have been reevaluated in ways that lead individuals to let go of some goals and invest more heavily in others. The result can be a reduction in rumination and a greater present focus.

Based on such observations and on his own close encounter with death, Wren-Lewis (2004) speculated on one of the key differences between the growth that follows close brushes with death and that which follows most traumas (e.g., loss of a loved one, infertility). He suggested that most traumas challenge benign world assumptions (e.g., the world is a fairly safe, predictable, controllable place), whereas a close encounter with death generally challenges more negative assumptions (e.g., I am not worthy, life is a vale of tears, it's every man for himself). By dropping their negative assumptions, individuals are free to live more in the present and be more self-accepting.

A Theoretical Integration

In this section, we use the multiple-goal assumptions (i.e., PDP model) to integrate the idea of posttraumatic growth into the goal progress model. Specifically, we highlight the main causal mechanisms in the Tedeschi and Calhoun (2004) and Wren-Lewis (2004) views of growth. Then we interpret those mechanisms in terms of multiple-goal progress.

Rebuilding the Worldview

According to Tedeschi and Calhoun (2004), traumatic events (positive or negative) violate individuals' assumptive worlds. When this happens, individuals must rebuild those worlds. Growth comes with the adoption of more realistic assumptions and the accrual of new insights and social support that may accompany the rebuilding. It is also important to note that, in this model, growth occurs after a real blockage. The trauma has, in fact, made it difficult, if not impossible, for individuals to make progress toward some of the important goals to which they were committed before the trauma.

How would we integrate this view of posttraumatic growth into the goal progress model? Recall that in the model, rumination is for doing, not simply for making sense. Specifically, the function of rumination is to help individuals resume progress toward their higher order goals. This view of rumination carries two implications. First, it implies that the violation of one's assumptive world is not inherently traumatic. It is traumatic only when the maintenance of a set of beliefs is crucial to goal progress. Individuals who adhere to the rules in their pursuit of long-term goals seem especially motivated to believe that the world is just (Hafer, 2000). After all, if the world were not just, then the current efforts of these individuals might not pay off. As a result, a threat to just-world beliefs would be more traumatic for these individuals than for individuals who are not committed to long-term goal pursuit by adhering to the rules.

Second, the goal progress view of rumination implies that an individual could develop a new, more veridical posttrauma worldview yet still ruminate. This would be the case if the new worldview did not allow the individual to make progress toward his or her goals. Altering one's worldview to make sense of the death of a child, for example, does not eliminate the loss of the child nor does it necessarily lessen the desire for the child. Consequently, the individual would still ruminate.

According to the goal progress model, therefore, additional considerations are needed to explain how traumatic experiences can lead to growth. Specifically, the model suggests that growth involves the restructuring of an individual's goal system in a way that makes progress toward the individual's higher order goals more likely. In PDP terms, posttraumatic growth is the result of the settling in to a more coherent local minimum.

Questioning Negative Worldviews

In the case of close brushes with death, the individual's goals are reprioritized but may not be actually blocked. In such cases, individuals can do anything they could before, but they make choices that are more congruent with their authentic values. According to Wren-Lewis (2004), this occurs because a close brush with death leads individuals to question their negative beliefs about the world (e.g., it is a dog-eat-dog world), and this, in turn, allows them to become more self-accepting and more present-focused.

Although there are many similarities between our own thinking and that of Wren-Lewis (2004), we have a slightly different interpretation of the causes of growth following a close brush with death. We suggest that individuals who believe that they are about to die examine the value of their goals and the adequacy of their pursuits. They evaluate these, however, in the context of no longer being alive. What seemed important during life (e.g., getting a promotion, losing weight) may not seem especially important as the end draws near. When individuals return from the brink, however, there may be no way for them to undo their reevaluation. What became trivial may still seem trivial. This reprioritization allows individuals to develop a greater focus on the goals that truly reflect the self, which, of course, is the very definition of psychological growth (e.g., Maslow, 1962; Rogers, 1961).

General Summary

Although there is good evidence for the basic goal progress model of rumination, there was reason to believe the model was incomplete in several ways. In this chapter, we tried to address those areas of incompleteness while maintaining the original model. The goal progress theory can now be summarized as follows:

Individuals pursue multiple goals at the same time. In doing so, they may find that their pursuit of some goals facilitates or impairs their pursuit of other goals. Environmental events may also facilitate or impair pursuit of various goals. This means that individuals will almost always find themselves with some of their important higher order goals unattained. It is likely, therefore, that individuals will frequently experience heightened accessibility of thoughts related to those goals. When this accessibility manifests itself in recurrent conscious thoughts about the goal, we refer to the thoughts as rumination. Rumination is not always pleasant or productive, but its function is to return individuals back to progress toward their important higher order goals.

Because individuals are unlikely to attain perfect satisfaction of all their important goals simultaneously, they often settle for the best they can do under the circumstances. In PDP terms, this is referred to as a local minimum. Although individuals may attempt to make slight changes here and there to improve their situation, the changes tend to have little long-term effect and may even make things worse (i.e., more unattained goals). Therefore, individuals tend to remain more or less in their same situation. Real growth is likely only with a more dramatic change in the individual's goal system.

As unpleasant as they are, traumatic events can sometimes lead individuals to reevaluate their goal structure. They can do so either by actually eliminating the goal as an option or simply by forcing individuals to evaluate their goals in a new context (e.g., being at death's door). Restructuring their goal systems can free individuals to invest in goals that are more congruent with their core values. In PDP terms, reevaluation may move individuals into a more coherent local minimum.

In this way, the original goal progress model can maintain its basic assumptions yet also account for multiple goals, disengagement and reengagement, the pursuit of authentic versus inauthentic goals, and some positive and negative effects of trauma. We are anxious to see the validity of these suggestions tested. If the suggestions prove sustainable, it may be possible to develop techniques to promote personal growth that do not require the individual undergoing a life-changing trauma.

References

Branfman, F. (1996). *A matter of life and death.* Retrieved November 28, 2004 from http://archive.salon.com/weekly/yalom960805.html.

Brothers, S. C., & Maddux, J. E. (2003). The goal of biological parenthood and emotional distress from infertility: Linking parenthood to happiness. *Journal of Applied Social Psychology, 33,* 248–262.

Bruner, J. S. (1957). On perceptual readiness. *Psychological Review, 64,* 123–152.

Butterfield, E. C. (1954). The interruption of tasks: Methodological, factual, and theoretical issues. *Psychological Bulletin, 62,* 309–322.

Carver, C. S. (1996). Goal engagement and the human experience. In R. S. Wyer, Jr. (Ed.), *Ruminative thoughts* (pp. 49–61). Hillsdale, NJ: Erlbaum.

Flett, G. L., Madorsky, D., & Hewitt, P. L. (2002). Perfectionism cognitions, rumination, and psychological distress. *Journal of Rational-Emotive and Cognitive Behavior Therapy, 20,* 33–47.

Greenberg, J., Koole, S. L., & Pyszczynski, T. (2004). *Handbook of experimental existential psychology.* New York: Guilford Press.

Grof, S., & Halifax, J. (1977). *Human encounter with death.* New York: Dutton.

Hafer, C. (2000). Investment in long-term goals and commitment to just means drive the need to believe in a just world. *Personality and Social Psychology Bulletin, 26,* 1059–1073.

Higgins, E. T., Rholes, W. S., & Jones, C. R. (1977). Category accessibility and impression formation. *Journal of Experimental Social Psychology, 13,* 141–154.

Janoff-Bulman, R. (1992). *Shattered assumptions: Towards a new psychology of trauma.* New York: Free Press.

Klinger, E. (1996). The contents of thoughts: Interference as the downside of adaptive normal mechanisms in thought flow. In I. Sarason & G. R. Pierce (Eds.), *Cognitive interference: Theories, methods, and findings* (pp. 3–23). Hillsdale, NJ: Erlbaum.

Koole, S. L., Smeets, K., van Knippenberg, A., & Dijksterhuis, A. (1999). The cessation of rumination through self-affirmation. *Journal of Personality and Social Psychology, 77,* 111–125.

Kuhl, D. (2002). *What dying people want: Practical wisdom for the end of life.* New York: Public Affairs.

Lavallee, L. F., & Campbell, J. D. (1995). Impact of personal goals on self-regulation processes elicited by daily negative events. *Journal of Personality and Social Psychology, 69,* 341–352.

Lewin, K. (1938). *The conceptual representation and the measurement of psychological forces.* Durham, NC: Duke University Press.

Martin, L. L., Campbell, W. K., & & Henry, C. D. (2004). The roar of awakening: Mortality acknowledgement as a call to authentic living. In J. Greenberg, S. L. Koole, & T. Pyszczynski (Eds.), *Handbook of experimental existential psychology* (pp. 431–448). New York: Guilford Press.

Martin, L. L., Shrira, I., & Startup, H. (2004). Rumination as a function of goal progress, stop-rules, and cerebral lateralization. In C. Papageorgiou & A. Wells (Eds.), *Depressive rumination: Nature, theory, and treatment* (pp. 153–175). Hoboken, NJ: Wiley.

Martin, L. L., Strack, F., & Stapel, D. A. (2001). How the mind moves: Knowledge accessibility and the fine-tuning of the cognitive system. In A. Tesser & N. Schwarz (Eds.), *Blackwell international handbook of social psychology: Vol. 1. Intraindividual processes* (pp. 236–256). London: Blackwell.

Martin, L. L., & Tesser, A. (1989). Toward a motivational and structural theory of ruminative thought. In J. S. Uleman & J. A. Bargh, (Eds.), *Unintended thought* (pp. 306–326). New York: Guilford Press.

Martin, L. L., & Tesser, A. (1996). Some ruminative thoughts. In R. S. Wyer (Ed.), *Advances in social cognition* (Vol. 9, pp. 1–47). Mahwah, NJ: Erlbaum.

Martin, L. L., Tesser, A., & McIntosh, W. D. (1993). Wanting but not having: The effects of unattained goals on thoughts and feelings. In D. M. Wegner & J. W. Pennebaker (Eds.), *Handbook of mental control* (pp. 552–572). Englewood Cliffs, NJ: Prentice-Hall.

Maslow, A. (1962). *Toward a psychology of being.* Oxford, UK: Van Nostrand.

McIntosh, W. D. (1996). When does goal nonattainment lead to negative emotional reactions, and when doesn't it?: The role of linking and rumination. In L. L. Martin & A. Tesser, (Eds.), *Striving and feeling: Interactions among goals, affect, and self-regulation* (pp. 53–77). Mahwah, NJ: Erlbaum.

McIntosh, W. D., Harlow, T. F., & Martin, L. L. (1995). Linkers and nonlinkers: Goal beliefs as a moderator of the effects of everyday hassles on rumination, depression, and physical complaints. *Journal of Applied Social Psychology, 25,* 1231–1244.

McIntosh, W. D., & Martin, L. L. (1992). The cybernetics of happiness: The relation of goal attainment, rumination, and affect. In M. S. Clark (Ed.), *Emotion and social behavior* (pp. 222–246). Thousand Oaks, CA: Sage.

McIntosh, W. D., Martin, L. L., & Jones, J. B., III (2001). Goal orientations and the search for confirmatory affect. *Journal of Psychology: Interdisciplinary and Applied, 135,* 5–16.

Millar, K. U., Tesser, A., & Millar, M. G. (1988). The effects of a threatening life event on behavior sequences and intrusive thought: A self-disruption explanation. *Cognitive Therapy and Research, 12,* 441–457.

Moskowitz, G. B. (2002). Preconscious effects of temporary goals on attention. *Journal of Experimental Social Psychology, 38,* 397–404.

Parkes, C. M. (1971). Psycho-social transitions: A field for study. *Social Science and Medicine, 5,* 101–115.

Riemann, B. C., & McNally, R. J. (1995). Cognitive processing of personally relevant information. *Cognition and Emotion, 9,* 325–340.

Rogers, C. R. (1961). *On becoming a person.* New York: Houghton-Mifflin.

Rothermund, K. (2003). Automatic vigilance for task-related information: Perseverance after failure and inhibition after success. *Memory and Cognition, 31,* 343–352.

Rumelhart, D. E., & McClelland, J. L. (Eds.). (1986). *Parallel distributed processing: Explorations in the microstructure of cognition* (Vol. 1). Cambridge, MA: MIT Press.

Schooler, J. W., Fallshore, M., & Fiore, S. M. (1995). Epilogue: Putting insight into perspective. In R. J. Sternberg & J. E. Davidson (Eds.), *The nature of insight* (pp. 559–587). Cambridge, MA: MIT Press.

Sheldon, K. M., & Kasser, T. (2001). Goals, congruence, and positive well-being: New empirical support for humanistic theories. *Journal of Humanistic Psychology, 41,* 30–50.

Steele, C. (1988). The psychology of self-affirmation: Sustaining the integrity of the self. In L. Berkowitz (Ed.), *Advances in experimental social psychology, 21,* 261–302.

Tedeschi, R. G., & Calhoun, L. G. (2004). Posttraumatic growth: Conceptual foundations and empirical evidence. *Psychological Inquiry, 15,* 1–18.

Weiner, B. (1972). *Theories of motivation: From mechanism to cognition.* Chicago: Rand McNally.

Wren-Lewis, J. (2004). The implications of near-death experiences for understanding posttraumatic growth. *Psychological Inquiry, 15,* 90–93.

Wrosch, C., Scheier, M. F., Miller, G. E., & Carver, C. S. (2003). Adaptive self-regulation of unattainable goals: Goal disengagement, goal reengagement, and subjective well-being. *Personality and Social Psychology Bulletin, 29,* 1494–1508.

Zeigarnik, B. (1938). On finished and unfinished tasks. In W. D. Ellis (Ed.), *A source book of gestalt psychology* (pp. 300–314). New York: Harcourt, Brace, & World. (Original work published 1927)

10

The Road Not Taken

Counterfactual Thinking Over Time

LAWRENCE J. SANNA
SETH E. CARTER
EULENA M. SMALL

Two roads diverged in a yellow wood,
And sorry I could not travel both
                              Robert Frost

In the well-known Frost poem, the traveler comes to a fork in the road and decides which way to go. After much mental deliberation, the person eventually chooses the road "less traveled." However, by so doing, the traveler also forgoes possibilities of the road not chosen. What might have happened if the alternative route had been taken instead? The figurative appeal of the poem lies in suggesting that we are all left with tough choices and that in many cases life events as they occur also leave us pondering what might have happened instead. Psychologists have studied people's conceptions of "the road not taken" in the form of *counterfactual thinking*. Counterfactuals involve mentally simulating "what might have been" in contrast to what was and what is. They focus on alternatives to the *past* that did not actually happen but that could be imagined having happened instead, typified by "if only," "at least," or "what if" (Miller, Turnbull, & McFarland, 1990; Roese, 1997; Roese & Olson, 1995, Sanna, 2000).

What are the causes and consequences of thinking counterfactually? Counterfactuals occur spontaneously (Sanna & Turley, 1996; Sanna, Parks, et al., 2003) and vary by number, intensity, and duration (Sanna & Turley-Ames, 2000). They exemplify an interplay between people's thoughts, feelings, and behaviors due to relationships with affective reactions (Gleicher et al., 1990; Landman, 1987; Connolly & Zeelenberg, 2002), accident and victim compensation (Macrae & Milne, 1992; Turley, Sanna, & Reiter, 1995), coping and

163

causal assignment (Holman & Silver, 1998; Lipe, 1991; Spellman & Mandel, 1999), and future preparation (Nasco & Marsh, 1999; Roese, 1994; Sanna, 1997). Counterfactual thoughts have implications not only at the individual level—as most initial research had emphasized—but also at the level of groups (Kray & Galinsky, 2003) and organizations (Goerke, Moller, Schulz-Hardt, Napiersky, & Frey, 2004). The importance of counterfactuals across levels makes them particularly compelling.

In keeping with the theme of this book, we describe both theory and research on counterfactual thinking while simultaneously considering relationships not only to the past but also to the future and present. We discuss the interplay of these thoughts with people's feelings and behaviors. Counterfactuals are placed within a broader context of mental simulations (Sanna, 2000; Sanna, Carter, & Burkley, 2005; Sanna, Small, & Cook, 2004; Sanna, Stocker, & Clarke, 2003), including past retrospections, present assessments, and future anticipations. We outline the *TEMPO* (*Time, Environment, Motivation, Personality*, and *Outcome*) model as an integrative framework to synthesize ideas about counterfactuals at the individual, group, and organizational levels. This explicitly places mental simulations within the context of judgments over time. Finally, we offer conclusions and suggest applications to other phenomena, such as temporal biases, personality processes and strategies, and automaticity and coping with life events.

Counterfactuals: A Brief Historical Background

Initial theorizing, perhaps quite naturally, emphasized the counterfactuals of individuals, but more recent research also focuses on group and organizational contexts. Counterfactuals are *if-then* conditional propositions (Johnson-Laird & Byrne, 2002; Roese, Sanna, & Galinsky, 2005) whereby reality is compared with imagined alternatives. They can be personal (e.g., "If only I had married Norma my life might be immeasurably happier"), historical (e.g., "At least the Nazis did not develop the atomic bomb first"; Cowley, 1999; Tetlock & Belkin, 1996) or whimsically scientific ("What if the moon did not exist?"; Comins, 1993). In fact, the ability to think counterfactually may be so central to human functioning that it is viewed as an essential component to consciousness and intelligence (Hofstadter, 1979).

Simulation Heuristic and Norm Theory

Most psychological interest in counterfactual thinking was stimulated by Kahneman and Tversky's (1982) discussion of the *simulation heuristic*, a process whereby people "run through" or imagine various possible alternatives when determining responses. Einhorn and Hogarth (1981) similarly suggested that counterfactuals are "based on a mental simulation in which 'what might be,' or 'what might have been,' is combined with 'what is'" (p. 456). The simulation heuristic plays a crucial role in counterfactual thinking, as the imagined alternatives have several implications for people's thoughts, feelings, and behaviors (Kahneman & Tversky, 1982).

People are more apt to change surprising or *abnormal* events by returning them to typical or *normal* states than vice versa (Kahneman & Tversky, 1982; Miller et al., 1990). Kahneman and Miller's (1986) *norm theory* suggests that normality can be *postcomputed*. Exemplars from memory create *norms*, and these can be independent of prior expectations (Byrne, 2002; Medvec, Madey, & Gilovich, 1995). An example is two people missing plane flights, one by 30 minutes and another by 5 minutes (Kahneman & Tversky, 1982). Counterfactuals are more readily available in the latter case, as it is easier to imagine having shaved off only 5 minutes than a full 30 minutes. Prior expectations and objective situations are identical (both people expected to make flights but did not), but the relative availability of counterfactuals accounts for differing feelings— people say they have greater regret when flights are missed by 5 minutes than by 30 minutes (Miller et al., 1990; Sanna & Turley-Ames, 2000). Groups of people in juries (Cantelloni & Milesi, 2001) and organizations (Morris & Moore, 2000) are similarly influenced by close outcomes when deciding how to allocate rewards and punishments, as well as when distributing other resources.

Two-Stage Model and Goals

Roese (1997; Roese & Olson, 1997) proposed a *two-stage model*, which separates factors that influence counterfactual *activation* and *content*. Negative affect activates counterfactuals, "turning on" the process. Normality then dictates the content of counterfactuals, what people think about. The two-stage model and norm theory diverge in that negative affect, not norm violation, initiates counterfactual generation (Roese et al., 2005). People may construct *upward* counterfactuals that contrast realities with better alternatives (e.g., "If only we had listed our home at a higher price, we might have made more money on the sale"); these are useful for future preparation or *self-improvement*. *Downward* counterfactuals contrast realities with worse alternatives (e.g., "At least we reallocated our assets, or we might have lost even more of our retirement investment") and are useful for self-enhancement or *mood repair* (Markman, Gavanski, Sherman, & McMullen, 1993; Roese, 1994; Sanna, Turley-Ames, & Meier, 1999).

Retrospective and prospective motivational goals may be served by mentally simulating alternatives. Sanna, Chang, and Meier (2001) demonstrated that people retrospectively engage in *mood repair* or *mood maintenance* and prospectively engage in *self-improvement* or *self-protection*. Each motive can be cued by positive and negative life events and accompanying good and bad feelings. We elaborate on these motivational goals later. Mood repair can be achieved by downward simulations after past failures; mood maintenance can be achieved by downward simulations after past successes; and self-improvement and self-protection can be achieved by upward simulations when anticipating future performances (Sanna, Chang, & Meier, 2001; Sirois, 2004). Counterfactuals may analogously serve diverse motives within groups (Naquin & Tynan, 2003; Sanna, Chang, & Carter, 2004) and organizations (Goerke et al., 2004), although fewer studies directly test these particular motives at these levels.

The TEMPO Model: Mental Simulations Over Time

The TEMPO model places counterfactuals into a broader integrative framework of mental simulations over time, including thoughts about the past, present, and future. It incorporates prior theorizing (e.g., contrasts with reality, goals and motives) and the imagination, goals, and affect (IGoA) model (Sanna, 2000; Sanna et al., 2005; Sanna, Small, & Cook, 2004; Sanna, Stocker, & Clarke, 2003), while also explicitly recognizing the role of time, environment, motivation, personality, and outcome. The TEMPO model is outlined in figure 10.1.

Time and Motivation

We suggest that there are three underlying dimensions to mental simulations. First, they differ by time. This is illustrated ranging from future (T_{-x}, T_{-2}, T_{-1}, etc.) to present (T_0) to past (T_{+1}, T_{+x}, etc.), but of course infinite divisions of this dimension are possible. *Retrospective* simulations focus on the past, exemplified by counterfactuals (Miller et al., 1990; Roese, 1997). *Prospective* simulations focus on the future, exemplified by prefactuals of "what may be" (Sanna, 1996, 1999). Second, mental simulations can be *goal-based* or *reactive*, referring to whether there are clear underlying motives or not. Some simulations are motivationally based (Sanna, Chang, & Meier, 2001; Taylor & Schneider, 1989); others occur without much premeditation or purpose (Klinger, 1977). Third, mental simulations can be *acquisitive* or *aversive*. Acquisitive refers to promoting or retaining something good or positive; aversive refers to preventing or protecting against negative possibilities (Arkin & Shepperd, 1989; Higgins, 1998).

Outcome

Mental simulations of particular directions are triggered by positive or negative outcomes in the present (T_0). Numerous life events, such as failures and successes, are associated with bad and good moods (Brown & Mankowski, 1993).

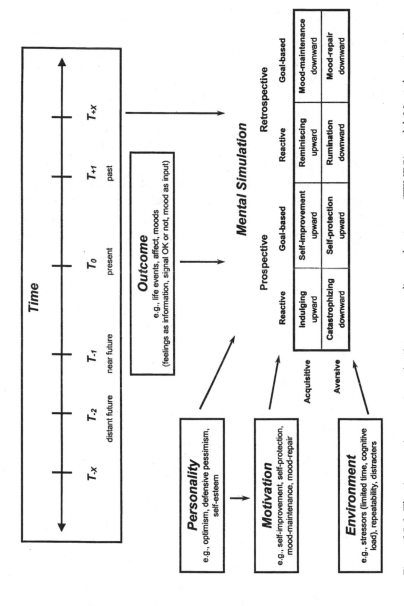

Figure 10.1. The time, environment, motivation, personality, and outcome (TEMPO) model. Mental contrasting underlies goal-based simulations, whereas mental assimilation underlies reactive simulations.

Markman et al. (1993) found downward counterfactuals most often, particularly after successes, and upward counterfactuals after failures, particularly on repeatable tasks. Manipulated moods produce an identical pattern. Bad and good moods make people think about upward and downward counterfactuals, because feelings serve as information about people's present states (Sanna, Meier, & Turley-Ames, 1998; Schwarz & Clore, 1996). People view their lives negatively in bad moods (e.g., "I am a failure" or "There is a problem") but positively in good moods (e.g., "I am a success" or "Things are fine"). Moods can be input to counterfactuals (Sanna, Meier, & Wegner, 2001).

We suggest that *mental contrasting* and *assimilation* provide mechanisms for how life events and moods influence simulations (Oettingen, Pak, & Schnetter, 2001; Sanna, 2000; Schwarz & Bless, 1992). Counterfactuals contrast realities with alternatives (Miller et al., 1990; Roese, 1997), as do prefactuals (Sanna, 1998, 1999). Oettingen et al. (2001) suggested that comparing desired futures with present realities underlies goal setting, a mental contrasting. We extend this idea to include all goal-based simulations. Mood informs the present in a congruent manner (positive in good mood, negative in bad mood), and mental contrasting produces the goal-based simulations. Reactive mental simulations do not involve contrasts. For example, Oettingen et al. (2001) found that people can "indulge" in free fantasies by focusing only on the future without an explicit contrast with the present (Oettingen, 1996; McMullen, 1997). We extend this idea to all reactive mental simulations, which focus on only the future or the past, a mental assimilation. The results are mental simulations congruent in direction with moods.

Mental Simulations

The combination of time, motivation, and outcome leads to a variety of prospective and retrospective mental simulations, examples of which are depicted in figure 10.1. These can be either goal-based or reactive, acquisitive or aversive.

Prospective Mental Simulations: What May Be

> And looked down one as far as I could
> To where it bent in the undergrowth.

Self-Improvement People can be motivated to improve traits, abilities, or well-being (Collins, 1996; Taylor & Lobel, 1989). Negative feelings often instigate motives to get better (Taylor & Schneider, 1989). Generating alternatives is useful for goal attainment (Martin & Tesser, 1989), and people mentally simulate better possibilities when preparing for the future (Nasco & Marsh, 1999; Roese, 1994; Sanna, 1996). We propose that self-improvement is prospective, acquisitive, and goal based. It involves comparing present realities with better futures, as does the original view of mental contrasting (Oettingen et al., 2001).

Self-Protection   People can protect themselves from negative possibilities by "bracing for loss" (Shepperd, Findley-Klein, Kwavnick, Walker, & Perez, 2000; Shepperd, Ouellette, & Fernandez, 1996). Defensive pessimism (Norem & Cantor, 1986; Sanna, 1996) and self-handicapping (Berglas & Jones, 1978; Sanna & Mark, 1995) are strategies that, in part, involve self-protection. Generating upward prefactuals has also been shown to help people protect themselves from possible future failure (Sanna, 1999; Sanna & Meier, 2000). We propose that self-protection is prospective, aversive, and goal-based and involves a mental contrast with the present.

Indulging   Oettingen et al. (2001) suggested that people can look to the future without specific goals in mind, a process called *indulging*. People simulate desired futures without a contrast with the present or with only a weak contrast. Indulging is a free fantasy in which people "enjoy the desired future in the here and now" (Oettingen et al., 2001, p. 737; Oettingen, 1996). Work on goal setting (Oettingen et al., 2001) and counterfactual work that indicates that people assimilate upward simulations (McMullen, 1997; Sanna, 1997, 2000) provide evidence for indulging. We propose that indulging is prospective, acquisitive, and reactive and that it occurs by mental assimilation.

Catastrophizing   Catastrophizing entails simulating negative "what if" scenarios (Kendall & Ingram, 1987) and worrying about bad things that may transpire (Vasey & Borkovec, 1992). The person carries on an internal dialogue characterized by problem-specific pessimism, feelings of inadequacy, and despair (Davey, Jubb, & Cameron, 1996). Catastrophizing is linked through lifestyles to negative events (Peterson, Seligman, Yurko, Martin, & Friedman, 1998). We view catastrophizing as prospective, aversive, and reactive and as involving mental assimilation.

Retrospective Mental Simulations: What Might Have Been

> Yet knowing how way leads on to way,
> I doubted if I should ever come back.

Mood maintenance   People in happy moods, or those who have experienced positive life events such as successes, think in ways that preserve positive feelings. The motive underlying this is *mood maintenance* (Isen, 1987). Happy people generate larger numbers of downward counterfactuals, and they report high enjoyment in doing so (Sanna, Meier, & Wegner, 2001). People in organizations similarly generate downward counterfactuals to maintain good moods (Goerke et al., 2004). We propose that mood maintenance is retrospective, and goal-based and that it involves a contrast of pleasant reality with worse alternatives to perpetuate positive affect.

Mood Repair   People in bad moods, or those who have experienced negative life events such as failures, work to reinstate positive feelings. The underlying motive is *mood repair* (Erber & Erber, 1994; Sedikides & Strube, 1997). Downward counterfactuals can repair mood in both individual (Sanna, Meier, & Turley-Ames, 1998; Sanna et al., 1999) and group settings (Naquin & Tynan, 2003; Sanna, Chang, & Carter, 2004). We suggest that mood repair is retrospective and goal-based and that it involves contrasting negative realities with worse alternatives to regain positive feelings.

Reminiscing   People reminisce by thinking about positive aspects of their lives, with a focus on past accomplishments, achievements, or successes (Fivush, Haden, & Reese, 1996; Strack, Schwarz, & Gschneidinger, 1985). Those who reminisce about past glories (Strack et al., 1985) and assimilate these thoughts to present states experience an increased sense of well-being (McMullen, 1997; Sanna, 1997). We propose that reminiscing is retrospective and reactive and that it involves a mental assimilation of upward, or positive, thoughts focusing only on the past.

Rumination   Ruminations are persistent or reoccurring thoughts about past events that focus on negatives or are associated with bad moods (Nolen-Hoeksema, 1996). They are respondent (Klinger, 1977) and have little to do with goals. Ruminations intensify reactions to negative life events. For example, men who ruminated about losing a partner to AIDS had bad feelings and prolonged periods of depression (Nolen-Hoeksema, McBride, & Larson, 1997). Viewed in this way, we suggest that ruminations are retrospective and aversive and that they do not entail a contrast with a present state—that is, they involve mental assimilation.

Personality

Personality characteristics, processes, or strategies may be related to counterfactuals and other mental simulations. This can also be tied directly to particular motivations. Sanna (2000) has connected several individual differences to mental simulations. Within the TEMPO model, personality may represent more global macro-goals or macro-reactions. For example, *defensive pessimism, pessimism*, and *optimism* present a comparison of how people might use prospective (T_{-2}, T_{-1}) versus retrospective (T_{+1}) mental simulations (Sanna, 1996, 1998; Sanna & Chang, 2003): Defensive pessimists use upward prefactual simulations prospectively, but optimists use downward counterfactual simulations retrospectively. Defensive pessimists' strategy involves a combination of self-improvement and self-protective motives, whereas that of optimists involves a mood-repair motive. Both strategies make use of mental contrasting.

Self-esteem refers to people's feelings of self-worth (Brown & Mankowski, 1993). Persons with low self-esteem are governed by self-protective motives, whereas persons with high self-esteem are governed by acquisitive motives. Similar to optimists, persons with high self-esteem use downward counterfactuals (T_{+1}) to repair moods (Sanna, Meier, & Turley-Ames, 1998; Sanna, Turley-Ames, & Meier, 1999); persons with low self-esteem do not. Although both use upward prefactuals (T_{-2} vs. T_{-1}), individuals with low self-esteem contrast them in a self-protective fashion (Sanna & Meier, 2000), similar to defensive pessimists. Individuals with high self-esteem assimilate upward prefactuals. Other individual differences may fit this model (Sanna, 2000). Other motives (Helgeson & Mickelson, 1995) may also underlie mental simulations. This might inform a myriad of personality differences, as mental simulations may be one distinguishing underlying process. Groups and organizations may similarly exhibit particular "personalities" (Chatman & Barsade, 1996; Kets-deVries & Miller, 1986), and these might also be related to particular mental simulations.

Environment

The fact that positive and negative life events and moods (T_0) trigger simulations of a particular direction may enlighten people's automatic and controlled responses and their coping and well-being. As we described, the TEMPO model suggests that feelings influence reactive simulations in a mood-congruent manner. Just as assimilating upward simulations leads to good moods (McMullen, 1997), good moods lead to upward simulations (Sanna, 2000). Feelings thus influence thoughts directly, and reactive simulations are assimilated to people's current states. Mental contrasting, however, involves comparisons of future (Oettingen et al., 2001) or past with the present. The TEMPO model suggests that feelings influence perceptions of the present directly (Sanna, 2000; Sanna et al., 1999). Goal-based mental simulations are contrasted with this present. Mood maintenance is a reaction to positive feelings, and self-improvement, self-protection, and mood repair are reactions to negative feelings (Sanna, Chang, & Meier, 2001).

One intriguing implication of this is the effect of environmental stressors such as limited time or cognitive load. When simulations activated by feelings (upward for negative, downward for positive) match that in figure 10.1, responses are automatic. When there is a mismatch, responses are effortful. Moods and the four goal-based simulations have been tested (Sanna, Chang, & Meier, 2001). To access automatic responses, some people were put under time pressure (Bargh, 1994; Smith & DeCoster, 2000). In bad moods, with no time pressure, quick reactions arose for upward simulations for self-improvement or self-protection (matches); slow reactions, for downward simulations for mood repair (mismatch). In good moods without time pressure, quick reactions arose for downward simulations for mood maintenance (match). Under time pressure, responses were quick for upward and downward simulations in bad and good moods, consistent with that activated by feelings. This match-versus-mismatch idea may extend to reactive simulations and to groups and organizations put under environmental pressures or constraints. Task repeatability can moderate this effect (Sanna, Chang, & Meier, 2001).

Some Conclusions and Further Implications

We believe that much may be gained by pursuing a more inclusive conception of counterfactual thinking within the context of other mental simulations over time and by explicitly considering the relation between these thoughts and people's feelings and behaviors. Our TEMPO model attempts to articulate relationships between what we believe to be conceptually related areas but which have thus far appeared mostly in separate literatures. We conclude by offering a few other possible implications and future applications of this approach.

Judgments and Biases Over Time

Figure 10.1 depicts the temporal orientation related to several temporal biases: confidence changes, planning fallacy, affective forecasting (impact bias), and hindsight bias. *Confidence change* research compares distant (T_{-2}) and near (T_{-1}) futures. People who anticipated immediate tests were less confident in their eventual success than those who anticipated distant tests (Gilovich, Kerr, & Medvec, 1993; Nisan, 1972). Shepperd et al. (1996) suggested that people brace for the worst or possible loss by reducing their confidence in success over time (Shepperd et al., 2000). Confidence changes over time may be related to increases in upward self-protective mental simulations from T_{-2} to T_{-1} (Sanna, 1999; Sanna & Meier, 2000).

Planning fallacy research (Buehler, Griffin, & Ross, 1994; Kahneman & Tversky, 1979) shows that people underestimate task completion time in the distant future (T_{-2}) compared with actual completion at the time of a deadline (T_0). People adopt an optimistic "narrow focus on successful future plans" (Buehler, Griffin, & MacDonald, 1997, p. 239) at a distance. The affective forecasting *impact bias* (Wilson, Wheatley, Meyers, Gilbert, & Axom, 2000) compares predicted feelings (e.g., T_{-2}) with actual feelings after events (T_{+1}), presuming that people "think too much about the focal event" (p. 833) when predicting. Planning fallacy may be due to more indulging at T_{-2}; people "enjoy the desired future in the here and now" (Oettingen et al., 2001, p. 737), resulting in undue optimism. Impact bias may be similarly due to indulging (when predicting success feelings) and catastrophizing (when predicting failure feelings) at T_{-2}. People may also inadequately account for other processes such as mood repair (Gilbert, Pinel, Wilson, Blumberg, & Wheatley, 1998) at T_{+1} when predicting future feelings at T_{-2}.

Hindsight bias research indicates that once event outcomes are known (T_{+1}), people believe they "knew all along" what would happen even though their pre-event predictions (T_{-2}) indicated otherwise (Guilbault, Bryant, Brockway, & Posavac, 2004; Fischhoff, 1975). The past is also viewed as particularly inevitable after experiencing positive versus negative events (Louie, 1999), suggesting the operation of mood-maintenance and mood-repair motives at T_{+1}, respectively. Within the TEMPO model, in addition to particular motives, there may be at least one other process that all temporal biases share: whether thoughts emphasizing focal or alternative events come to mind most easily (Sanna & Schwarz, 2004). Possible applications of mental simulations to understanding the production, and reduction, of temporal biases at the individual, group, and organizational level may lead to more effective decision making.

Judgments of Individuals, Groups, and Organizations

We already mentioned implications for counterfactuals beyond individuals to groups (Sanna, Chang, & Carter, 2004) and organizations (Goerke et al., 2004; Morris & Moore, 2000) throughout this chapter, although research is sometimes sparse. Thinking about better possibilities—upward counterfactuals—in social dilemmas has positive consequences as people are more cooperative (Parks, Sanna, & Posey, 2003). After negotiations, upward counterfactuals may have negative consequences by focusing people on missed opportunities (Galinsky, Seiden, Kim, & Medvec, 2002; Naquin, 2003). Similar to social comparisons (Collins, 1996), upward counterfactuals can be a source of future preparation or a source of unfavorable comparison. In the TEMPO model, both begin with negative present states. But the former involve self-improvement in which positive futures are contrasted with negative realities, whereas the latter involve a more ruminative focus and assimilating negative present states. The key would be to try to move people and groups from ruminations to self-improvement.

Jury groups are also influenced by counterfactual thinking (Bothwell & Duhon, 1994; Cantellani & Milesi, 2001). This is especially important as counterfactuals can affect blame assignment, compensation, or punishments (Bothwell & Duhon, 1994; Macrae & Milne, 1992; Turley et al., 1995), and quite literally could come down to a matter of life or death. In fact, what people see as fair compensation more generally, as well as their affective responses at the individual, group, and organizational levels, may depend on counterfactuals (Mark & Folger, 1984; Shaw, Wild, & Colquitt, 2003). Kray and Galinsky (2003; Galinsky & Kray, 2004) have shown that groups can be primed with counterfactual mindsets, and this may help them to consider all relevant alternatives before making a decision. This might aid in more effective group decision making, depending on the particular circumstances. In short, applications beyond individuals appear to be particularly wide open areas for future investigation.

Coda

> Two roads diverged in a wood, and I—
> I took the one less traveled by,
> And that has made all the difference.

Researchers and theorists in many areas are interested not only in counterfactuals but also in other conceptually related mental simulations, although they have approached these topics in slightly different ways. Our chapter instead takes a more integrative perspective on judgments over time. The TEMPO model organizes current developments and diverse findings while affording new insights into the interplay between people's thoughts, feelings, and behaviors. Of course, no model can profess to be a sole way to look at the field. However, through this synthesis, we believe not only that a greater understanding of existing findings may be achieved but also that novel and unique avenues for future research may be opened. We hope that this chapter in some small sense gives readers at least an opportunity to ponder a possible counterfactual road less traveled, and perhaps that just might turn out to make all the difference.

Acknowledgments

Portions of this chapter were completed while Lawrence J. Sanna was a visiting scholar at the Fuqua School of Business, Duke University. We thank the Imagination, Goals, and Affect (IGoA, or ego) laboratory group members at the University of North Carolina at Chapel Hill for their comments on this chapter.

Note

All quotations in each section are from "The Road Not Taken" (Frost, 1920).

References

Arkin, R. M., & Shepperd, J. A. (1989). Self-presentation styles in organizations. In R. A. Giacalone & P. Rosenfeld (Eds.), *Impression management in the organization* (pp. 125–139). Hillsdale, NJ: Erlbaum.

Bargh, J. A. (1994). The four horsemen of automaticity: Awareness, intention, efficiency, and control in social cognition. In R. S. Wyer, Jr., & T. K. Srull (Eds.), *Handbook of social cognition* (2nd ed., Vol. 1, pp. 1–40). Hillsdale, NJ: Erlbaum.

Berglas, S., & Jones, E. E. (1978). Drug choice as a self-handicapping strategy in response to noncontingent success. *Journal of Personality and Social Psychology, 36*, 405–417.

Bothwell, R. K., & Duhon, K. W. (1994). Counterfactual thinking and plaintiff compensation. *Journal of Social Psychology, 134*, 705–706.

Brown, J. D., & Mankowski, T. A. (1993). Self-esteem, mood, and self-evaluation: Changes in mood and the way you see you. *Journal of Personality and Social Psychology, 64*, 421–430.

Buehler, R., Griffin, D., & MacDonald, H. (1997). The role of motivated reasoning in optimistic time predictions. *Personality and Social Psychology Bulletin, 23*, 238–247.

Buehler, R., Griffin, D., & Ross, M. (1994). Exploring the "planning fallacy": Why people underestimate their task completion times. *Journal of Personality and Social Psychology, 67*, 366–381.

Byrne, R. M. J. (2002). Mental models and counterfactual thoughts about what might have been. *Trends in Cognitive Science, 6*, 426–431.

Cantellani, P., & Milesi, P. (2001). Counterfactuals and roles: Mock victims' and perpetrators' accounts of judicial cases. *European Journal of Social Psychology, 31*, 247–264.

Chatman, J. A., & Barsade, S. G. (1996). Personality, culture, and cooperation: Evidence from a business simulation. *Administrative Science Quarterly, 40*, 423–443.

Collins, R. L. (1996). For better or worse: The impact of upward social comparison on self-evaluations. *Psychological Bulletin, 119*, 51–69.

Comins, N. F. (1993). *What if the moon didn't exist? Voyages to Earths that might have been.* New York: Harper Collins.

Connolly, T., & Zeelenberg, M. (2002). Regret in decision making. *Current Directions in Psychological Science, 11*, 212–216.

Cowley, R. (Ed.). (1999). *What if? The world's foremost historians imagine what might have been.* New York: Putnam.

Davey, G. C. L, Jubb, M., & Cameron, C. (1996). Catastrophic worrying as a function of changes in problem-solving confidence. *Cognitive Therapy and Research, 20,* 333–344.

Einhorn, H. J., & Hogarth, R. M. (1981). Behavioral decision theory: Processes of judgment and choice. *Annual Review of Psychology, 32,* 53–88.

Erber, R., & Erber, M. W. (1994). Beyond mood and social judgment: Mood incongruent recall and regulation. *European Journal of Social Psychology, 24,* 79–88.

Fischhoff, B. (1975). Hindsight ≠ foresight: The effect of outcome knowledge on judgment under uncertainty. *Journal of Experimental Psychology: Human Perception and Performance, 1,* 288–299.

Fivush, R., Haden, C., & Reese, E. (1996). Remembering, recounting, and reminiscing: The development of autobiographical memory in social context. In D. Rubin (Ed.), *Remembering our past: Studies in autobiographical memory* (pp. 341–359). New York: Cambridge University Press.

Frost, R. (1920). *Mountain interval.* New York: Holt.

Galinsky, A. D., & Kray, L. J. (2004). From thinking about what might have been to sharing what we know: The role of counterfactual mind-sets in information sharing in groups. *Journal of Experimental Social Psychology, 40,* 606–618.

Galinsky, A. D., Seiden, V. L., Kim, P. H., & Medvec, V. H. (2002). The dissatisfaction of having your first offer accepted: The role of counterfactual thinking in negotiations. *Personality and Social Psychology Bulletin, 28,* 271–283.

Gilbert, D. T., Pinel, E. C., Wilson, T. D., Blumberg, S. J., & Wheatley, T. P. (1998). Immune neglect: A source of durability bias in affective forecasting. *Journal of Personality and Social Psychology, 59,* 617–638.

Gilovich, T., Kerr, M., & Medvec, V. H. (1993). Effect of temporal perspective on subjective confidence. *Journal of Personality and Social Psychology, 64,* 552–560.

Gleicher, F., Kost, K. A., Baker, S. M., Strathman, A. J., Richman, S. A., & Sherman, S. J. (1990). The role of counterfactual thinking in judgments of affect. *Personality and Social Psychology Bulletin, 16,* 284–295.

Goerke, M., Moller, J., Schulz-Hardt, S., Napiersky, U., & Frey, D. (2004). "It's not my fault—but only I can change it": Counterfactual and prefactual thoughts of managers. *Journal of Applied Psychology, 89,* 279–292.

Guilbault, R. L., Bryant, F. B., Brockway, J. H., & Posavac, E. J. (2004). A meta-analysis of research on hindsight bias. *Basic and Applied Social Psychology, 26,* 103–117.

Higgins, E. T. (1998). Promotion and prevention: Regulatory focus as a motivational principle. In M. P. Zanna (Ed.), *Advances in experimental social psychology* (Vol. 23, pp. 305–331). New York: Academic Press.

Helgeson, V. S., & Mickelson, K. D. (1995). Motives for social comparison. *Personality and Social Psychology Bulletin, 21,* 1200–1209.

Hofstadter, D. R. (1979). *Gödel, Escher, Bach: An eternal golden braid.* New York: Vintage Books.

Holman, E. A., & Silver, R. C. (1998). Getting "stuck" in the past: Temporal orientation and coping with trauma. *Journal of Personality and Social Psychology, 74,* 1146–1163.

Isen, A. M. (1987). Affect, cognition, and social behavior. In L. Berkowitz (Ed.), *Ad-*

vances in experimental social psychology (Vol. 20, pp. 203–253). San Diego, CA: Academic Press.

Johnson-Laird, P. N., & Byrne, R. M. J. (2002). Conditionals: A theory of meaning, pragmatics, and inference. *Psychological Review, 109*, 646–678.

Kahneman, D., & Miller, D. T. (1986). Norm theory: Comparing reality to its alternatives. *Psychological Review, 93*, 136–153.

Kahneman, D., & Tversky, A. (1979). Intuitive prediction: Biases and corrective procedures. *Management Science, 12*, 313–327.

Kahneman, D., & Tversky, A. (1982). The simulation heuristic. In D. Kahneman, P. Slovic, & A. Tversky (Eds.), *Judgment under uncertainty: Heuristics and biases* (pp. 201–208). New York: Cambridge University Press.

Kendall, P. C., & Ingram, R. E. (1987). The future for cognitive assessment of anxiety: Let's get specific. In L. Michaelson & L. M. Ascher (Eds.), *Anxiety and stress disorders: Cognitive-behavioral assessment and treatment* (pp. 89–104). New York: Guilford Press.

Kets-deVries, M. F., & Miller, D. (1986). Personality, culture, and organization. *Academy of Management Review, 11*, 266–279.

Klinger, E. (1977). *Meaning and void: Inner experience and the incentives in people's lives.* Minneapolis: University of Minnesota Press.

Kray, L. J., & Galinsky, A. D. (2003). The debiasing effect of counterfactual mind-sets: Increasing the search for disconfirmatory information in group decisions. *Organizational Behavior and Human Decision Processes, 91*, 69–81.

Landman, J. (1987). Regret and elation following action and inaction: Affective responses to positive versus negative outcomes. *Personality and Social Psychology Bulletin, 13*, 524–536.

Lipe, M. G. (1991). Counterfactual thinking as a framework for attribution theories. *Psychological Bulletin, 109*, 456–471.

Louie, T. A. (1999). Decision makers' hindsight bias after receiving favorable and unfavorable feedback. *Journal of Applied Psychology, 84*, 29–41.

Macrae, C. N., & Milne, A. B. (1992). A curry for your thoughts: Empathic effects on counterfactual thinking. *Personality and Social Psychology Bulletin, 18*, 625–630.

Mark, M. M., & Folger, R. (1984). Responses to relative deprivation: A conceptual framework. In P. Shaver (Ed.), *Review of personality and social psychology: Emotions, relationships, and health* (Vol. 5, pp. 192–218). Beverly Hills, CA: Sage.

Markman, K. D., Gavanski, I., Sherman, S. J., & McMullen, M. N. (1993). The mental simulation of better and worse possible worlds. *Journal of Experimental Social Psychology, 29*, 87–109.

Martin, L. L., & Tesser, A. (1989). Toward a motivational and structural theory of ruminative thought. In J. S. Uleman & J. A. Bargh (Eds.), *Unintended thought* (pp. 306–326). New York: Guilford Press.

McMullen, M. N. (1997). Affective assimilation and contrast in counterfactual thinking. *Journal of Experimental Social Psychology, 33*, 77–100.

Medvec, V. H., Madey, S. F., & Gilovich, T. (1995). When less is more: Counterfactual thinking and satisfaction among Olympic athletes. *Journal of Personality and Social Psychology, 69,* 603–610.

Miller, D. T., Turnbull, W., & McFarland, C. (1990). Counterfactual thinking and social perception: Thinking about what might have been. In M. P. Zanna (Ed.), *Advances in experimental social psychology* (Vol. 23, pp. 305–331). New York: Academic Press.

Morris, M. W., & Moore, P. C. (2000). The lessons we (don't) learn: Counterfactual thinking and organizational accountability after a close call. *Administrative Science Quarterly, 45,* 737–765.

Naquin, C. E. (2003). The agony of opportunity in negotiation: Number of negotiable issues, counterfactual thinking, and feelings of satisfaction. *Organizational Behavior and Human Decision Processes, 91,* 97–107.

Naquin, C. E., & Tynan, R. O. (2003). The team halo effect: Why teams are not blamed for their failures. *Journal of Applied Psychology, 88,* 332–340.

Nasco, S. A., & Marsh, K. L. (1999). Gaining control through counterfactual thinking. *Personality and Social Psychology Bulletin, 25,* 556–568.

Nisan, M. (1972). Dimension of time in relation to choice behavior and achievement orientation. *Journal of Personality and Social Psychology, 21,* 175–182.

Nolen-Hoeksema, S. (1996). Chewing the cud and other ruminations. In R. S. Wyer (Ed.), *Ruminative thoughts: Advances in social cognition* (Vol. 9, pp. 135–144). Mahwah, NJ: Erlbaum.

Nolen-Hoeksema, S., McBride, A., & Larson, J. (1997). Rumination and psychological distress among bereaved partners. *Journal of Personality and Social Psychology, 72,* 855–862.

Norem, J. K., & Cantor, N. (1986). Defensive pessimism: "Harnessing" anxiety as motivation. *Journal of Personality and Social Psychology, 51,* 1208–1217.

Oettingen, G. (1996). Positive fantasy and motivation. In P. M. Gollwitzer & J. A. Bargh (Eds.), *The psychology of action: Linking cognition and motivation to behavior* (pp. 236–259). New York: Guilford Press.

Oettingen, G., Pak, H., & Schnetter, K. (2001). Self-regulation and goal-setting: Turning free fantasies about the future into binding goals. *Journal of Personality and Social Psychology, 80,* 736–753.

Parks, C. D., Sanna, L. J., & Posey, D. C. (2003). Retrospection in social dilemmas: How thinking about the past affects future cooperation. *Journal of Personality and Social Psychology, 84,* 988–996.

Peterson, C., Seligman, M. E. P., Yurko, K. H., Martin, L. R., & Friedman, H. S. (1998). Catastrophizing and untimely death. *Psychological Science, 9,* 127–130.

Roese, N. J. (1994). The functional basis of counterfactual thinking. *Journal of Personality and Social Psychology, 66,* 805–818.

Roese, N. J. (1997). Counterfactual thinking. *Psychological Bulletin, 121,* 133–148.

Roese, N. J., & Olson, J. M. (Eds.). (1995). *What might have been: The social psychology of counterfactual thinking.* Hillsdale, NJ: Erlbaum.

Roese, N. J., & Olson, J. M. (1997). Counterfactual thinking: The intersection of affect and function. In M. P. Zanna (Ed.), *Advances in experimental social psychology* (Vol. 29, pp. 1–59). San Diego, CA: Academic Press.

Roese, N. J., Sanna, L. J., & Galinsky, A. D. (2005). The mechanics of imagination:

Automaticity and control in counterfactual thinking. In R. R. Hassin, J. S. Uleman, & J. A. Bargh (Eds.), *The new unconscious* (pp. 138–170). New York: Oxford University Press.

Sanna, L. J. (1996). Defensive pessimism, optimism, and simulating alternatives: Some ups and downs of prefactual and counterfactual thinking. *Journal of Personality and Social Psychology, 71,* 1020–1036.

Sanna, L. J. (1997). Self-efficacy and counterfactual thinking: Up a creek with and without a paddle. *Personality and Social Psychology Bulletin, 23,* 654–666.

Sanna, L. J. (1998). Defensive pessimism and optimism: The bitter-sweet influence of mood on performance and prefactual and counterfactual thinking. *Cognition and Emotion, 12,* 635–665.

Sanna, L. J. (1999). Mental simulations, affect, and subjective confidence: Timing is everything. *Psychological Science, 10,* 339–345.

Sanna, L. J. (2000). Mental simulation, affect, and personality: A conceptual framework. *Current Directions in Psychological Science, 9,* 168–173.

Sanna, L. J., Carter, S. E., & Burkley, E. (2005). Yesterday, today, and tomorrow: Counterfactual thinking and beyond. In A. J. Strathman & J. A. Joireman (Eds.), *Understanding behavior in the context of time: Theory, research, and application* (pp. 165–185). Mahwah, NJ: Erlbaum.

Sanna, L. J., & Chang, E. C. (2003). The past is not what it used to be: Optimists' use of retroactive pessimism to diminish the sting of failure. *Journal of Research in Personality, 37,* 388–404.

Sanna, L. J., Chang, E. C., & Carter, S. E. (2004). All our troubles seem so far away: Temporal pattern to accessible alternatives and retrospective team appraisals. *Personality and Social Psychology Bulletin, 30,* 1359–1371.

Sanna, L. J., Chang, E. C., & Meier, S. (2001). Counterfactual thinking and self-motives. *Personality and Social Psychology Bulletin, 27,* 1023 1034.

Sanna, L. J., & Mark, M. M. (1995). Self-handicapping, expected evaluation, and performance: Accentuating the positive and attenuating the negative. *Organizational Behavior and Human Decision Processes, 64,* 84–102.

Sanna, L. J., & Meier, S. (2000). Looking for clouds in a silver lining: Self-esteem, mental simulations, and temporal confidence changes. *Journal of Research in Personality, 34,* 236–251.

Sanna, L. J., Meier, S., & Turley-Ames, K. J. (1998). Mood, self-esteem, and counterfactuals: Externally attributed moods limit self-enhancement strategies. *Social Cognition, 16,* 267–286.

Sanna, L. J., Meier, S., & Wegner, E. C. (2001). Counterfactuals and motivation: Mood as input to affective enjoyment and preparation. *British Journal of Social Psychology, 40,* 235–256.

Sanna, L. J., Parks, C. D., Meier, S., Chang, E. C., Kassin, B. R., Lechter, J. L., et al. (2003). A game of inches: Spontaneous use of counterfactuals by broadcasters during Major League Baseball playoffs. *Journal of Applied Social Psychology, 33,* 455–475.

Sanna, L. J., & Schwarz, N. (2004). Integrating temporal biases: The interplay of focal thoughts and accessibility experiences. *Psychological Science, 15,* 474–481.

Sanna, L. J., Small, E. M., & Cook, L. M. (2004). Social problem solving and mental simulation: Heuristics and biases on the route to effective decision making. In E. C. Chang, T. J. D'Zurilla, & L. J. Sanna (Eds.), *Social problem solving: Theory, research, and training* (pp. 135–149). Washington, DC: American Psychological Association.

Sanna, L. J., Stocker, S. L., & Clarke, J. A. (2003). Rumination, imagination, and personality: Specters of the past and future in the present. In E. C. Chang & L. J. Sanna (Eds.), *Virtue, vice, and personality: The complexity of behavior* (pp. 105–124). Washington, DC: American Psychological Association.

Sanna, L. J., & Turley, K. J. (1996). Antecedents to spontaneous counterfactual thinking: Effects of expectancy violation and outcome valence. *Personality and Social Psychology Bulletin, 22*, 906–919.

Sanna, L. J., & Turley-Ames, K. J. (2000). Counterfactual intensity. *European Journal of Social Psychology, 30*, 273–296.

Sanna, L. J., Turley-Ames, K. J., & Meier, S. (1999). Mood, self-esteem, and simulated alternatives: Thought-provoking affective influences on counterfactual direction. *Journal of Personality and Social Psychology, 76*, 543–558.

Schwarz, N., & Bless, H. (1992). Constructing reality and its alternatives: An inclusion/exclusion model of assimilation and contrast in social judgment. In L. L. Martin & A. Tesser (Eds.), *The construction of social judgments* (pp. 217–245). Hillsdale, NJ: Erlbaum.

Schwarz, N., & Clore, G. L. (1996). Feelings as phenomenal experiences. In E. T. Higgins & A. W. Kruglanski (Eds.), *Social psychology: Handbook of basic principles* (pp. 433–465). New York: Guilford Press.

Sedikides, C., & Strube, M. J. (1997). Self-evaluation: To thine own self be good, to thine own self be sure, to thine own self be true, and to thine own self be better. In M. P. Zanna (Ed.), *Advances in experimental social psychology* (Vol. 29, pp. 209–269). San Diego, CA: Academic Press.

Shaw, J. C., Wild, E., & Colquitt, J. A. (2003). To justify or excuse? A meta-analytic review of the effects of explanations. *Journal of Applied Psychology, 88*, 444–458.

Shepperd, J. A., Findley-Klein, C., Kwavnick, K. D., Walker, D., & Perez, S. (2000). Bracing for loss. *Journal of Personality and Social Psychology, 78*, 620–634.

Shepperd, J. A., Ouellette, J. A., & Fernandez, J. K. (1996). Abandoning unrealistic optimism: Performance estimates and the temporal proximity of self-relevant feedback. *Journal of Personality and Social Psychology, 70*, 844–855.

Sirois, F. M. (2004). Procrastination and counterfactual thinking: Avoiding what might have been. *British Journal of Social Psychology, 43*, 269–286.

Smith, E. R., & DeCoster, J. (2000). Dual-process models in social and cognitive psychology: Conceptual integration and links to underlying memory systems. *Personality and Social Psychology Review, 4*, 108–131.

Spellman, B. A., & Mandel, D. R. (1999). When possibility informs reality: Counterfactual thinking as a cue to causality. *Current Directions in Psychological Science, 8*, 120–123.

Strack, F., Schwarz, N., & Gschneidinger, E. (1985). Happiness and reminiscing: The role of time perspective, affect, and mode of thinking. *Journal of Personality and Social Psychology, 49,* 1460–1469.

Taylor, S. E., & Lobel, M. (1989). Social comparison activity under threat: Downward evaluation and upward contact. *Psychological Review, 96,* 569–575.

Taylor, S. E., & Schneider, S. K. (1989). Coping and the simulation of events. *Social Cognition, 7,* 174–194.

Tetlock, P. E., & Belkin, A. (Eds.). (1996). *Counterfactual thought experiments in world politics: Logical, methodological, and psychological perspectives.* Princeton, NJ: Princeton University Press.

Turley, K. J., Sanna, L. J., & Reiter, R. L. (1995). Counterfactual thinking and perceptions of rape. *Basic and Applied Social Psychology, 17,* 285–303.

Vasey, M. W., & Borkovec, T. D. (1992). A catastrophizing assessment of worrisome thoughts. *Cognitive Therapy and Research, 16,* 505–520.

Wilson, T. D., Wheatley, T., Meyers, J. M., Gilbert, D. T., & Axom, D. (2000). Focalism: A source of durability bias in affective forecasting. *Journal of Personality and Social Psychology, 78,* 821–836.

11

Explaining the Past, Predicting the Future

BERTRAM F. MALLE
CHUCK TATE

The Cognitive Apparatus of Explanation

Classic Attribution Theory

The psychological literature on explanation was born in the 1950s and 1960s, with seminal contributions by Heider (1958), Jones and Davis (1965), and Kelley (1967). Putting important differences aside (see Malle, 2004, chapter 1), all these authors identified cognitive inference as the underlying mechanism by which explanation is achieved. Specifically, explanations are based on inference from observation, past experience, and knowledge structures (Abelson & Lalljee, 1988). According to traditional attribution theories, social perceivers wonder primarily whether a person cause or a situation cause explains the event in question. For example, did she invite him to dinner because of something about her (e.g., her friendly personality) or because of something about him (e.g., his irresistible charm)? Researchers tried to identify the rules of inference people follow when making these person-situation attributions, and Kelley's (1967) covariation model was revolutionary in this respect, specifying the inferential integration of multiple pieces of information in a process akin to analysis of variance.

Traditional attribution theories suffered from a number of shortcomings. First, the theories narrowed the kinds of explanations people seek to only two types (person vs. situation attributions), and even though some theorists expanded this set (Abramson, Seligman, & Teasdale, 1978; Weiner, 1985), the assumption remained that people select "types of causes" in terms of their abstract features (internal-external, stable-unstable, global-specific). Evidence was accumulating, however, that people explain behavior with a variety of conceptual entities, such as goals, reasons, and preconditions (Buss, 1978; McClure, 2002; McClure & Hilton, 1997; Read, 1987).

A second and related shortcoming was that traditional attribution theories considered explanations of generic events, thereby failing to distinguish, as people do, between explanations for intentional and other types of events (Malle & Knobe, 1997b). Actually, Heider (1958) did make this distinction under the labels "personal vs. impersonal causality," but this concept pair was mistakenly interpreted as the distinction between person and situation causes and folded into Kelley's scheme (Malle, 2004; Malle & Ickes, 2000). The first and second shortcomings are related because the genuine variety of explanation types (goals, reasons, causes, etc.) suddenly makes sense when we separate out intentional from unintentional events.

A third shortcoming was that covariation inference was considered the only process that generates explanations. Even though such inference may play an important role in certain contexts, other processes for generating explanations clearly play a role as well (Abelson & Lalljee, 1988; Ahn, Kalish, Medin, & Gelman, 1995; Andrews, 2003; Malle, 2004, chapter 5). For example, explainers sometimes directly recall a particular goal or purpose and at other times simulate the agent's reasoning or experience in order to arrive at a plausible explanation.

Over the past decade, our research group has attempted to mend the shortcomings of attribution theory, integrate the important criticisms voiced over the years, and offer a comprehensive model of explanation that takes into account conceptual, cognitive, linguistic, and social aspects of explanation (Knobe & Malle, 2002; Malle, 1999, 2001, 2004, in press; Malle, Knobe, O'Laughlin, Pearce, & Nelson, 2000; O'Laughlin & Malle, 2002). Here we summarize the major features of our folk-conceptual theory of explanation in order to develop new ideas about the temporal dimension of explanation.

The Folk-Conceptual Theory of Explanation

The name *folk-conceptual theory* was chosen because the theory highlights the folk concepts by which people make sense of mind and behavior—concepts such as intention and intentionality, reasons, enabling factors, and the like. Besides this conceptual layer, the theory has two other layers: psychological processes by which people generate explanations and the linguistic tools by which they express explanations. Finally, the model is embedded in considerations of social functions that explanations serve, including impression management, conversational clarification, persuasion, and propaganda (Malle, 2004).

We now introduce the three layers of the theory and then apply them to an analysis of temporal aspects of explanation.

First Layer: Conceptual Framework and
Modes of Explanation

The theory's first and fundamental layer describes the *conceptual framework* that underlies behavior explanations. As Heider (1958) argued, people sharply distinguish between intentional and unintentional behavior. Moreover, a close inspection of the folk concept of intentionality (Malle & Knobe, 1997a) suggested that people employ at least three different modes of explanation for intentional actions (Malle, 1999, 2001): reason explanations, causal history of reason explanations, and enabling-factor explanations.

Most often, people explain an action by the *reasons* for which the agent performed the action. Reasons are typically beliefs and desires in light of which and on the grounds of which the agent decided to act. That is, reasons have two defining features: agents are *aware* of their reasons, and agents consider their reasons to be *rational grounds* for acting. For example:

> I am going to read some proverbs *because they are supposed to be extremely wise, and I need some wisdom in my life.*

Second, people explain some actions by the *causal history* of those reasons—if, for example, the reasons themselves are not known or are of little interest. Causal history or reason explanations refer to context, personality, culture, or unconscious processes that led up to (lay in the history of) an agent's consideration of certain beliefs or desires as reasons for acting. However, causal history factors are not themselves reasons. For a causal history explanation to be appropriate, the agent need not be aware of the causal history factor, nor does the factor have to provide any rational grounds for acting. Like reasons, causal history explanations account for intentional action; but, unlike reasons, they do not conform to the constraints of awareness and rationality. To sharpen the contrast between reason explanations and causal history explanations, Table 11.1 juxtaposes both explanation modes for the same actions.

Third, occasionally people are not interested in what motivated an agent's action but what made it possible that the action was successfully performed (Malle et al., 2000; McClure & Hilton, 1997). These *enabling factor* explanations refer to processes inside or outside the agent that facilitated or permitted (i.e., enabled) the successful action performance.

Whereas people's concept of intentional action provides three distinct modes of explanation, their concept of unintentional behavior is far simpler. Unintentional behaviors are treated like any other events (e.g., physical or biological)—"mechanically" brought about without the necessary involvement of intention,

Table 11.1. Examples of reason explanations and CHR explanations that were distinguished reliably by social perceivers

Behavior	Reasons	CHR explanations
Nancy chose not to vote in the last election.	None of the candidates appealed to her.	Her mom died that week.
	She wasn't interested in the issues.	She doesn't realize that every vote counts.
Ian worked 14 hours a day last month.	To make more money	He is driven to achieve.
	He wants to get ahead.	That's the cultural norm.

Note: Adapted from O'Laughlin and Malle (2002). Behaviors and explanations were selected from Malle (1999) and Malle et al. (2000).

awareness, or rationality. People explain such events with *causes* as the single mode of explanation.

The proposed folk-conceptual model of behavior explanation thus includes four modes of explanation, each of which has a distinct conceptual basis and distinct functions. The theory also identifies specific types of explanation within each mode—for example, belief reasons and desire reasons that are linguistically marked (as mental states) or not. We return shortly to these more specific types.

Second Layer: Psychological Processes in
Generating Explanations

The second layer of the folk-conceptual theory concerns the *psychological processes* that govern the actual construction of explanations (for more details, see Malle, 2004, chapter 5). In constructing explanations, people have to solve two problems (not necessarily in a fixed order). The first is to choose among the various explanatory tools they have available (i.e., four modes and various types of explanation within each). Three factors appear to determine these choices: (1) features of the behavior to be explained (e.g., intentionality, difficulty); (2) pragmatic goals (e.g., impression management, audience design); and (3) information resources (e.g., knowledge structures, perceived action context). These determinants of explanation choice are systematically related to the kinds of explanations people offer. Studies have shown, for example, that the choice between reasons and causal history explanations is primarily a function of knowledge and impression management goals; the choice of enabling factors (rather than reasons or causal histories) is a function of behavior difficulty and audience design; and the choice between causes and any of the other three explanation modes is a function of judgments about the behavior's intentionality, as well as additional impression management goals, e.g., averting blame by portraying an ambiguous behavior as unintentional. (For evidence, see Malle, 1999; Malle, Knobe, & Nelson, 2005; Malle et al., 2000; O'Laughlin & Malle, 2002).

The second problem in constructing explanations is that people must select *specific* reasons, causes, and so on (not just a generic "belief reason" or "situation cause"), and they do so by relying on a variety of cognitive strategies. These strategies include retrieving information from knowledge structures, projection of one's own beliefs and preferences, simulation of another person's reasoning or experience, and, occasionally, covariation analysis. Research has just begun to examine which processes are used for which kinds of explanation modes and in response to which psychological determinants of explanation, such as pragmatic goals and information resources. (See Malle, 2004, chapter 5, for an initial, qualitative exploration.)

Third Layer: Linguistic Expression

The third layer of the theory identifies the specific *linguistic forms* speakers have available in their language to express behavior explanations. People can exploit these linguistic forms when using explanations as a tool of social influence. For example, to distance themselves from an agent's reasons, observers explicitly mark those reasons as the other person's mental states (e.g., Why did she refuse dessert?—"Because *she thinks* she's been gaining weight" vs. "Because she's been gaining weight"; Malle et al., 2000). Similarly, when people watch a video displaying them from a third-person perspective, they seem to distance themselves from their own reasons by increasing the use of mental state markers (Malle, Heim, & Knorek, 2005.).

We now apply this model of explanations to a consideration of temporal aspects of explanation. An analysis of such temporal factors must take all three layers of explanation into account. The conceptual level enumerates the different modes and types of explanation that can vary with changing temporal perspective or passage of time. The psychological process level surveys the cognitive routes people take to construct explanations, permitting us to examine in detail how explanations of past, recent, and future events may be differentially constructed. Finally, the linguistic level alerts us to the variations in language that might reflect either underlying psychological processes or social functions and practices that govern explanations.

Temporal Aspects of Explanations

We can distinguish at least two temporal aspects of explanation. First, how do explanations of a given event change as time passes after the event? For example, does a person's immediate explanation of a transgression differ from an explanation offered years later? Second, do people offer only explanations of past and present events (that actually occurred), or do they ever explain future events? If so, do such future explanations vary either in the modes of explanation they employ or the cognitive processes from which they are constructed?

Traditional research is available only on the first question, so we begin with a brief review of this research.

Do Explanations Change Over Time?

Classic Research

About a dozen studies in the social-psychological literature discuss effects of time on attribution patterns. We set aside four studies that concern not behavior explanations but trait inferences (i.e., the fundamental attribution error; Burger, 1991; Truchot, Maure, & Patte, 2003; Wright & Wells, 1985) or estimations of contributions to joint outcomes (Burger & Rodman, 1983). Of the remaining studies, five show a pattern of actors increasing person attributions for successes but increasing situation attributions for failures, which the authors consider evidence for a time-dependent strengthening of the self-serving bias (Burger, 1985, 1986; Burger & Huntzinger, 1985; Moore, Sherrod, Liu, & Underwood, 1979; see also Burger & Pavelich, 1994). Two additional studies showed an increase of situational attributions for interpersonal interactions (Funder & Van Ness, 1983; Miller & Porter, 1980), and one showed no change (Frank & Gilovich, 1989), but it is unclear whether the events explained (interpersonal interactions) were perceived as undesirable, akin to failures. Finally, one study documented an increase of stable attributions for actors, a finding that is compatible with the previous ones in that the stable factors were typically positive (e.g., desirable personality traits).

We cannot draw compelling conclusions from these findings. One difficulty in generalizing the results is that in most studies the specific outcomes (success or failure) were manipulated by the experimenter, and participants essentially had to explain a fabricated reality (Burger, 1986; Burger & Huntzinger, 1985; Sanna & Swim, 1992). It may not be surprising that some number of participants in the failure condition attributed this surprising outcome to situational circumstances, because the failure feedback may have been discordant both with their experience in the experiment and their personal performance history. More important, studies that showed a reasonably consistent time effect focused on achievement outcomes, which are not the dominant events people explain (Malle & Knobe, 1997b). Indeed, the pattern of self-serving change over time disappears when we expand the sample of events explained. In a meta-analysis of the actor-observer asymmetry in attribution (Malle, 2005; see also Malle, in press), 102 studies assessed attributions immediately after the event, and 70 studies assessed delayed attributions. If a self-serving bias increases over time, we would expect that for positive events actors should increase person attributions (weakening the actor-observer asymmetry), and for negative events they should increase situation attributions (strengthening the actor-observer asymmetry). There was a trend showing that actors increase their person attributions for positive events, but the same trend held true for negative events, which does not support the hypothesis that the self-serving bias increases over time.

Perhaps the most serious limitation of traditional studies on time and attribution is that there is no theoretical model that predicts the findings (or its exceptions). Why would people increase situational attributions, why would they decrease them, or why would they do both, depending on the outcome? Why the person-situation dimension rather than the stability dimension or the other way around? As in other instances (e.g., Knobe & Malle, 2002; Malle et al., 2000), there are no readily available theoretical principles that predict variations in person-situation attributions as a function of critical variables. The only candidate theory, Kelley's covariation model, doesn't actually predict person-situation attributions very well (Ahn et al., 1995; Malle, 2002), but that aside, the model has little to say about self-serving time changes in attributions. Covariation considerations predict changes in attributions only when new information becomes available (e.g., a systematic increase in consistency information, leading to a situational shift; Lau, 1984), but the whole notion of time effects in attribution presumes a *lack* of new information; otherwise, time itself wouldn't be the critical force of change.

A possibly more fruitful alternative approach is to investigate time effects on behavior explanations across the full range of unintentional and intentional events, taking into account the entire set of explanatory tools people bring to the task and considering the specific psychological determinants that govern such explanations. The following section develops this approach in more detail and, in particular, offers testable hypotheses about time effects on explanation. Our major claim is that there is no single psychological process that mediates between passing time and changes in explanation. Rather, time can affect explanations in different ways, depending on the specific process that changes over time.

Folk-Conceptual Analysis of Explanations Across Time

Our approach relies on the folk-conceptual theory of explanations, which identifies the modes and types of explanations people use and the psychological processes that determine this use. If we can identify the psychological processes that actually change over time, then we can rely on known relationships between these processes and modes of explanation to predict how explanations change over time. There is no perfect, and certainly no one-to-one, relationship between psychological processes and explanatory tools, but there is growing evidence that systematic relationships exist (Malle, 2004, chapter 5). To make our point, we focus on explanations of *intentional* behavior, both because they demand more complex explanatory tools and because the strength of the folk-conceptual approach is most salient in this domain. (For considerations of unintentional behaviors, see Malle, 2004.)

The three determinants of choosing modes and types of explanation introduced earlier are *behavior features*, *pragmatic goals*, and *information resources*, and we can explore time effects for each of them.

1. *Behavior features* that are critical for explanatory choices include at least two. Intentionality determines whether explainers will choose cause explanations (for unintentional events) or other explanation modes (for intentional behavior); behavior difficulty determines whether explainers will choose enabling factor explanations or other explanations of intentional behavior. These behavior features can be set aside for our analysis, however, because they must remain constant across time when we examine temporal change in explanations. Unless people explain the *same* behavior at two different times (with the same intentionality and difficulty), we cannot assess time effects; rather, we would assess effects of new information.

2. *Pragmatic goals* partially determine the choice between reasons and causal history of reason (CHR) explanations for intentional actions. One important pragmatic goal is impression management. When trying to make the agent (self or other) look good and rational for having performed a positive action, explainers typically increase their use of reasons relative to CHRs (Malle et al., 2000); by contrast, when limiting blame for negative actions, explainers typically increase their use of CHRs relative to reasons (Nelson & Malle, 2005). Another important pragmatic goal is parsimony in conversation (Grice, 1975). For example, when explaining a whole series of actions to an audience, explainers tend to decrease their use of reasons because there are too many distinct reasons to mention (potentially a different one for each action in the series). As a result, explainers tend to increase their use of CHRs, because a single CHR can precede a variety of different reasons and thereby provide a succinct explanation for the complex series of events (O'Laughlin & Malle, 2002). For example, a mother who was asked why she goes shopping several times a week replied: "Because I have three children." The series of shopping acts is parsimoniously explained by offering this causal history of having three children because it underlies the variety of specific reasons she has for shopping each individual time (e.g., buying more milk, a new supply of diapers, or a special carpet cleaner for crayon stains).

The question is whether these processes of impression management and conversational parsimony change over time. Impression management, we suggest, may not be rigidly connected with passing time, but more often than not, impression management pressures for a given action will decrease over time because the action was performed by a "past self," whereas impression management typically applies to the "present self."[1] (This point applies to observer explanations just as to actor explanations but far more frequently to the latter.) This process would therefore predict a decrease in reasons for positive actions and a decrease of CHRs for negative actions.

Conversational parsimony per se is unlikely to change over time, but there is one condition under which passing time can elicit parsimony considerations: when the initial action has been repeated and therefore, at a later time, is explained as part of a whole series of actions. Perhaps we don't want to consider this an explanation of truly the *same* action, but if we do, time will increase the demand for parsimony and thereby the likelihood of CHR explanations.

3. *Information resources* represent the broadest determinant of explanatory choice. They are anchored by stable knowledge structures at one end and context-immediate information access at the other, with additional resources in between.

Stable knowledge structures are unlikely to change over time, so to the extent that explanations are based on these structures, we predict no notable change of explanations over time.

Context-immediate information access, at the other extreme, refers to information that is available right there at the time of acting. To analyze its impact profile over time, we need to distinguish the actor perspective from the observer perspective. From the actor perspective, this kind of access will yield information about facts, affordances, or constraints of the immediate context, which will translate into reasons and especially *unmarked belief reasons*—beliefs that are not explicitly marked by a mental state verb (e.g., "Why are you watering the plants?"—"Well, [I see that] their soil is dry!") To the extent that the actor's initial explanation is guided by such context-immediate information, a later explanation (after time has passed) may well retrieve the same reason content from memory but will now mark the reason with a mental state verb ("*I saw* that their soil was dry").[2] This predicted increase in markers is supported by the finding that episodic memories over time shift toward a third-person visual perspective (Nigro & Neisser, 1983) and that actors in third-person perspective increase their use of mental state inferences (Malle, Heim, & Knorek, 2005; see Moore et al., 1979, for a similar argument).

From the perspective of an observer who is present at the time of action, immediate information may similarly refer to contextual facts and constraints, but these have to be translated into ascriptions of belief reasons to the agent. In addition, immediate information also includes the perception of the "moving body," which is likely to elicit ascriptions of desires and intentions (Baird & Baldwin, 2001). Ascriptions of both belief and desire reasons (which may be based at least in part on "simulation" processes—e.g., Gordon, 1986, 1992; Goldman, 1989, 2001) will typically be marked with mental state verbs ("She thought"; "He wanted") to identify states of "that mind over there." Over time observers will retrieve far less of this immediate (often perceptual) information, which may reduce their ability to ascribe mental states to the agent (perhaps because of limited simulation opportunities), and in that case observers may resort increasingly to causal history of reason explanations. Thus, for actors, the fading of context-immediate information should primarily affect the formulation of their explanations (increasing the use of mental state markers), but for observers, this fading should decrease their overall ascriptions of reasons.

A final type of information resource is the actor's direct recall of her reasons for acting. In some number of intentional actions, actors deliberate about their decision to act (i.e., they consider reasons for or against courses of action), and in those cases an actor who explains her action can easily recruit the very reasons (beliefs, desires) for which she acted (Brewer, 1994; Russell & D'Hollosy, 1992). Such direct recall may fade, at first weakly, but more noticeably with passing time, especially for insignificant actions. An example: One of us bikes home up a hill on a route that has a fork in the road such that a decision has to be made to take the shorter and steeper path or the longer and more gently sloped path. It is virtually impossible to recall the reasons for taking the longer, flatter route this day a year ago, even though on that day, especially within minutes of the decision, the reasons were almost certainly directly recalled. This fading of direct recall will undermine the actor's offering of reasons, especially context-sensitive reasons, which are typically beliefs.

Even without a parallel analysis of explanations for unintentional behavior, we feel confident in our conclusion that time has no uniform effect on explanatory choices. One must take into account the various determinants of explanations and the perspectives of actor and observer; only then can mere time passing be translated into actual explanatory changes.

Do People Explain Future Events (and How)?

The second important temporal aspect of behavior explanations is not oriented toward the past but the future. The question we would like to explore is to what extent people explain future behaviors, and if they do, how.

It may appear somewhat paradoxical to wonder whether people *explain* future behavior. After all, explanation is often defined as a clarification of events that already happened (e.g., Heider, 1958; Hempel & Oppenheim, 1948; Salmon, 1989). This is a reasonable position, but we still would like to examine whether the same *processes* that give rise to explanations of past behaviors can sometimes generate what look like explanations of future behaviors. In the end, these explanations may come close to *predictions* of future behaviors, which will make the tenor of our subsequent section yet more plausible: that predictions of future events are closely tied to explanatory processes.

The best case for explanations of future events can be made in the domain of *reason explanations* for intentional behavior. The agent's deliberation process (rudimentary as it may be in some cases) consists of the consideration of reasons, primarily desires for certain outcomes and beliefs about ways to achieve those outcomes. This reasoning process weighs the motivational and rational grounds for forming various intentions, and the reasoning process ends when the agent settles on an intention to act for particular reasons (Malle & Knobe, 2001; Mele, 1992, 2003). Schematically:

Reasons [beliefs, desires] → intention to *A* → action *A*.

The folk conception of intentional action and its underlying reasoning process is such that an explanation of the *completed action*, were it performed, would refer to the agent's reasons for which she chose that action; and so would an explanation of the *intention* to act, even if the action has not yet been performed (Malle, 1999). Nothing guarantees that actions are performed. Lara may deliberate and then decide to go to the movies tonight, but something comes up and she doesn't go. Nonetheless, at the time of the decision, and even later on, we can explain why she decided to go to the movies by pointing to her reasons—for example, because it was Thursday night and the film was about to leave the theater.

Every intention (e.g., "I am going to *A*") is future directed. This is nicely driven home by the fact that in many languages the future tense either stems from or is closely related to intention verbs, as in the English "I will . . ." (Bybee, Perkins, & Pagliuca, 1994). And because intentions are explained by the reasons for which the intention was formed, people explain at least some future events—those that are intended (but not yet performed) actions. Consider the following examples (from students' diaries and audiotaped conversations; Malle & Knobe, 1997b; Malle et al., 2005):

Since I'll be gone she's going to take Lara out instead.
I'm not going to apply for "live-out" *'cause I don't want to step on anybody's toes.*

Reason explanations dominate these explanations of future events, though under rare circumstances, an intended future action might be explained by reference to a causal history of reason factor. We could not find a real example in our database of explanations, but the following constructed example appears plausible:

She intends to buy, not rent, *because she is from a rich family.*

Perhaps more likely would be a reformulation as a pure prediction: "She *will* buy, not rent, because she grew up in a rich family." CHR explanations of intended future actions are rare because, when explicitly announcing an agent's intention, the speaker is normally expected to clarify the agent's motives for intending to act, which requires reason explanations. This demand for reason explanations should be particularly true for actors explaining their own intended future actions. Announcing one's own intention comes with a strong conversational expectation to justify and clarify that intention with one's reasons for adopting it; CHR explanations do not meet this expectation. Rarely would an actor say, "I intend to buy, not rent, because I grew up in a rich family."

Enabling factor explanations cannot be used to explain intended future events, because these explanations account for the successful performance of actions, not for their motives and intentions. We can, however, *predict* that somebody will likely succeed in clearing 7 feet in high jumping because he or she has trained for 6 months or that a team will succeed in finishing a project because it started early enough.

Similarly, neither actors nor observers can explain future *unintentional* events; they can only predict them. Consider the following examples:

> When I started taking those math classes I thought, "This is going to be hard *'cause I really hate math."*
> I will hopefully get alumni status, *'cause when you affiliate to another chapter, that's what you get.*

In each of these cases, the *because* clause offers a cause that makes it likely for the future event to obtain, and in that sense most would call this a prediction, not an explanation. In addition, the *because* clause has a second function: It provides *backing* or *evidence* for the claim that the future event will obtain. Claim backings are most transparent when the *because* clause does not cite any causal factor at all, as in the following example:

> Joe is going to be angry *because I have seen him react to conflict before.*

Clearly, Joe's anger will not be caused by the speaker's having seen Joe react that way before. What the speaker does in the *because* clause is back up, provide evidence for, the prediction that Joe will be angry. Davies (1979) proposed a criterion that distinguishes clear cases of claim backing from explanation: Claim backings can be formulated only in the canonical order of "event + because," whereas explanations can also be formulated in the inverse order, "because + event." For example, it makes no sense to say, "Because I have seen him react to conflict before, Joe is going to be angry." The infelicitous use of the inverse order exposes the *because* clause as a pure claim backing.[3]

In sum, we suggest that *because* clauses paired with future event statements can be explanations of intended future events, predictions made on the basis of identified causes, or predictions with pure claim backing. This range already suggests a close relationship between explanations and predictions. We now explore more thoroughly the topic of prediction and inspect once more the particular role of explanatory processes in predictions.

The Cognitive Apparatus of Prediction

Existing Prediction Literature

To date, psychological studies of prediction have largely used likelihood estimates as a method of shedding light on this phenomenon. Likelihood estimates are studied under different names (e.g., subjective probability) and have been related to a wide variety of judgment and decision-making topics such as choice (see Dawes, 1998, for a review), alternative outcomes (Windschitl & Wells, 1998), anticipated regret (e.g., Zeelenberg, 1999), risk (e.g., Slovic, 2000), contrast effects in social judgments (e.g., Schwarz & Bless, 1992), and affective forecasting (e.g., Gilbert, Lieberman, Morewedge, & Wilson, 2004). In addition, virtually all prediction studies have some standard of accuracy against which predictions are examined. This accuracy focus has allowed researchers to uncover heuristics and biases people use when making predictions (e.g., Kahneman & Tversky, 1973; MacDonald & Ross, 1999; Peterson & Pitz, 1986) and to compare human thinking to regression models or other statistical methods of prediction (e.g., Kahneman & Tversky, 1982a; Snook, Canter, & Bennell, 2002).

Compared to work on accuracy of predictions, far less research has focused on *how* humans are able to predict in the first place. Studying the accuracy of predictions is only an indirect method of examining the processes underlying prediction because accuracy is a result of comparing a predicted outcome to what actually happened, not a focus on how the person generated or evaluated that prediction in the first place. In fact, the underlying processes of prediction have remained virtually unstudied since the work by Kahneman and Tversky (1973), who provided an initial answer by arguing (using accuracy data) that humans make predictions using representativeness (i.e., stereotypical associations and/or expectations).

Types of Predictions

The Simulation Heuristic

Some years after their proposal that prediction relies on representativeness, Kahneman and Tversky (1982b) developed five "scenarios" (or kinds) of mental simulations. Three of these focused on mentally simulating possible futures, and the remaining two pertained to mental simulation of the past. The scenarios about the past are currently studied under the heading of "counterfactual thinking" in social and cognitive psychology, but less research has examined the first three scenarios concerning future thinking. The future-oriented scenarios were called (1) *prediction*, (2) *assessing the probability of a specified event*, and (3) *assessing conditioned probabilities* (Kahneman & Tversky, 1982b, p. 202). Briefly, *prediction* concerns how individuals generate predictions, such as that two strangers will "get on famously" (Kahneman & Tversky, 1982b, p. 202). *Assessing the probability of a specified event* concerns a specified target event and "the 'ease' with which this target state can be produced" (Kahneman & Tversky, 1982b, p. 202). An example of this scenario would be: What is the likelihood of an American invasion of Iran in the next decade? Here, the invasion is the specified target state, and, according to Kahneman and Tversky, a person evaluates the ease with which the target state can be imagined or simulated. Most studies of prediction focus on this kind of scenario because the operationalization of prediction as likelihood estimates or subjective probabilities is amenable to studying the ease with which specified target outcomes can be imagined. The specification of the outcome also usually allows for testing of these estimates against some standard of accuracy. Finally, *assessing conditioned probabilities* refers to simulating future events under initial conditions. For example, a person might be asked: "If civil war breaks out in Saudi Arabia, what are the likely consequences?" (Kahneman & Tversky, 1982b, p. 202). This task requires a person to assume a state of affairs that may or may not be consistent with reality (e.g., civil war in Saudi Arabia might or might not be happening currently). After accepting the conditional, it then appears that a person can focus on the "ease" with which the specified target event can be imagined.

A New Fourfold Typology of Prediction

We believe that the simulation heuristic provides a good starting point for distinguishing among types of predictions, but by itself it does not cover the full range of prediction types or processes. When examining the structure of predictions, it appears that virtually all predictions have three elements: (1) the outcome or event that is predicted, (2) the starting conditions in light of which the prediction is made, and (3) some sort of connection between outcome and starting conditions. This tripartite structure of prediction can be depicted as $S \rightarrow O$, wherein S represents the starting conditions, O represents the outcome, and $\rightarrow$ represents some connection that "leads to" the outcome given the starting conditions. This conceptual structure serves as the cornerstone for the new typology of prediction that we propose and develop here. The typology focuses on whether the starting conditions S and outcome O are explicitly specified or left unspecified. These considerations result in a 2×2 model encompassing four types of prediction (see Table 11.2).

Table 11.2. Fourfold Typology of Prediction.

Starting Conditions	Outcome	
	Specified	Unspecified
Specified	Fully Specified **SO**	Starting Conditions Specified **S**
Unspecified	Outcome Specified **O**	Unspecified **U**

*Fully Specified Predictions (**SO**).* Type SO predictions have specified starting conditions and a specified outcome. In language, this kind of prediction might be stated as "Given that [S], how likely is it that [O]?"

*Outcome-Specified Predictions (**O**).* Type O predictions have unspecified starting conditions and a specified outcome. In language, this kind of prediction might be stated as "How likely is it that [O] will happen?"

*Starting-Conditions-Specified Predictions (**S**).* Type S predictions have specified starting conditions and an unspecified outcome. In language, this kind of prediction might be stated as "Given [S], what will happen?"

Unspecified Predictions (U). Type U predictions contain both unspecified starting conditions and an unspecified outcome. In language, this kind of prediction might be stated as "What will happen?" Such formulations of predictions, however, may be inconsistent with conversational norms (Grice, 1975), and listeners might therefore move to specify at least one of the elements, thereby shifting to a Type SO, Type O, or Type S prediction.

A Comparison of the Two Models

The fourfold typology of prediction subsumes and clarifies the three scenarios of prediction offered by Kahneman and Tversky's (1982b) analysis. The *prediction* scenario is analyzed as having specified starting conditions but unspecified outcomes (Type S). *Assessing the probability of a specified event* can be either a Type SO or a Type O prediction, as both these types involve specified outcomes. Our new typology distinguishes, however, between the two contexts in which a specified event can be evaluated: with or without a specified set of starting conditions. This distinction enables the investigation of cognitive strategies for identifying starting conditions when relevant (i.e., for Type O predictions). Finally, *assessing conditioned probabilities* is analyzed as a Type SO prediction, which is fully specified.

From Simulation to Multiple Cognitive Processes

We propose one more addition to Kahneman and Tversky's (1982b) analysis of prediction. Kahneman and Tversky subsumed all forms of prediction under the simulation heuristic, relying on the intuition that to predict the future people have to simulate it. But much work in cognitive science over the past 20 years strongly suggests that simulation is a unique cognitive process, and not all prediction relies on this process. Simulation is best considered a process of running an analogous "model" of the to-be-predicted domain and, akin to a computer simulation, arriving at a likely outcome that is then formulated as a prediction about the domain (e.g., Gordon, 1986; Goldman, 1989). Simulation understood this way is very different from theoretical or rule-driven inferences, which are often the basis of prediction (Gopnik & Wellman, 1994; Rips, 1994). One can easily make a prediction about a future event without literally simulating the steps that lead up to this event; one might, instead, use past experience to take a best guess or rely on a general rule to predict the event. These distinct processes underlying prediction must somehow be incorporated into a theory of prediction.

Regardless of whether starting conditions and outcomes are explicitly stated or left implicit, we assume that all cases of prediction can be modeled by the general $S \rightarrow O$ structure, which is the basis for the preceding fourfold typology. But a theory of prediction must specify in more detail the nature of the connection operator (the "leads to" connections). We propose that the connections between S and O can be characterized by two generic strategies—simulation and inference—and we identify three different forms that the inference strategy can take. Moreover, we propose that all the connections are, to varying degrees, explanatory in nature. That is, they provide some explanation of how the starting conditions lead to the outcome. As a result, we propose a total of four *explanatory strategies* (simulation and three forms of inference), which all specify, to varying degrees, the connection or relationship between starting conditions and a predicted outcome.

Four Explanatory Strategies for Prediction

The proposed explanatory strategies characterize subjective human experience and can be construed as cognitive tools that people have at their disposal. The explanatory strategies described here were developed from examining various literatures in philosophy (see Reschler, 1997, for a review) and cognitive, social, and developmental psychology, such as behavior explanation (e.g., Malle, 1999, 2004), inductive inference and rule-based inference (see Sloman, 1996, for a review), causal inference (e.g., Cohen, Rundell, Spellman, & Cashon,

1999), and theory of mind (e.g., German & Leslie, 2000; Gordon, 1986). The four explanatory strategies gleaned from these reviews are: (1) noncontradiction, (2) association (induction), (3) derivability (deduction), and (4) scenario generation (simulation).

Noncontradiction is a minimal connection between S and O such that there is no apparent contradiction between the outcome and both the starting conditions and other relevant knowledge. For instance, when predicting that a party will be wild and crazy, a participant in one of our studies provided the following explanation: "There'll be some crazy happenings because, I don't know, it's a party and stuff like that can happen." That is, the outcome does not seem to contradict the assumed starting conditions and other relevant knowledge, lending some plausibility to the predicted event. In addition to providing a minimal requirement for predicting events at above-zero probabilities, noncontradiction might be useful for situations in which a person has little knowledge about the domain. In this case, the person can at least predict that an outcome is "somewhat likely" because it does not appear to contradict what else is known. To be sure, noncontradiction is not what one might characterize as a full-fledged prediction, because the mechanism through which the outcome is believed to result remains unspecified; yet this strategy provides the necessary foundation for developing full-fledged predictions, as any predicted outcome must be possible given the starting conditions and other relevant knowledge.

Association draws a correlational or stereotypical connection between the starting conditions and the outcome. This strategy includes representativeness as Kahneman and Tversky (1973) defined it and was inspired by literature on inductive inference (see Sloman, 1996, for a review). This strategy is qualitatively different from noncontradiction in that association at least hints at a causal mechanism (or process) through which the outcome ensues given the starting conditions. In this manner, association begins to resemble full-fledged prediction. Interestingly, association-based predictions are comparable to causal history of reason explanations (see the second section of this chapter) in that the association strategy, too, mentions factors that led up to or lay in the history of an event without offering details about the mechanism by which the event came about. Nevertheless, association-based predictions are broader than CHR explanations because they are believed to be domain-general, not merely applicable to intentional actions. Examples of associative explanations include "The Los Angeles Lakers always beat the Chicago Bulls, so this time will not be any different" (empirical association) or "good students don't cheat, so she won't" (stereotypical association). It should be noted that one can use the same strategy for nonhuman objects, such as physical or natural events: "Old Faithful spouts everyday, so today will be no different."

Derivability provides a deduction of the outcome from the starting conditions together with a rule, law, or psychological principle. This explanatory strategy mirrors rule-based inference (Sloman, 1996) and the *theory theory* position in theory of mind research (Gopnik & Wellman, 1994). This strategy is different from noncontradiction and association in that derivability actually identifies a causal mechanism or process that connects the starting conditions and outcome. Reason explanations of intentional action resemble derivability-based predictions in that they posit a particular mechanism (e.g., belief-desire reasoning leading to intentions and actions) and thus connect specific starting conditions (particular belief or desire reasons) with the outcome (the action). In the realm of physical events, derivability-based prediction uses laws or rules such as gravity or force to provide a connection between starting conditions and outcome, thus going beyond past co-occurrences of two events or stereotypical associations. An example of a derivability explanation for human behavior would be: "Christine will invite Diego to the party because she is interested in him." Here, Christine's interest in Diego serves as the deductive premise from which it is very likely that she will ask him to the party, in light of the general principle that people pursue that in which they are interested. An example of derivability in a physical domain would be: "Given that the structural supports for the bridge are weak, it will probably collapse."

Scenario generation provides a story or simulation of the events unfolding over time, as in a film or narrative. This strategy was inspired by Pennington and Hastle's (1993) story model of decision making, simulation theory in the theory of mind literature (e.g., Gordon, 1986), and the underlying theme of Kahneman and Tversky's simulation heuristic. This strategy is distinguishable from the inference strategies described earlier because scenario generation fills in concrete steps between the starting conditions and the outcome, typically relying on a wealth of domain-relevant knowledge in order to create complex causal chains. To simulate a predicted event, the person creates an explanatory structure that resembles a story, often containing a plot (the starting condition-outcome connection) and subplots (starting condition-starting condition connections). Take the example of a person predicting the victory of a sports team by envisioning a scenario in which the team trails in the first half, rallies in the second, and beats the opponent at the buzzer.

We now provide initial empirical support for the distinction among these four strategies. In particular, we examined whether these strategies (1) can be identified in people's introspections about how they generate predictions and (2) have systematic relationships to the four types of prediction we proposed earlier and to different content domains of prediction.

Explanatory Strategies and Prediction
Types: Initial Support for the Model

We first conducted a study that examined the efficacy of the proposed model of explanatory strategies and prediction typology in characterizing actual predictions that people encounter, generate, and evaluate in daily life. We used a diary methodology in which nine participants recorded predictions over a 4-day period that either they or someone else had generated. Participants were required to record 12 predictions during this interval but were allowed to record as many as 20. For each recorded prediction (their own or another person's), participants were asked to speculate on what was going on in their own minds (or what they believed was going on in the other person's mind) just before making the prediction.

Of the 180 records across participants, only 130 were valid predictions. The remaining entries were either desires (e.g., "I want to go the game"), wonderings (e.g., "am I hungry?"), or statements (e.g., "I don't like work"). Of the 130 valid records, 106 (81.5%) were coded as specified-outcome (Type O) predictions, 16 (12.3%) were coded as fully specified (Type SO) predictions, and 8 (6.2%) were coded as specified-starting-condition (Type S) predictions. None of the valid records were codable as unspecified (Type U) predictions.

A total of 116 records provided valid responses to the question of what was going on in the mind of the predictor just before making the prediction. Of these, 82 (70.6%) were coded as *derivability* predictions (e.g., "DeShaun Foster isn't playing, so their offense will be weak [and, therefore, their team will lose]"; "I've done all the right things on time [so I will get a good grade]"). Furthermore, 20 (17.2%) were coded as *association* predictions (e.g., "I beat him by 22 yesterday"; "I've saved a person on Sunday for the past 3 weeks [so I will save a person this week too]"), 11 (9.5%) were coded as *noncontradiction* predictions (e.g., restating the predictive thought or simply agreeing with it; e.g., "[there will be some crazy happenings at a party] because stuff like that happens"), and 3 (2.5%) were coded as scenario generation (e.g., "I can see us getting down by a few points early but then coming back strong in the second half").

The relative proportion of the types of predictions and explanation strategies should be interpreted with caution. With the relatively small number of predictions chosen (20 each across nine people), these proportions might not be representative. Additionally, the proportions may be influenced by the diary methodology. For instance, specified-outcome (Type O) predictions might be the most frequent in this sample because starting conditions for familiar outcomes are often left implicit. Relative proportions of prediction types and explanatory strategies notwithstanding, these results do suggest that the proposed prediction typology characterizes people's naturally occurring predictions quite well[4] and that people rely on all four proposed explanatory strategies when constructing or analyzing predictions.

Our next step was to examine more systematically whether explanatory strategies vary by type of prediction and by content domain. To this end, we interviewed 11 participants and asked them to generate or evaluate a total of nine predictions. We created the prediction question so that they fell into a 3 (domain) × 3 (prediction type) design. Predictions were of Type SO, Type O, and Type S. Domains included (1) natural or physical events (e.g., occurrence of tornadoes in a region, the spouting of geysers), (2) the actions of strangers (e.g., the United States Congress, the university basketball team), and (3) the actions of intimates (i.e., close others—friends, family—and the self). An example of a prediction question is: "How likely is it that the United States government will find Osama bin Laden?" (Type O prediction in the strangers domain). Participants' responses to each prediction question were coded into one of the four explanatory strategies (noncontradiction, association, derivability, or scenario generation).

The data were analyzed using a repeated measures analysis of variance on the number of times participants provided a specific explanatory strategy by domain and prediction. Of note, there was a main effect for explanatory strategies such that scenario generation-based predictions ($M = .13$) were listed least frequently and association-based predictions ($M = .50$) were listed most frequently. Noncontradiction-based predictions ($M = .14$) and derivability-based predictions showed intermediate frequency ($M = .22$).

There was also a significant interaction between explanatory strategies and domain. The results, displayed in Figure 11.1, are somewhat complex but show distinct patterns for the four explanatory strategies. Noncontradiction-based predictions tended to be provided significantly more in the nature domain ($M =$

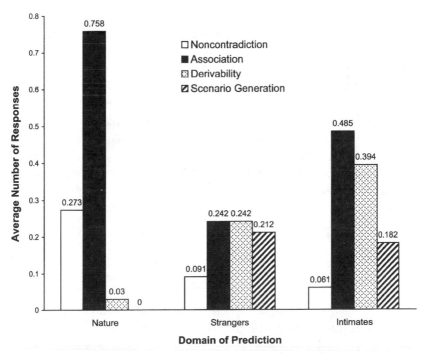

Figure 11.1. Predictions based on different explanatory strategies function as a domain of prediction.

.27) than in the human domain ($M = .08$). Association-based predictions were also listed significantly more often in the nature domain ($M = .76$) than in the human domain ($M = .36$) and significantly more often for intimates ($M = .49$) than for strangers ($M = .24$). Derivability-based predictions were provided significantly more often in the human domain ($M = .32$) than in the nature domain ($M = .03$). Finally, scenario generation predictions occurred significantly more often in the human domain ($M = .20$) than in the nature domain ($M = 0$).

These results suggest that people use explanatory strategies differently depending on the domain of prediction. Noncontradiction and association strategies appear to be preferred over derivability and scenario generation strategies in the nature domain, presumably because it is easier to predict natural events by either associating past occurrences or simply finding no good reason why it should not happen again in the future. Derivations and scenarios, in contrast, might be harder to generate in the nature domain because undergraduate students normally do not have extensive knowledge about such topics as weather patterns, behavior of sharks, or the functioning of geysers.

In the human domain, noncontradiction-based predictions are close to zero, but, for strangers, the three other explanatory strategies occur equally often. This result suggests that when predicting human action for those with whom the predictor has little familiarity, elaborated inference strategies and simulation are equally preferred. Yet association explanations show a further familiarity effect such that they are used even more to predict the behavior of intimates. This finding makes sense to the extent that people have more past history information about close friends, family, and the self than about sports teams or congressional bodies. The lack of a difference between strangers and intimates in using derivability and scenario generation suggest that these two strategies work well for predicting the behaviors for people in general—well known or not.

In sum, these initial studies provide some basis for adopting a model of prediction that distinguishes between multiple types of prediction and multiple explanatory strategies in service of prediction. Moreover, the use of these strategies appears to vary with task, domain, and knowledge. In the concluding section, we relate the folk-conceptual theory of explanation to this new model of prediction and ask more generally to what extent prediction and explanation are served by the same psychological processes.

Summary and Conclusion

We have introduced a model of prediction that postulates two kinds of cognitive processes with which people construct predictions: simulation and inference. We elaborated the category of inference by distinguishing assessment of noncontradiction, reliance on association, and derivation from principles. In the section on explanations, we introduced a number of psychological pro-

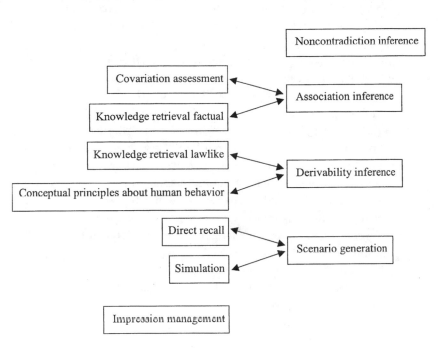

Processes in Explanations   **Processes in Prediction**

Figure 11.2. Unique and shared cognitive processes in explanation and prediction.

cesses that underlie explanations, in particular impression management, retrieval from knowledge structures, direct recall, simulation, and covariation assessment. It is now time to relate these two sets of processes. Our claim is that explanations and predictions overlap to a considerable extent because they share a number of cognitive processes—processes that support the agent's attempt to construct the judgment at issue, whether it be an explanation or a prediction.

Figure 11.2 shows the psychological processes that we identified as underlying explanations and predictions, respectively. Some processes are unique to explanations, and at least one process is unique to predictions; but the two kinds of judgments have at least three processes in common. Their labels are different, but the cognitive operations they point to are the same.

First, covariation assessment and factual knowledge retrieval in explanations correspond to association-based prediction. In all of these cases, stored knowledge about past events and their co-occurrence supports the goal of explaining or predicting. Second, explanations based on retrieval of lawlike knowledge or reliance on conceptual principles (e.g., that reasons engender intentions) correspond to derivability-based predictions. In these cases, given information is connected with unknown information by means of laws or principles. Third, simulation and direct recall of explanations correspond to scenario generation for predictions. Here, the person mentally goes through the actual steps (e.g., of belief-desire reasoning) that explain or predict the outcome in question.

More generally, both explanations and predictions are underdetermined by the data—that is, the available information does not favor a single explanation or prediction. For explanations we know the outcome but not the starting conditions, and for predictions we know the starting conditions but not the outcome. Events in closed physical systems may be the extreme case in which explanation and prediction are, as Hempel and Oppenheim (1948) proposed, symmetric. However, in everyday situations, in which people explain human action and experience, institutional events, and complex natural patterns, predictions are more underdetermined because the unknown (the outcome) has not yet happened. Predictions' more serious underdetermination also results in their being cognitively more demanding (Bartsch, 1998; Robinson & Mitchell, 1995; Moses & Flavell, 1990) and less accurate (Clarke & Blake, 1997).

In addition to this difference in underdetermination, the functions of explanations and predictions differ as well. The thirst for meaning inherent in explanations (Malle, 2004) is powerful and cannot be quenched by predictions alone. Predictions may provide hope for reaching an understanding (as when scientific theories make competing predictions and wait for reality to select one as correct), but it is the explanation following the outcome that provides meaning. Explanations can also settle social tension and uncertainty, whereas predictions normally cannot. Finally, predictions when paired with *intentions* can support social coordination, whereas explanations cannot by themselves solve coordination problems because these problems necessarily reach into the future.

These differences notwithstanding, this chapter has emphasized the similarities between explanation and prediction—similarities that exist primarily at the cognitive level. In attempting to master the social and physical world, the human mind relies on a toolbox of cognitive strategies and operations of which some uniquely support explanations, some uniquely support predictions, but a good number support both.

Acknowledgments

Thanks to Lisa A. Johnson and Meghan Bean for coding the explanatory strategies in the described studies.

Notes

1. This prediction seemingly contradicts the studies in the literature that found increasing self-servingness for explanations of achievement outcomes over time. But as we argued earlier, unintentional outcomes and intentional actions may be differentially affected by passing time. Relatedly, a self-serving bias is not a result of impression management but an opportunity to exploit ambiguity and vague memories for self-protective purposes. In fact, if participants in the achievement outcome studies were managing their impressions in front of a real audience, they might not present themselves as self-serving but as modest.

2. This situation may be comparable to a visual perspective switch in which an actor sees herself on video as if from an observer's viewpoint (famously manipulated by Storms, 1973). In a recent study we found that switching actors' visual perspective this way increases their use of mental state markers for their own belief reasons ("I thought"; "I assumed"), more than doubling their normally quite low frequency of marker use (Malle, Heim, & Knorek, 2005).

3. One can say, however, "Because I have seen him react to conflict before, *I believe that* Joe is going to be scared," making the claim and its backing transparent.

4. Although we did not observe any unspecified (Type U) predictions, recall that our discussion of the typology suggests that people may turn such predictions into one of the other three types, consequently making the expected frequency of Type U predictions very low.

References

Abelson, R. P., & Lalljee, M. (1988). Knowledge structures and causal explanations. In D. J. Hilton (Ed.), *Contemporary science and natural explanation: Commonsense conceptions of causality* (pp. 175–203). Brighton, UK: Harvester.

Abramson, L. Y., Seligman, M. E. P., & Teasdale, J. D. (1978). Learned helplessness in humans: Critique and reformulation. *Journal of Abnormal Psychology, 87*, 49–74.

Ahn, W., Kalish, C. W., Medin, D. L., & Gelman, S. A. (1995). The role of covariation versus mechanism information in causal attribution. *Cognition, 54*, 299–352.

Andrews, K. (2003). Knowing mental states: The asymmetry of psychological prediction and explanation. In Q. Smith & A. Jokic (Eds.), *Consciousness: New philosophical perspectives* (pp. 201–219). Oxford: Oxford University Press.

Baird, J. A., & Baldwin, D. A. (2001). Making sense of human behavior: Action parsing and intentional inference. In B. F. Malle, L. J. Moses, & D. A. Baldwin (Eds.), *Intentions and intentionality: Foundations of social cognition* (pp. 193–206). Cambridge, MA: MIT Press.

Bartsch, K. (1998). False belief prediction and explanation: Which develops first and why it matters. *International Journal of Behavioral Development, 22*, 423–428.

Brewer, W. F. (1994). Autobiographical memory and survey research. In N. Schwarz

& S. Sudman (Ed.), *Autobiographical memory and the validity of retrospective reports* (pp. 11–20). New York: Springer.

Burger, J. M. (1985). Temporal effects on attributions for academic performances and reflected-glory basking. *Social Psychology Quarterly, 48,* 330–336.

Burger, J. M. (1986). Temporal effects on attributions: Actor and observer differences. *Social Cognition, 4,* 377–387.

Burger, J. M. (1991). Changes in attributions over time: The ephemeral fundamental attribution error. *Social Cognition, 9,* 182–193.

Burger, J. M., & Huntzinger, R. M. (1985). Temporal effects on attributions for one's own behavior: The role of task outcome. *Journal of Experimental Social Psychology, 21,* 247–261.

Burger, J. M., & Pavelich, J. L. (1994). Attributions for presidential elections: The situational shift over time. *Basic and Applied Social Psychology, 15,* 359–371.

Burger, J. M., & Rodman, J. L. (1983). Attributions of responsibility for group tasks: The egocentric bias and the actor-observer difference. *Journal of Personality and Social Psychology, 45,* 1232–1242.

Buss, A. R. (1978). Causes and reasons in attribution theory: A conceptual critique. *Journal of Personality and Social Psychology, 36,* 1311–1321.

Bybee, J., Perkins, R., & Pagliuca, W. (1994). *The evolution of grammar: Tense, aspect, and modality in the languages of the world.* Chicago: University of Chicago Press.

Clarke, D. D., & Blake, H. (1997). The inverse forecast effect. *Journal of Social Behavior and Personality, 12,* 999–1018.

Cohen, L. B., Rundell, L. J., Spellman, B. A., & Cashon, C. H. (1999). Infants' perception of causal chains. *Psychological Science, 10,* 412–418.

Davies, E. C. (1979). *On the semantics of syntax: Mood and condition in English.* London: Croom Helm.

Dawes, R. M. (1998). Behavioral decision making and judgment. In D. T. Gilbert, S. T. Fiske, & G. Lindzey (Eds.), *The handbook of social psychology* (4th ed., vol. 1, pp. 497–548). New York: McGraw-Hill.

Frank, M. G., & Gilovich, T. (1989). Effect of memory perspective on retrospective causal attributions. *Journal of Personality and Social Psychology, 57,* 399–403.

Funder, D. C., & Van Ness, M. J. (1983). On the nature and accuracy of attributions that change over time. *Journal of Personality, 51,* 17–33.

German, T. P., & Leslie, A. M. (2000). Attending to and learning about mental states. In P. Mitchell & K. J. Riggs (Eds.), *Children's reasoning and the mind* (pp. 229–252). London: Psychological Press.

Gilbert, D. T., Lieberman, M. D., Morewedge, C. K., & Wilson, T. D. (2004). The peculiar longevity of things not so bad. *Psychological Science, 15,* 14–19.

Goldman, A. I. (1989). Interpretation psychologized. *Mind and Language, 4,* 161–185.

Goldman, A. I. (2001). Desire, intention, and the simulation theory. In B. F. Malle, L. J. Moses, & D. A. Baldwin (Eds.), *Intentions and intentionality: Foundations of social cognition* (pp. 207–225). Cambridge, MA: MIT Press.

Gopnik, A., & Wellman, H. M. (1994). The theory theory. In L. A. Hirschfeld and S. A. Gelman (Eds.), *Mapping the mind: Domain specificity in cognition and culture* (pp. 257–293). New York: Cambridge University Press.

Gordon, R. M. (1986). Folk psychology as simulation. *Mind and Language, 1*, 158–171.

Gordon, R. M. (1992). The simulation theory: Objections and misconceptions. *Mind and Language, 7*, 11–34.

Grice, H. P. (1975). Logic and conversation. In P. Cole & J. L. Morgan (Eds.), *Syntax and semantics: Vol. 3. Speech acts* (pp. 41–58). New York: Academic Press.

Heider, F. (1958). *The psychology of interpersonal relations.* New York: Wiley.

Hempel, C. G., & Oppenheim, P. (1948). Studies in the logic of explanation. *Philosophy of Science, 15*, 135–175.

Jones, E. E., & Davis, K. E. (1965). From acts to dispositions: The attribution process in person perception. In L. Berkowitz (Ed.), *Advances in experimental social psychology* (Vol. 2, pp. 219–266). New York: Academic Press.

Kahneman, D., & Tversky, A. (1973). On the psychology of prediction. *Psychological Review, 80*, 237–251.

Kahneman, D., & Tversky, A. (1982a). Intuitive prediction: Biases and corrective procedures. In D. Kahneman, P. Slovic, & A. Tversky (Eds.), *Judgment under uncertainty: Heuristics and biases* (pp. 414–421). New York: Cambridge University Press.

Kahneman, D., & Tversky, A. (1982b). The simulation heuristic. In D. Kahneman, P. Slovic, & A. Tversky (Eds.), *Judgment under uncertainty: Heuristics and biases* (pp. 201–210). New York: Cambridge University Press.

Kelley, H. H. (1967). Attribution theory in social psychology. In D. Levine (Ed.), *Nebraska Symposium on Motivation* (Vol. 15, pp. 192–240). Lincoln: University of Nebraska Press.

Knobe, J., & Malle, B. F. (2002). Self and other in the explanation of behavior: 30 years later. *Psychologica Belgica, 42*, 113–130.

Lau, R. R. (1984). Dynamics of the attribution process. *Journal of Personality and Social Psychology, 46*, 1017–1028.

MacDonald, T. K., & Ross, M. (1999). Assessing the accuracy of predictions about dating relationships: How and why do lovers' predictions differ from those made by observers? *Personality and Social Psychology Bulletin, 25*, 1417–1429.

Malle, B. F. (1999). How people explain behavior: A new theoretical framework. *Personality and Social Psychology Review, 3*, 23–48.

Malle, B. F. (2001). Folk explanations of intentional action. In B. F. Malle, L. J. Moses, & D. A. Baldwin (Eds.), *Intentions and intentionality: Foundations of social cognition* (pp. 265–286). Cambridge, MA: MIT Press.

Malle, B. F. (2002). Verbs of interpersonal causality and the folk theory of mind and behavior. In M. Shibatani (Ed.), *The grammar of causation and interpersonal manipulation* (pp. 57–83). Amsterdam: Benjamins.

Malle, B. F. (2004). *How the mind explains behavior: Folk explanations, meaning, and social interaction.* Cambridge, MA: MIT Press.

Malle, B. F. (2005). *The actor-observer asymmetry in causal attribution: A (surprising) meta-analysis.* Manuscript in preparation.

Malle, B. F. (in press). Self-other asymmetries in behavior explanations: Myth and reality. In M. D. Alicke, D. Dunning, & J. I. Krueger (Eds.), *The self in social perception* (pp. 155–178). New York: Psychology Press.

Malle, B. F., Heim, K., Knorek, J. (2005). *Storms revisited: Visual perspective and actor-observer asymmetries in explanation.* Manuscript in preparation.

Malle, B. F., & Ickes, W. (2000). Fritz Heider: Philosopher and psychologist. In G. A. Kimble & M. Wertheimer (Eds.), *Portraits of pioneers in psychology* (Vol. 4, pp. 193–214). Washington, DC: American Psychological Assoication.

Malle, B. F., & Knobe, J. (1997a). The folk concept of intentionality. *Journal of Experimental Social Psychology, 33,* 101–121.

Malle, B. F., & Knobe, J. (1997b). Which behaviors do people explain? A basic actor-observer asymmetry. *Journal of Personality and Social Psychology, 72,* 288–304.

Malle, B. F., & Knobe, J. (2001). The distinction between desire and intention: A folk-conceptual analysis. In B. F. Malle, L. J. Moses, & D. A. Baldwin (Eds.), *Intentions and intentionality: Foundations of social cognition* (pp. 45–67). Cambridge, MA: MIT Press.

Malle, B. F., Knobe, J., & Nelson, S. (2005). *Actor-observer asymmetries in folk explanations of behavior: New answers to an old question.* Manuscript in preparation.

Malle, B. F., Knobe, J., O'Laughlin, M., Pearce, G. E., & Nelson, S. E. (2000). Conceptual structure and social functions of behavior explanations: Beyond person—situation attributions. *Journal of Personality and Social Psychology, 79,* 309–326.

McClure, J. (2002). Goal-based explanations of actions and outcomes. In W. Stroebe & M. Hewstone (Eds.), *European review of social psychology* (Vol. 12, pp. 201–235). Wiley.

McClure, J., & Hilton, D. (1997). For you can't always get what you want: When preconditions are better explanations than goals. *British Journal of Social Psychology, 36,* 223–240.

Mele, A. R. (1992). *Springs of action: Understanding intentional behavior.* New York: Oxford University Press.

Mele, A. R. (2003). *Motivation and agency.* New York: Oxford University Press.

Miller, D. T., & Porter, C. A. (1980). Effects of temporal perspective on the attribution process. *Journal of Personality and Social Psychology, 34,* 532–541.

Moore, B. S., Sherrod, D. R., Liu, T. J., & Underwood, B. (1979). The dispositional shift in attribution over time. *Journal of Personality and Social Psychology, 15,* 553–569.

Moses, L. J., & Flavell, J. H. (1990). Inferring false beliefs from actions and reactions. *Child Development, 61,* 929–945.

Nelson, S., & Malle, B. F. (2005). *Self-serving biases in explanations of intentional behavior.* Manuscript in preparation.

Nigro, G., & Neisser, U. (1983). Point of view in personal memories. *Cognitive Psychology, 15,* 467–482.

O'Laughlin, M. J., &. Malle, B. F. (2002). How people explain actions performed by groups and individuals. *Journal of Personality and Social Psychology, 82,* 33–48.

Pennington, N., & Hastie, R. (1993). Reasoning in explanation-based decision making. *Cognition, 49,* 123–163.

Peterson, D. K., & Pitz, G. F. (1986). Effects of amount of information on predictions of uncertain quantities. *Acta Psychologica, 61,* 299–241.

Read, S. J. (1987). Constructing causal scenarios: A knowledge structure approach to causal reasoning. *Journal of Personality and Social Psychology, 52*, 288–302.

Reschler, N. (1997). *Predicting the future: An introduction to the theory of forecasting.* New York: State University of New York Press.

Rips, L. J. (1994). Deduction and its cognitive basis. In R. J. Sternberg (Ed.), *Thinking and problem solving* (pp. 149–178). San Diego, CA: Academic Press.

Robinson, E. J., & Mitchell, P. (1995). Masking of children's early understanding of the representational mind: Backwards explanation versus prediction. *Child Development, 66*, 1022–1039.

Russell, E. W., & D'Hollosy, M. E. (1992). Memory and attention. *Journal of Clinical Psychology, 48*, 530–538.

Salmon, W. C. (1989). *Four decades of scientific explanation.* Minneapolis, MN: University of Minnesota Press.

Sanna, L. J., & Swim, J. K. (1992). Temporal perspective and attributions: The role of causal stability and certainty. *Basic and Applied Social Psychology, 13*, 371–387.

Schwarz, N., & Bless, H. (1992). Constructing reality and its alternatives: An inclusion/exclusion model of assimilation and contrast effects in social judgments. In L. L. Martin & A. Tesser (Eds.), *The construction of social judgments* (pp. 217–245). Hillsdale, NJ: Erlbaum.

Sloman, S. (1996). The empirical case for two reasoning systems. *Psychological Bulletin, 119*, 3–22.

Slovic, P. (Ed.). (2000). *The perception of risk.* Sterling, VA: Earthscan.

Snook, B., Canter, D., & Bennell, C. (2002). Predicting the home location of serial offenders: A preliminary comparison of the accuracy of human judges with a geographic profiling system. *Behavioral Sciences and the Law, 20*, 109–118.

Storms, M. D. (1973). Videotape and the attribution process: Reversing actors' and observers' points of view. *Journal of Personality and Social Psychology, 27*, 165–175.

Truchot, D., Maure, G., & Patte, S. (2003). Do attributions change over time when the actor's behavior is hedonically relevant to the perceiver? *Journal of Social Psychology, 143*, 202–208.

Weiner, B. (1985). An attributional theory of achievement-related emotion and motivation. *Psychological Review, 29*, 548–573.

Windschitl, P. D., & Wells, G. L. (1998). The alternative-outcomes effect. *Journal of Personality and Social Psychology, 75*, 1411–1423.

Wright, E. F., & Wells, G. L. (1985). Does group discussion attenuate the dispositional bias? *Journal of Applied Social Psychology, 15*, 531–546.

Zeelenberg, M. (1999). Anticipated regret, expected feedback and behavioral decision making. *Journal of Behavioral Decision Making, 12*, 93–106.

12

Looking Backward With an Eye on the Future

Propositions Toward a Theory of Regret Regulation

MARCEL ZEELENBERG
RIK PIETERS

Regret is the emotion we feel when we realize or imagine that our present situation would have been better had we made different decisions. It is a negative emotion reflecting a retrospective evaluation of a decision. It is an awful feeling, coupled with a clear sense of self-blame concerning its causes and strong wishes to undo the current situation. Regret is also a universal experience that people like to avoid, deny, or suppress but try to manage or regulate when they are experiencing it.

This regulatory aspect of regret has not yet received much systematic attention, though studies are surely available. Research findings are scattered across different fields, and the only systematic treatment of regret was published more than 10 years ago (Landman, 1993), before the bulk of experimental work was published. This increased attention is easily demonstrated by the following simple exercise.

We searched for articles that mentioned regret in either the title or abstract via Web applications such as Web of Science, PsychLit, EconLit, REPEC, and JSTOR. We tracked the number of articles per year to show the development of interest in regret in academic publications since 1945. The result is offered in Figure 12.1. Clearly, our coarse procedure may have missed some relevant articles and picked up some irrelevant ones, but the trend is unmistakably: From the 1990s onwards, there has been a sharp increase in publications on regret. This increase has produced many robust findings, some of which are reviewed in the next sections.

Here, we attempt to provide an overview of the relevant studies and theoriz-

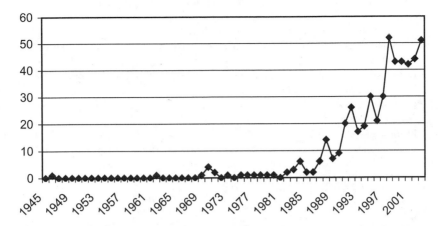

Figure 12.1. Interest in regret over time: Growth of publications. Note: Based on a survey of publication databases.

ing by advancing a set of seven propositions that both capture the current state of the art in the research on regret, and—we hope—stimulate further research about this highly relevant and consequential emotion. The propositions are presented in Table 12.1, and they form the common thread in the sections to come. They also form the basis of our theory of regret regulation, which we develop in this chapter. Our theory is a pragmatic theory that stresses that emotions exist for the sake of behavioral guidance. Put differently, the theory assumes that "feeling is for doing" (Zeelenberg & Pieters, in press). Such an approach is needed to understand what the experience of regret entails, which behaviors it motivates, and how it can shape subsequent decision making. Our regret regulation theory thus acknowledges that regret bridges the past and the future in the present. The theory is still embryonic—this is our first attempt to write it down—and hence it should be handled with care. Before turning to the propositions that are the building blocks of our theory, let us start by examining how common and aversive regret actually is to decision makers.

The Universality of Regret

Regret is a widespread emotion that all of us seem familiar with. Barry Cadish (2001) published a book called *Damn! Reflections on Life's Biggest Regrets* based on personal regrets that were provided by adults and teenagers from different countries via the website RegretsOnly.com. He concluded that "regrets are universal; nearly everyone has them. Regrets transcend age, gender, race, culture,

Table 12.1.   Propositions Concerning the Experience and Regulation of Regret

1. Regret is an aversive, cognitive emotion that people are motivated to regulate.
2. Regret is experienced when people realize or imagine that their present situation would have been better had they decided differently in the past.
3. Regret is distinct from other specific emotions, such as disappointment, and from general negative affect on the basis of its phenomenology and behavioral consequences.
4. Regret can be experienced about past ("retrospective regret") and future ("anticipated or prospective regret") decisions.
5. Regret can be experienced about decision processes ("process regret") and decision outcomes ("outcome regret").
6. Regret aversion is distinct from risk aversion.
7. Regret regulation strategies are decision-, alternative-, or feeling-focused and implemented based on their accessibility and their instrumentality to the current overarching goal.

nationality, religion, language, social status, and geographic location" (p. 2). The ubiquity of regret is also apparent in a study of verbal expressions of emotions. Shimanoff (1984) found that regret was the most frequently named negative emotion (only love was mentioned more frequently). In fact, Festinger (1964, p. 99) already suggested this when discussing the nature of postdecisional dissonance: "Phenomenally, such salience of dissonance might be experienced as a feeling of regret, something that most of us have felt, probably, at one time or another."

From a theoretical stance, as well, it has been suggested that regret is prevalent (Humberstone, 1980). The idea is that some decisions are bound to produce regret. Betting on a horse race (or any other event) is an example of such a decision. Imagine placing a bet on a horse and losing. You may regret wasting the money. But, even if the horse wins, you may regret not having placed more money on it. Thus, whether we like it or not, the painful feeling of regret is well known to most, if not all, of us.

What Regret Is

Although we described regret at the outset of this chapter, it may still be useful to provide, in somewhat more detail, what the experience of regret entails (see also Gilovich & Medvec, 1995, and Landman, 1993). First, regret is generally not considered to be one of the basic emotions. This probably stems from the fact that it is a rather complex emotional experience that both stems from and produces higher order cognitive processes. Feeling regret requires the ability to imagine other possibilities than the current state of the world. One has to reflect on one's choices and the outcomes generated by these choices, but one also has to reflect on what other outcomes might have been obtained by making a different choice. Put differently, regret is a counterfactual emotion (Kahneman & Miller, 1986).

Because of the cognitive complexity, the ability to feel regret is acquired relatively late in our emotional development. Babies can feel fear, anger, and sadness, but regret arises roughly at the age of 7. In a study by Guttentag and Ferrell (2004), it was found that the emotional responses of 7-year-olds took into account the comparison of what is with what might have been, whereas those of 5-year-olds did not.

Taking these findings together, we conceive of regret as a cognitive emotion (instead of an emotional cognition) because it contains all the elements that are typical of emotional experiences, as we explain next. This conception leads to the first proposition.

Proposition 1: *Regret is an aversive, cognitive emotion that people are motivated to regulate.*

An important issue in understanding regret and its regulatory processes is the question of how it feels. What is the phenomenology of this emotion? What is its experiential content? This is vital information if one is interested in the behavioral consequences of regret, because the experiential content of an emotion contains and expresses its motivational components (Zeelenberg & Pieters, in press). According to Roseman, Wiest, and Swartz (1994), the experiential content consists of feelings, thoughts, emotivational goals, action tendencies, and actions. Feelings are perceived physical or mental sensations. Feelings include all sorts of subjective experiences, such as feeling a lump in the throat (in case of sadness) and feeling ready to explode (in case of anger). Thoughts refer to ideas, conceptions, or opinions produced by mental activity. Emotivational goals describe the aims or ends that govern discrete emotions (wanting to avoid danger in case of fear, or wanting to recover from loss in case of sadness). Action tendencies are impulses or inclinations to respond with a particular action to the situation at hand. Actions include actual behavior that may or may not be purposive. Although emotivational goals, action tendencies, and actions are all motivational in quality, they vary in degree of concreteness and implementation, with emotivational goals being more abstract states to strive for and actions being more concrete and implemented to attain the emotivational goal.

Regret comprises the following experiential qualities (Roseman et al. 1994; Zeelenberg, Van Dijk, Manstead, & Van der Pligt, 1998): It is accompanied by feelings that one should have known better, by a sinking feeling, by thoughts about the mistake one has made and the opportunities lost, by tendencies to kick oneself and to correct one's mistake, by wanting to undo the event and get a second chance, and by actually doing this if given the opportunity. Put differently, regret is experienced as an aversive state that focuses our attention on our own role in the occurrence of a regretted outcome. It is thus a cognitively based emotion that motivates us to think about how the negative event could have happened and how we could change it, or how we could prevent its future occurrence. Together, these characteristics imply:

Proposition 2: *Regret is experienced when people realize or imagine that their present situation would have been better had they decided differently in the past.*

Proposition 2 reflects two important preconditions for regret: first, an element of personal agency, and second, the realization that another decision would have been better. Regret is not experienced if one was not a causal agent or if no other decision would have led to a better outcome. We return to this idea of personal agency soon, after describing how regret differs from related emotions.

The Distinctiveness of Regret

Why would one study the specific emotion regret, rather than other specific emotions, or just the general valence of the emotional experience? The research presented by Roseman et al. (1994), Zeelenberg, Van Dijk, Manstead, and Van der Pligt (1998), and Zeelenberg and Pieters (1999, 2004a) demonstrates that regret can be distinguished from other emotional experiences (e.g., disappointment, guilt, and shame) on the basis of its experiential content and behavioral consequences. This is important because different specific emotions have been found to affect judgment and behavior in different ways (Bougie, Pieters, & Zeelenberg, 2003; Lerner & Keltner, 2000; Raghunathan & Pham, 1999). For example, in a study in which the behavioral consequences of regret and disappointment were explicitly compared, distinct effects of both emotions were found (Zeelenberg & Pieters, 1999). This study examined consumers' emotional and behavioral responses to dissatisfaction with services. Regret predicted switching to another service provider, whereas disappointment predicted complaining to the service provider and talking to others about the bad experience. Moreover, there was a tendency for higher levels of regret to result in *less* talking to others.

Regret also has different effects than does general negative affect. In a large-scale survey of consumer responses to failed services, Zeelenberg and Pieters (2004a) found that regret about having chosen a service influenced postconsumption behaviors significantly, over and above the effect of the general dissatisfaction with the service and the service provider. Thus:

Proposition 3: *Regret is distinct from other specific emotions, such as disappointment, and from general negative affect on the basis of its phenomenology and behavioral consequences.*

The role of personal agency in regret, but not in disappointment, is illustrated in Table 12.2. It depicts the choice between the actions A and B. The out-

Table 12.2. Outcomes of Actions A and B for Each Possible State of the World

Actions	States of the World			
	S1 (25%)	S2 (25%)	S3 (25%)	S4 (25%)
A	$100	$50	$25	$0
B	$0	$100	$50	$25

Note: This table depicts a choice between actions A and B, for which the outcomes depend on the state of the world that occurs. Each state of the world has a probability of 25%.

come of the two actions depends on the occurrence of one of four possible states of the world. A decision maker will feel regret after having chosen action A and state-of-the-world S2 occurs. Regret occurs because the decision maker knows that given this state of the world, action B would have resulted in a much better outcome. If we simplify this situation by taking away one of the two actions (that is, taking away the choice), decision makers cannot experience regret anymore, because they cannot compare the outcomes of different actions.

Disappointment, also a counterfactual emotion, is assumed to originate from a comparison between the factual outcome and an outcome that might have been had another state of the world occurred. A decision maker would feel disappointment if he or she chose action B and state-of-the-world S4 occurred. The outcome obtained in this combination, $25, is worse than the majority of outcomes that would have occurred in another state of the world. Note that although one should experience disappointment when confronted with this outcome, one should not experience regret, because the outcome of the rejected action would be even worse. Also note that when we take away choice, decision makers can still feel disappointment when the obtained outcome is lower than expected. To summarize, one may be disappointed by the rainy weather (which is beyond our control), but one cannot regret it (although one may regret the decision not to carry an umbrella).

This strong link between regret and choice also clarifies the relation between the experience of regret and the responsibility for the negative decision outcome, and it is consistent with many other studies in the field of emotion theory (Frijda, Kuipers, & Ter Schure, 1989; Gilovich & Medvec, 1995). Regret is directly related to personal agency in choice, and without choice there would be no regret. In this respect, regret is a unique emotion.

Lineage and Types of Regret

Regret has attracted research attention in many domains, both theoretical and applied. Examples are marketing (Inman, Dyer, & Jia, 1997; Simonson, 1992), law (Guthrie, 1999; Prentice & Koehler, 2003), organizational behavior (Goerke, Moller, & Schulz-Hardt, 2004; Maitlis & Ozcelik, 2004), medicine (Brehaut et al., 2003; Djulbegovic, Hozo, Schwartz, & McMasters, 1999), cross-cultural psychology (Gilovich, Wang, Regan, & Nishina, 2003) and neuroeconomics (Camille, Coricelli, Sallet, Pradat-Diehl, Duhamel, & Sirigu, 2004; Coricelli, Critchley, Joffily, O'Doherty, Sirigu, & Dolan, 2005), and of course the disciplines in which regret research sprouted, economics (Bell, 1982, Loomes & Sugden, 1982), and psychology (Kahneman & Tversky, 1982).

Interest in regret originated in the literature on economic decision making. Researchers in this field have argued that we may base our decisions on a "minimax regret" principle (e.g., Luce & Raiffa, 1957; Savage, 1951). According to this principle, one first computes the maximum of possible regret for each option (regret is defined as the difference between the actual outcome of the chosen option and the highest possible outcome of the rejected options). Then one chooses the option with the lowest maximum regret. This minimax regret has been criticized as being overly pessimistic because it ignores the probabilities of the possible outcomes and may hence be relevant only in cases of complete uncertainty.

The later developed regret theories in economics (Bell, 1982; Loomes & Sugden, 1982; Sage & White, 1983; see also Larrick, 1993) took the probability of regret into account to provide a more plausible account for the influence of regret. Direct tests of predictions derived from regret theory did not provide unequivocal support (e.g., Harless, 1992; Leland, 1998; Starmer & Sugden, 1993), but the main psychological assumptions have been supported (for a review, see Zeelenberg, 1999). These assumptions are that we may experience emotions as a consequence of our decisions. Decision makers experience regret when they know that the outcome of the rejected option would have been better and rejoicing when they know that the outcome of the rejected option would have been worse. Another assumption is that these emotions have an impact on how we evaluate decision outcomes. And the most important assumption is that this impact of regret is taken into account before we decide and thus may play an important role in determining what we choose.

Parallel to the developments in economics, psychological research focused on questions such as: Do we regret our actions more than our inactions (Gilovich & Medvec, 1995; Kahneman & Tversky 1982; Zeelenberg, van den Bos, van Dijk, & Pieters, 2002)? What are the things we regret (Landman, 1993)? How does regret relate to counterfactual thinking (Roese, 1997; Sanna, Carter, & Small, this volume; Zeelenberg, Van Dijk, Van der Pligt, et al., 1998)? How does regret differ from related emotions?

Interestingly, economists and psychologists appear to have started out studying regret for different reasons, or they initially studied different types of regret. Economists were primarily interested in how effects of possible future regret affect our current decisions, and thus they focused on prospective or anticipated regrets. This is understandable given their focus on predicting future choice.

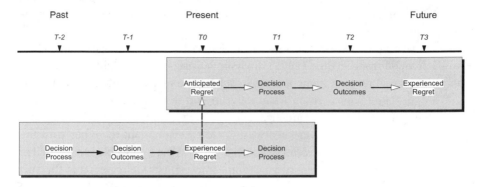

Figure 12.2. Experience and regulation of regret over time.

Psychologists, on the other hand, more often studied the antecedents and consequences of regret that is currently experienced, and thus they focused on retrospective regrets. Nowadays, researchers from different fields study both types of regret, retrospective and prospective regret. We express the existence of these different regrets as:

> Proposition 4: *Regret can be experienced about past ("retrospective regret") and future ("anticipated or prospective regret") decisions.*

Figure 12.2 clarifies the distinction between these two different regrets and how they are related. There is some discussion about whether anticipated regret is an emotion or a mere (cognitive) prediction about an emotion. Frijda (2004), as a case in point, believes that anticipated emotions, including anticipated regret, are predictions, referring to them as "virtual emotions." We believe that to the extent that the prospect of future regret feeds into the present experience, and thus acquires the experiential qualities of any other emotion, it is an emotion, albeit cognitively based. Figure 12.2 indicates how anticipated regret about future decisions may depend on experienced regret about the past, as when people who regret having lost a bet on a horse in the previous race contemplate how to decide for the next.

Objects of Regret

As proposition 2 expressed, regret is experienced when decisions go awry. Yet which aspect of decisions is regretted? We argue that, in addition to the decision outcomes, the decision process may independently produce regret. That is, a decision process that is bad in comparison to an alternative decision process can be regretted even if the decision outcomes are good. Figure 12.2 expresses the two sources of regret and how they may affect both anticipated and experienced regret.

An example of how one may still experience regret despite a good outcome is borrowed from Sugden (1985). Imagine leaving a party slightly intoxicated. You decide to drive home and do so safely. The morning after, however, you might regret your decision when reflecting on what might have occurred. In line with this example, Connolly and Zeelenberg (2002) postulated two components of regret, one associated with outcome evaluation, the other with the feeling of having made a choice poorly. Regret, taken as a whole, is supposed to be a combination of these two decision components: One regrets that the outcome contrasts poorly with the counterfactual outcome and/or that the decision was made in an unjustified way.

We recently tested the idea of two sources of regret in the context of intention-behavior consistency (Pieters & Zeelenberg, 2005). More precisely, we examined the regret that people experience when they behave in ways not originally intended. These studies show that intention-behavior inconsistency, which is often hard to justify, amplifies regret independent of the outcomes of the behavior. This inconsistency effect was obtained in different research contexts: using a scenario approach, asking people about autobiographical memories of regrettable events, and via a longitudinal study of a significant real-life decision, namely, voting in national elections. The results of these studies clearly indicated that a bad decision process had an impact on regret independent of the quality of the decision outcomes. In fact, the crucial mediating factor was whether the decision process was judged to be sensible and wise, that is, justifiable. These findings may explain other effects of decision processes on regret (see also Inman & Zeelenberg, 2002), which we are currently investigating. Proposition 5 concerns the objects of regret.

Proposition 5: *Regret can be experienced about decision processes ("process regret") and decision outcomes ("outcome regret").*

Risk Versus Regret

Regret aversion has sometimes been equated to risk aversion, as illustrated by the saying that one should be "better safe than sorry." A series of studies has demonstrated that anticipated regret can promote both risk-avoiding and risk-seeking tendencies (Zeelenberg et al., 1996; Zeelenberg & Pieters, 2004b). Which tendency prevails, risk seeking or risk avoidance, depends on which option shields the decision maker from feedback on forgone outcomes. Zeelenberg et al. (1996) found that when participants were given a choice between a risky and a safe gamble, those who expected to receive feedback on the safe option, regardless of their choice, were likely to choose this safe option. They thereby protected themselves from potentially threatening feedback on the forgone outcome. Likewise, those who expected to receive feedback on the risky option tended to choose the risky option. This is summarized in the following:

Proposition 6: *Regret aversion is distinct from risk aversion.*

Thus decision makers are motivated to avoid regret but are unlikely to always succeed in this. One reason is the sheer amount of decisions that we have to make. No one will make the right choice in all of those. And, as we argued earlier, some decisions will always produce regret. How do we cope with these regrets?

What If Decisions Go or Might Go Awry?

Which specific strategies do decision makers use to manage their regrets over time? This question is central in the development of our theory of regret regulation. According to this theory, the experiential qualities of regret (proposition 3) contain the seeds of the strategies that people use to regulate regret. People want to undo the decision and kick themselves when they experience regret, and its aversiveness stimulates specific behaviors to prevent regret (proposition 6). Because there is, as yet, little systematic research on regret regulation strategies, the proposed theory should be considered conjectural.

Proposition 7: *Regret regulation strategies are decision-, alternative-, or feeling-focused and implemented based on their accessibility and their instrumentality to the current overarching goal.*

The main strategic options for regret regulation are the same for anticipated and experienced regret, although the specific mechanics differ, as shown in Table 12.3. People can employ decision-focused, alternative-focused, and feeling-focused regulation strategies. Decision-focused strategies aim at the specific decision process and outcomes at hand. Alternative-focus strategies deal with the unchosen alternative, and feeling-focused strategies address the experience of regret directly rather than indirectly as the previous two do. We would like to stress that we expect that not all regulation strategies will be equally successful and that some actually increase long-term regret. Importantly, to date not all possible strategies have been equally extensively researched, which opens up many avenues for research.

Table 12.3.   Regret Regulation Strategies

Prevent future regret:
  1. *Decision-focused*
        a. Increase decision quality
        b. Increase decision justifiability
        c. Transfer decision responsibility
        d. Delay or avoid decision
  2. *Alternative-focused*
        a. Ensure decision reversibility
        b. Avoid feedback about forgone alternatives
  3. *Feeling-focused*
        a. Anticipate regret
Manage current regret:
  1. *Decision-focused*
        a. Undo decision
        b. Bolster decision quality
        c. Justify decision
        d. Deny responsibility for the decision
  2. *Alternative-focused*
        a. Reverse decision (switch to alternative)
        b. Reappraise quality of alternative
  3. *Feeling-focused*
        a. Suppress or deny regret

Anticipated Regret Regulation Strategies

Improve Decision Quality

To prevent future regret, people may try to improve the quality of the decision process and outcomes, for instance, by increased internal (memory) or external information search. They may also attempt to do so by applying decision rules that use as much of the available information as possible, such as a linear-compensatory one. In this way, regret stimulates increased decision effort and learning and should be conducive to reducing long-term regret, except when all the decision effort in hindsight turns out to have been in vain.

Delay or Avoid Decision

Also, people may simply delay decisions or avoid making them (Table 12.3, 1d; Janis & Mann, 1977). That is, they can become decision averse (Beattie, Baron, Hershey, & Spranca, 1994). Making no decision prevents regret, simply because one cannot make the "wrong" decisions. However, such a strategy is not likely to be useful, because many situations require a decision. Moreover, there may be long-term disadvantages to decision avoidance, because eventually we may well regret our inactive decision attitude (Gilovich & Medvec,

1995). Postponement or other kinds of decision delay have the same disadvantages as avoiding decisions. In addition, to the extent that the anticipated regret over making the wrong decision enhances rumination during the period of postponement, the decision conflict may only mount, and the resulting experienced regret may be enhanced, as well, if indeed the decision goes awry.

Increase Decision Justifiability

A fruitful way of avoiding regrets is to opt for "normal" choices. When choosing between a well-known brand and a cheaper brand, potential regret is minimized by opting for the well-known brand (Simonson, 1992). This also explains why default options produce less regret than switch decisions, at least when there is no good reason for either of the two (Inman & Zeelenberg, 2002). And it may account for the fact that intention-behavior consistency, being a "norm," lowers regret independent of the decision outcomes (Pieters & Zeelenberg 2005).

Transfer Decision Responsibility

As indicated earlier, regret arises when one is personally responsible for bad decisions. Thus one strategy to reduce future regret is transferring the responsibility of a potentially regrettable decision to others. Most frequently, this occurs when assigning responsibility to experts, such as investment advisors, marriage counselors, or partners ("I did what you told me to"). There are more strategies to deal with responsibility of anticipated future regret as well. Farnsworth (1998; p. 19), in his book on regret in the context of contract law, writes, "If you sometimes had 'past Regrets' because of unexpected difficulties in performing, you could allay your 'future Fears' by including in your agreement a force majeure clause, excusing you from performing should such difficulties arise." The link between experienced and anticipated regret in Figure 12.2 expresses this idea.

Ensure Decision Reversibility

If one cannot improve the decision quality, for example because of an inherently uncertain future, nor increase the decision justifiability, transfer responsibility to another agent, or postpone the decision, then decision makers may aim to increase the reversibility of a decision once it is taken. That is, they may anticipate future regret over being stuck with a suboptimal choice and aim for reversible choices to prevent this. Thus consumers' anticipations of regret are attenuated and their impact on choice is diminished when they receive lowest-price guarantees (McConnell et al., 2000). What's more, insurances have been shown to have similar effects (Hetts, Boninger, Armor, Gleicher, & Nathanson, 2000). Thus, when decisions or their consequences can be reversed, less regret is anticipated. Interestingly, it is not yet clear that retrospective regret is influenced in a similar way. Gilbert and Ebert (2002) recently found that people indeed prefer reversible decisions to irreversible ones but that the irreversible decisions resulted in more satisfaction, perhaps because reversibility raises counterfactual thinking, which then feeds regret.

Avoid Feedback About Forgone Alternatives

Because regret stems from outcome comparisons, decision makers can avoid regret by avoiding feedback about unchosen options. This tendency was described in the discussion of proposition 6.

Anticipate Regret

Sometimes the anticipation of possible regret is deemed to make the experience less aversive, as when people prepare to feel pain at the dentist. Put differently, when we expect the worst, it can only be better. We must note that this works only when it does not affect our choices. It can be counterproductive when, for example, it leads people to avoid decisions or to choose different options.

The regulatory aspects of anticipated regret are thus aimed at preventing regret from happening or ameliorating its potential occurrence. What happens when we do experience this emotion is described next, with a focus on strategies that differ from those for anticipated regret. Again, there are three basic strategies: decision-, alternative-, and regret-focused. Specific strategies that differ from those for anticipated regret are emphasized.

Experienced Regret Regulation Strategies

We stated and showed earlier that regret most clearly induces decision reversals or undoing behaviors. In Table 12.3 we distinguish between two specific expressions of this: undoing a decision (yes-no decision; e.g., not buying the house) and reversing a decision (multiple choice; e.g., studying law instead of literature). Although both undo the original decision, one is focused mostly on the current act and the other mostly on the alternatives. Thus they appear in two different places in Table 12.3, but they are discussed here jointly because of their resemblance. Because of their centrality to regret regulation, undoing and reversing are discussed first and more extensively than other strategies.

Undo or Reverse Decision

According to Festinger (1964), if a decision maker who experiences regret "were given the opportunity to reconsider, he should show some inclination to reverse his decision" (p. 100). Festinger and Walster (1964) induced postdecisional regret in participants and provided them with the opportunity to switch to another option. They did this by having participants in one condition rank several haircuts on attractiveness. The one ranked as most attractive could be obtained for free. Because this task implied a decision, it was expected to produce some dissonance, and hence regret. Participants in the other condition also ranked the attractiveness of the haircuts, but they were unaware of the fact that they subsequently could choose one for free. Because in this condition the ranking did not imply a decision, dissonance and the accompanying regret were expected not to appear. When the participants were subsequently asked to choose a coupon for a free haircut, it was expected that participants who knew this in advance would feel more regret and would show more decision reversals than participants who did not know in advance that they would get a haircut for free. This was indeed what Festinger and Walster found. Interestingly, the prediction that regret promotes switching is also consistent with Thibaut and Kelley's (1959, pp. 80–81) reasoning about regret in relationships. They argued that a comparison with a forgone alternative "provides a standard in terms of which decisions about remaining in or leaving the relationship are made." Recent research shows that the more we elaborate on our decisions, the stronger these effects are (Carmon, Wertenbroch & Zeelenberg, 2003).

Undoing previous decisions occurs frequently; for example, after buying a product that proves to be suboptimal, regret can motivate us to ask for our money back or to switch to another supplier of services or product the next time around (Zeelenberg, Van der Pligt, & Manstead, 1998; Zeelenberg & Pieters, 1999; 2004b). In both instances, regret can help us to satisfy our needs in the best possible way. It protects us from wasting money and helps us to maintain good social relationships. Interestingly, regret may also be functional via its influence on cognitions. Instead of going back to the shop, we can imagine various ways in which the outcome could have been more favorable to us. So regret not only helps us to remember our mistakes and missed opportunities and motivates us to engage in reparative action, but by means of mental undoing it also prepares us to behave more appropriately when we are confronted with similar choices in the future.

Sometimes decision makers show reluctance to acknowledge regret's existence. They may actively deny or suppress it. To disclose feelings of regret, it seems, is to admit failure, and that is the sign of a weak person, even outside the realms of presidential election campaigns. Classic examples of such an attitude ring through in Frank Sinatra's "My Way" and Edith Piaf's "Non je ne regrette rien." Some contemporary writings even seem to promote some sort of regret denial. In Helen Fielding's (2003) novel *Olivia Joules and the Overactive Imagination,* the main character writes down a number of rules for living. Rule 15 states, "Don't regret anything. Remember there wasn't anything else that could have happened, given who you were and the state of the world at that moment. The only thing you can change is the present, so learn from the past" (p. 94). Interestingly, her rule 16 applies when rule 15 appears to be violated: "If you start regretting something and thinking, 'I should have done . . . ' always add, 'but then I might have been run over by a lorry or blown up by a Japanese-manned torpedo' " (p. 94).

Not all regret regulation strategies have been empirically examined in detail, and this is an important topic for future research. For instance, people may bolster their decisions and downplay the rejected alternatives similarly to the ways proposed in cognitive dissonance and self-perception theories (see also Gilovich, Medvec, & Chen, 1995) in order to live with their decisions. Then they reappraise the decision process and outcomes and how these match their preferences and come to the conclusion that the chosen option is actually the best. Also, one critical way to avoid or reduce regret once the outcomes of decisions become known is to justify the chosen decision. Yet so far we know little about the conditions in which such strategies are preferred over others, and more research is dearly needed.

Toward a Theory of Regret Regulation

In this chapter we have advanced a set of propositions that capture an important element of the psychology of regret. We argued that regret is an aversive, cognitively based emotion that people are motivated to regulate. It is a functional emotion that influences decision making in ways that are relevant to our goals and concerns. Regret is experienced when people realize or imagine that their present situation would have been better had they decided differently in the past. It is distinct from other specific emotions such as disappointment, guilt, and general negative affect on the basis of its phenomenology and behavioral consequences. It can be experienced about decision processes ("process regret") and decision outcomes ("outcome regret"). It can be experienced about past ("experienced or retrospective regret") and future ("anticipated or prospective regret") decisions. Experienced regret has a retrospective element that informs us about the level of goal achievement and a prospective element in that it shapes our future behavior. Anticipated regret has a prospective element that signals us when decisions would be regrettable and a retrospective element that looks backward from the future to guide our present decisions. We have provided evidence that regret regulation strategies aim to minimize the responsibility for the decision and the availability of counterfactual information and to maximize the quality, justifiability, and reversibility of the decision and the suppression of regret. We speculate that the strategies chosen are the ones most accessible and instrumental for the current overarching goal. The seven broad propositions that we offered form the basis for a theory of regret regulation, which is currently "under construction." This theory of regret regulation should be able to explain the current findings and produce new, testable predictions concerning the regulatory processes that are associated with the experience of regret, several of which we offered here.

The Benefits of Regret Regulation

Although the direct experience of regret is aversive, it may induce decision makers to undo decisions and thereby to maximize utility. The painful experience and anticipation of regret may also lead to learning and to behavioral adaptations and thereby to avoiding future regrets. As Shefrin and Statman stated, "both the unpleasant pain of regret and the pleasurable glow of pride can lead to learning. They help us to remember clearly both bad and good choices" (1985, p. 57). Yet over and above these long-term benefits of regret for decision making over time, experiencing and expressing regret may also carry direct gains. In fact, although decision makers are often reluctant to acknowledge regret, as we showed, at other times they may be quite willing to express regret because of the expected immediate social gains. As a case in point, expressions of regret on the part of the accused may be mitigating factors in U.S. courts, and it is at the discretion of the judge to instruct the jury explicitly to take this regret into account when determining the penalty. Thus Senior Master Sergeant Larry R. Hopkins, in *United States v. Hopkins* (No. 01–0739/AF) indicated, "I have made a lot of mistakes and poor decisions," "I lost my discipline and my self-control," and "I took many actions which I now regret," and that he accepted "full responsibility" for his actions, expressed sorrow, and apologized to his unit, his commander, his friends, and his family. He was convicted and sentenced to confinement of 1 year and reduction to a lower pay grade, which he appealed as being too high because the judge had not explicitly instructed the jury to take his "I'm sorry" into account. Hopkins felt that he should have gotten less for his decisions involving assault, assault consummated by a battery, falsifying a visa application, making and uttering bad checks, dishonorable failure to pay just debts, adultery, and bigamy. Judge

Howard P. Sweeney of the United States Court of Appeals for the Armed Forces decided on April 12, 2002, that the original judge's decision was justified. Clearly, even enthusiastically voiced regrets cannot mitigate all bad decisions and their outcomes. But the more important lesson is that public expressions of regret are socially counted on and can be factored in when penalizing an individual for bad decisions. The theory of regret regulation that we called for should consider the conditions under which the experience and expression of regret are enhanced, rather than inhibited, and thus explicate when it is good to feel bad and to communicate it.

Coda

In this chapter we have argued that a pragmatic approach to regret is needed to understand the experience and regulation of regret. Regret bridges the past and the future in the present, and the theory of regret regulation builds on this. Clearly, regret is the prototypical decision-making emotion because it entails systematic attempts to maximize utility over time by comparing decision processes and outcomes to what might have been and by informing the self and others about this. Regret is also an inevitable part of life's experience, because almost any decision could have been better in hindsight, and even after having picked the right alternative, one may regret having lost the opportunity to learn about the wrong one. In fact, because it distinguishes us from other species, regret is intrinsically human. We hope that a fuller understanding of the experience of regret and its idiosyncratic regulatory processes will lead to better insight into the psychology of decision making. And this may eventually also lead to fewer regrets.

References

Beattie, J., Baron, J., Hershey, J. C., & Spranca, M. D. (1994). Psychological determinants of decision attitude. *Journal of Behavioral Decision Making, 7*, 129–144.

Bell, D. E. (1982). Regret in decision making under uncertainty. *Operations Research, 30*, 961–981.

Bougie, R., Pieters, R., & Zeelenberg, M. (2003). Angry customers don't come back, they get back: The experience and behavioral implications of anger and dissatisfaction in services. *Journal of the Academy of Marketing Sciences, 31*, 377–391.

Brehaut, J. C., O'Connor, A. M., Wood, T. J., Hack, T. F., Siminoff, L., Gordon, E., & Feldman-Stewart, D. (2003). Validation of a decision regret scale. *Medical Decision Making, 23*, 281–292.

Cadish, B. (2001). *Damn! Reflections on life's biggest regrets.* Kansas City, MO: Andrew McMeel.

Camille, N., Coricelli, G., Sallet, J., Pradat-Diehl, P., Duhamel, J. R., & Sirigu, A.

(2004). The involvement of the orbitofrontal cortex in the experience of regret. *Science, 304,* 1167–1170.

Carmon, Z., Wertenbroch, K., & Zeelenberg, M. (2003). Option attachment: When deliberating makes choosing feel like losing. *Journal of Consumer Research 30,* 15–29.

Connolly, T., & Zeelenberg, M. (2002). Regret and decision making. *Current Directions in Psychological Science, 11,* 212–216.

Coricelli, C., Critchley, H. D., Joffily, M., O'Doherty, J. P., Sirigu, A., & Dolan, R. J. (2005). Regret and its avoidance: A neuroimaging study of choice behavior. *Nature Neuroscience, 8,* 1255–1262.

Djulbegovic, B., Hozo, I., Schwartz, A., & McMasters, K. M. (1999). Acceptable regret in medical decision making. *Medical Hypotheses, 53,* 253–259.

Farnsworth, E. A. (1998). *Changing your mind: The law of regretted decisions.* New Haven, CT: Yale University Press.

Festinger, L. (1964). *Conflict, decision, and dissonance.* Stanford, CA: Stanford University Press.

Festinger, L., & Walster, E. (1964). Post-decision regret and decision reversal. In L. Festinger (Ed.), *Conflict, decision, and dissonance* (pp. 100–112). Stanford, CA: Stanford University Press.

Fielding, H. (2003). *Olivia Joules and the overactive imagination.* London: Picador.

Frijda, N. H. (2004). Emotion and action. In A.S.R. Manstead, N. H. Frijda, & A. H. Fischer (Eds.), *Feelings and emotions: The Amsterdam symposium* (pp. 158–173). Cambridge: Cambridge University Press.

Frijda, N. H., Kuipers, P., & Ter Schure, E. (1989). Relations among emotion, appraisal, and emotional action readiness. *Journal of Personality and Social Psychology, 57,* 212–228.

Gilbert, D. T., & Ebert, J. E. J. (2002). Decisions and revisions: The affective forecasting of changeable outcomes. *Journal of Personality and Social Psychology, 82,* 503–514.

Gilovich, T., & Medvec, V. H. (1995). The experience of regret: What, when, and why. *Psychological Review, 102,* 379–395.

Gilovich, T., Medvec, V. H., & Chen, S. (1995). Commission, omission and dissonance reduction: Coping with regret in the Monty Hall problem. *Personality and Social Psychology Bulletin, 21,* 182–190.

Gilovich, T., Wang, R. X. F., Regan, D., & Nishina, S. (2003). Regrets of action and inaction across cultures. *Journal of Cross-Cultural Psychology, 34,* 61–71.

Goerke, M., Moller, J., & Schulz-Hardt, S. (2004). "It's not my fault—But only I can change it": Counterfactual and prefactual thoughts of managers. *Journal of Applied Psychology, 89,* 279–292.

Guthrie, C. (1999). Better settle than sorry: The regret aversion theory of litigation behavior. *University of Illinois Law Review, 1,* 43–90.

Guttentag, R., & Ferrell, J. (2004). Reality compared with its alternatives: Age differences in judgments of regret and relief. *Developmental Psychology, 5,* 764–775.

Harless, D. W. (1992). Actions versus prospects: The effect of problem presentation on regret. *American Economic Review, 82,* 634–649.

Hetts, J. J., Boninger, D. S., Armor, D. A., Gleicher, F., & Nathanson, A. (2000). The influence of anticipated counterfactual regret on behavior. *Psychology and Marketing, 17,* 345–368.

Humberstone, I. L. (1980). You'll regret it. *Analysis, 40,* 175–176.

Inman, J. J., Dyer, J. S., & Jia, J. (1997). A generalized utility model of disappointment and regret effects on post-choice valuation. *Marketing Science, 16,* 97–111.

Inman, J. J., & Zeelenberg, M. (2002). Regret repeat versus switch decisions: The attenuation role of decision justifiability. *Journal of Consumer Research, 29,* 116–128.

Janis, I. L., & Mann, L. (1977). *Decision making.* New York: Free Press.

Kahneman, D., & Miller, D. T. (1986). Norm theory: Comparing reality to its alternatives. *Psychological Review, 93,* 136–153.

Kahneman, D., & Tversky, A. (1982). The psychology of preferences. *Scientific American, 246,* 160–173.

Landman, J. (1993). *Regret: The persistence of the possible.* New York: Oxford University Press.

Larrick, R. P. (1993). Motivational factors in decision theories: The role of self-protection. *Psychological Bulletin, 113,* 440–450.

Leland, J. W. (1998). Similarity judgments in choice under uncertainty: A reinterpretation of the predictions of regret theory. *Management Science, 44,* 659–672.

Lerner, J. S., & Keltner, D. (2000). Beyond valence: Toward a model of emotion-specific influences on judgment and choice. *Cognition and Emotion, 14,* 473–493.

Loomes, G., & Sugden, R. (1982). Regret theory: An alternative theory of rational choice under uncertainty. *Economic Journal, 92,* 805–824.

Luce, R. D., & Raiffa, H. (1957) *Games and decisions.* New York: Wiley.

Maitlis, S., & Ozcelik H. (2004). Toxic decision processes: A study of emotion and organizational decision making. *Organization Science, 15,* 375–393.

McConnell, A. R., Niedermeier, K. E., Leibold, J. M., El-Alayli, A. G., Chin, P. P., & Kuiper, N. M. (2000). What if I find it cheaper someplace else?: Role of prefactual thinking and anticipated regret in consumer behavior. *Psychology and Marketing, 17,* 281–298.

Pieters, R., & Zeelenberg, M. (2005). On bad decisions and deciding badly: When intention-behavior inconsistency is regrettable. *Organizational Behavior and Human Decision Processes, 97,* 18–30.

Prentice, R. A., & Koehler, J. J. (2003). A normality bias in legal decision making. *Cornell Law Review, 88,* 583–650.

Raghunathan, R., & Pham, M. T. (1999). All negative moods are not equal: Motivational influences of anxiety and sadness on decision making. *Organizational Behavior and Human Decision Processes, 79,* 56–77.

Roese, N. J. (1997). Counterfactual thinking. *Psychological Bulletin, 121,* 133–148.

Roseman, I. J., Wiest, C., & Swartz, T. S. (1994). Phenomenology, behaviors, and goals differentiate discrete emotions. *Journal of Personality and Social Psychology, 67,* 206–211.

Sage, A. P., & White, E. B. (1983). Decision and information structures in regret models of judgment and choice. *IEEE, Transactions on Systems, Man, and Cybernetics, 13,* 136–145.

Savage, L. J. (1951). The theory of statistical decision. *Journal of the American Statistical Association, 46*, 55–67.

Shefrin, H., & Statman, M. (1985). The disposition to sell winners too early and ride losers too long: Theory and evidence. *Journal of Finance, 40*, 777–790.

Shimanoff, S. B. (1984). Commonly named emotions in everyday conversations. *Perceptual and Motor Skills, 58*, 514.

Simonson, I. (1992). The influence of anticipating regret and responsibility on purchase decisions. *Journal of Consumer Research, 19*, 105–118.

Starmer, C., & Sugden, R. (1993). Testing for juxtaposition effects and event splitting. *Journal of Risk and Uncertainty, 6*, 235–254.

Sugden, R. (1985). Regret, recrimination and rationality. *Theory and Decision, 19*, 77–99.

Thibaut, J. W., & Kelley, H. H. (1959), *The social psychology of groups.* New York: Wiley.

United States v. Hopkins. (2002). (No. 01-0739/AF). http://www.armfor.uscourts.gov/opinions/2002Term/01-0739.pdf.

Zeelenberg, M. (1999). Anticipated regret, expected feedback and behavioral decision-making. *Journal of Behavioral Decision Making, 12*, 93–106.

Zeelenberg, M., Beattie, J., Van der Pligt, J., & de Vries, N. K. (1996). Consequences of regret aversion: Effects of expected feedback on risky decision making. *Organizational Behavior and Human Decision Processes, 65*, 148–158.

Zeelenberg, M., & Pieters, R. (1999). On service delivery that might have been: Behavioral responses to disappointment and regret. *Journal of Service Research, 2*, 86–97.

Zeelenberg, M., & Pieters, R. (2004a). Beyond valence in customer dissatisfaction: A review and new findings on behavioral responses to regret and disappointment in failed services. *Journal of Business Research, 57*, 445–455.

Zeelenberg, M., & Pieters, R. (2004b). Consequences of regret aversion in real life: The case of the Dutch postcode lottery. *Organizational Behavior and Human Decision Processes, 93*, 155–168.

Zeelenberg, M., & Pieters, R. (2005). Feeling is for doing: A pragmatic approach to the study of emotions in economic behavior. In D. De Cremer, M. Zeelenberg, & K. Murnighan (Eds.), *Social psychology and economics.* Mahwah, NJ: Erlbaum.

Zeelenberg, M., Van den Bos, K., van Dijk, E., & Pieters, R. (2002). The inaction effect in the psychology of regret. *Journal of Personality and Social Psychology, 82*, 314–327.

Zeelenberg, M., Van der Pligt, J., & Manstead, A.S.R. (1998). Undoing regret on Dutch television: Apologizing for interpersonal regrets involving actions and inactions. *Personality and Social Psychology Bulletin, 24*, 1113–1119.

Zeelenberg, M., Van Dijk, W. W., Manstead, A.S.R., & Van der Pligt, J. (1998). The experience of regret and disappointment. *Cognition and Emotion, 12*, 221–230.

Zeelenberg, M., Van Dijk, W. W., Van der Pligt, J., Manstead, A.S.R., Van Empelen, P., & Reinderman, D. (1998). Emotional reactions to the outcomes of decisions: The role of counterfactual thought in the experience of regret and disappointment. *Organizational Behavior and Human Decision Processes, 75*, 117–141.

13

Looking Back on What We Knew and When We Knew It

The Role of Time in the Development of Hindsight Bias

FRED B. BRYANT
ADAM DeHOEK

> Life is lived forwards, but understood backwards.
>
> Søren Kierkegaard

You are watching a television game show in which contestants compete to win cash by correctly answering a series of true-false questions testing their general knowledge. As the correct answer to each question is revealed, you begin to believe that you are better than most people in discriminating true and false factual questions and that you could get rich as a contestant on the show. Is this really the case—are you good at distinguishing true and false questions, or is it a retrospective illusion? Is your predictive foresight really as good as it seems, or does it just seem better when viewed retrospectively in hindsight?

A small private airplane crashes in the desert. After taking 2 years to sift through the available evidence, a team of independent investigators concludes that pilot error caused the accident. At that point in time, a senior investigator reviews the same body of evidence and is asked to draw her own conclusion about the cause of the accident. Before reviewing the evidence, she knows the research team concluded that pilot error caused the accident. As she studies the evidence, she begins to grow more and more confident that pilot error caused the accident. But did knowing the research team's earlier conclusion make her more likely to reach that same conclusion than she would have been otherwise?

A hurricane spins its way across the Caribbean toward the Florida coast. At first, meteorologists predict the hurricane will make landfall at a popular beach resort, and nearby residents begin to prepare. But over time, it becomes increasingly evident that the storm will miss the resort, residents stop preparing, and the hurricane comes ashore elsewhere. Just afterward, residents remember having gradually learned near the end that the storm would miss them; but a week later, they believe they knew from the start they would be spared. As hurricanes come and go over time, this process is repeated, and residents begin to feel safe living in hurricane territory, based on the belief that they can predict from the outset whether or not hurricanes will hit them. Can residents actually predict the course of hurricanes well in advance, or does it just seem like it to them retrospectively?

Each of these hypothetical scenarios—the game show, the accident investigation, the hurricane forecasting—represents a classic, prototypical example of hindsight bias in operation. Hindsight bias occurs when knowing the outcome of an event distorts one's memory of what one had earlier expected the outcome to be (Fischhoff, 1975). Once people know the outcome of an event, they tend to believe that they knew it would happen all along. An outcome that may have seemed unlikely prior to its occurrence is afterward seen as inevitable, unavoidable, and foreseeable. Thus hindsight distorts the past, making foresight appear more accurate than it actually was (Fischhoff, 1975).

A Temporal Perspective on Hindsight Bias

At the heart of the concept of hindsight bias is the distinction between (1) what one knew, expected, or predicted *before* learning the actual outcome (foresight) versus (2) what one remembers knowing, expecting, or predicting beforehand *after* learning the actual outcome (hindsight). As Fischhoff (1976) noted concerning the distinction between a priori prediction and post hoc explanation:

> Common sense appears to hold that the two are highly interrelated because of perceived similarities in the underlying processes and because increased prowess in one is seen as conferring increased prowess in the other. When we manage to explain the past, we feel we have increased our ability to predict the future. The main perceived difference seems to be that we can adequately explain more things than we can predict because we know more in hindsight than in foresight. (p. 443)

In other words, past events appear simpler and easier to understand than future events because these events have already occurred. When an event is over, it has definite outcomes, and the reasons for these outcomes are more easily examined and understood. Even though people might not have predicted a particular outcome beforehand, once that outcome has happened, they can often find reasons to support it. People's retrospective search for causes to explain the observed outcome after the fact is of narrower specificity compared with their prospective attempts to predict the outcome beforehand.

By definition, time is integral to the very concept of hindsight. But exactly how and in what ways does time influence the development of hindsight bias? Clearly, time is a necessary ingredient in hindsight bias. It requires time for foresight to become hindsight and for people to be able to look back on what they knew earlier before a particular outcome occurred. Indeed, it is the very passage of time itself that eventually transforms what we know from the prospective expectation of predictive foresight to the retrospective remembrance of postdictive hindsight.

Yet beyond these simple chronological effects, time also plays an integral role in our experience of hindsight bias in reaction to ongoing life events as they unfold in real time in the world around us. It requires the passage of time for a future event to approach, unfold in the present, and recede into the past; for people's future expectations about the event to be either confirmed or disconfirmed and then recede into the past; and for people to try to recall afterward what they thought would happen before the event occurred. Time not only establishes the accuracy of foresight but also erodes the accuracy of hindsight.

In this chapter, we address the question of how time influences hindsight bias. We begin by briefly summarizing the three dominant methodological paradigms researchers have used to study hindsight judgments, considering the influence of time in relation to each of these dominant experimental approaches and highlighting relations between foresight (a priori prediction) and hindsight (a posteriori reconstruction) within each research paradigm. We then consider prevailing theoretical models of the processes that underlie the development of hindsight bias over time. We conclude by comparing and contrasting the role time plays within each mediational model, constructing an integrative temporal model and suggesting potentially fruitful avenues for future research on the role of time in the development of hindsight bias.

Three Dominant Approaches to Studying Hindsight Bias

A comprehensive meta-analysis of the first 35 years of research on hindsight bias (Guilbault, Bryant, Brockway, & Posavac, 2004) found that researchers have primarily employed one of three methodological paradigms: (1) almanac questions, (2) case histories, or (3) real-world events. Each of these research procedures provides a different means of measuring the strength of hindsight bias. Note that temporal concerns vary across the different types of methodological paradigms, with almanac questions and case histories more often studied using cross-sectional experiments (not directly examining temporal effects) and real-world events more often studied using longitudinal survey designs (directly examining temporal effects).

Foresight and Hindsight in Relation to Almanac Questions

Almanac questions focus on the accuracy of one's general knowledge—in particular, the perceived likelihood that specific factual information is true or untrue. For example, "In what country is the world's second highest mountain located—India or Pakistan?"). In studies using such general knowledge questions, respondents are asked to estimate the probability that they would have known the correct answer, with some respondents first learning the correct answer (i.e., Pakistan) and thus making the likelihood judgment retrospectively (postdictively) and other respondents not learning the correct answer and thus making this likelihood judgment prospectively (predictively). The critical issue here is whether being given the correct answer increases the perceived likelihood that one's general knowledge was accurate beforehand, compared with foresight judgments of the accuracy of general knowledge when not being given the correct answer. The research evidence indicates that seeing the correct answer before giving your response makes you more likely to believe you knew it all along (Guilbault et al., 2004).

Research using almanac questions to study the relationship between prospection and retrospection is based on the assumption that the primary influence of time on these two constructs is in transforming foresight into hindsight. Within this conceptual framework, what one knows before learning the correct information is considered static and unchanging over time. Before learning the truth, one either does or does not know the correct answer. But after the truth is revealed, there can be no more foresight concerning the outcome, only hindsight in recalling what one believed earlier (Fischhoff & Beyeth, 1975). Viewed from this perspective, foresight changes only when it becomes hindsight; and once established, hindsight bias is stable. This static temporal viewpoint is consistent with the notion that outcome knowledge produces an immediate, automatic cognitive assimilation of the past to the present (Fischhoff, 1975, 1977).

Foresight and Hindsight in Relation to Case Histories

Hindsight has been studied not only in relation to the accuracy of general knowledge but also in relation to specific case histories, in which people are asked to judge the likelihood that a particular event has occurred in a single concrete instance. For example, researchers have asked physicians to: (1) review reports of medical case histories with the correct diagnosis either labeled on the cover (making physician judgments retrospective) or unlabeled on the cover (making physician judgments prospective); and then (2) estimate the probability that they think they would have assigned to that particular diagnosis (e.g., Arkes, Wortman, Saville, & Harkness, 1981). The critical issue here is whether being given the correct diagnosis increases the perceived likelihood that one would have predicted this diagnosis prospectively, compared with actual prospective predictions made before receiving the correct diagnosis. As is the case with almanac questions, research reveals that knowing the actual outcome for a case history before making one's own prediction makes a person more likely to believe that he or she knew it all along (Guilbault et al., 2004).

Like studies using almanac questions, research using case histories to investigate the relationship between prospection and retrospection are also founded on the assumption that the primary influence of time on these two constructs occurs when foresight becomes hindsight. Within this conceptual framework, both what one would have predicted *before* learning the correct diagnosis and what one thinks one would have predicted beforehand *after* learning the correct diagnosis are considered largely static and unchanging over time.

Foresight and Hindsight in Relation to Real-World Events

Unlike studies that use almanac questions or case histories to investigate hindsight bias, research on judgments of the likelihood of unfolding real-life events assumes that both foresight and hindsight are dynamic and evolve over time. As an upcoming event approaches in time, people often look forward and anticipate it. People often have expectations about the likelihood that the upcoming event will actually occur, and, if it does, how it will eventually turn out. Then, after some time, the anticipated event either does or does not occur. As time passes, people may look back on what they believed earlier before the event occurred, and they may make retrospective judgments about how likely they thought it was beforehand that the event would occur. At first, they may recall the surprisingness of the outcome. But over time, people may come to believe that they knew from the start exactly what would happen and how things would later unfold.

These phenomena are perhaps most obvious in relation to a special class of relatively common real-world events (Guerin, 1982) that can be anticipated or imagined because of their scheduled or publicized nature, as with the outcome of sporting events (Roese & Maniar, 1997), elections (Leary, 1982), legislative votes (Dietrich & Olson, 1993), labor strikes (Pennington, 1981), and legal trials (Gilbertson, Dietrich, Olson, & Guenther, 1994). In many circumstances, foresight improves as events draw closer in time, eventually making more accurate short-range forecasts possible (Bryant & Guilbault, 2002). But after the event occurs, if the outcome is surprising, it may take time for hindsight to develop, until the outcome's unexpected nature becomes less salient and outcome-related information becomes less accessible (Sanna, Schwarz, & Stocker, 2002; Tversky & Kahneman, 1973). In such cases, both foresight and hindsight may change over time, the former becoming more accurate, the latter becoming less so.

Evidence that supports the dynamic nature of foresight and hindsight in relation to unfolding real-life events comes from longitudinal studies of two highly publicized trials in the United States. One study (Bryant & Brockway, 1997) concerned reactions to the 1995 murder acquittal of O. J. Simpson; the other (Bryant & Guilbault, 2002), reactions to the acquittal of President Clinton in the 1999 U.S. Senate impeachment trial. Using a single pretest and two posttests, Bryant and Brockway (1997) found that 2 days after the Simpson verdict, respondents showed no hindsight distortion concerning the prior probability of acquittal but that 1 week after the verdict, retrospective estimates of the prior probability of acquittal were higher than prospective estimates. Thus it took time for hindsight bias to develop in relation to Simpson's acquittal. Bryant and Brockway (1997) speculated that hindsight bias may not emerge as long as (1) people can accurately recall their earlier prospective estimates (Hell, Gigerenzer, Gauggel, Mall, & Mueller, 1988); (2) people are unable to construct a plausible explanation for the outcome (Nario & Branscombe, 1995); or (3) the media continue to publicize the surprising and unforeseeable nature of the actual outcome.

Extending this longitudinal work to study another widely publicized trial, Bryant and Guilbault (2002) used two pretests and two posttests to investigate changes over time in both foresight and hindsight in response to the Clinton impeachment verdict. Specifically, college students made prospective probability estimates concerning the Senate verdict both 22 days beforehand (distal pretest) and 3 days beforehand (proximal pretest), and they made retrospective probability estimates both 4 days after the verdict (immediate posttest) and 11 days after the verdict (delayed posttest). With respect to *foresight*, students evidenced a shift between the two pretests toward greater prospective accuracy in their estimates of the likelihood of acquittal. Content analysis of archived national news reports suggested that media predictions about the impending vote produced this temporal increase in the accuracy of foresight. With respect to *hindsight*, at the immediate posttest students accurately recalled that their prospective estimates of the likelihood of conviction had shifted toward greater accuracy as the verdict approached. But 1 week later, they incorrectly believed they had been more certain all along that Clinton would be acquitted. With time, students came to believe they knew it all along.

Bryant and Guilbault's (2002) findings demonstrate that whether hindsight emerges in relation to a real-world event depends not only on how long after the event people make retrospective judgments but also on how long before the event people focus these retrospective judgments. Participants never distorted the recent past—at that point they really had determined what was going to happen, based on media reports—but instead, eventually over time they came to distort the distant past and to believe that they knew from the start what was going to happen. With the passage of time after the event, the proximal pretest faded into the distant past, and people lost sight of the fact that their foresight became accurate only at the "eleventh hour." At the end of this chapter, we incorporate these temporal influences in an integrative theoretical model of how time influences the development of hindsight bias in response to unfolding real-world events.

The Impact of Time on Cognitive, Affective, and Behavioral Responses to Unfolding Life Events

This new way of thinking about hindsight bias as a dynamic phenomenon has interesting implications for human thoughts, feelings, and behaviors in relation to unfolding real-world events. Because short-range forecasts are typically more accurate than long-range forecasts, predictions often grow more accurate as future events grow closer in time. Bryant and Guilbault's (2002) longitudinal data suggest that whenever more accurate short-range foresight replaces less accurate longer range foresight, eventually people will come to equate the two forms of foresight retrospectively. Consider a few examples.

Stock Investment

Just before the stock market plummets, a well-informed investor accurately forecasts the impending crisis and sells all of his shares of stock, narrowly avoiding a major financial loss. Although immediately after the event he accurately recalls having foreseen only at the last minute what was about to happen, over time the investor's beliefs about how long beforehand he foresaw the market crash may well change. As the close call recedes into the past, he may mistakenly come to believe that he knew long beforehand exactly when to sell and that he is therefore invulnerable to future financial risks. Ironically, this illusion of invulnerability would put the investor at greater objective risk if it reduced his likelihood of taking preventive action (Perloff, 1983). Thus the passage of time both improves the prospective accuracy of foresight and impairs the retrospective accuracy of hindsight, creating a rich interplay between the two temporal perspectives in relation to unfolding real-life events.

Medicine

Physicians and medical staff forecast the outcome of a problem pregnancy with increasing accuracy as time goes by, until eventually it becomes clear whether or not the mother is going to carry the baby to full term. Immediately after the birth outcome (either positive or negative), the mother may recall having realized the eventual outcome only shortly before it happened. But over time, as she looks back on what she knew and when she knew it, she may come to believe that she knew all along that things would turn out the way they did. Such an effect might promote a false sense of security by enhancing beliefs in the power, precision, and prescience of modern medicine. This might well put pregnant women at greater medical risk if it makes them less likely to engage in health precautions because they think that their birth outcome is no longer uncertain. Research indicates that physicians and medical staff are no more immune to hindsight bias than is the mother herself (Guilbault et al., 2004).

Politics

Three months before the U.S. presidential election, national polls show that the two candidates are "neck and neck," dead-even approaching the November election. But then just days before the election, it becomes evident from voter polls that one candidate has surged ahead of the other in a key electoral state, and this candidate in fact goes on to win the election. At first, voters remember having figured out at the end which candidate would win, as their foresight became more accurate just before the election. But later, with time, voters eventually forget what they learned only at the end of the election and come to believe that they knew all along what would happen. This effect would enhance the perceived long-range predictability of election outcomes and might reduce people's likelihood of voting if they believe the outcome is already determined and grow disinterested. Viewed within this temporal perspective, people distort not so much what they knew, but rather when they came to know it.

Warfare

As a final case in point, consider how such temporal changes in hindsight bias might explain reactions to war among both the victors and the vanquished. As victory approaches near the end of a war, foresight becomes more accurate. After warfare ends in victory, at first the victors recall having foreseen the outcome only at the end of the war. But with time, citizens, troops, and leaders alike come to believe that there was never any doubt that they would win the war. Over time this belief in the inevitability of victory might well breed a national sense of "manifest destiny" in military matters. On the other hand, the same effect should also occur for the nation that loses the war, but with the opposite consequences. As defeat becomes evident at the end of a war, foresight also becomes more accurate among the vanquished. After the war ends in defeat, at first the vanquished recall foreseeing the outcome only at the end of the war. But with time, citizens, troops, and leaders all come to believe that their efforts were doomed from the outset. Over time this belief in the inevitability and foreseeability of defeat might well breed a sense of "wholesale betrayal" among the populace toward its leaders, as citizens blame and seek to punish the negligent "scapegoats" they see as responsible for faulty decision making (Fischhoff, 1975; Myers, 1999).

The Timing of Foresight and Hindsight in Relation to Real-World Events

Based on their longitudinal results, Bryant and Guilbault (2002) drew several speculative conclusions about how the timing of shifts in the accuracy of foresight influence temporal shifts in the accuracy of hindsight. In particular, these researchers speculated that the sooner beforehand one figures out what is going to happen, the faster will be the development of hindsight bias after the event occurs. In other words, the later in time (closer to the event) one's foresight becomes accurate, the longer it will take for hindsight bias to develop. Hindsight should take longest to develop when foresight becomes accurate only immediately before the event occurs. Under these circumstances, information about the prior uncertainty and last-minute clarity of foresight should remain accessible for the longest time. Thus the later the shift in the accuracy of foresight, the greater the expected delay in the onset of hindsight bias.

Bryant and Guilbault (2002) further speculated that the more effort one has expended in trying to predict the impending outcome, the stronger will be the hindsight bias after the event, the quicker hindsight bias will develop after the event, and the farther hindsight bias will extend back into the past. In such cases, exerting effort to gain predictive control beforehand would be expected to heighten perceived control (Langer, 1975; Wortman, 1975). For example, in a laboratory experiment in which Harvard undergraduates tried to guess the outcome of 30 coin tosses, Langer and Roth (1975) found that participants who actively tried to predict the outcomes afterward recalled more successes, predicted more future successes, and perceived themselves as having greater innate ability at the coin-toss prediction task (regardless of how successful they were), compared with ratings made by observers who merely watched.

Theoretical Explanations for Hindsight Bias

We have described how hindsight bias develops over time, but the question remains—why does time have these effects on retrospective judgments? Why does foresight differ depending on whether it is judged prospectively or retrospectively? In this section we review prevailing thought on this matter. We then compare and contrast alternative mediating mechanisms proposed to explain hindsight bias in terms of the presumed role of time in the underlying causal process.

Because hindsight bias has traditionally been conceptualized as static, immediate, and automatic, most prior researchers have treated hindsight as being relatively invariant over time. For example, Fischhoff (1975) argued that the change between doubt about an outcome preceding an event and certainty about an outcome after receiving relevant information happens all at once the moment the outcome is revealed. Fischhoff's theory of "creeping determinism" presumes that outcome information is automatically integrated into an individual's knowledge immediately after the knowledge is taken in. Once they learn the outcome, people are no longer able to distinguish it from what they knew previously. Most prior work on hindsight bias has adopted this theoretical framework in assuming that hindsight bias reflects a stable, irreversible perceptual change that occurs the instant foresight changes to hindsight. Attesting to the robustness of hindsight bias, meta-analysis reveals that experimental interventions aimed at reducing hindsight bias are typically ineffective (Guilbault et al., 2004).

Because of the presumed immediacy, temporal stability, and irreversibility of hindsight bias, most studies of hindsight bias have been cross-sectional (Guilbault et al., 2004). For example, Fischhoff (1975) used four historical events to study hindsight: the nineteenth-century war between the British and the Gurkas of Nepal; a 1967 civil uprising in Atlanta, Georgia; and two clinical cases. For each situation, the experimenter gave a brief description of the event or case, along with either a list of possible outcomes (the foresight condition) or the "actual" outcome (the hindsight condition). Each of the possible outcomes in the foresight condition ruled out the other possible outcomes. In addition, the experimenter varied the "actual" outcome that was presented to the participants in the hindsight condition. Therefore, some participants received an "actual" outcome that was not the true outcome. To end the experiment, participants were asked to judge the probability of each possible outcome as if they did not know the outcome information. Those in the hindsight condition showed greater reporting of the "actual" outcome than did participants in the foresight condition. This classic between-subjects randomized experiment is a prime example of the cross-sectional experimental design that researchers have typically adopted in testing hypotheses about hindsight bias.

In contrast, a temporal perspective that allows for changes in both foresight and hindsight requires longitudinal research designs in which the same individuals are measured repeatedly over time. Along these lines, designs that include multiple posttests allow for both immediate and delayed hindsight judgments to determine whether or not it takes time for hindsight bias to develop (Bryant & Brockway, 1997). Adding a second layer of temporal complexity, designs that include both multiple pretests and multiple posttests provide measures not only of immediate and delayed hindsight but also of hindsight in relation to both distal and proximal foresight (Bryant & Guilbault, 2002). Including multiple pretests enables researchers to examine changes in the accuracy of foresight; combined with multiple posttests, it allows researchers to examine temporal changes in retrospective beliefs about when foresight became accurate. Also, including a separate "posttest only" cross-sectional sample helps rule out testing, history, and maturation as threats to internal validity (Bryant & Guilbault, 2002; Cook & Campbell, 1978).

Motivational and Cognitive Mechanisms

In a comprehensive conceptual review of the hindsight literature, Hawkins and Hastie (1990) explicated potential causes of hindsight bias in terms of a blend of motivational and cognitive processes people use when judging an event's likelihood retrospectively.

Motivated Response Adjustment

Hindsight bias may reflect a form of motivated response adjustment in which participants strive to present themselves favorably (Hawkins & Hastie, 1990). Fischhoff (1975) hypothesized that people wish to appear as accurate as possible in their judgments of past events, while also wishing to appear realistic, rather than clairvoyant. Along these lines, Campbell and Tesser (1983) found that individual differences in both need for positive self-presentation and self-rated ego involvement in the judgment task were positively correlated with the strength of observed hindsight effects. Also supporting a self-serving motivational interpretation, Bryant and Guilbault (2002) found that hindsight bias emerged for one's own personal estimates of prior probability but not for one's beliefs about the estimates of the average person or one's best friend.

Besides ego enhancement, another motivational mechanism that may underlie hindsight bias is the need for security, which may motivate people to exaggerate the degree to which important events are predictable, particularly when outcomes are more serious (Walster, 1967). Still other research has investigated retroactive pessimism, a form of self-protective hindsight motivated by the need to regulate disappointment when outcomes fall short of expectations (Tykocinski, Pick, & Kedmi, 2002). Although hindsight bias no doubt has a motivational component in some situations, retrospective distortion cannot be completely explained in this manner. For example, Hawkins and Hastie (1990) deemed it unlikely that people are motivated to see themselves as more knowledgeable about obscure almanac trivia than they actually are, though trivia buffs might disagree.

Anchoring on the Current Belief and Adjusting

As noted earlier, Hawkins and Hastie (1990) also suggested specific cognitive processes that influence hindsight effects. One of these processes occurs when participants anchor on the current postoutcome belief and then try to adjust their retrospective response toward how they would respond if they were ignorant of the outcome. In hindsight, participants would obviously assign a 100% probability of knowing the outcome. From this vantage point of absolute certainty, participants must now retrospectively estimate how uncertain they were before learning the outcome. Such adjustments are notoriously inaccurate and typically demonstrate hindsight probabilities that are higher than they should be (Lopes, 1982; Slovic & Lichtenstein, 1971; Tversky & Kahneman, 1974).

Rejudgment

Another cognitive process that may underlie hindsight bias occurs when people "rejudge" the outcome to reconstruct their earlier foresight. The process of rejudging unfolds in three stages, in which people sample, evaluate, and integrate the available evidence.

Sampling Evidence

In rejudgment, participants first sample evidence related to the judgment from their memories or from the outside world. Once individuals become aware of an outcome, they seek out relevant evidence with respect to the topic (Hastie & Park, 1986). Such evidence is available in a countless variety of forms, from print media to Internet websites. When an outcome is known, subsequent judgments are most likely to be influenced by evidence that is consistent (as opposed to inconsistent) with the outcome. Such evidence is more likely to be accessible in memory (Dellarosa & Bourne, 1984; Sanna et al., 2002). With respect to hindsight, Slovic and Fischhoff (1977) argued that only the outcome is considered as a cue for retrieving information about an issue or event, but in cases of foresight, there are many sources of evidence from which to draw, none more salient than another, as the outcome is still undetermined. Thus, once an outcome is known, evidence relating to that outcome becomes more salient, whereas information that is inconsistent with the known outcome loses accessibility.

Evaluating Evidence

After sampling the evidence, participants first evaluate the evidence they have obtained before making a judgment. Concerning this process, Fischhoff (1975) argued that people assimilate knowledge and information into what they already know about a particular situation. In hindsight, observers will attempt to combine all they know about an event into a coherent whole to make more sense of the outcome. In addition, observers evaluate evidence within the context of what they already know about the outcome. For example, participants may add causal inferences never presented by the experimenter to link what they know about the beginning, middle, and final outcome of an event (Pennington & Hastie, 1986, 1987, 1988; Trabasso & van den Broek, 1985).

As an alternative conceptual approach, other theorists have proposed the so-called "Reconstruction After Feedback with Take the Best" (RAFT) model to explain the process of evidence evaluation (Hoffrage, Hertwig, & Gigerenzer, 2000). The basic idea of the RAFT model is that when a person receives any feedback or correct information after making his or her initial judgment, this information updates the knowledge base that underlies the initial judgment. Therefore, if individuals cannot remember their initial judgments, they will reconstruct them from what they currently know about the situation, that being the updated information. Thus feedback information indirectly affects an individual's memory by revising the knowledge used in reconstruction. Feedback information especially aids in filling in the information that was elusive during the original judgment. The RAFT model suggests that hindsight bias is not a flaw in human cognition but rather an adaptive tool that helps people disregard information that is now either irrelevant or inaccurate (Hoffrage et al., 2000).

Integrating Evidence

In the last stage of rejudgment, participants combine the implications of all pieces of information in order to form a final, unitary judgment. In some previous research, the mechanism for predicting this ultimate response has been an algebraic formula (e.g., Anderson, 1981). The integration of information occurs in this model when each piece of information is weighted for credibility, authority, relevance, and importance and then the weighted implications are summed to yield a judgment on which a choice or decision is based (Hawkins & Hastie, 1990). By learning from the outcome, individuals change their generic model of causal relations in the situation that they are currently considering. Therefore, outcome knowledge will influence the weights that people place on various components, and this will in turn influence their final retrospective judgments of foresight.

Within the integration stage, hindsight bias is seen in a more "benign" light, as it is regarded as a side effect of the adaptive learning process. As Hawkins and Hastie (1990) noted in distinguishing between this phase of evidence integration and the previous phase of evidence evaluation, the latter applies only to immediately relevant, case-specific items of evidence, whereas the former refers to the influence of the learning process on a participant's generic model (which will shape many related cases within a given domain). If outcome feedback generalizes to different judgments, then it would be plausible to implicate the process of evidence integration. However, if the effect of outcome feedback is limited to a certain situation, then this would signal the process of evidence evaluation.

Recalling the Old Belief

A final cognitive process that may lead to hindsight bias involves recalling the old belief (Hawkins & Hastie, 1990). This is the simplest form of recall strategy, in which people first search their long-term memory for old beliefs regarding a specific question or outcome and then respond consistently with memory. Both Fischhoff (1977) and Wood (1978) believed that their research participants were able to recall roughly two thirds of original pretest estimates. Consistent with this notion, Hell et al. (1988) concluded that hindsight bias cannot occur until one forgets one's original judgment.

Although direct recall of information is a plausible strategy for people to use in some situations (e.g., almanac questions and events of great personal significance), it is unlikely to hold across all events (Hawkins & Hastie, 1990). Identical responding in original and postfeedback judgment ratings by itself is not conclusive evidence for the effectiveness of recall. Although accuracy is necessary if direct recall is at work, accuracy is insufficient to suggest that direct recall was the mechanism underlying the second response (Hawkins & Hastie, 1990). In addition, direct recall is irrelevant when considering cross-sectional studies. In between-groups experiments, two groups are measured once, and neither has a second measurement; thus direct recall provides an insufficient explanation for hindsight bias. This fact further strengthens the argument that more hindsight studies should be longitudinal. Moreover, although it is evident that these theoretical explanations contribute to our understanding of hindsight bias, no one theory furnishes a full explanation of all observed effects.

The Influence of Time on Alternative Mediational Mechanisms

Note that the passage of time has different effects on hindsight depending on the particular motivational or cognitive process at work. And depending on the situation, the amount of time necessary for hindsight bias to develop after an event can vary, with time either producing hindsight bias immediately after the event by transforming prospection into retrospection or gradually producing hindsight bias by eroding the accuracy of foresight. We now explicate the impact of time on the motivational and cognitive mechanisms presumed to produce hindsight bias. We then synthesize these temporal influences in an integrative conceptual model of how time shapes the trajectory of retrospective judgments of foresight. As the following theoretical analysis illustrates, time has no one single influence on hindsight judgments of foresight but rather affects the retrospective accuracy of hindsight differently as a function of the underlying causal mechanism involved.

Motivational Mechanisms

If the mechanism through which hindsight effects occur is motivational, then time might be expected to have very little effect. Once the actual outcome is known, it is impossible to return to a time when it was unknown, and immediately afterward people should be motivated to think they knew it all along to enhance their self-esteem. However, motivational concerns may also cause a delay in the emergence of hindsight bias immediately after the outcome. For example, people may downplay their predictive accuracy just after the outcome to avoid being seen as boastful, especially if they think their superior foresight is obvious. Thus self-presentational modesty may initially motivate people to underrate their prospective accuracy. But as time passes, they may later exaggerate their predictive prowess if they believe others are unaware of it (Baumeister & Jones, 1978; Schlenker, Miller, & Leary, 1983). Thus, especially after unexpected outcomes, time may delay the onset of ego-motivated hindsight bias until initial self-presentational concerns have faded.

Anchoring on Current Belief and Adjusting

As with motivational mechanisms, when people engage in the cognitive process of anchoring the current belief and adjusting retrospective judgments accordingly, the passage of time is also presumed to have little effect except when unveiling the actual outcome of an event. Once an event occurs, the postoutcome probability of having predicted the actual outcome should not change over time. Nevertheless, with some real-life events, media publicity about the surprising nature of the actual outcome may temporarily suppress this cognitive form of hindsight bias after an event by preserving memories of the inaccuracy of foresight (Bryant & Guilbault, 1997). Yet, once these biased hindsight judgments have formed, the cognitive process of anchoring on the current belief and adjusting would presumably be unaffected by the passage of time.

Rejudgment

In stark contrast, time is presumed to have profound effects on the cognitive processes that underlie rejudgment as a determinant of hindsight bias. Time not only allows for three successive stages of rejudgment—sampling, evaluating, and integrating evidence—but also produces different qualitative effects depending on at which stage of evidence rejudgment is involved. In the case of *sampling evidence*, although all of the necessary information was available before the event occurred, all of this information held equal relevance at that point in time. In this case, as time passes, outcome-related evidence becomes more relevant than other information. In *evidence evaluation*, the passage of time encourages a schema to be created for all that is known about the event for use in making sense of the event. In addition, over time outcome information updates and revises one's knowledge about an event. Before knowing the outcome, a schema cannot be created, as the event has not occurred. In other words, the information surrounding the event is incomplete before the event occurs. Thus time facilitates the development of a schema for the event. In *evidence integration*, the passage of time influences the weights people place on each of the various pieces of information relevant to the event, such that information that had more impact before the event has less impact afterward and vice versa.

Recalling the Old Belief

Regarding the most basic cognitive process with respect to hindsight effects—recalling the old belief—the passage of time eventually causes one to forget an event or an earlier judgment, thereby allowing hindsight distortion to occur. Thus, when recalling the old belief is the mediating mechanism, time produces an interval during which the onset of hindsight effects is delayed. It takes time for information associated with the future event to be replaced by new outcome-specific information. Hindsight effects occur only after time has changed the old information or made it no longer accessible. Furthermore, it seems reasonable to assume that once people have forgotten their old beliefs, they would be unlikely to suddenly remember them again later. Thus, within the simplest cognitive mediational framework, time has its effects on hindsight bias primarily in delaying the onset of retrospective distortion until memory of foresight eventually fades and becomes inaccessible.

Toward an Integrative Temporal Model

Based on this theoretical analysis, we propose a temporal sequence through which time can influence judgments of foresight in relation to unfolding real-world events in several different ways, depending on whether or not the event has occurred and the nature of the cognitive or motivational mechanism assumed to underlie hindsight bias.

1. *Before an event* occurs, time can improve the accuracy of prospective foresight through short-range forecasting as the future event approaches in time.
2. *When an event occurs*, by definition time irrevocably transforms prospective foresight into retrospective hindsight.
3. *After an event occurs*, time can increase the strength of hindsight bias by blurring the distinction between proximal short-range foresight and distal long-range foresight.
4. *After an event occurs*, time can temporarily delay the onset of hindsight bias, as when:
   (a) An initial need for modesty in disclosing one's predictive prowess gradually disappears
   (b) Widespread media publicity about the inaccuracy of foresight following unexpected outcomes gradually ceases
   (c) An accurate memory of foresight gradually fades over time
5. *After an event occurs*, time's effects vary qualitatively across the stages of rejudgment:
   (a) When people *sample evidence*, time makes outcome-related information more relevant
   (b) When people *evaluate evidence*, time cultivates a more complete schema about the event, updates outcome information, and revises personal knowledge about the event
   (c) When people *integrate evidence*, time increases the weight given to outcome-related information and decreases the weight given to information about other possible outcomes

Table 13.1 summarizes the chronological sequence of these temporal effects on judgments of foresight made before (prospectively) and after (retrospectively) an unfolding real-world event.

Table 13.1. Effects of time on the development of hindsight bias in relation to an unfolding real-world event

Chronological Sequence	Effect of Time on Judgments of Foresight
I. *Before the Event*	
Prospective foresight	
Distal long-range forecasts	Prediction of outcome is relatively inaccurate
Proximal short-range forecasts	Greater accuracy in predicting outcome
II. *When the Event Occurs*	Foresight changes to hindsight
III. *After the Event*	
Retrospective hindsight	
Immediate recall	Recall of foresight is relatively accurate
Delayed recall	Less accuracy in recalling distal foresight
Temporary delay in hindsight bias	
Mediating mechanism:	
Motivational processes	Initial self-presentational modesty gradually fades
Cognitive processes	Publicity about faulty foresight gradually fades
Recalling the old belief	Accurate memory of foresight gradually fades
Emergence of hindsight bias	
Mediating mechanism	
Rejudgment	
Sampling evidence	Outcome-related evidence becomes more relevant
Evaluating evidence	Knowledge base updated; event schema completed
Integrating evidence	Outcome-related evidence weighted more heavily

Additional Directions for Future Research on Time and Hindsight Bias

Although we have synthesized existing theory and research to construct an integrative model of the effects of time on hindsight bias, a host of unanswered theoretical questions remain. For example, future work is needed to explore hindsight bias in relation to when events *actually occur* versus when one *thought prospectively* they *would occur* (as opposed to studying beliefs about the probability of an event's occurrence). Although this type of temporal judgment is irrelevant when the event is scheduled to occur at a fixed time (e.g., as with an election or a sports competition), it is relevant when the event in question may never occur (e.g., as with an earthquake, a terrorist attack, or the election of a female U.S. president).

We also know nothing about how people make *long-range forecasts* of what the distant future will or will not bring in their lives, about how they revise these long-range forecasts over time, and about how they look back on their earlier long-range forecasts in light of the changing present. Extending our longitudinal temporal perspective, we can speculate that if people's vision of the distant future has been gradually disconfirmed over the course of their lifetime, then over time they will come to believe that they really knew all along that it was bound to turn out that way. For truly, people live life looking forward in foresight but understand it looking backward in hindsight.

Acknowledgments

The authors wish to thank Jennifer Brockway, Rebecca Guilbault Devlin, and Scott Tindale for insights into the temporal processes underlying the development of hindsight bias, and Linda Perloff, Emil Posavac, Larry Sanna, and Ed Chang for helpful feedback on an earlier draft of this chapter.

References

Anderson, N. H. (1981). *Foundations of information integration theory.* New York: Academic Press.

Arkes, H. R., Wortman, R. L., Saville, P. D., & Harkness, A. R. (1981). Hindsight bias among physicians weighing the likelihood of diagnoses. *Journal of Applied Psychology, 66,* 252–254.

Baumeister, R. F., & Jones, E. E. (1978). When self-presentation is constrained by the target's prior knowledge: Consistency and compensation. *Journal of Personality and Social Psychology, 36,* 608–618.

Bryant, F. B., & Brockway, J. H. (1997). Hindsight bias in reaction to the verdict in the O.J. Simpson criminal trial. *Basic and Applied Social Psychology, 19,* 225–241.

Bryant, F. B., & Guilbault, R. L. (2002). "I knew it all along" eventually: The development of hindsight bias in reaction to the Clinton impeachment verdict. *Basic and Applied Social Psychology, 24,* 27–41.

Campbell, J. D., & Tesser, A. (1983). Motivational interpretations of hindsight bias: An individual difference analysis. *Journal of Personality, 51,* 605–620.

Cook, T. D., & Campbell, D. T. (1978). *Quasi-experimentation: Design and analysis issues for field settings.* Chicago: Rand McNally.

Dellarosa, D., & Bourne, L. E., Jr. (1984). Decisions and memory: Differential retrievability of consistent and contradictory evidence. *Journal of Verbal Learning and Verbal Behavior, 23,* 669–682.

Dietrich, D., & Olson, M. (1993). A demonstration of hindsight bias using the Thomas confirmation vote. *Psychological Reports, 72,* 377–378.

Fischhoff, B. (1975). Hindsight ≠ foresight: The effect of outcome knowledge on judgments under uncertainty. *Journal of Experimental Psychology: Human Perception and Performance, 1,* 288–299.

Fischhoff, B. (1976). Attribution theory and judgment under uncertainty. In J. H. Harvey, W. J. Ickes, & R. Kidd (Eds.), *New directions in attribution research* (Vol. 1, pp. 421–452). Hillsdale, NJ: Erlbaum.

Fischhoff, B. (1977). Perceived informativeness of facts. *Journal of Experimental Psychology: Human Perception and Performance, 3,* 349–358.

Fischhoff, B., & Beyeth, R. (1975). "I knew it would happen": Remembered probabilities of once-future things. *Organizational Behavior and Human Performance, 13,* 1–16.

Gilbertson, L. J., Dietrich, D., Olson, M., & Guenther, R. K. (1994). A study of hindsight bias: The Rodney King case in retrospect. *Psychological Reports, 74,* 383–386.

Guerin, B. (1982). Salience and hindsight biases in judgments of world events. *Psychological Reports, 50,* 411–414.

Guilbault, R. L., Bryant, F. B., Brockway, J. H., & Posavac, E. J. (2004). A meta-analysis of research on hindsight bias. *Basic and Applied Social Psychology, 26,* 103–117.

Hastie, R., & Park, B. (1986). The relationship between memory and judgment depends on whether the judgment task is online or memory-based. *Psychological Review, 93,* 258–268.

Hawkins, S. A., & Hastie, R. (1990). Hindsight: Biased judgments of past events after the outcomes are known. *Psychological Bulletin, 107,* 311–327.

Hell, W., Gigerenzer, G., Gauggel, S., Mall, M., & Mueller, M. (1988). Hindsight bias: An interaction of automatic and motivational factors? *Memory and Cognition, 16,* 533–538.

Hoffrage, U., Hertwig, R., & Gigerenzer, G. (2000). Hindsight bias: A by-product of knowledge updating? *Journal of Experimental Psychology, 26,* 566–581.

Langer, E. J. (1975). The illusion of control. *Journal of Personality and Social Psychology, 32,* 311–328.

Langer, E. J., & Roth, J. (1975). Heads I win, tails it's chance: The illusion of control as a function of the sequence of outcomes in a purely chance task. *Journal of Personality and Social Psychology, 32,* 951–955.

Leary, M. R. (1982). Hindsight distortion and the 1980 presidential election. *Personality and Social Psychology Bulletin, 8,* 257–263.

Lopes, L. L. (1982). *Toward a procedural theory of judgment* (Tech. Rep. No. 17). Madison: University of Wisconsin, Wisconsin Human Information Processing Program.

Myers, D. G. (1999). *Social psychology* (6th ed.). Boston: McGraw-Hill.

Nario, M. R., & Branscombe, N. R. (1995). Comparison processes in hindsight and causal attribution. *Personality and Social Psychology Bulletin, 21,* 1244–1255.

Pennington, N. (1981). The British foremen's strike of 1977/78: An investigation of judgements in foresight and hindsight. *British Journal of Social and Clinical Psychology, 20,* 89–96.

Pennington, N., & Hastie, R. (1986). Evidence evaluation in complex decision making. *Journal of Personality and Social Psychology, 51,* 242–258.

Pennington, N., & Hastie, R. (1987). Explanation-based decision making. In *Proceedings of the Ninth Annual Conference of the Cognitive Science Society* (pp. 682–690). Hillsdale, NJ: Erlbaum.

Pennington, N., & Hastie, R. (1988). Explanation-based decision making: Effects of memory structure on judgment. *Journal of Experimental Psychology: Learning, Memory, and Cognition, 14,* 521–533.

Perloff, L. S. (1983). Perceptions of vulnerability to victimization. *Journal of Social Issues, 39,* 41–61.

Roese, N. J., & Maniar, S. D. (1997). Perceptions of purple: Counterfactual and hindsight judgments at Northwestern Wildcats football games. *Personality and Social Psychology Bulletin, 23,* 1245–1253.

Sanna, L. J., Schwarz, N., & Stocker, S. L. (2002). When debiasing backfires: Accessible content and accessibility experiences in debiasing hindsight. *Journal of Experimental Psychology: Learning, Memory, and Cognition, 28,* 497–502.

Schlenker, B. R., Miller, R. S., & Leary, M. R. (1983). Self-presentation as a function of the validity and quality of past performance. *Representative Research in Social Psychology, 13,* 2–14.

Slovic, P., & Fischhoff, B. (1977). On the psychology of experimental surprises. *Journal of Experimental Psychology: Human Perception and Performance, 3,* 544–551.

Slovic, P., & Lichtenstein, S. (1971). Comparison of Bayesian and regression approaches to the study of human information processing in judgment. *Organizational Behavior and Human Performance, 6,* 649–744.

Trabasso, T., & Van den Broek, P. (1985). Causal thinking and the representation of narrative events. *Journal of Memory and Language, 24,* 612–630.

Tversky, A., & Kahneman, D. (1973). Availability: A heuristic for judging frequency and probability. *Cognitive Psychology, 5,* 207–232.

Tversky, A., & Kahneman, D. (1974). Judgment under uncertainty: Heuristics and biases. *Science, 185,* 1124–1131.

Tykocinski, O. E., Pick, D., & Kedmi, D. (2002). Retroactive pessimism: A different kind of hindsight bias. *European Journal of Social Psychology, 32,* 577–588.

Walster, E. (1967). "Second guessing" important events. *Human Relations, 20,* 239–249.

Wood, G. (1978). The knew-it-all-along effect. *Journal of Experimental Psychology: Human Perception and Performance, 4,* 345–353.

Wortman, C. B. (1975). Some determinants of perceived control. *Journal of Personality and Social Psychology, 31,* 282–294.

14

How Do You Feel About It Now and When Did It Happen?

Judgments of Emotion and Judgments of Time in Autobiographical Memory

JOHN J. SKOWRONSKI
W. RICHARD WALKER
JOHN E. EDLUND

The characteristics of memory have long been a target of theorists, writers, and philosophers, and references to ideas about memory are spread throughout many ancient tomes (for overviews, see Herrmann & Chaffin, 1988; Robinson, 1986). For example, the writings of Augustine (354–430 A.D.) make reference to autobiographical memories in a discussion of "sense memories." Augustine argued that false memories are possible when "we fancy we remember as though we had done or seen it, when we never did or saw at all" (Augustine, trans. 1872, book 12, chap. 15). Augustine also pondered the relation between memory and the self. Foreshadowing modern interest in that topic (see Beike, Lampinen, & Behrend, 2004), Augustine considered memory to be a place in which identity is forged and in which we continually relive original experience and refashion everything we remember (Augustine, 1872). More recently, Mark Twain anticipated research examining false memories when he wrote (1924, p. 96): "When I was younger, I could remember anything, whether it had happened or not; but my faculties are decaying now and soon I shall be so I cannot remember any but the things that never happened." He also shows appreciation for the relation between memory and emotion when he wrote in an 1882 letter to George W. Cable (cited in Cardwell, 1953, p. 85): "I ought to be ashamed, but I never remember anything whatever except humiliation. If by some lucky chance there had been humiliation mixed in, I could remember every detail of that day for a thousand years."

Early theoretical psychologists showed a similar interest in autobiographical memory. For example, William James discussed the topic of autobiographical memory as it relates to ideas about associationism when he wrote (1900, pp. 117–118):

> Suppose I am silent for a moment, and then say in commanding accents: "Remember! Recollect!" Does your faculty of memory obey the order, and reproduce any definite image for your past? Certainly not. It stands staring into vacancy, and asking, "What kind of a thing do you wish me to remember?" It needs in short, a *cue*. But, if I say, . . . remember what you had for breakfast . . . ; then your faculty of memory immediately produces the required result: the 'cue' determines its vast set of potentialities toward a particular point.

Of course, it was only at the turn of the nineteenth century that psychology finally got around to doing much research on the topics that had stimulated such theoretical and philosophical interest. For example, anticipating modern research that examines so-called flashbulb memories (e.g., R. Brown & Kulik, 1982), Colegrove (1899) conducted personal interviews in which people were asked to recall where they were when they heard that Lincoln had been assassinated. In another early study, this one examining imagery in autobiographical memory, Galton (1883) devised a questionnaire asking respondents to visualize something definite (e.g., their breakfast tables) and then to describe aspects of the brightness, clarity, and apparent location of the resultant visual images.

However, research exploring autobiographical memory progressed at only a relatively modest pace throughout the first three quarters of the twentieth century. One reason for this modest pace was that such research was not a part of the mainstream of research in psychology, particularly among memory researchers. During the first half of the twentieth century, the world of memory research became the domain of research in the tradition of Ebbinghaus (1885/1964): The characteristics stimuli used in such research were well-known from pretesting, were often relatively low in personal meaning, and were presented in precise locations, at precise times, and in precise ways (an approach that some still see as fundamental to progress in psychology; see Banaji & Crowder, 1989). Bartlett (1932, 1935) argued that such stimuli stripped memory research of the elements that were essential to an understanding of memory, and some of his research can be seen as a reaction against this trend. In the absence of much interest from memory researchers, the study of autobiographical memory was largely left to researchers in other subareas of psychology.

However, in the spirit of Bartlett, spurred by theoretical and technical advances, the latter quarter of the twentieth century witnessed a resurgence of interest in autobiographical memory research. One spur to this research came from Tulving's work (1974), which gave researchers a theoretically driven reason to look at autobiographical memories. Tulving's theorizing implied that if one wanted to understand the properties of the episodic memory subsystem, one needed to specifically study the memories (episodic, autobiographical) that belonged to that subsystem. In addition, statistical methods, such as multiple regression, helped researchers to compensate for the loss of control over stimuli that invariably accompanies autobiographical memory research. As a consequence of these and other factors, autobiographical memory has come to be a mainstream topic of memory research.

Nonetheless, because memory researchers were late arrivals to the stage, current autobiographical memory research continues to be characterized by a diversity of theories and methods. This diversity is well illustrated by a partial listing of the topics that autobiographical memory researchers are currently trying to grapple with: (1) the neural substrates of such memories and how defects in those substrates affect memory formation and retrieval (Conway, Pleydell-Pearce, Whitecross, & Sharpe, 2003); (2) how such memories contribute to the construction of the self (Conway, Singer, & Tagini, 2004; Fivush, 2004; Singer & Blagov, 2004) and how the self shapes the events that are remembered (Sedikides, Green, & Pinter, 2004); (3) the impact of culture and social interactions on the development of, and content of, autobiographical memories (Fivush, 1994; Fivush & Nelson, 2004; Wang, 2001); (4) the development of false autobiographical memories and their behavioral implications (Bernstein, Laney, Morris, & Loftus, 2005; Loftus & Pickrell, 1995); (5) how clinical syndromes that affect autobiographical memories can inform us about neural and functional aspects of such memories (Klein, German, Cosmides, & Gabriel, 2004); (6) the kinds of real-world functions that autobiographical memories might serve (Bluck, Alea, Habermas, & Rubin, 2005); (7) the extent to which various self-report measures of autobiographical memories reflect the same underlying construct or reflect different constructs (Rubin, Shrauf, & Greenberg, 2003); and (8) the structure of autobiographical memories (N. R. Brown, 2005).

Some of this autobiographical memory research relates directly to this book's theme, *judgments over time.* In fact, we think that two of our own lines of research pertain to this theme especially well. The first of these is concerned with the emotions that accompany recall of autobiographical memories and how and why the intensity of those emotions might change across time. The second of these lines of research is concerned with time itself—the extent to which people know the time at which an autobiographical event occurred and the structures and mechanisms that accompany and influence such knowledge. We consider each of these topics in turn in the sections that follow.

You Struck Out and Lost the Championship Game: How Do You *Feel* About It Now?

People sometimes get emotional when they remember some events in their lives: Memories of the death of a sibling may be accompanied by feelings of sadness; memories of one's own wedding may be accompanied by feelings of happiness. In fact, the emotions that are activated by such memories can be so powerful that recall of autobiographical memories can be used as a method of mood induction (Baker & Gutterfreund, 1993; Brewer, Doughtie, & Lubin, 1980). In fact, as in people with posttraumatic stress syndrome, some autobiographical memories can be accompanied by emotions that are overwhelmingly powerful (Ehlers & Clark, 2000; Rubin, Feldman, & Beckham, 2004). However, one might claim that such long-lasting and persistent emotions are the exception rather than the rule. Certainly, the everyday experience of most people suggests that the affect associated with most autobiographical events fades over time (as captured, at least for negative events, by the phrase "time heals all wounds").

Some of our recent research has explored this fading of the affect that accompanies recalled autobiographical memories. One of the consistent findings in this research is that fading tends to be greater for the unpleasant emotions associated with autobiographical events than for the pleasant emotions associated with such events. This pattern has been termed the *fading affect bias* (Skowronski, Gibbons, Vogl, & Walker, 2004; Walker, Skowronski, Gibbons, Vogl, & Thompson, 2003; Walker, Vogl, & Thompson, 1997; for an overview, see Walker, Skowronski, & Thompson, 2003).

Although the fading affect bias has been known for some time, it has been the focus of only a few studies (Cason, 1932; Holmes, 1970). Hence it is fertile ground for new research. One focus of our recent research has been to ensure that the fading affect bias is a valid phenomenon. For example, some might suggest that the fading affect bias is a consequence of memory distortion. This possibility is raised by the fact that some studies that evinced the bias (e.g., Cason, 1932) used a retrospective memory procedure. In this procedure participants first recalled autobiographical events and then rated both the emotions experienced when the events originally occurred and the emotions prompted by recalling the event.

In such a procedure, perceivers might distort their memory for the emotions accompanying the original event. Indeed, several studies have shown that memory for emotions can evince such retrospective distortion (Feldman-Barrett, 1997; Safer, Levine, & Drapalski, 2002). Such results raise the possibility that the fading affect bias is a consequence of these distortions. That is, if people recall that their initial emotional response to a negative event was more extreme than it actually was, the apparent enhanced fading of emotion for the negative event over time would be exaggerated.

However, the results of several studies suggest that the fading affect bias is not a consequence of retrospective distortion in memory for negative emotion. For example, in a retrospective memory study, Walker, Skowronski, Gibbons, et al. (2003) found no difference in the initial intensity of emotions accompanying positive and negative events. If the fading affect bias were caused by retrospective memory distortions, the perceived initial intensity of negative emotions should have been greater than the perceived initial intensity of positive emotions. In addition, the results of four fading affect bias studies (Holmes, 1970; Walker et al., 1997) that used a diary methodology contradict the distortion argument. Participants in these studies kept a diary of life events in which they rated each event's valence and emotional intensity. A fading affect bias was observed in all four studies. Because the initial emotionality ratings obtained in these studies were made at the time of each event's occurrence, there can be no retrospective distortion in the memory for the intensity of the emotions experienced at event occurrence.

An additional focus of our recent research has been to explore some of the moderators of the fading affect bias. For example, one might expect that the extent to which the affect associated with an event fades might be related to an event's self-relevance. However, from a theoretical perspective, the exact nature of this effect is unclear. Positions that emphasize the fact that the self tends to be self-enhancing and self-protective (e.g., Sedikides & Strube, 1997) would seem to suggest that high self-relevance should be associated with low negativity and high positivity. On the other hand, because of the sensitive nature of such events, events with high self-relevance might be especially likely to provoke emotional reactions compared with less self-relevant events. Recent results (Ritchie, Skowronski, Wood, Vogl, Walker, & Gibbons, 2005) are more consistent with this latter idea. These results suggest that the affect associated with negative events is particularly robust across time when events are highly self-relevant or are perceived to be psychologically "open."

Another of the moderators of the fading affect bias is the disposition of the participant. Walker, Skowronski, Gibbons, et al. (2003) assessed an individual's dysphoria level and related that dysphoria level to the magnitude of the fading affect bias. They found that people with dysphoria showed less of a fading affect bias than those without dysphoria. This overall reduction was due to differences between individuals with dysphoria and those without in their responses to both positive and negative events. Positive events faded more, and negative events faded less, for people with dysphoria than for people without dysphoria.

Several questions are left unanswered by this research. One of these questions is the extent to which these results are unique to a dysphoric disposition. Tim Ritchie, a research team member at Northern Illinois University, has suggested that the dysphoria results of Walker, Skowronski, Gibbons, et al. (2003) explored only one side of the dispositional affect issue. If positive and negative dispositional affectivity have some degree of independence (as suggested by measures such as the Positive and Negative Affect Schedule [PANAS]; Watson, Clark, & Tellegen, 1988), then the magnitude of the fading affect bias ought to be affected by an individual's level of euphoria, independently of his or her level of dysphoria. Research is currently under way that examines this issue.

A second question left unanswered by the original dysphoria research is whether the extent to which people with and without dysphoria experience the fading affect bias is determined by the affect that is already in place when people recall events. That is, in accord with models such as the Affect Infusion Model (Forgas, 2001), it could be that the affect that people perceive in response to event recall could be contaminated by the affective state that they are in prior to recall. Moreover, such a mechanism might potentially account for the entire fading affect bias. That is, if people are generally in a good mood prior to their rating of the affect experienced at event recall, that preexisting positive affect could bias the event-specific affect ratings so that the positive events seem to be more positive and the negative events less negative than would otherwise be the case. Tim Ritchie is conducting a study that should address this concern. He is manipulating mood (e.g., via a music induction) to examine the impact of this manipulation on the fading affect bias. The primary interest is to see whether the fading affect bias is totally determined by mood at recall, is only partially affected by mood at recall, or is relatively impervious to mood at recall.

One other affect-related question that is left unaddressed in prior research is whether the fading affect bias might be caused by a confound between valence and activity level in the emotions prompted by event recall. That is, some emotion theorists (e.g., Russell, 1980) have suggested that emotions might be conceptually derived from two underlying constructs, valence (positive-negative) and activity level (active-passive). It may be that active emotions (ecstatic, angry) associated with autobiographical events fade more rapidly across time than passive emotions (sad, satisfied). It may also be the case that negative autobiographical events tend to be associated with a higher emotion activity level than positive autobiographical events. If this were the case, then the fading affect bias could, in fact, be potentially accounted for by this heightened activity level.

Another research team member at Northern Illinois University, Nicolette Jones, will be exploring this idea. She will ask participants to recall events related to different emotions. These emotions will be selected to reflect different underlying combinations of valence and activity level. This will allow her to disentangle the effects of valence and activity level, control for the possible valence/activity level confound, and allow her see whether a fading affect bias emerges across different emotions.

If the bias is relatively impervious to mood and occurs across emotion types, as we hope, then it would be useful to explore how other variables, such as event processing, affect the bias. We have already made progress in this regard. In Skowronski, Gibbons, et al. (2004), we explored the extent to which the magnitude of the fading affect bias was related to social discourse. That is, one of the characteristics of autobiographical memories is that they are shared with others, and we wondered whether such sharing altered the magnitude of the bias. This possibility was suggested by two lines of work. One of those, of course, was Pennebaker's research (e.g., Pennebaker, 2000; Mehl & Pennebaker, 2003). This research suggests that discussing traumatic events with others (or even preparing to discuss those events) seems to ease emotional adjustment to those events. The second line of work comes from the dysphoria literature. This work suggests that people with dysphoria may have impoverished social networks (Holahan, Moos, Holahan, Cronkite, & Randall, 2004), which obviously provide fewer opportunities for autobiographical disclosures.

These studies imply that the magnitude of the fading affect bias ought to be related to the frequency with which events are socially disclosed. Study 2 of Skowronski, Gibbons, et al. (2004) demonstrated this relation by showing that social disclosure frequency is, indeed, related to the fading of affect. Participants in that study reported that negative events that were frequently disclosed produced less negative affect at recall than events that were infrequently disclosed. However, although the effect was weaker, disclosure frequency was also related to the fading of positive affect. That is, the affect associated with positive events that were discussed frequently faded less than did the affect associated with infrequently discussed positive events. An additional study replicated this outcome and also showed an independent effect of disclosure breadth on the fading affect bias. Independently of disclosure frequency, the greater the number of different types of people with whom negative events were disclosed, the more the emotions associated with those negative events faded. In comparison, the greater the number of different types of people with whom positive events were disclosed, the less positive events faded—and it was this latter breadth effect that was the more robust of the two.

Of course, these correlational studies do not demonstrate that the extent to which emotions faded was causally altered by social disclosure. This cause-and-effect relation was demonstrated in Study 4 of Skowronski, Gibbons, et al. (2004). Participants in that study recalled autobiographical memories. At a later time, they came to an experimental session in which these memories were discussed with others. Skowronski and colleagues manipulated the disclosure frequencies so that an event was discussed either 0, 2, or 3 times. In the latter two conditions, each disclosure was to a different person. Later, people were asked to recall the events and to report the intensity of affect prompted by the recall of each. The results (see Figure 14.1) were clear: Discussing events with

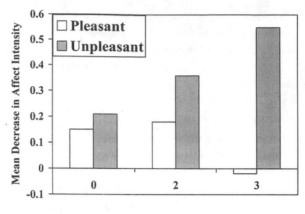

Manipulated Frequency of Social Disclosure

Figure 14.1. The relation between social disclosure frequency and the fading of emotions associated with positive and negative autobiographical events (from Skowronski et al., 2004).

others altered the affect produced by those events at recall. Discussing negative events increased the fading of the emotions associated with those events. In addition, although the effect was modest, discussing positive events decreased the fading of the emotions associated with those events.

A recent set of studies (Ritchie et al., 2005) explored whether these results were related to mere rehearsal of the events or whether it was the social nature of the rehearsals that was crucial. In these studies people were asked to report, for each recalled autobiographical event, the number of times they engaged in various kinds of private rehearsals and the number of times they rehearsed each event in the course of discourse with others. The data show that only the social rehearsals were associated with heightened fading of negative affect and diminished fading of positive affect. Because these studies were correlational, a recently completed study (Skowronski, Heider, Scherer, & Walker, 2005) tried to duplicate this outcome using an experimental methodology. Participants in this study were asked to disclose some autobiographical events to others either 0 or 3 times (each rehearsal was with a different person). They also participated in a task in which they answered an interaction partner's questions about one of several additional autobiographical events, but these events were never actually disclosed to the interaction partner. However, these events needed to be rehearsed to answer the questions. Events were rehearsed in this way either 0 or 3 times. It is expected that the social disclosure conditions will replicate the results of our prior study: that, with increasing disclosure frequency, fading of negative events will increase and fading of positive events will decrease. However, the condition of interest here is the condition in which the events were rehearsed but not disclosed. If the correlational results described earlier are replicated, then one might expect the extent to which affect fades to be unaffected by those trials on which events are rehearsed but not disclosed.

Even if this result is obtained, much remains to be done to understand why social discourse affects the emotions associated with recalled autobiographical events. Although some research (e.g., Petrie, Fontanilla, Thomas, Booth, & Pennebaker, 2004) suggests that even preparing to make a social communication (e.g., private writing) might have such effects, one cannot help but think that the overtly social aspects of interactions might also play a role. It may be the case that the consolation that one receives from a friend after a broken relationship or the expressions of admiration and support that one provokes in friends when telling a success story might also serve to affect the emotions later experienced when recalling the event that was disclosed.

You Hit A Home Run to Win the Championship: How Do You Know *When* That Event Occurred?

We are involved in a second line of research that pertains to the "judgments over time" theme of this book. Some of this research explored peoples' judgments about the time at which events occurred in their lives (Betz & Skowronski, 1997; Skowronski, Betz, Thompson, & Larsen, 1995; Skowronski, Betz, Thompson, & Shannon, 1991; Thompson, Skowronski, & Betz, 1993; Thompson, Skowronski, & Lee, 1988a,b). In these studies, participants kept dated diaries of autobiographical events. Later, they were given a blank calendar and were asked to report the exact date on which each event occurred.

These studies yielded a host of interesting findings. First, they showed that people typically provided erroneous event dates. This outcome matched peoples' self-reports, which indicated that they only infrequently knew exactly when an event occurred. Interestingly, females were more likely than males to provide such exact dates, an outcome that Skowronski and Thompson (1990) speculated was caused by the differing roles of males and females in society. They argued that females are often given the role of date keeper, inducing them to feel responsible for keeping track of the important dates on which certain events occurred (e.g., the first kiss, the first date, all the birthdays of relatives, etc.). They suggested that this habitual date-keeping activity made it more likely that females would know the exact dates of autobiographical events than males. This notion also suggests that when females incorrectly dated events, the magnitude of the errors that they made should equal the magnitude of males' errors. This idea was confirmed by analyses of the inaccurate date estimates.

The fact that date knowledge was so infrequently exact obviously implies that the dates that people provided were often estimated. Unsurprisingly, the magnitude of the errors that people made increased with the age of the event.

What was a bit more surprising was the relative consistency of the effect: Error magnitude increased by roughly 1 day with each 7-day increase in an event's age and did so across relatively long time frames (see Skowronski, Walker, & Betz, 2004). The research team speculated that people were using their event memories to concoct event estimates. That this should occur is seemingly obvious—if one recalls that an event occurred when snow was on the ground, one would probably suspect that the event occurred in winter. Indeed, self-reported event memorability did predict the accuracy of the event dates that were provided. Moreover, in participants' self-reports of the process by which they obtained event dates, they indicated that they did sometimes use their ability to remember event details to reconstruct the time at which an event occurred.

However, not only were the event date estimates erroneous, but they were also systematically biased by several variables. Many of these variables reflect the action of top-down knowledge on peoples' date judgments. One of these variables is the presence of a bounded time period specifying the starting and ending points between which events must have occurred. Many of the studies conducted in this line of research used such bounded periods—typically the beginning and end of academic terms. The presence of such boundaries tended to produce *telescoping effects* in the date estimates. When the events were recent, the events tended to be misdated in the direction of being older than they were (*backward telescoping*); when the events were old, the events tended to be misdated in the direction of being younger then they were (*forward telescoping*).

Peoples' self-reports of their dating strategies suggested that they used a number of different kinds of information in these reconstructions. These included memory clarity, memory accessibility, the use of prototypic temporal event information (knowledge of the day, week, or month), the use of general reference periods (e.g., it happened in summer), and counts of the number of events that intervened between two other events. The fact that people use such strategies was verified by some of the error patterns observed in the date estimates. For example, peoples' estimates tended to be biased by their knowledge of the *day of the week* on which an event occurred. Skowronski et al. (1991) first showed that the errors in peoples' date estimates showed a peculiar "scalloping" pattern: The most frequent errors in date estimates were at multiples of 7 days (7, 14, 21, etc.; see Figure 14.2). Such error patterns reflect the fact that a standard blank calendar that included day of the week was used to cue date estimates and that people had day-of-week knowledge available to them that was cued by these day-of-week labels. Hence, the calendar might prompt people to recall that an event happened on a Thursday, but not *which* Thursday. However, the day-of-week information was not the only temporal information available to the temporal estimates. This was confirmed by the fact that misestimates were most likely to occur for the Thursday that was 1 week removed from the actual date of occurrence and were least likely to occur for the Thursday that was the farthest removed (within the bounded period) from the actual date.

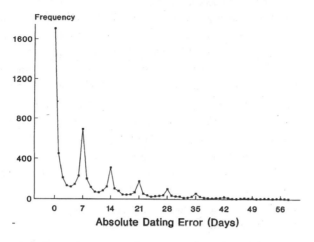

Figure 14.2. The relation between error magnitude and error frequency reflects the extent to which day-of-week knowledge affects date estimation (from Skowronski et al., 1991).

Betz and Skowronski (1997) demonstrated that evidence of the biasing effects of such day of week knowledge emerges in date estimates in other ways. For example, they demonstrated that within-week day transposition errors also seem to follow from top-down knowledge about the nature of events that occur within a given week. They argued that for many college students the week is segmented into subunits. One such segmenting pattern seems to be early school week (Monday and Tuesday), late school week (Wednesday and Thursday), and weekend (Friday through Sunday). Betz and Skowronski (1997) showed that people were more likely to make dating errors within a particular day-of-week segment than between day-of-week segments. Hence, it was relatively likely that a person would misdate a Monday event as occurring on a Tuesday; but it was relatively less likely that the person would misdate a Sunday event as occurring on a Monday.

Asymmetries in the error patterns were also seemingly reflective of the action of top-down within-week knowledge of events on date estimates. For example, Saturday events were relatively likely to be misplaced as occurring on a Sunday, but Sunday events were relatively unlikely to be misplaced as occurring on a Saturday. Such asymmetries may have to do with the types of events that people listed for those dates. The tendency may have been for participants to list Saturday events that were "all-purpose" events that could have occurred on any of the weekend days (e.g., I watched a football game with friends). In comparison, Sunday events (e.g., went to church) may have tended to be highly specific to Sundays.

Gibbons and Thompson (2001) showed that these day-of-week error patterns are caused by use of the calendar as a cuing device. In a series of experiments, they found that the frequency with which multiple-of-7 errors appeared dropped when participants were not given calendars as a date estimation aid. This dissipation occurred despite the fact that most participants were able recall the day of the week on which an event occurred. Hence, without a calendar available, that day-of-week knowledge was apparently not used in formulating date estimates. Gibbons and Thompson (2001) found that the calendars had another effect on event dating: Estimates tended to be more accurate when a blank calendar was provided than when it was not.

Data from Thompson et al. (1993) suggested that one of the other strategies that people use in event dating is a "landmark" strategy. In this strategy, people first date a "landmark" event and date other events relative to that landmark event. For example, one typical landmark event is the start of a connected event sequence, such as the start of a vacation. To estimate the dates of all the vacation events listed in one's diary, one simply has to establish the date of the initial event, then date all the vacation events relative to that initially dated landmark. Thompson and colleagues (1993) showed evidence for such a dating strategy by showing that there were frequent "error runs" in the date estimates. That is, when examining error patterns, clusters of similarly misdated events (e.g., a series of events on 5 consecutive days, all of which were misdated by 7 days) occurred at a rate greater than that expected by chance. The presence of such clusters would be expected if some date estimates were established by fixing event dates relative to a landmark event that was itself misdated.

Responses of participants in these studies to the request that they provide dates for autobiographical events were also potentially informative. It seemed that for many participants, the process of determining event dates was subjectively difficult and, indeed, even painful (especially when people realized that they did not have a clue as to when some events occurred). These observations contributed to our belief that temporal knowledge was something that was obtained only via reconstructive processes that were relatively effortful in nature.

This belief has been challenged by our recent studies of temporal order judgments (Skowronski, Walker, & Betz, 2003, 2004). In these studies, participants were again asked to list events in a dated diary. Later, the events were presented to each participant two at a time, and the participant was asked to indicate the correct ordering of events. Response latency and accuracy were recorded.

Initial studies yielded two sensible results. The first of these is that the older events became, the more difficult the ordering judgment became. The second result was *a temporal distance effect* in the data: Controlling for the ages of the events that were involved, the farther apart in age the two events were, the easier (faster, more accurate) the judgment became. It was this temporal distance effect that led us to reconsider the notion that event age estimates were always obtained with great difficulty. Contradicting this notion, for events that were far apart in age, event order judgments were made with great speed and accuracy.

This observation suggested that there was some characteristic of event representations that allowed rapid identification of at least some rudimentary forms of temporal knowledge.

One possibility is that autobiographical events are linked to semantic information that has temporal implications (see Conway & Pleydell-Pearce, 2000). That is, there may be a "header" or "tag" linked to an event that identifies the broad period in which the event occurred. This tag could be "graduate school" or "my first job" or "when I was a kid." Hence, when events are separated by long periods of time, temporal discriminations may be easy because the temporal orderings are specified by the tags ("when I was a kid" comes before "graduate school"). When events are relatively close in time, such event tags may not be present, and people may have to repeatedly access fine-grained event knowledge in their attempt to determine event orders. Such repeated access should be difficult, which should be indicated by responses that take a long time and are often incorrect.

One of the implications of these conjectures is that order judgments that involve events from two different time periods should be easier than order judgments that involve events from the same time period, even when the absolute time difference between the events is held constant. In our team's most recent studies, we have probed for such effects in the context of an individual's academic life history, which is conveniently segmented into periods that are similar for most people (grade school vs. high school vs. college; freshman vs. sophomore vs. junior vs. senior). Our preliminary analyses of the data from these studies have yielded exactly the expected pattern—order judgments are easier for two events that cross major time period boundaries than for events that both occurred within the same time period, even when the absolute time between their occurrence is the same (Skowronski, 2004; Skowronski, Ritchie, et al., 2005).

We also realized that some of the data from our first series of event dating studies could also be viewed as consistent with the semantic tag idea. After all, even though peoples' estimates of the dates of old events were often erroneous, they also seemed to contain a kernel of truth. That is, though erroneous, the event dates provided by people for old events were not random guesses—people knew that they were old. This relatively general temporal knowledge could come from the semantic labels that characterized the time periods in which the events occurred. Such labels could provide a first approximation of an event's date.

However, even in the face of such supportive data, we wondered whether the presence of semantic headers or tags serves as the sole explanation for the ease with which people could make some temporal order judgments and for the kernel of truth that seems to characterize some date judgments. Our pondering has led us to a second conjecture: that one context for autobiographical memories is the "state of the self" (which we term the *self-image*). Broadly defined, this self-image is composed of one's memory of one's physical and psychological characteristics at the time an event occurred. We hypothesize that one's self-image may be linked to events and might be activated by event recall. Hence, this self-image can serve as another "rough and ready" cue that can help to place an event in temporal context. For example, one might be able to get a sense of how old an event is by comparing the self-image activated by event recall to the current self-image. Self-images that are highly discrepant imply old events; self-images that are congruent imply recent events. Similarly, when trying to decide which of two events is more recent, the event that prompts recall of a self-image that is more discrepant from the current self is the event that will be judged to be older.

This notion has some interesting and testable implications. For example, it predicts that, controlling for the absolute passage of time between events, temporal order judgments will be easier for those who see themselves as having changed substantially in a given period of time when compared with those who see themselves as relatively stable. One way to test this would be to compare the temporal order judgments of high school students, who presumably see substantial self-changes across the 4-year span of high school, with those of adults, who, in general, probably have a relatively constant self-image across a 4-year time span. However, not all adults experience such stability. A second study could compare the temporal order judgments of adults who have experienced rapid self-concept change in a given period of time with the judgments of those similarly aged adults who have not. Ross and Wilson (2002) have already taken a step in this direction by showing that event outcomes that are substantially different from the current self and that could potentially derogate the current self "feel" old. Although it has not been shown that such feelings alter more objective estimates of time (e.g., date of occurrence), Ross and Wilson's results certainly suggest that such effects might be detectable with at least some measures.

Nonetheless, although conceptually straightforward, conducting the studies that we have suggested presents several methodological difficulties. One of these difficulties would be controlling for the notion that self-concept change might be noted in memory by semantic tags that label lifetime periods ("when I was a freshman," "before my divorce"). One would expect that such tags might often accompany, and even index, rapid changes in the self-image. Hence, to look at the self-as-a-standard idea, one needs to find a way to eliminate the potential influence of such tags (or at least, to hold the influence of such tags constant). A second difficulty would be that the recalled self-image linked to a memory may not be veridical but instead may be distorted. Similarly, the current self-image might also be distorted. Such distortions can occur in the service of sharpening the distinction between one's past and present (see Cameron, Wilson, & Ross, 2004). Such instability in memories for self-images might distort their usefulness as a temporal cue, causing people to ignore them when they need to pinpoint event dates or event orders with relative accuracy.

Coda

People interact with their pasts in a number of ways. They try to remember the details of events, they try to remember when such events happened, and they experience alterations in emotions as a result of some of the events that are recalled. The research that is described in this chapter describes some findings that relate to these interactions.

These results suggest that people are generally better able to retain the positive emotions that accompany positive events than the negative emotions that accompany negative events. As with many psychological phenomena, there are exceptions: This trend does not occur for some people (e.g., those with dysphoria) and may be significantly lessened for some events (e.g., self-relevant ones). Moreover, some extreme events (e.g., highly traumatic ones) that we simply do not capture in our studies of everyday memory might be especially likely to yield results that are inconsistent with our typical findings.

However, our findings provide some hope for optimism, even for those traumatic events. These results suggest, as do those of Pennebaker (2000), that communicating negative events to other people might be a good way to dissipate the negativity associated with those negative life events. Moreover, these results go beyond Pennebaker's in showing that the emotions that are associated with positive events can also be affected by social disclosure. That is, in addition to removing "the agony of defeat," talking to people about the good events in your life helps you to retain "the thrill of victory."

People also try to put these recalled events in temporal context. The extent to which this task is easy or difficult partially depends on the level of precision required in the judgment. People can seemingly place events in broad lifetime periods with relative ease. However, given that some of those lifetime periods are temporally imprecise (e.g., "when I was a kid"), there will often be considerable error in such rapid judgments. That error can be reduced by resorting to a host of cues that a person has at her or his disposal. The use of such cues often requires attention and effort—for example, making inferences about temporal periods from the recollected details of events. The fact that such inferences are necessary also implies that there can be systematic error in the judgments that people provide, and evidence of such error is vividly portrayed in the day-of-week error frequency data that are depicted in Figure 14.2.

Although seemingly disparate, these two phenomena, judgments of emotions and judgments about time, are united in an important way. They show that peoples' knowledge of their lives is not determined by a passive "readout" of a stored memory trace or even by a passive readout of one's current emotional state. Instead, people must constantly attend to past and present information, make judgments about that information, and make additional judgments based on their judgments about that information. Was I really so happy when I hit that home run that I sprinted around the bases, or do I just believe that because people have often told me that I did it? Were the leaves on the trees at the ballpark turning color, and does that mean that the game was played in the autumn? Am I happy when I think about that memory now because the memory makes me happy, or am I happy because I just got a paper published? These questions illustrate the fact that memory and judgment processes work hand in hand to determine peoples' perceptions of their past, present, and future. We hope that the research that we have discussed in this chapter gives you a better sense of how memory and judgment processes operate when people think about events in their lives, when those events occurred, and how remembering those events makes them feel.

Acknowledgment

We thank the NIH for facilitating this chapter via a grant (MH063724–01) awarded to John Skowronski.

References

Augustine. (1872). *On the Trinity, Bk. 12.* In M. Dods (Ed.), & A. W. Haddan (Trans.), *The works of Aurelius Augustine. A new translation.* Edinburgh: T&T Clark. Retrieved October 25, 2005, from http://www.logoslibrary.org/augustine/trinity/1215.html.

Baker, R. C., & Gutterfreund, D. G. (1993). The effects of written autobiographical recollection induction procedures on mood. *Journal of Clinical Psychology, 49,* 563–568.

Bartlett, F. C. (1932). *Remembering: A study in experimental and social psychology.* Oxford, UK: Macmillan.

Bartlett, F. C. (1935). Remembering. *Scientia Bologna, 57,* 221–226.

Banaji, M. R., & Crowder, R. G. (1989). The bankruptcy of everyday memory. *American Psychologist, 44,* 1185–1193.

Beike, D. R., Lampinen, J. M., & Behrend, D. A. (Eds.). (2004). *The self and memory.* New York: Psychology Press.

Bernstein, D. M., Laney, C., Morris, E. K., & Loftus, E. F. (2005). False memories about food can lead to food avoidance. *Social Cognition, 23,* 11–34.

Betz, A. L., & Skowronski, J. J. (1997). Self-events and other-events: Temporal dating and event memory. *Memory and Cognition, 25(5),* 701–714.

Bluck, S., Alea, N., Habermas, T., & Rubin, D. (2005). A tale of three functions: The self-reported uses of autobiographical memory. *Social Cognition, 23,* 91–117.

Brewer, D., Doughtie, E. B., & Lubin, B. (1980). Induction of mood and mood shift. *Journal of Clinical Psychology, 36,* 215–226.

Brown, N. R. (2005). On the prevalence of event clusters in autobiographical memory. *Social Cognition, 23,* 35–69.

Brown, R., & Kulik, J. (1982). Flashbulb memories. In U. Neisser (Ed.), *Memory observed: Remembering in natural contexts* (pp. 23–40). San Francisco: Freeman.

Cameron, J. J., Wilson, A. E., & Ross, M. (2004). Autobiographical memory and self assessment. In D. R. Beike, J. M. Lampinen, & D. A. Behrend (Eds.), *The self and memory* (pp. 207–226). New York: Psychology Press.

Cardwell, G. (1953). *Twins of genius.* East Lansing: Michigan State College Press.

Cason, H. (1932). The learning and retention of pleasant and unpleasant activities. *Archives of Psychology, 134,* 1–96.

Colegrove, F. (1899). Individual memories. *American Journal of Psychology, 10,* 228–255.

Conway, M. A., & Pleydell-Pearce, C. W. (2000). The construction of autobiographical memories in the self-memory system. *Psychological Review, 107,* 261–288.

Conway, M. A., Pleydell-Pearce, C. W., Whitecross, S. E., & Sharpe, H. (2003). Neurophysiological correlates of memory for experienced and imagined events. *Neuropsychologia, 41,* 334–340.

Conway, M. A., Singer, J. A., & Tagini, A. (2004). The self and autobiographical memory: Correspondence and coherence. *Social Cognition, 22,* 491–529.

Ebbinghaus, H. (1964). *Memory: A contribution to experimental psychology [Über das Gedächtnis: Untershungen zur experimentellen Psychologie]* (H. A. Ruger, Trans.). New York: Dover. (Original work published 1885)

Ehlers, A., & Clark, D. M. (2000). A cognitive model of posttraumatic stress disorder. *Behaviour Research and Therapy, 38,* 319–345.

Feldman-Barrett, L. (1997). The relationship among momentary emotion experiences, personality descriptions, and retrospective ratings of emotion. *Personality and Social Psychology Bulletin, 23,* 1100–1110.

Fivush, R. (1994). Constructing narrative, emotion, and self in parent-child conversations about the past. In U. Neisser & R. Fivush (Eds.), *The remembering self: Construction and accuracy in the self-narrative* (pp. 136–157). Cambridge, UK: Cambridge University Press.

Fivush, R. (2004). The silenced self: Constructing self from memories spoken and unspoken. In D. R. Beike, J. M. Lampinen, & D. A. Behrend (Eds.), *The self and memory* (pp. 75–94). New York: Psychology Press.

Fivush, R., & Nelson, K. (2004). Culture and language in the emergence of autobiographical memory. *Psychological Science, 15,* 573–577.

Forgas, J. P. (2001) The affect infusion model (AIM): An integrative theory of mood effects on cognition and judgments. In L. L. Martin & G. L. Clore (Eds.), *Theories of mood and cognition: A user's guidebook* (pp. 99–134). Mahwah, NJ: Erlbaum.

Galton, F. (1883). *Inquiries into human faculty and its development.* London: Macmillan.

Gibbons, J. A., & Thompson, C. P. (2001). Using a calendar in event dating. *Applied Cognitive Psychology, 15,* 33–44.

Herrmann, D. J., & Chaffin, R. (Eds.).(1988). *Memory in historical perspective: The literature before Ebbinghaus.* New York: Springer-Verlag.

Holahan, C. J., Moos, R. H., Holahan, C. K., Cronkite, R. C., & Randall, P. K. (2004). Unipolar depression, life context vulnerabilities, and drinking to cope. *Journal of Consulting and Clinical Psychology, 72,* 269–275.

Holmes, D. S. (1970). Differential change in affective intensity and the forgetting of unpleasant personal experiences. *Journal of Personality and Social Psychology, 3,* 234–239.

James, W. (1900). *Talks to teachers on psychology and to students on some of life's ideals.* New York: Holt.

Klein, S. B., German, T. P., Cosmides, L., & Gabriel, R. (2004). A theory of autobiographical memory: Necessary components and disorders resulting from their loss. *Social Cognition, 22,* 460–490.

Loftus, E. F., & Pickrell, J. E. (1995). The formation of false memories. *Psychiatric Annals, 25,* 720–725.

Mehl, M. R., & Pennebaker, J. W. (2003). The social dynamics of a cultural upheaval: Social interactions surrounding September 11, 2001. *Psychological Science, 14,* 579–585.

Pennebaker, J. W. (2000). The effects of traumatic disclosure on physical and mental health: The values of writing and talking about upsetting events. In J. M. Violanti, D. Paton, & C. Dunning (Eds.), *Posttraumatic stress intervention: Challenges, issues, and perspectives* (pp. 97–114). Springfield, IL: Thomas.

Petrie, K. J., Fontanilla, I., Thomas, M. G., Booth, R. J., & Pennebaker, J. W. (2004). Effect of written emotional expression on immune function in patients with human immunodeficiency virus infection: A randomized trial. *Psychosomatic Medicine, 66,* 272–275.

Ritchie, T. D., Skowronski, J. J., Wood, S. E., Walker, W. R., Vogl, R. J., & Gibbons, J. A. (2005). *Event self-importance, event rehearsal, and the fading affect bias in autobiographical memory.* Unpublished manuscript.

Robinson, J. A. (1986). Autobiographical memory: A historical prologue. In D. C. Rubin (Ed.), *Autobiographical memory* (pp. 19–24). New York: Cambridge University Press.

Ross, M., & Wilson, A. E. (2002). It feels like yesterday: Self-esteem, valence of personal past experiences, and judgments of subjective distance. *Journal of Personality and Social Psychology, 82,* 792–803.

Rubin, D. C., Feldman, M. E., & Beckham, J. C. (2004). Reliving, emotions, and fragmentation in the autobiographical memories of veterans diagnosed with PTSD. *Applied Cognitive Psychology, 18,* 17–35.

Rubin, D. C., Schrauf, R. W., & Greenberg, D. L. (2003). Belief and recollection of autobiographical memories. *Memory and Cognition, 31,* 887–901.

Russell, J. A. (1980). A circumplex model of affect. *Journal of Personality and Social Psychology, 39,* 1161–1178.

Safer, M. A., Levine, L. J., & Drapalski, A. L. (2002). Distortion in memory for emotions: The contributions of personality and post-event knowledge. *Personality and Social Psychology Bulletin, 28,* 1495–1507.

Sedikides, C., Green, J. D., & Pinter, B. (2004). Self-protective memory. In D. R. Beike,

J. M. Lampinen, & D. A. Behrend (Eds.), *The self and memory* (pp. 161–180). New York: Psychology Press.

Sedikides, C., & Strube, M. J. (1997). Self-evaluation: To thine own self be good, to thine own self be sure, to thine own self be true, and to thine own self be better. In M. P. Zanna (Ed.), *Advances in experimental social psychology* (Vol. 29, pp. 209–270). San Diego, CA: Academic Press.

Singer, J. A., & Blagov, P. (2004). The integrative function of narrative processing: Autobiographical memory, self-defining memories, and the life story of identity. In D. R. Beike, J. M. Lampinen, & D. A. Behrend (Eds.), *The self and memory* (pp. 117–138). New York: Psychology Press.

Skowronski, J. J. (2004, May). *When was I? Thoughts and data concerning our ability to place autobiographical events in time.* Paper presented at the University of Nijmegen, Nijmegen, The Netherlands.

Skowronski, J. J., Betz, A. L., Thompson, C. P., & Larsen, S. F. (1995). Long-term performance in autobiographical event dating: Patterns of accuracy and error across a two-and-a-half-year time span. In A. F. Heay & L. E. Bourne (Eds.), *Learning and memory of knowledge and skills: Durability and specificity* (pp. 206–233). Thousand Oaks, CA: Sage.

Skowronski, J. J., Betz, A. L., Thompson, C. P., & Shannon, L. (1991). Social memory in everyday life: Recall of self-events and other-events. *Journal of Personality and Social Psychology, 60,* 831 843.

Skowronski, J. J., Gibbons, J. A., Vogl, R. J., & Walker, W. R. (2004). The effect of social disclosure on the intensity of affect provoked by autobiographical memories. *Self and Identity, 3,* 285–309.

Skowronski, J. J., Heider, J. D., Scherer, C. R., & Walker, W. R. (2005). [Fading affect for rehearsed and non-rehearsed events activated in a social context]. Unpublished raw data.

Skowronski, J. J., Ritchie, T. D., Walker, W. R., Betz, A. L., Sedikides, C., Bethencourt, L. A., et al. (2005). *Ordering our world: The quest for traces of temporal organization in autobiographical memory.* Unpublished manuscript.

Skowronski, J. J., & Thompson, C. P. (1990). Reconstructing the dates of personal events: Gender differences in accuracy. *Applied Cognitive Psychology, 4,* 371–381.

Skowronski, J. J., Walker, W. R., & Betz, A. L. (2003). Ordering our world: An examination of time in autobiographical memory. *Memory, 11,* 247–260.

Skowronski, J. J., Walker, W. R., & Betz, A. L. (2004). Who was I when that happened? The timekeeping self in autobiographical memory. In D. R. Beike, J. M. Lampinen, & D. A. Behrend (Eds.), *The self and memory* (pp. 183–206). New York: Psychology Press.

Thompson, C. P., Skowronski, J. J., & Betz, A. L. (1993). The use of partial temporal information in dating personal events. *Memory and Cognition, 21,* 352–360.

Thompson, C. P., Skowronski, J. J., & Lee, D. J. (1988a). Telescoping in dating naturally occurring events. *Memory and Cognition, 16,* 461–468.

Thompson, C. P., Skowronski, J. J., & Lee, D. J. (1988b). Reconstructing the date of a personal event. In M. M. Gruneberg, P. E. Morris, & N. Sykes (Eds.), *Practical aspects of memory: Current research and issues: Vol. 1. Memory in everyday life* (pp. 241–246). Oxford, UK: Wiley.

Tulving, E. (1972). Episodic and semantic distinction. In E. Tulving & W. Donaldson (Eds.), *Organization of memory* (pp. 381–384). New York: Academic Press.

Twain, M. (1924). *Mark Twain's autobiography.* New York: Harper & Brothers.

Walker, W. R., Skowronski, J. J., Gibbons, J. A., Vogl, R. J., & Thompson, C. P. (2003). On the emotions that accompany autobiographical memory: Dysphoria disrupts the fading affect bias. *Cognition and Emotion, 17,* 703–723.

Walker, W. R., Skowronski, J. J., & Thompson, C. P. (2003). Life is pleasant . . . and memory helps to keep it that way! *Review of General Psychology, 7,* 203–210.

Walker, W. R., Vogl, R. J., & Thompson, C. P. (1997). Autobiographical memory: Unpleasantness fades faster than pleasantness over time. *Applied Cognitive Psychology, 11,* 399–413.

Wang, Q. (2001). Culture effects on adults' earliest childhood recollection and self-description: Implications for the relation between memory and the self. *Journal of Personality and Social Psychology, 81,* 220–233.

Watson, D., Clark, L. A., & Tellegen, A. (1988). Development and validation of brief measures of positive and negative affect: The PANAS scales. *Journal of Personality and Social Psychology, 54,* 1063–1070.

15

Remembering and Misremembering Emotions

LINDA J. LEVINE
MARTIN A. SAFER
HEATHER C. LENCH

"Tell me about your vacation . . . your accident . . . your wedding. . . ." When remembering life experiences, individuals often relate not just what happened but also how they remembered feeling at the time. Indeed, the most meaningful and memorable experiences of our lives are typically those that evoked strong emotions such as joy, fear, anger, or shame. Although most research on emotional memories focuses on how well people remember the events that elicited emotion (e.g., Reisberg & Heuer, 2004), this chapter addresses a different question: How well do people remember their own past emotions?

Investigating memory for emotions is of practical, as well as theoretical, importance. Remembering past emotions helps people make decisions about the future. Indeed, people's preferences, goals, and behavior are often shaped by their memories of the emotions elicited by specific situations. We typically seek to repeat circumstances and activities that we remember as resulting in positive emotions, and we try to avoid or change circumstances that we remember as resulting in negative emotions (Kahneman, Fredrickson, Schreiber, & Redelmeier, 1993). Moreover, a person's memory of past emotional reactions plays a vital role in the construction of personal identity (Neimeyer & Metzler, 1994). Generalizing from such memories, people come to view themselves as easygoing or hot-tempered, sentimental or dispassionate. Also, researchers and clinicians often ask people to rate the intensity and frequency with which they have experienced affective states such as depression and anger over the past weeks or months (Christianson & Safer, 1996; Thomas & Diener, 1990). Diagnostic and treatment decisions concerning mental disorders are based partly on self-reports of this type. Thus there are many different reasons to investigate how people remember past emotions.

Interestingly, investigators have taken radically different positions on whether and how people remember past emotions. Some argue that emotion is stored in memory directly, whereas others argue that emotions must first be transformed into cognitive representations. Similarly, there are theoretical debates as to whether emotion is stored in memory indelibly or, like other features of autobiographical memories, is subject to forgetting and reconstruction over time. In this chapter, we discuss different ways that emotions are represented in memory, whether representations of past emotions are accurate, and the sources and direction of bias when they are inaccurate.

How Are Emotions Stored in Memory?

There is a long-standing debate within psychology as to whether emotions per se are stored in memory (for a review, see B. Ross, 1991). Some investigators argue that emotion cannot be stored in memory but must be reconstructed based on knowledge concerning the circumstances in which the emotion was experienced. According to this view, when asked to remember emotions, people retrieve not the fleeting emotional experience but a redescription of it based on memory for relevant details concerning the event (episodic knowledge) or based on beliefs about how one is likely to have felt (semantic knowledge) (Robinson & Clore, 2002a,b). Remembering the circumstances in which an emotion was experienced also may cause people to experience a similar but new emotion in the present (Wyer, Clore, & Isbell, 1999), and it is this new emotion that is then reported. As William James put it, "The revivability in memory of the emotions, like that of all the feelings of the lower senses, is very small. . . . [W]e can produce, not remembrances of the old grief or rapture, but new griefs and raptures, by summing up a lively thought of their exciting cause" (1890/1918, vol. 2, p. 474).

Others argue not only that emotions are stored in memory but also that they are stored permanently and accurately (Fanselow & Gale, 2003; LeDoux, 1996; van der Kolk, 1994). This contrasting claim, that emotions can leave indelible memory traces, is based primarily on findings that conditioned fear is remarkably long lasting. Indeed, even after being extinguished, classically conditioned avoidance responses can be reinstated by exposure to a stressful stimulus. Thus extinction modifies behavior, but it does not seem to erase the original emotional memory (e.g., LeDoux, 1992).

The conflict between these claims is more apparent than real. Its resolution lies in noting that emotion can be represented in memory in at least two levels, with each level having unique properties. These levels closely parallel the distinction between explicit and implicit memory for cognitive material (e.g., LeDoux, 1996; Leventhal & Scherer, 1987; Tobias, Kilhstrom, & Schacter, 1992). Consider the following experience: While staying in a hotel in Turkey, I (LJL) leaned against a large porcelain sink that shattered and fell out of the wall. The broken porcelain severed much of my left wrist, resulting in months of severe pain, three operations, and more than a year of physical therapy. How do I remember this emotional experience? Deliberate attempts to remember it are not very successful and, mercifully, do not lead to reexperiencing the physical sensations of pain (Morley, 1993). I simply recall having described the pain at the time as combining feelings of extreme heat and pressure. I recall having felt anxious, but retrieval of this verbal descriptor does not constitute retrieval of the emotion. However, more than 10 years after the accident, in response to the slight unsteadiness of a sink, I experienced sudden, intense anxiety and immediately jumped back.

The pallid verbal descriptors of anxiety and pain fit well with claims that affective states are evanescent. When people make deliberate attempts to recall past emotions, they reconstruct how they must have felt from episodic details or retrieve semantic descriptors (Robinson & Clore, 2002a). These explicit memories are flexible and accessible across situations and do not depend on the presence of specific retrieval cues (Eichenbaum, 1992). In contrast, my reaction to the unsteady sink 10 years later suggests that emotion is also stored in memory as emotion and not simply reconstructed based on cognitive representations. This reaction suggests a level of representation of emotion in memory that is vivid and long lasting but accessible only in the presence of specific contextual cues.

Implicit memory for emotions has been studied primarily in the context of conditioned behavior in animals. Animals behave in a manner consistent with retaining representations of the valence, intensity, and circumstances of past emotional experiences (Mackintosh, 1983). Indeed, Weinberger, Gold, and Sternberg (1984) found that memory for emotional experiences affected rats' subsequent behavior even when an emotion-eliciting event and epinephrine injection occurred under deep anesthesia so that no conscious memory for the event was accessible. Similarly, experimental and case studies of humans with traumatic and organic amnesias show that memory for emotion can be demonstrated in the absence of conscious memory for the emotion-eliciting event (Christianson & Safer, 1996; Tobias et al., 1992).

Thus emotions can be represented in memory in two ways: Explicit representations of emotional experience can be reconstructed based on the retrieval of episodic and semantic knowledge. A more direct, implicit representation also can be stored of emotional valence and intensity (and likely of discrete emotions such as sadness, anger, and fear). Explicit and implicit memories for emotions have different properties. They differ with respect to whether they are consciously controlled or automatic, with respect to the specificity of the retrieval cues needed to elicit them, and with respect to their effects on ongoing cognition and behavior. Explicit memory for emotion can be retrieved (or reconstructed) at will in a broad range of circumstances. For example, I (LJL) have dispassionately related the broken sink incident in different settings over the years. Explicit memories provide information that can be used intentionally to guide decisions to seek out or avoid situations in the future. In contrast, implicit memory for emotion is evoked involuntarily in the presence of relatively specific retrieval cues that bear a close resemblance to the situation in which the emotion was originally experienced. Even in the absence of conscious recollection and appraisal of an experience, stored representations of past emotional experience can elicit an emotional reaction in the present. When implicit memory for emotion becomes accessible, the resulting experience shares many of the properties of the original emotional experience. It is vivid and commandeers attention, thought, and behavior in the service of attaining goals or avoiding goal failure. Thus, even after 10 years, a loose sink evokes a feeling of anxiety and motivates avoidance behavior.

Animal research using lesions or drugs to inactivate specific brain regions, human and animal research on conditioning under anesthesia, and research on amnesiacs indicates that explicit and implicit memory for emotion are dissociable (Christianson, 1992; Daum, Flor, Brodbeck, & Birbaumer, 1996; Tobias et al., 1992; Witvliet, 1997) and rely on different neural systems (LeDoux, 1996; Ochsner & Schacter, 2003; Schacter, Chiu, & Ochsner, 1993). Because they can be retrieved independently, it is possible for the two types of information to conflict. For example, a parent's memory of foreign travel with teens may include conscious recollections of having had a great time, as well as implicit memories of exasperation that come to mind only when taking the next trip.

Bias in Memory for Emotions

The coexistence and possible conflict between explicit and implicit representations of emotion raises the issue of which is accurate: explicit memory, implicit memory, both, or neither. Researchers who have focused on explicit memory for emotion have generally stressed its inaccuracy and have noted that people often overestimate the intensity of past emotions. Researchers who have focused on implicit memory for emotion, particularly fearful memories, have argued that emotional memories are stored permanently and accurately. In this section, we review evidence that both explicit and implicit memory for emotions are subject to forgetting and bias. Moreover, emotions can be recalled as either more or less intense than initially reported. We argue that the direction of bias depends on current goals and appraisals of the emotion-eliciting event, as well as recent or current emotional experience.

Bias in Explicit Memory for Emotion

Overestimation of Past Emotions

Most research on explicit memory for emotion has shown moderate correlations between the intensity of emotion initially reported and the intensity recalled ($r = .50$ or higher). Relative accuracy across individuals, however, does not guarantee fidelity of recall for any one individual, and, indeed, biases in explicit memory for emotion have been demonstrated for many types of experiences (for reviews, see Robinson & Clore, 2002a; Fredrickson, 2000). In many cases, the direction of bias has been toward overestimation in recalling the intensity of past emotions (for a review, see Safer & Keuler, 2002). Examples include the overestimation by depressed patients of the intensity of previous reportedly depression (Schrader, Davis, Stefanovic, & Christie, 1990), overestimation of negative affect at the time of their first relapse by smokers who were trying to quit (Shiffman, Hufford, Hickcox, Paty, Gnys, & Kassel, 1997), overestimation by blood donors of their predonation anxiety (Breckler, 1994), and overestimation of both positive and negative emotion experienced on vacation (Wirtz, Kruger, Scollon, & Diener, 2003).

Several mechanisms may underlie overestimation of emotional intensity. Because emotional intensity reflects people's appraisals of an event's importance and relevance to their goals and concerns (Frijda, Ortony, Sonnemans, & Clore, 1992), the most salient moments when remembering past experiences are often the moments of peak intensity. When estimating how they felt over the course of an extended emotional experience, moments of peak intensity are most likely to come to mind. As a result, peak affect contributes disproportionally to estimates of overall emotional experience, in comparison with moments of lesser or neutral affect (Fredrickson & Kahneman, 1993; Hedges, Jandorf, & Stone, 1985; Wilson, Meyers, & Gilbert, 2003; Wirtz et al., 2003). In addition, the process of thinking about and trying to remember an experience may lead to reporting the experience as being more intense (Knowles, 1988; Tesser, 1978). There may also be motivational reasons for overestimating past emotions. For example, McFarland and Alvaro (2000) found that, following traumatic events, people perceive "growth" or improvement in feelings and personal attributes by exaggerating pretrauma negative feelings and attributes. The more they derogated their past, the better they felt in the present (also see Conway & Ross, 1984).

The Role of Current Appraisals

The intensity of past emotions is not always overestimated, however. Drawing on appraisal theories of emotion, Levine (1997) argued that the reconstruction of explicit memory for emotions can consist of either over- or underestimation. "Appraisal" refers to a person's conscious or unconscious evaluation of the relationship between a stimulus and his or her well-being (Arnold, 1960; Lazarus, 1991). According to appraisal theories, people experience emotions primarily when they evaluate circumstances as being relevant to their goals, desires, or values. Specific types of appraisals elicit specific emotional responses (e.g., Frijda, 1987; Levine, 1996; Oatley & Johnson-Laird, 1987; Scherer, Schorr, & Johnstone, 2001; Smith & Lazarus, 1993; Stein & Levine, 1987; Weiner, 1985). Levine (1997) proposed that when gaps exist in people's memories for past emotions, emotional memories are reconstructed based on recall of the emotion-eliciting circumstances and their appraisals of those circumstances. If people's appraisals have changed since the occurrence of the emotion-eliciting event, they should show a bias toward recalling emotions that are consistent with their current appraisals. If memories for emotions are reconstructed in this manner, one would not expect to find a general tendency to overestimate or underestimate the intensity of past emotions. Whether emotions are over- or underestimated should depend on how people's interpretations of the emotion-eliciting event have changed over time (also see Ross, 1989; Eich, Reeves, Jaeger, & Graff-Radford, 1985).

To test these claims, Levine (1997) assessed people's memory for the emotions evoked by Ross Perot's abrupt withdrawal from his United States presidential candidacy in July of 1992. Perot's supporters described their initial emotional reactions and their appraisals of Perot shortly after his withdrawal. After Perot reentered the presidential race and participated in the November 1992 election, supporters again recalled their initial emotions and described their current appraisals of Perot. Systematic changes in memory for emotions were found in the direction of supporters' current appraisals. For example, loyal supporters who wished that Perot had been elected in November overestimated how hopeful they had felt when Perot first dropped out of the race and underestimated how angry they had felt. In contrast, those who had turned against Perot underestimated how hopeful they had felt and demonstrated stable recall of anger.

Even when the emotions in question are evoked by sudden and devastating losses, people appear to draw on their current appraisals to help them infer how they must have felt. For example, the September 11, 2001, attacks evoked intense distress in people throughout the United States (e.g., Silver, Holman, McIntosh, Poulin, & Gil-Rivas, 2002). Levine, Whalen, Henker, and Jamner (2005) asked parents and adolescents to recall their initial emotional reactions to the attacks 3 months and 8 months after the attacks. Their current appraisals of the impact of the attacks were also assessed. The results showed that parents recalled increased distress over time, whereas adolescents recalled decreased distress. These differences between parents and adolescents were predicted by their current appraisals of the terrorist attacks, with those viewing the attacks as more consequential recalling their emotions as more intense than those who viewed the attacks as having less impact.

Because these data are correlational, however, one cannot be certain that changes in appraisals actually cause changes in how emotions are remembered. So Safer, Levine, and Drapalski (2002) conducted an experiment that assessed college students' memories for how anxious they felt before a midterm exam. Students were randomly assigned to one of two groups. One group learned their exam grades before recalling their pre-exam emotions. The other group did not yet know their grades when they recalled their emotions. In contrast to those who had not yet learned their grades, students who learned that they had done well on the exam underestimated how anxious they had felt before the exam. Students who learned that they had done poorly overestimated how anxious they had felt. Thus current beliefs about their grades led to distortions in students' memories for their past feelings of anxiety.

In general, our studies have shown that, the greater the change in people's goals and beliefs concerning an emotion-eliciting event, the greater the instability in their memories for past emotions. Moreover, as would be predicted by appraisal theories, changes in specific appraisals are associated with instability in memory for specific emotions. For example, change in beliefs about whether an outcome was desirable is associated with bias in memory for happiness, but not for surprise. Change in beliefs about whether an outcome was expected is associated with bias in memory for surprise, but not for happiness (Levine, Prohaska, Burgess, Rice, & Laulhere, 2001).

Individual Differences

People differ in how they appraise emotional experiences, and so it is not surprising that individuals also differ in their tendencies to overestimate or underestimate past emotions. Safer and Keuler (2002) found that among clients terminating psychotherapy, those who reported being high on negative traits such as neuroticism tended to overestimate in recalling their prepsychotherapy emotional distress. Those who scored high on positive traits such as ego strength tended to underestimate their prepsychotherapy distress. Cutler, Larsen, and Bunce (1996) had participants rate their moods twice daily for 4 weeks. Participants with a repressive coping style underestimated daily unpleasant affect, whereas participants high in anxiety overestimated unpleasant affect (also see Feldman Barrett, 1997). Individual difference measures reflect people's ongoing emotional states and appraisals, and these, in turn, affect what is remembered about past emotions (Safer et al., 2002). Thus enduring personality traits, as well as current appraisals, are associated with bias in explicit memory for emotions.

Bias in Implicit Memory for Emotion

Implicit memory for emotion is also subject to fading over time and to biases that can consist of either over- or underestimation. Animal research indicates that conditioned fear responses can be maintained, virtually unchanged, for months. Such findings have led to claims that implicit fear memories are permanent (e.g., Fanselow & Gale, 2003). In most conditioning studies, the animal lives in a benign environment, is placed in a novel context and exposed to an aversive stimulus, and is then returned to its previous, uneventful existence (Hendersen, 1985). In real life, though, after a frightening event occurs, other experiences follow that may be better or worse than the initial frightening one. What happens to conditioned fear in cases like that?

Hendersen (1985) created a laboratory analogue to such real-life experiences. Rats underwent a series of conditioning trials in which a tone preceded a shock and repeated pairings led to a conditioned fear response to the tone. After either 1 day or 60 days, the rats received a couple of gratuitous shocks (i.e., shocks that were not preceded by the tone) that were either milder or stronger than the level of shock used during conditioning. When reexposed to the tone, those rats that had recently received mild shocks showed less fear in response to the tone than those that had recently received strong shocks. Importantly, the difference in the intensity of the fear response following the mild versus strong gratuitous shocks was much greater at 60 days than at 1 day. Thus, over time, memory for the intensity of fear had become increasingly malleable—increasingly subject to bias in the direction of recent experience.

These findings conflict with claims that implicit memory for emotion is indelible. Interestingly, implicit memory for cognitive material (e.g., neutral words and pictures) was also once thought to be immune to forgetting and bias. Recent studies, however, reveal similar patterns of forgetting and bias for explicit and implicit cognitive representations (e.g., Lustig & Hasher, 2001; McBride & Dosher, 1999).

In summary, emotions can be stored in memory at different levels, but both explicit and implicit memories for emotions become increasingly malleable over time. Both over- and underestimation of past emotions occur, and the link between changing appraisals of events and biases in memory for emotion is now well documented. Bartlett (1932) stated that "the past is continually being remade, reconstructed in the interests of the present" (p. 309). The findings reviewed herein demonstrate that this is true of the emotional past as well. Irrespective of whether the emotions in question were mild or intense, positive or negative, concerned others or the self, people drew on current (or habitual) goals and interpretations concerning prior events to help them infer how they must have felt (Levine & Safer, 2002). Recent experience also biases implicit memory and can lead to underestimation, as well as overestimation, of past emotions (Hendersen, 1985).

Functions of Remembering and Misremembering Emotions

In his delightfully titled chapter, "But What the Hell Is It For?" Alan Baddeley (1988) argued that, whenever we come across a clear and replicable phenomenon, we should place a high priority on figuring out what role that phenomenon plays in normal human activity. So, why are emotions stored in memory? Why do memories for emotions fade over time? Why are these memories reconstructed in directions consistent with current experience, goals, and interpretations of events?

Why Remember Emotions?

The utility of remembering emotion is obvious. According to appraisal theory (e.g., Scherer, Schorr, & Johnstone, 2001), emotions provide essential information about the relation between environmental events and people's goals. Happiness signals that circumstances are consistent with goals and values and should be maintained. Negative emotions signal that circumstances threaten goals and must be avoided or changed. Thus emotion provides information that guides concurrent, goal-directed behavior.

Memory for emotion also guides people's preferences, intentions, and behavior (e.g., Hendersen, 1985; Levine, 1997; Levine et al., 2001; Loewenstein & Schkade, 1999; Robinson, 1980). People choose to seek out or avoid particular experiences based in part on their memories for how experiences made them feel. For example, a person who remembers leaving the Nemesis roller coaster feeling terrified, shaky, and nauseated is likely to forgo that ride in the future. An inability to draw on emotion memories, which can occur in certain patients with frontal lobe lesions, leads to markedly poor judgments and decisions (Damasio, 1994). Remembering emotions is also efficient. Zajonc (1980) argued that emotions can be remembered long after details concerning the events that elicited them have been forgotten. Recalling past emotions thus alleviates the need to store detailed descriptions of events, while letting people know whether to seek out or avoid similar situations in the future.

Why Forget Emotions?

If emotions are so important for guiding goal-directed action, why forget them? It has been argued that forgetting aspects of emotional experience hinders people's ability to both learn from the past and make informed choices for the future (Wilson et al., 2003). There are risks, however, in remembering too much. As William James put it, "Selection is the very keel on which our mental ship is built. And in this case of memory its utility is obvious. If we remembered everything, we should on most occasions be as ill off as if we remembered nothing" (1890/1950, vol. 1, p. 680).

From infancy through adolescence and into adulthood, people experience emotional ups and down on a daily, even an hourly, basis. Intense emotional experiences are also far from rare (Kochanska, Coy, Tiebkes, & Husarek, 1998; Larson & Richards, 1994). A memory system that preserved each of these experiences indelibly would be too unwieldy to serve the functions of guiding preference, intention, and behavior. Moreover, memories for emotions may no longer be useful guides if circumstances have changed or if a person's goals and beliefs have changed. The more time passes, the more likely it is that both circumstances and individuals will have changed. As a result, recent memories generally serve as more useful guides to goal-directed behavior than distant memories. Thus, it is at least efficient, and at most a product of evolutionary design, that emotional memories fade over time (Hendersen, 1985; also see Schacter, 2001).

Why Reconstruct Memories for Emotion?

As memory for emotion fades over time, it becomes more subject to modification based on subsequent experience, goals, and beliefs. Why reconstruct memory for emotions? One could argue that reconstructing emotional memories not only makes them more useful but also makes them more accurate. To determine whether a given representation is accurate, one first has to know what it is supposed to be representing. If emotional memories are records of actual past internal states, then certainly, reconstruction leads to inaccuracy. But the fundamental contribution of appraisal theory is that emotions are not simply internal states of arousal and valence. Emotions signal the perceived relationship between circumstances and an individual's goals and values. If memories for emotions are records of the ongoing relationship between past events and an individual's goals, then updating these records based on current goals and beliefs makes them more accurate. In the same way, updating a map when new roads are built makes it more accurate. In short, the primary function of memory may be to guide future behavior rather than to keep an exact record of the past. Because emotional memories are informed by current appraisals of the emotion-eliciting situation, rather than being perfectly faithful to the past, they may serve as a more relevant guide for future behavior (Levine & Safer, 2002).

Future Consequences of Misremembering Emotions

We have described different ways in which memories for emotions can be stored and different factors that influence how emotions are remembered. Next, we examine how memory for emotion influences future feelings, cognitions, and behaviors. A widely believed truism is that people seek to repeat pleasant experiences and to avoid unpleasant experiences. Kahneman et al. (1993) have argued that people prefer to repeat, not necessarily the experiences that actually gave them the most pleasure, but the experiences that have left them with the most favorable memories. Similarly, people prefer to avoid experiences that left them with the least favorable memories. Just as perceptual illusions can illuminate the mechanisms underlying ordinary perception, the effect of memory for emotion on future choice and behavior is particularly apparent when people's remembered feelings differ from their concurrent ratings of an experience. Thus, in emphasizing misremembered emotions, our aim is not to downplay the importance of accurately remembered emotions but to highlight the ways in which memory for emotion guides future thoughts, feelings, and behaviors.

Misremembering Emotion Can Influence Future Choice

Wirtz et al. (2003) compared students' predicted, actual, and remembered emotions over their spring-break vacations. Students rated their actual (or current) emotions seven times a day at random intervals, every day during the vacation. The researchers found that students later overestimated in recalling the intensity of both positive and negative emotion. Nevertheless, it was their remembered emotional reactions, rather than their predicted or actual emotions, that best predicted intentions to repeat that vacation in the future. Thus students were not particularly accurate in remembering how they had felt, but remembered emotion was the map they used to guide their future choices.

Similarly, studies have shown that memory of pain, not just the actual experience of pain, affects future behavior. Pain includes both sensory and affective experience. Redelmeier, Katz, and Kahneman (2003) investigated memory for the pain caused by colonoscopy. They compared control patients with those for whom the colonoscope remained in place for an additional 1 to 3 minutes, resulting in a period of relatively mild pain at the end of a moderately painful procedure. Consistent with findings that ending states are particularly salient in retrospective evaluations of emotional experience (Fredrickson, 2000; Kahneman et al., 1993), patients with this additional mild pain actually remembered the overall experience as less painful than the controls. These patients were also more likely than controls to repeat the procedure within 6 years, after controlling for prior colonoscopy, abnormal findings, and procedural indications. Thus the pain remembered, rather than the pain actually experienced, affected the decision to repeat the procedure in the future.

Misremembering Emotion Can Promote Goal-Directed Behavior

Memory distortions are typically viewed as problematic. In the case of emotion, memory distortions have been described as interfering with people's ability to learn from past emotional experiences (e.g., Wilson et al., 2001, 2003). Misremembering emotion, though, can also promote goal achievement. Fredrickson (2000) argued that people's tendency to focus on the peaks and ends of affective experiences may be best understood in terms of promoting goal-directed behavior and coping. Peaks and ends may dominate memories of affective experiences not because of perceptual salience but because of the personal meaning captured by those points in time. When people are engaged in goal-directed behavior, end affect is of particular importance because it symbolizes the outcome of the activity (e.g., success or failure) and whether or not it was worthwhile. Peak affect is important because it defines the personal capacity that would be needed to face the experience again.

Loewenstein's (1999) discussion of the emotions and goals of mountaineers is consistent with the view that the salience of emotions at the end of an experience serves to promote goal achievement. He describes mountaineers' accounts of forgetting the boredom, discomfort, and fear they endured throughout much of an expedition after achieving their goal of reaching the summit. One mountaineer, for instance, described conditions during a climb in the Alps as "harshly uncomfortable, miserable and exhausting." After achieving the summit however, he reported that, "my memory edited out the anxiety and tension and fed me happy recollections of superb climbing, the spectacular positions we had been in, feeling confident and safe, knowing we were going to succeed" (Simpson, 1993, as cited in Loewenstein, 1999, p. 319). Arguably, accurate and detailed recall of the moment-to-moment struggles en route to goal achievement would result in fewer mountains climbed, children born and raised, research projects conducted, and articles written.

Exaggerating negative emotions can also promote goal-directed behavior. For example, Safer et al. (2002) found that students who did poorly on their midterm exams recalled more pre-exam anxiety than they had actually reported. Exaggerating pre-exam anxiety was associating with planning to study more for the final exam, even after controlling for exam grades.

The overestimation of past emotions in the service of goal-directed behavior can have negative, as well as positive, consequences. This occurs when memory distortion promotes short-term goals (such as avoiding pain and distress) at the expense of long-term goals (such as restoring health). In such cases, it may be advantageous to minimize exaggeration of past feelings of pain and distress. For example, Chen, Zeltzer, Craske, and Katz (1999) found that children tended to exaggerate in recalling the negative affect and discomfort caused by lumbar punctures in the treatment of leukemia. This exaggeration heightened distress when the children prepared to undergo subsequent lumbar punctures. Rather than trying to teach the children new coping skills, Chen et al. (1999) used a memory reframing procedure to try to keep them from remembering the distress as more extreme than their actual experience.

Specifically, a therapist interviewed children for about 15 minutes immediately following the first puncture and encouraged them to remember as accurately as possible their actual, successful coping responses. The therapist also reminded the children about their successful coping just prior to their next lumbar puncture. Compared with controls, children who engaged in memory reframing did not exaggerate in remembering their distress, and they were calmer when they had to undergo the next lumbar puncture. Thus keeping individuals from exaggerating negative affect in memory may be particularly valuable for those who have to undergo repeated stressful experiences, such as medical procedures, in the service of broader goals.

Misremembering Emotion Can Facilitate Coping

Misremembering past emotion may also facilitate people's ability to cope with ongoing challenges. For example, Safer and Keuler (2002) found that approximately two thirds of clients who terminated psychotherapy overestimated in remembering their pretherapy distress, thereby apparently perceiving a greater positive change with therapy than was warranted. Clients who did not show objective improvement in therapy were particularly likely to overestimate in remembering their pretherapy distress. In contrast, after people have successfully coped with past emotion-eliciting events, overestimation of previous emotions seems to diminish. Thus clients who improved the most in therapy tended to underestimate past distress. Good current functioning was associated with the retrospective reappraisal that past negative experiences were "not so bad." Safer, Bonanno, and Field (2001) found similar memory biases in a sample of widows and widowers who were coping with the midlife death of a spouse.

A vital ongoing challenge is that of maintaining positive long-term relationships. Research shows that misremembering the emotional past of an ongoing relationship can contribute to its future quality. In a longitudinal study, Karney and Coombs (2000) had wives rate their satisfaction with their marriages at 10-year intervals. At the 10-year and 20-year follow-ups, wives were also asked to remember their satisfaction ratings from 10 years earlier. They found that, across the first 20 years of marriage, wives' satisfaction tended to decline linearly. After 10 years, however, wives remembered the past more negatively than they actually reported, possibly in keeping with the common belief that good relationships improve and deepen over time. Importantly, the degree of memory bias at 10 years predicted satisfaction over the next 10 years of marriage. Karney and Coombs (2000) concluded that memory bias may be a mechanism that serves to maintain satisfaction in long-term relationships (also see Sprecher, 1999).

The study just described concerned explicit memory for relationship satisfaction. A study that examined a more implicit measure of memory for emotion found that such memories could predict future relationship commitment. Buehlman, Gottman, and Katz (1992) asked married couples to reminisce about the history of their relationship. Observer ratings of the emotions elicited while couples were reminiscing predicted divorce over the next 3 years with 94% accuracy. This oral history interview predicted divorce better than the couples' self-reports of their current marital satisfaction (which may be based on explicit episodic and semantic memory) and better than an observational measure of how couples solved relationship problems. The emotions expressed while reminiscing may result from implicit memories and may reveal a level of distress that couples do not want to acknowledge.

Future Directions and Conclusions

An understudied issue concerns individual differences in remembered and forecasted emotions. Kihlstrom noted that, "what a person can and cannot remember, and the way in which personal experiences are reconstructed, may be more revealing of the individual's personality than the most sophisticated trait measure" (1981, p. 137). Systematic patterns of memory distortion for emotion may help to define personality and may be a basis for self-ratings of personality (Safer & Keuler, 2002; Safer et al., 2002). For example, people who self-report as high on neuroticism are likely to overestimate in recalling the intensity of negative emotions and underestimate in recalling the intensity of positive emotions (Feldman Barrett, 1997). In turn, people who consistently overestimate past negative feelings and underestimate past positive feelings are likely to develop an autobiographical memory "database" that will lead them to self-report as high on neuroticism. In current studies, we are assessing the relationship between traits such as neuroticism and optimism and people's predicted, actual, and recalled responses to emotional events. We hope to use this data to explore the potentially cyclical relationship between personality characteristics, distortion in memory for emotions, and predictions concerning future affective experiences.

Another fascinating issue for future research concerns the interaction of appraisals, explicit memory for emotion, and implicit memory for emotion. We know that changes in goals and appraisals can bias explicit memories of emotion, but can they also bias implicit memories of emotion, including memories other than fear? For example, some therapeutic treatments for posttraumatic stress disorder assume that implicit emotional memories, particularly intrusive, disturbing memories from a traumatic experience, can be neutralized by reexperiencing them, changing how they are interpreted, and framing them within a flexible narrative that fits into a person's life story (van der Hart, Brown, & van der Kolk, 1989). Thus empirical research on processes that influence the accessibility and accuracy of implicit memory for emotion would have important implications for clinical practice (also see Metcalfe & Jacobs, 1998). Another potentially important area for research is how individuals experience and resolve discrepancies between implicit and explicit memories for an emotional experience (Fazio & Olson, 2003).

In conclusion, emotions provide critical information about the relevance of events to people's goals. It is essential that this information be stored in memory and just as essential that these memories be informed by subsequent learning. We have reviewed evidence that emotions are represented in at least two different forms in memory: explicit and implicit. Explicit memories are based on semantic and episodic knowledge and can be retrieved in a flexible manner in different circumstances. Typically, these memories inform but do not overpower people's preferences, intentions, and actions. In contrast, implicit memories of emotion come to mind in the presence of cues that resemble the context in which the emotional event occurred. Retrieval of implicit memory for emotion is experienced as current emotion, with many of the properties of the initial emotional state. When accessible, these memories can strongly direct attention, thinking, and behavior toward avoiding dangerous or aversive states and toward attaining desired states. Thus explicit and implicit memories have very different properties.

One property that they share, though, is that both types of memories are subject to bias and can represent past emotion as either more or less intense than originally experienced. It is well documented that explicit recall of past emotions may be biased by current goals and appraisals concerning the emotion-eliciting event. Much less is known about biases in implicit memory for emotion, but research suggests that it, too, may be biased by current or recent experience. Both types of biasing can be viewed as updating memories of emotions so that they can more precisely guide future thoughts, intentions, and behaviors.

References

Arnold, M. B. (1960). *Emotion and personality.* New York: Columbia University Press.

Baddeley, A. (1988). But what the hell is it for? In M. M. Gruneberg & P. E. Morris (Eds.), *Practical aspects of memory: Current research and issues: Vol. 1. Memory in everyday life* (pp. 3–18). Oxford, UK: Wiley.

Bartlett, F. C. (1932). *Remembering: A study in experimental and social psychology.* Cambridge, UK: Cambridge University Press.

Breckler, S. (1994). Memory for the experience of donating blood: Just how bad was it? *Basic and Applied Social Psychology, 15,* 467–488.

Buehlman, K. T., Gottman, J. M., & Katz, L. F. (1992). How a couple views their past predicts their future: Predicting divorce from an Oral History Interview. *Journal of Family Psychology, 5,* 295–318.

Chen, E., Zeltzer, L. K., Craske, M. G., & Katz, E. R. (1999). Alteration of memory in the reduction of children's distress during repeated aversive medical procedures. *Journal of Consulting and Clinical Psychology, 67,* 481–490.

Christianson, S.-Å. (1992). Remembering emotional events: Potential mechanisms. In S. Christianson (Ed.), *The handbook of emotion and memory: Research and theory* (pp. 307–340). Hillsdale, NJ: Erlbaum.

Christianson, S.-Å., & Safer, M. A. (1996). Emotional events and emotions in autobiographical memories. In D. C. Rubin (Ed.), *Remembering our past* (pp. 218–243). New York: Cambridge University Press.

Conway, M., & Ross, M. (1984). Getting what you want by revising what you had. *Journal of Personality and Social Psychology, 47,* 738–748.

Cutler, S. E., Larsen, R. J., & Bunce, S. C. (1996). Repressive coping style and the experience and recall of emotion: A naturalistic study of daily affect. *Journal of Personality, 64,* 379–405.

Damasio, A. R. (1994). *Descartes' error: Emotion, reason, and the human brain.* New York: Grosset/Putnam.

Daum, I., Flor, H., Brodbeck, S., & Birbaumer, N. (1996). Autobiographical memory for emotional events in amnesia. *Behavioral Neurology, 9,* 57–67.

Eich, E., Reeves, J. L., Jaeger, B., & Graff-Radford, S. B. (1985). Memory for pain: Relation between past and present pain intensity. *Pain, 23,* 375–379.

Eichenbaum, H. (1992). The hippocampal system and declarative memory in animals. *Journal of Cognitive Neuroscience, 4,* 217–231.

Fanselow, M. S., & Gale, G. D. (2003). The amygdala, fear, and memory. *Annals of the New York Academy of Sciences, 985,* 125–134.

Fazio, R. H., & Olson, M. A. (2003). Implicit measures in social cognition research: Their meaning and use. *Annual Review of Psychology, 54,* 297–327.

Feldman Barrett, L. (1997). The relationship among momentary emotion experiences, personality descriptions, and retrospective ratings of emotion. *Personality and Social Psychology Bulletin, 23,* 1100–1110.

Fredrickson, B. L. (2000). Extracting meaning from past affective experiences: The importance of peaks, ends, and specific emotions. *Cognition and Emotion, 14,* 577–606.

Fredrickson, B. L., & Kahneman, D. (1993). Duration neglect in retrospective evaluations of affective episodes. *Journal of Personality and Social Psychology, 65,* 45–55.

Frijda, N. H. (1987). Emotion, cognitive structure, and action tendency. Cognition and Emotion, 1, 115–143.

Frijda, N. H., Ortony, A., Sonnemans, J., & Clore, G. L. (1992). The complexity of intensity: Issues concerning the structure of emotion intensity. In M. S. Clark (Ed.), *Emotion* (pp. 60–89). Newbury Park, CA: Sage.

Hedges, S. M., Jandorf, L., & Stone, A. A. (1985). Meaning of daily mood assessments. *Journal of Personality and Social Psychology, 48,* 428–434.

Hendersen, R. W. (1985). Fearful memories: The motivational significance of forgetting. In F. R. Brush & J. B. Overmier (Eds.), *Affect, conditioning, and cognition: Essays on the determinants of behavior* (pp. 43–53). Hillsdale, NJ: Erlbaum.

James, W. (1950). *The principles of psychology* (Vol. 2). New York: Holt. (Original work published 1890)

Kahneman, D., Fredrickson, B. L., Schreiber, C. A., & Redelmeier, D. A. (1993). When more pain is preferred to less: Adding a better end. *Psychological Science, 4,* 401–405.

Karney, B. R., & Coombs, R. H. (2000). Memory bias in long-term close relationships: Consistency or improvement? *Personality and Social Psychology Bulletin, 26,* 959–970.

Kihlstrom, J. F. (1981). Personality and memory. In N. Cantor & J. F. Kihlstrom (Eds.), *Personality, cognition, and social interaction* (pp. 123–149). Hillsdale, NJ: Erlbaum.

Knowles, E. S. (1988). Item context effects on personality scales: Measuring changes the measure. *Journal of Personality and Social Psychology, 55,* 312–320.

Kochanska, G., Coy, K. C., Tiebkes, T. L., & Husarek, S. J. (1998). Individual differences in emotionality in infancy. *Child Development, 69,* 375–390.

Larson, R., & Richards, M. H. (1994). *Divergent realities: The emotional lives of mothers, fathers, and adolescents.* New York: Basic Books.

Lazarus, R. S. (1991). *Emotion and adaptation.* New York: Oxford University Press.

LeDoux, J. (1996). *The emotional brain.* New York: Touchstone.

LeDoux, J. E. (1992). Emotion as memory: Anatomical systems underlying indelible neural traces. In S.-Å. Christianson (Ed.), *The handbook of emotion and memory: Research and theory* (pp. 269–288). Hillsdale, NJ: Erlbaum.

Leventhal, H., & Scherer, K. (1987). The relationship of emotion to cognition: A functional approach to a semantic controversy. *Cognition and Emotion, 1,* 3–28.

Levine, L. J. (1996). The anatomy of disappointment: A naturalistic test of appraisal models of sadness, anger, and hope. *Cognition and Emotion, 10,* 337–359.

Levine, L. J. (1997). Reconstructing memory for emotions. *Journal of Experimental Psychology: General, 126,* 165–177.

Levine, L. J., Prohaska, V., Burgess, S. L., Rice, J. A., & Laulhere, T. M. (2001). Remembering past emotions: The role of current appraisals. *Cognition and Emotion, 15*, 393–417.

Levine, L. J., & Safer, M. A. (2002). Sources of bias in memory for emotions. *Current Directions in Psychological Science, 11*, 169–173.

Levine, L. J., Whalen, C. K., Henker, B., & Jamner, L. D. (2005). Looking back on September 11, 2001: Appraised impact and memory for emotions in adolescents and adults. *Journal of Adolescent Research, 20*, 497–523.

Loewenstein, G. (1999). Because it is there: The challenge of mountaineering . . . for utility theory. *Kyklos, 52*, 315–344.

Loewenstein, G., & Schkade, D. (1999). Wouldn't it be nice? Predicting future feelings. In D. Kahneman, E. Diener, & N. Schwarz (Eds.), *Well-being: The foundations of hedonic psychology* (pp. 85–105). New York: Sage.

Lustig, C., & Hasher, L. (2001). Implicit memory is not immune to interference. *Psychological Review, 127*, 629–650.

Mackintosh, N. J. (1983). *Conditioning and associative learning.* New York: Oxford University Press.

McBride, D. M., & Dosher, B. A. (1999). Forgetting rates are comparable in conscious and automatic memory: A process-dissociation study. *Journal of Experimental Psychology: Learning, Memory, and Cognition, 25*, 583–607.

McFarland, C., & Alvaro, C. (2000). The impact of motivation on temporal comparisons: Coping with traumatic events by perceiving personal growth. *Journal of Personality and Social Psychology, 79*, 327–343.

Metcalfe, J., & Jacobs, W. J. (1998). Emotional memory: The effects of stress on the "cool" and "hot" memory systems. In D. L. Medin (Ed.), *The psychology of learning and motivation: Advances in research and theory* (Vol. 38, pp. 188–222). New York: Academic Press.

Morley, S. (1993). Vivid memory for "everyday" pains. *Pain, 55*, 55–62.

Neimeyer, G. J., & Metzler, A. E. (1994). Personal identity and autobiographical recall. In U. Neisser & R. Fivush (Eds.), *The remembering self: Construction and accuracy in the self-narrative* (pp. 105–135). Cambridge, UK: Cambridge University Press.

Oatley, K., & Johnson-Laird, P. N. (1987). Toward a cognitive theory of emotions. *Cognition and Emotion, 1*, 29–50.

Ochsner, K. N., & Schacter, D. L. (2003). Remembering emotional events: A social cognitive neuroscience approach. In R. J. Davidson, K. R. Scherer, & H. Goldsmith, (Eds.), *Handbook of the affective sciences (pp. 643–660).* New York: Oxford University Press.

Redelmeier, D. A., Katz, J., & Kahneman, D. (2003). Memories of colonoscopy: A randomized trial. *Pain, 104*, 187–194.

Reisberg, D., & Heuer, F. (2004). Memory for emotional events. In D. Reisberg & P. Hertel (Eds.), *Memory and emotion* (pp. 3–41). New York: Oxford University Press.

Robinson, J. A. (1980). Affect and retrieval of personal memories. *Motivation and Emotion, 4*, 149–174.

Robinson, M. D., & Clore, G. L. (2002a). Belief and feeling: Evidence for an accessibility model of emotional self-report. *Psychological Bulletin, 128*, 934–960.

Robinson, M. D., & Clore, G. L. (2002b). Episodic and semantic knowledge in emotional self-report: Evidence for two judgment processes. *Journal of Personality and Social Psychology, 83,* 198–215.

Ross, B. M. (1991). *Remembering the personal past: Descriptions of autobiographical memory.* London: Oxford University Press.

Ross, M. (1989). The relation of implicit theories to the construction of personal histories. *Psychological Review, 96,* 341–357.

Safer, M. A., Bonanno, G. A., & Field, N. P. (2001). "It was never that bad": Biased recall of grief and long-term adjustment to the death of a spouse. *Memory, 9,* 195–204.

Safer, M. A., & Keuler, D. J. (2002). Individual differences in misremembering prepsychotherapy distress: Personality and memory distortion. *Emotion, 2,* 162–178.

Safer, M. A., Levine, L. J., & Drapalski, A. (2002). Distortion in memory for emotions: The contributions of personality and post-event knowledge. *Personality and Social Psychology Bulletin, 28,* 1495–1507.

Schacter, D. L. (2001). *The seven sins of memory: How the mind forgets and remembers.* New York: Houghton Mifflin.

Schacter, D. L., Chiu, C. Y. P., & Ochsner, K. N. (1993). Implicit memory: A selective review. *Annual Review of Neuroscience, 16,* 159–182.

Scherer, K. R., Schorr, A., & Johnstone, T. (2001). *Appraisal processes in emotion: Theory, method, and research.* New York: Oxford University Press.

Schrader, G., Davis, A., Stefanovic, S., & Christie, P. (1990). The recollection of affect. *Psychological Medicine, 20,* 105–109.

Shiffman, S., Hufford, M., Hickcox, M., Paty, J. A., Gnys, M., & Kassel, J. O. (1997). Remember that? A comparison of real-time versus retrospective recall of smoking lapses. *Journal of Consulting and Clinical Psychology, 65,* 292–300.

Silver, R. C., Holman, E. A., McIntosh, D. N., Poulin, M., & Gil-Rivas, V. (2002). Nationwide longitudinal study of the psychological responses to September 11. *Journal of the American Medical Association, 288,* 1235–1244.

Smith, C. A., & Lazarus, R. S. (1993). Appraisal components, core relational themes, and the emotions. *Cognition and Emotion, 7,* 233–269.

Sprecher, S. (1999). "I love you more today than yesterday": Romantic partners' perception of changes in love and related affect over time. *Journal of Personality and Social Psychology, 76,* 46–53.

Stein, N. L., & Levine, L. J. (1987). Thinking about feelings: The development and organization of emotional knowledge. In R. E. Snow & M. Farr (Eds.), *Aptitude, learning, and instruction: Vol. 3. Cognition, conation, and affect* (pp. 165–197). Hillsdale, NJ: Erlbaum.

Tesser, A. (1978). Self-generated attitude change. In L. Berkowitz (Ed.), *Advances in experimental social psychology* (Vol. 11, pp. 289–338). New York: Academic Press.

Thomas, D. L., & Diener, E. (1990). Memory accuracy in the recall of emotions. *Journal of Personality and Social Psychology, 59,* 291–297.

Tobias, B. A., Kihlstrom, J. F., & Schacter, D. L. (1992). Emotion and implicit memory. In S.-A. Christianson (Ed.), *The handbook of emotion and memory: Research and theory* (pp. 67–92). Hillsdale, NJ: Erlbaum.

van der Hart, O., Brown, P., & van der Kolk, B. A. (1989). Pierre Janet's treatment of post-traumatic stress disorder. *Journal of Traumatic Stress, 2,* 379–395.

van der Kolk, B. A. (1994). The body keeps the score: Memory and the evolving psychobiology of posttraumatic stress. *Harvard Review of Psychiatry, 1,* 263–265.

Weinberger, N. M., Gold, P. E., & Sternberg, D. B. (1984). Epinephrine enables Pavlovian fear conditioning under anesthesia. *Science, 223,* 605–606.

Weiner, B. (1985). An attributional theory of achievement motivation and emotion. *Psychological Review, 92,* 548–573.

Wilson, T. D., Meyers, J., & Gilbert, D. T. (2001). Lessons from the past: Do people learn from experience that emotional reactions are short-lived? *Personality and Social Psychology Bulletin, 27,* 1648–1661.

Wilson, T. D., Meyers, J., & Gilbert, D. T. (2003). "How happy was I, anyway?": A retrospective impact bias. *Social Cognition, 21,* 421–446.

Wirtz, D., Kruger, J., Scollon, C. N., & Diener, E. (2003). What to do on spring break? The role of predicted, on-line, and remembered experience in future choice. *Psychological Science, 14,* 520–524.

Witvliet, C. V. O. (1997). Traumatic intrusive imagery as an emotional memory phenomenon: A review of research and explanatory information processing theories. *Clinical Psychology Review, 17,* 509–536.

Wyer, R. S., Clore, G. L., & Isbell, L. M. (1999). Affect and information processing. In M. Zanna (Ed.), *Advances in experimental social psychology* (Vol. 31, pp. 1–77). San Diego, CA: Academic Press.

Zajonc, R. B. (1980). Feeling and thinking: Preferences need no inferences. *American Psychologist, 35,* 151–175.

16

Future as Epilogue

Some Conclusions on Judgments Over Time

LAWRENCE J. SANNA
EDWARD C. CHANG

Study the past if you would define the future.
                    Confucius (551–479 B.C.)

The chapters in this volume give testimony to the importance of considering the variety of complex and intriguing ways in which people make judgments over time. Our lives are not static. Instead, they are continually changing over time, and thus taking into account temporal variables is potentially relevant to almost every aspect of our lives. We began this volume by suggesting that temporal variables are critically important when people consider the antecedents and consequences of their judgments within a variety of settings, including interpersonal, intrapersonal, economic, or broader societal ones. The authors of the individual chapters, in their own unique ways, have illustrated this point well.

As the various chapter authors have so eloquently suggested, variables normally associated mainly with a future perspective (abandoning optimism, defensive pessimism, perfectionism, predicting feelings and choices, considering future consequences, hope, and fantasy realization) can also be greatly influenced by people's pasts. Conversely, variables associated mainly with a past perspective (rumination, counterfactuals, attribution, regret, hindsight bias, autobiographical memory, and remembering emotions) can also have enormous implications for people's futures. In one way or another, all authors additionally suggest that temporal variables are by their very nature fluid: The future becomes the present and the present fades into the past. Thus, although we chose to organize our volume around thinking about the future and the past, it is important to reemphasize what we believe to be the reciprocal relationships among thoughts, feelings, and behaviors, intertwined with the past,

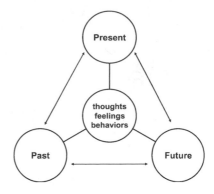

Figure 16.1. Reciprocal interrelationships between thoughts, feelings, and behaviors within the context of past, present, and future temporal perspectives.

present, and future perspectives (Figure 16.1). Each variable can serve as both cause and effect.

It is not our purpose within this brief epilogue to summarize everything that is contained within the many preceding chapters. The authors of those chapters have already proffered excellent reviews of the literature, proposed several intriguing models, suggested future research, and articulated many areas in need of more attention. However, we did want to end our book by making a few concluding remarks and some final observations. This concluding chapter thus focuses on some more general overarching themes, questions, and issues. We merely provide examples within each section for the purpose of illustration, and our discussion should not be viewed as an exhaustive list of all that is relevant within the individual chapters.

Relations Between Past, Present, and Future

It may be easy for us to say that people's conceptions of the past, present, and future are interrelated and also that they have reciprocal influences on each other. To many, this would seem like a very reasonable suggestion. However, research that directly bears on relations between past, present, and future is actually quite sparse. Within our book, it may also appear at first that there is a "missing present." That is, there is no corresponding section dealing specifically with the present, as there are for thinking about the future and the past. But a closer inspection of the individual chapters reveals that the present might always be a part of people's judgments. The present is now. Of course, one major issue here is that what is now is also very fleeting. It is now only for a brief instant. How people conceive of what is the present, or what is the now, certainly seems to be deserving of more intense investigation (and similar things can be said about investigating how people actually conceive of the past and the future).

What is clear from several chapters in this volume is that the present may, at least sometimes, serve as a benchmark for comparing the past and future. On the one hand, the present can be contrasted with the future. Oettingen and Thorpe (chapter 8) demonstrate how this leads to the development of expectations and goal setting if the present is viewed as standing in the way of desired futures. On the other hand, the present can also be contrasted with the past. Sanna, Carter, and Small (chapter 10) describe how contrasts form a basis for counterfactual thinking, and Zeelenberg and Pieters (chapter 12) show that such contrasts may underlie both retrospective and anticipated regret. But the future and the past may additionally be assimilated to the present, becoming part of the "now." It is likely that research on judgments over time would benefit from considering the possibility of simultaneous assimilation and contrast mechanisms (Collins, 1996; Mussweiler, 2003; Stapel & Winkielman, 1998), rather than each in isolation, as this may more accurately explain people's conceptions of the past, present, and future.

Information From Thoughts, Feelings, and Behaviors

People's thoughts, feelings, and behaviors can be informative. That is, if thinking about a particular course of action makes us feel good, we will likely do it. If the action produces positive consequences, we will likely do it again. We learn from past experiences what is good and bad. This information provides cues about how we should act in the future and about the meaning of our past actions. Of course, we are not always accurate. Van Boven and Kane (chapter 5) clearly describe how our experienced feelings and choices may differ and might not always lead to what we had previously expected. When will people use their thoughts and feelings in judgments over time? There might turn out to be many answers to this question, but an intriguing start may lie in what people perceive as informative. That is, people may not use their thoughts or feelings in judgments over time if they are led to question their meaningfulness or they are otherwise rendered uninformative (Schwarz, 1998; Schwarz & Clore, 1996).

There are several examples of this. Levine, Safer, and Lench (chapter 15) describe how people's current emotions can cloud their memories for past emotions. Martin and Tesser (chapter 9) explain how affect can indicate extent of goal attainment. Shepperd, Sweeny, and Carroll (chapter 2) show that people can abandon optimism in favor of pessimism to brace for possible bad news. In the former case, current emotions serve as a cue to the past, whereas in the latter two cases, current emotions serve as cues to the future. But affect does not influence judgments if it is rendered uninformative through the use of misattribution or other manipulations. For example, when people's anxiety could be attributed to caffeinated coffee rather than to the current situation, it did not influence optimistic predictions (Shepperd, Grace, Cole, & Klein, 2005). When people's thoughts were rendered uninformative, they similarly did not influence retrospective judgments (Sanna & Schwarz, 2003). More research that tests when people find thoughts, feelings, and behaviors informative in judgments over time is necessary.

Cognitive Versus Motivational Explanations

Many of the chapters also suggest that cognitive or motivational factors alone or in combination influence people's judgments over time. Skowronski, Walker, and Edlund (chapter 14) describe how memories for negative past events fade over time and also how people self-servingly reconstruct when events happened. One intriguing part of their analysis makes explicit the fact that perceived psychological distance from past events does not always match up to actual objective distance from events as measured by clock time. For example, negative past events can seem subjectively farther away than positive past events, even though they occurred at exactly the same time (Ross & Wilson, 2002). Malle and Tate (chapter 11) suggest how people's causal explanations for events can also be self-serving, and Bryant and DeHoek (chapter 13) illustrate how hindsight biases may serve a similar function. People may, for example, view past successes as inevitable, allowing them to take credit for success, and/or view past failures as less inevitable, allowing them to deny blame for failures (Louie, 1999).

Motivation clearly can be important. People might distance themselves from negative pasts, construct flattering causal explanations, or view successes as more inevitable, all in the service of making themselves feel better. They could also do this to maintain or restore positive impressions in their own eyes or in the eyes of other people. Cognition clearly can be important. For example, distant future events may be construed at more abstract, higher levels (Trope & Liberman, 2003), and this may influence people's judgments over time without any motivational influences. It is important for researchers to determine the many and varied influences of motivation and cognition, either independently or in conjunction, on people's judgments over time. When are motivations relevant or primary? When are cognitions relevant or primary? This may be a particularly difficult task. Most likely, both motivations and cognitions will be found to be operative under particular conditions, and studying their combined influences will undoubtedly produce results that are all the more fascinating (Kunda, 1990).

Individual Differences and Culture

The issues brought up in this volume can potentially apply across individuals and across cultures. However, it is important to recognize that there can be major qualifications to this assertion. Joireman, Strathman, and Balliet (chapter 6) describe how some people focus more on the immediate consequences of their actions, whereas others focus more on the long-term consequences of their actions. Snyder, Rand, and Ritschel (chapter 7) discuss how hopeful thoughts can influence emotions and behaviors through several mechanisms, ultimately affecting psychological and physical adjustment. Norem and Smith (chapter 3) discuss how defensive pessimists' strategy involves attempts to convince themselves that poor outcomes are likely or probable in order to use this as a motivating force to ensure that they will do well. This differs from what optimists do. As these examples illustrate, along with others (Waller, Conte, Gibson, & Carpenter, 2001; Zimbardo & Boyd, 1999), the role of individual differences or personality strategies can certainly play a significant role in judgments over time.

The role of culture was also alluded to in several chapters. Chang, Downey, and Lin (chapter 4) do this perhaps most explicitly. For example, within their model of perfectionism, these authors describe how studies that have considered cultural or racial variations have usually found significant differences between groups. Psychologists in a wide variety of areas have become increasingly aware of cultural issues (Diener, Oishi, & Lucas, 2003; Heine & Lehman, 1999; Markus & Kitayama, 1991). There are likely similar important cultural differences in people's judgments over time and also in their more general time conceptions. For example, some cultures may be monochronic, perceiving time in a linear sequential fashion, whereas other cultures may be polychronic, perceiving time in a nonlinear simultaneous fashion (Ancona, Okhuysen, & Perlow, 2001). Culture can have critical implications for people's thoughts, feelings, and behaviors. The diversity of cultural issues, along with developmental and possible age-related changes in judgments over time, may also prove extremely interesting.

Further Implications and Applications

There are many other possible connections that might be made across topics. These are both theoretical and applied. One obvious one is that several authors discuss goals. Oettingen and Thorpe (chapter 8) describe how goals initiate, whereas Martin and Tesser (chapter 9) elaborate on processes underlying blocked goals. Both Shepperd et al. (chapter 2) and Norem and Smith (chapter 3) discuss how people use strategies that facilitate goal attainment while simultaneously ensuring that they will continue to maintain positive self-views if goals are not met. It is interesting to speculate about possible relationships between mechanisms described by Oettingen and Thorpe and Martin and Tesser on the one hand and Shepperd et al. and Norem and Smith on the other. For example, could bracing for loss eliminate or reduce the likelihood of later ruminative thoughts? Could the attribution processes described by Malle and Tate (chapter 11) add to this by turning off the ruminative process should it begin? Individually, the topics covered in the specific chapters are interesting; combining them will likely prove even more so.

Several authors focus on decision making. Both Van Boven and Kane (chapter 5) and Zeelenberg and Pieters (chapter 12) describe antecedents and consequences of choosing—and failing to choose—whereas Sanna et al. (chapter 10) and Bryant and DeHoek (chapter 13) discuss biases in decision making. Skowronski et al. (chapter 14) and Levine et al. (chapter 15) add some general memory biases. We all are faced with a multitude of decisions throughout our lives. Thus these processes may have very broad applicability. Chang et al. (chapter 4) and Snyder et al. (chapter 7) discuss applications in clinical settings, whereas Joireman et al. (chapter 6) describe the general processes of growth and change. These topics illustrate just a few connections that might be made. Our discussion undoubtedly suffers from oversimplifying what has been said within the individual chapters. However, by bringing together diverse theory and research into a single volume, our goal was to correspondingly help bring greater awareness and appreciation of potential conceptual relations between seemingly disparate areas.

Coda

We hope that the individual contributions in this book express the vigor and excitement of studying judgments over time that we felt when embarking on this endeavor. It was our goal to bring together in one volume some of the exciting and diverse theory and research related to people's judgments over time. We feel this excitement even more strongly now. The chapter authors provide excellent reviews of the literature, propose interesting models, and also help to focus attention on issues that remain and suggest new and intriguing problems to be addressed. In this epilogue we have tried simply to give readers a flavor for the many possible implications of studying judgments over time by touching on a few more general overarching themes, questions, and issues. Undoubtedly, readers will find many more connections. This was precisely the point. In short, we hope that by studying the past in terms of what we know so far, readers can help define the future in terms of what we can know, while perhaps suggesting some initial steps in getting there from here. To us, this is the most exciting prospect of all.

References

Ancona, D. G., Okhuysen, G. A., & Perlow, L. A. (2001). Taking time to integrate temporal research. *Academy of Management Review, 26*, 512–529.

Collins, R. L. (1996). For better or worse: The impact of upward social comparison on self-evaluations. *Psychological Bulletin, 119*, 51–69.

Confucius. (1998). *Confucius: The analects* (D. C. Lau, Trans.). New York: Penguin Classics.

Diener, E., Oishi, S., & Lucas, R. E. (2003). Personality, culture, and subjective well-being: Emotional and cognitive evaluations of life. *Annual Review of Psychology, 54*, 403–425.

Heine, S. J., & Lehman, D. R. (1999). Culture, self-discrepancies, and self-satisfaction. *Personality and Social Psychology Bulletin, 25*, 915–925.

Mussweiler, T. (2003). Comparative processes in social judgment: Mechanisms and consequences. *Psychological Review, 110*, 472–489.

Kunda, Z. (1990). The case for motivated reasoning. *Psychological Bulletin, 108*, 480–498.

Louie, T. A. (1999). Decision makers' hindsight bias after receiving favorable and unfavorable feedback. *Journal of Applied Psychology, 84*, 29–41.

Markus, H. R., & Kitayama, S. (1991). Culture and the self: Implications for cognition, emotion, and motivation. *Psychological Review, 98*, 224–253.

Ross, M., & Wilson, A. E. (2002). It feels like yesterday: Self-esteem, valence of personal past experiences, and judgments of subjective distance. *Journal of Personality and Social Psychology, 82*, 792–803.

Sanna, L. J., & Schwarz, N. (2003). Debiasing the hindsight bias: The role of accessibility experiences and (mis)attributions. *Journal of Experimental Social Psychology, 39*, 287–295.

Schwarz, N. (1998). Accessible content and accessibility experiences: The interplay of declarative and experiential information in judgment. *Personality and Social Psychology Review, 2*, 87–99.

Schwarz, N., & Clore, G. L. (1996). Feelings as phenomenal experiences. In E. T. Higgins & A. W. Kruglanski (Eds.), *Social psychology: Handbook of basic principles* (pp. 433–465). New York: Guilford Press.

Shepperd, J. A., Grace, J., Cole, L. J., & Klein, C. (2005). Anxiety and outcome predictions. *Personality and Social Psychology Bulletin, 31*, 267–275.

Stapel, D. A., & Winkielman, P. (1998). Assimilation and contrast as a function of context-target similarity, distinctness, and dimensional relevance. *Personality and Social Psychology Bulletin, 24*, 634–646.

Trope, Y., & Liberman, N. (2003). Temporal construal. *Psychological Review, 110*, 403–421.

Waller, M. J., Conte, J. M., Gibson, C. B., & Carpenter, M. A. (2001). The effect of individual perceptions of deadlines on team performance. *Academy of Management Review, 26*, 586–600.

Zimbardo, P. G., & Boyd, J. N. (1999). Putting time in perspective: A valid, reliable individual differences metric. *Journal of Personality and Social Psychology, 77*, 1271–1288.

Author Index

Subject Index

affect for defensive pessimist
  goal pursuit, 41
  retrospection, 38
  strategy stability or change, 43–44
Affect Infusion Model, autobiographical
    memory, 256
affective arousal, empathy gaps, 71
agency
  hope theory, 101, 103
  listening, 114
  physical exercise, 114–115
  role of personal, in regret, 214–215
  self-talk, 114
aggression, consideration of future
    consequences, 85–86
agony of defeat, autobiographical
    memory, 265
airplane crash, hindsight bias, 230, 231
almanac questions, foresight and
    hindsight in relation to, 233
alternative-focused strategies, regret
    regulation, 220
anchoring current belief and adjusting
    hindsight bias, 241
  time influence, 244–245
anticipated regret, future decisions,
    217, 224–225
anticipation, regret, 222
anxiety
  defensive pessimism, 35, 39–42
  planning for worst, 39–40
appraisal
  individual differences in, of
      emotional experiences, 277–278
  remembering emotions, 279
  theories of emotion, 276–277
approach framework, goal, 109–110
assessing probability, prediction, 195
assimilation, mechanisms for events
    and moods influencing
    simulations, 168
association
  explanatory strategy for prediction,
      198, 200–202
  prediction process, 203
associationism, autobiographical
    memory, 252
assumptive worlds, sets of beliefs, 156
attribution, defensive pessimism, 37
attribution theory, explanation,
    182–183

autobiographical memory
  Affect Infusion Model, 256
  agony of defeat, 265
  associationism, 252
  backward telescoping, 260
  dating strategies, 260–262
  day-of-week error patterns, 260–262
  diversity of theories and methods,
      253
  dysphoria research, 255–256
  fading affect bias, 8, 254–258
  false memories, 251
  flashbulb memories, 252
  forward telescoping, 260
  home run winning championship,
      259–265
  judging when events occur, 259–265
  judgments of emotions and time,
      265–266
  judgments over time, 253
  landmark strategy, 262
  method of mood induction, 254
  roles of males and females in society,
      259
  semantic headers or tags, 263–265
  sense memories, 251
  social disclosure, 257–259
  striking out and losing championship
      game, 254–259
  telescoping effects, 260
  temporal distance effect, 262–263
  thrill of victory, 265
avoidance goals, hope, 102
awareness model, consideration of
    future consequences, 84–85

backward telescoping, autobiographical
    memory, 260
balance, goals, 111–112
because clauses, explaining future
    events, 193–194
behavior features, folk-conceptual
    analysis of explanations across
    time, 189
behaviors
  information from thoughts, feelings,
      and, 293–294
  reciprocal relationships with
      thoughts and feelings, 291–292
Being and Time, Heidegger, 4
beliefs, versus images, 121–122

benefits
abandoning optimism, 23–24
balancing, and costs, 24–26
bias. *See also* hindsight bias
counterfactual thinking, 172–173
explicit memory for emotions,
275–278
memory for emotions, 274–279
bracing for undesired outcome
downward shift in optimism, 21–23
future research, 29
brush with death, psychological
growth, 157
Buddha, perfectionism, 47

case histories, foresight and hindsight
in relation to, 233–234
catastrophe, prospective mental
simulations, 169
causal history, modes of explanation,
184–185
change over time
actor perspective for explanations
190–191
behavior features, 189
explanations, 187–191
folk-conceptual analysis of
explanations across time,
188–191
information resources, 190–191
pragmatic goals, 189–190
Chicken Little, adversity, 13
child-caregiver bond, hope, 105
choices. *See also* predictions
dispositional properties, 73–74
empathy gaps in predicted, 70–72
predictions for "cold" and "hot"
situations, 67–68
stability versus feelings, 72–73
Clinton impeachment, foresight and
hindsight, 235
cognitions
explanations of people's judgment
over time, 294
perfectionism, 54–56
cognitive processes, from simulation to
multiple, for prediction, 197
common sense, hindsight bias, 231
comparative optimism, bias toward
optimism, 13
completed action, explanation, 192

conceptions, past, present and future, 8
conceptual framework, explanation, 184
concern model, consideration of future
consequences (CFC), 84–85
confidence change research, judgments
and biases over time, 172
Confucius
past and future, 291
perfectionism, 47
consequences. *See* consideration of
future consequences (CFC)
consideration of future consequences
(CFC)
academic achievement, 85
aggression, 85–86
awareness model, 84–85
CFC scale, 83
concern model, 84–85
defining and measuring, 6, 82–84
emotions, 94
feedback loops and relevance of past,
93
health behavior, 85
integrative model, 88
mediation model, 84–85
moderation model, 84–85
precursors, 89–90
precursors and mediating
mechanisms of, 88
proenvironmental attitudes and
behavior, 87–88
prosocial organizational behavior, 86
risk taking, 85
role of feelings, 93–95
self-regulatory strength, self-efficacy,
and locus of control, 92–93
temporal construal, temporal
discounting, and delay of
gratification, 90–91
validity, 85–88
consideration of future consequences
scale, 83
content, two-stage model of
counterfactual thinking, 165
control, outcome, and optimism, 17
coping with challenges,
misremembering emotions,
283–284
costs
abandoning optimism, 23–24
balancing benefits and, 24–26

counterfactual thinking
  catastrophe, 169
  causes and consequences, 163–164
  confidence change research, 172
  defensive pessimism, 170–171
  environment, 171–172
  expectations versus fantasies, 127
  hindsight bias research, 173
  historical background, 164–166
  indulging, 169
  judgments and biases over time,
    172–173
  judgments of individuals, groups,
    and organizations, 173–174
  jury groups, 173–174
  mental simulations, 7, 168–170
  mood maintenance, 169–170
  mood repair, 170
  norm theory, 165
  optimism, 170–171
  outcome, 166, 168
  personality, 170–171
  planning fallacy research, 172–173
  prospective mental simulations,
    168–169
  reminiscing, 170
  retrospective mental simulations,
    169–170
  road not taken, 163, 174
  rumination, 170
  self-esteem, 171
  self-improvement, 168–169
  self-protection, 169
  simulation heuristic, 164–165
  TEMPO model (time, environment,
    motivation, personality, and
    outcome), 164, 166, 167
  time and motivation, 166
  two-stage model and goals,
    165–166
covariation assessment, explanation
    process, 203
creeping determinism, hindsight bias,
    239
cultures
  differences in judgments over time,
    295
  mental contrasting across, 137–138

data, scrutiny of, downward shift in
    optimism, 20

data acquisition, downward shift in
    optimism, 19
dating strategies, autobiographical
    memory, 260–262
day-of-week error patterns,
    autobiographical memory,
    260–262
death, close encounter with, 157
decision
  delaying or avoiding, 220–221
  ensuring, reversibility, 221–222
  improving, quality, 220
  increasing, justifiability, 221
  regret regulation strategies, 219, 220
  transferring responsibility, 221
  undoing or reversing, 223
decision-focused strategies, regret
    regulation, 220
decision making, 296
defensive pessimism
  affect and goal pursuit, 41
  affect and retrospection, 38
  affect and strategy stability or
    change, 43–44
  anxiety and performance in future,
    39–42
  brightness of future, 42–44
  downward shift in optimism, 23
  judgments, 44
  judgments about past behavior,
    38–39, 41–42
  past experience, 35–37
  personality and counterfactual
    thinking, 170
  planning for worst, 39–40
  possible selves, 42–43
  strategy, 6, 34–35
delay of gratification, consideration of
    future consequences, 88, 90–91
denial, regret regulation, 224
depressive symptoms, perfectionism, 61
derivability
  explanatory strategy for prediction,
    198–199, 200–202
  prediction process, 203
direct recall, explanation process, 203,
    204
disappointment
  downward shift in optimism
    avoiding, 21–22
  regret, 214–215

dispositional optimism, bias toward optimism, 13
dispositional properties, choice versus feelings, 73–74
dissonance reduction, predicted feelings, 69
distortions. *See also* misremembering emotions
memory, and goal-directed behavior, 282–283
downward counterfactuals, two-stage model, 165
durability bias, downward shift in optimism, 22
dysphoria research, autobiographical memory, 255–256

economics
abandoning optimism, 23–26
regret literature, 216
Egypt, Middle Kingdom, perfectionism, 47
emotional benefits, optimism, 14
emotions. *See also* remembering and misremembering emotions
bias in explicit memory for, 275–278
bias in implicit memory for, 278–279
consideration of future consequences (CFC), 93–95
explicit memory for, 273–274
forgetting, 280
hope theory, 106
implicit memory for, 273–274
memories of past, 8, 271–272
reconstructing memories for, 280–281
regret, 210, 211
storage in memory, 272–274
utility of remembering, 279
empathy gaps, predicted choice, 70–72
enabling factor
explanations for future events, 193
modes of explanation, 184
environment, TEMPO model for counterfactual thinking, 171–172
event occurrence, autobiographical memory, 259–265
excelling in mathematics, realizing fantasies of, 130–131
exercise, agency, 114–115
expectancy judgments, linking future and present, 136

expectations. *See also* fantasy realization
life courses, 4–5
motivational consequences of, versus fantasies, 123–127
versus fantasies, 121–127
experience
regret, 212, 224–225
regret over time, 217
explanation
classic attribution theory, 182–183
cognitive apparatus of, 182–186
cognitive processes in, and prediction, 203
cognitive versus motivational, influencing judgment over time, 294
conceptual framework and modes of, 184–185
folk-conceptual theory, 183–186
linguistic expression, 186
processes of, and prediction, 7
psychological processes in generating, 185–186
temporal aspects of, 186–194
theoretical, for hindsight bias, 239–240
underdetermination, 204
explicit memory for emotion
bias in, 275–278
future research, 285
individual differences, 277–278
overestimation of past emotions, 275
properties, 273–274
role of current appraisals, 276–277

fading affect bias, autobiographical memory, 254–258
false memories, 251
fantasy realization
about positive futures, 128–133
academic achievement, 124–125
beliefs versus images, 121–122
of excelling in mathematics, 130–131
expectations versus fantasies, 121–127
future and present linking to activate past, 128–137
mastering fantasies about negative futures, 133–136

rebuilding worldview, 158
restricting means of attaining goal,
    151–152
rumination as result of thwarted goal
    progress, 147–148
substitute means of attaining goal
    turning off rumination, 149–150
termination difficulty, 151–152
theoretical integration, 158
trauma, letting go, and growth,
    156–157
goal pursuit
    defensive pessimism, 41
    hope in present, 105–107
goals
    abilities and skills, 111
    anchors to future, 108–112
    balance and priorities, 111–112
    happiness pursuit, 109
    hope theory, 101–102
    two-stage model and, of
        counterfactual thinking, 165–166
    value systems and, 110–111
Greeks, perfectionism, 47
group judgments, counterfactual
    thinking, 173–174
growth, rumination, 156–157

happiness, pursuit as goal, 109
headers, autobiographical memory,
    263–265
health behavior, consideration of future
    consequences, 85
health benefits, optimism, 14
health domain, expectations versus
    fantasies, 127
Heidegger, Martin, *Being and Time*, 4
high standards of performance,
    performance perfectionism theory,
    53–54
hindsight bias
    anchoring current belief and
        adjusting, 241, 244–245
    Clinton impeachment, 235
    dominant approaches for studying,
        232–236
    effects of time on development of
        real-world event, 247
    factors influencing, 7
    foresight and hindsight in relation to
        almanac questions, 233

foresight and hindsight in relation to
    case histories, 233–234
foresight and hindsight in relation to
    real-world events, 234–236
future research on time and,
    247–248
hypothetical scenarios, 230–231
long-range forecasts, 247
medicine, 237
motivated response adjustment,
    240–241
motivational and cognitive
    mechanisms, 240–243
motivational mechanisms, 244
politics, 237
recalling old belief, 243, 245–246
rejudgment, 241–243, 245
stock investment, 236–237
temporal perspective on, 231–232
theoretical explanations for,
    239–240
time and alternative mediational
    mechanisms, 244–246
time and responses to unfolding life
    events, 236–238
time influence, 232
timing of foresight and hindsight in
    real-world events, 238–239
toward integrative temporal model,
    246–247
warfare, 237–238
hindsight bias research, counterfactual
    thinking, 173
hope
    abilities and skills, 111
    agency, 114–115
    approach framework, 109–110
    blending present and future in
        psychotherapy, 107–108
    goals and future, 108–112
    overview of research on, 6
    pathways, 112–114
    potential of pathways, 113–114
    prioritizing goals, 111–112
    pursuit of happiness, 109
    time commitment, 113
    value system and goals, 110–111
hope theory
    agency, 101, 103
    child-caregiver bond, 105
    goal-pursuit process, 106–107

normal perfectionists, adaptive
perfectionism, 51–52
norm theory, counterfactual thinking,
165

occurrence, event in autobiographical
memory, 259–265
optimism. *See also* abandoning
optimism
abandoning, and future events, 5
bias toward, 13–14
comparative, 13
departures from, 15–23
dispositional, 13
downward shift, 14
emotional and health benefits, 14
explanations for downward shifts, 18
personality and counterfactual
thinking, 170
unrealistic, 13
organization, human activities, 100
organizational citizenship behaviors,
consideration of future
consequences, 86
organizational judgments,
counterfactual thinking, 173–174
outcome
actual, and hindsight bias, 239–240
departure from optimism, 15–17
TEMPO model for counterfactual
thinking, 166, 168
outcome cognitions, perfectionism,
54–56
outcome predictions, preparedness and,
26–28
outcome regret, decision outcome, 218,
224
outcome-specified prediction (O),
typology of prediction, 196
overestimation, past emotions, 275
overestimations. *See* predictions

past. *See also* mental contrasting;
thinking about past
importance in hope theory, 103–104
lessons for goal pursuit, 104–105
linking future and past to activate,
128–137
overview of thinking about, 7–8
relations between, present, and
future, 292–293

past behavior, defensive pessimism,
38–39, 41–42
past emotions, memories of, 8
past experience
consideration of future
consequences, 93
defensive pessimism, 35–37
pathways
goals versus, 113
hope theory, 101, 103
potential, 113–114
roads to tomorrow, 112–114
time commitment, 113
values, 112–113
perfectionism
academic achievement and
depressive symptoms, 60–61
association between, and negative
affect, 50–51
Buddha and Confucius, 47
definition during Middle Kingdom, 47
development of Performance
Perfectionism Scale (PPS), 58–59
as distressful, 48–49
empirical status of performance,
theory, 58–61
as future distress maker, 49–51
Greeks, 47
high standards of performance,
53–54
learning from past, 51–52
linking past to present in seeking
future goals, 56–58
maladaptive, 6
model of internalization process, 57
multidimensional and
multifunctional model, 53–61
negative self-oriented performance,
55–56
negative socially prescribed
performance, 55–56
neurotic perfectionists, 52
normal perfectionists, 51
outline of model of performance,
across time, 56–58
performance perfectionism theory,
53–61
positive and negative psychological
functioning, 59–60
positive self-oriented performance,
55–56

positive socially prescribed
performance, 55–56
positive versus negative outcome
cognitions, 54–56
stress-generation model, 50–51
Performance Perfectionism Scale (PPS),
development, 58–59
performance perfectionism theory. *See
also* perfectionism
academic achievement and
depressive symptoms, 60–61
development of Performance
Perfectionism Scale (PPS), 58–59
empirical status, 58–61
high standards of performance,
53–54
outcome cognitions, 54–56
outline of model of, across time,
56–58
positive and negative psychological
functioning, 59–60
personality, TEMPO model for
counterfactual thinking, 170–171
pessimism. *See also* defensive pessimism
defensive, as strategy, 6, 34–35
philosophical history, time, 3–5
physical exercise, agency, 114–115
planning fallacy research, judgments
and biases over time, 172–173
politics, time and hindsight bias, 237
positive self-oriented performance
perfectionism, 55–56
positive socially prescribed
performance, perfectionism,
55–56
possible selves, defensive pessimism,
42–43
posttraumatic growth
integration into goal progress model,
158–159
rumination, 156–157
post-traumatic stress disorder, emotions
and negative events, 25–26
pragmatic goals, folk-conceptual
analysis of explanations across
time, 189–190
preconditions, regret, 214
precursors, consideration of future
consequences, 88, 89–90
predictions. *See also* choices; feelings
association, 198, 201

cognitive apparatus, 194–202
cognitive processes in explanation
and, 203
comparison of two models, 196
cultural differences, 75
derivability, 198–199, 201
developmental differences, 75
differences of predicted feelings and
choices, 72–74
different types of affect, 75–76
distinction between feelings and
choice, 72
downward shift from optimism,
15–23
empathy gaps in predicted choice,
70–72
explanatory strategies and prediction
types, 199–202
feelings and choices, 67–68
four explanatory strategies for,
197–199
fully specified predictions (SO), 196
future research, 74–76
impact bias in predicted feelings,
68–70
intentions, 204
literature, 194
new fourfold typology, 195–196
noncontradiction, 198, 201
outcome-specified predictions (O),
196
processes of explanation and, 7
scenario generation, 199, 201
simulation heuristic, 194–195
from simulation to multiple cognitive
processes, 197
starting-conditions-specified
predictions (S), 196
types, 194–196
underdetermination, 204
unspecified predictions (U), 196
preparedness, outcome predictions,
26–28
present
hope in, 105–107
relations between past, present, and
future, 292–293
priorities, goals, 111–112
probability, prediction, 195
process regret, decision processes, 218,
224

proenvironmental attitudes and behavior, consideration of future consequences, 87–88
professional achievement, expectations versus fantasies, 124–125
propositions, regret, 212
prosocial organizational behavior, consideration of future consequences, 86
prospective mental simulations, TEMPO model for counterfactual thinking, 168–169
prospective regret, future decisions, 217, 224–225
psychological distance, time context, 4
psychological functioning, perfectionism, 59–60
psychological growth, close brush with death, 157
psychological history, time, 3–5
psychological immune system, predicted feelings, 69
psychological literature, explanation, 182–183
psychological processes, generating explanations, 185–186
psychotherapy, blending present and future in, 107–108
publications, regret, 210–211
purposeful organization, human activities, 100

rational grounds, modes of explanation, 184
realization. *See* fantasy realization
real-world events
  foresight and hindsight in relation to, 234–236
  timing of foresight and hindsight, 238–239
reason explanations, future events, 191, 192–193
recalling old belief
  hindsight bias, 243
  time influence, 245–246
recovery from surgery, expectations versus fantasies, 126–127
regret
  anticipated, regulation strategies, 220–222

anticipated or prospective, 217
anticipating, 222
description, 212–214
disappointment, 214–215
distinctiveness of, 214–215
economic decision making, 216
experience and regulation of, over time, 217
interest in, over time, 211
lineage and types of, 215–217
motivation to regulate, 213–214
objects of, 217–218
outcome, 218
preconditions, 214
process, 218
publications, 211
regulation strategies, 219, 220
retrospective, 217
risk aversion, 219
risk versus, 218–224
role of personal agency, 214–215
theory and research, 7
universality of, 211–212
regret regulation
  anticipated, strategies, 220–222
  avoiding feedback about forgone alternatives, 222
  benefits of, 225–226
  delaying or avoiding decision, 220–221
  ensuring decision reversibility, 221–222
  experienced, strategies, 222–224
  improving decision quality, 220
  increasing decision justifiability, 221
  regret denial or suppression, 224
  toward theory of, 224–226
  transferring decision responsibility, 221
  undo or reverse decision, 223
regulation. *See also* regret regulation
  regret, 212
  regret over time, 217
reinterpretation paradigm, xenophobic fantasies, 134–135
rejudgment
  evaluating evidence, 242
  hindsight bias, 241–243
  integrating evidence, 242–243

sense memories, 251
simulation, explanation process, 203, 204
simulation heuristic
  counterfactual thinking, 164–165
  prediction, 194–195
skills, goals, 111
social disclosure, autobiographical memory, 257–259
socially prescribed performance perfectionism
  negative and positive, 55–56
  Performance Perfectionism Scale (PPS), 58–59
stability, choice versus feelings, 72–73
standards of performance, performance perfectionism theory, 53–54
starting-conditions-specified predictions (S), typology of prediction, 196
stock investment, time and hindsight bias, 236–237
strategies, explanatory, for prediction, 197–199
strategy change, defensive pessimism, 44
stress-generation model, perfectionism, 50–51
suppression, regret regulation, 224
surgery, recovery from, expectations versus fantasies, 126–127

tags, autobiographical memory, 263–265
telescoping effects, autobiographical memory, 260
television game show, hindsight bias, 230, 231
temporal aspects of explanations
  behavior features, 189
  classic explanation research, 187–188
  enabling factor explanations, 193
  explanations changing over time, 187–191
  explanations of future events, 191–194
  folk-conceptual analysis of explanations across time, 188–191

information resources, 190–191
pragmatic goals, 189–190
reason explanations, 192–193
temporal construal, consideration of future consequences, 88, 90–91
temporal discounting, consideration of future consequences, 88, 90–91
temporal distance effect, autobiographical memory, 262–263
TEMPO (time, environment, motivation, personality, and outcome) model. *See also* counterfactual thinking
counterfactual thinking, 164, 166, 167
environment, 171–172
mental stimulations, 168–170
outcome, 166, 168
outline, 167
personality, 170–171
prospective mental simulations, 168–169
retrospective mental simulations, 169–170
time and motivation, 166
thinking, counterfactual. *See* counterfactual thinking
thinking about future
  overview, 5–7
  thinking about past versus, 122–123
thinking about past
  overview, 7–8
  versus thinking about future, 122–123
thoughts
  hope theory, 106
  information from, feelings, and behaviors, 293–294
  reciprocal relationships with feelings and behaviors, 291–292
thrill of victory, autobiographical memory, 265
time. *See also* autobiographical memory; judgments
  development of hindsight bias, 247
  foresight and hindsight in real-world events, 238–239